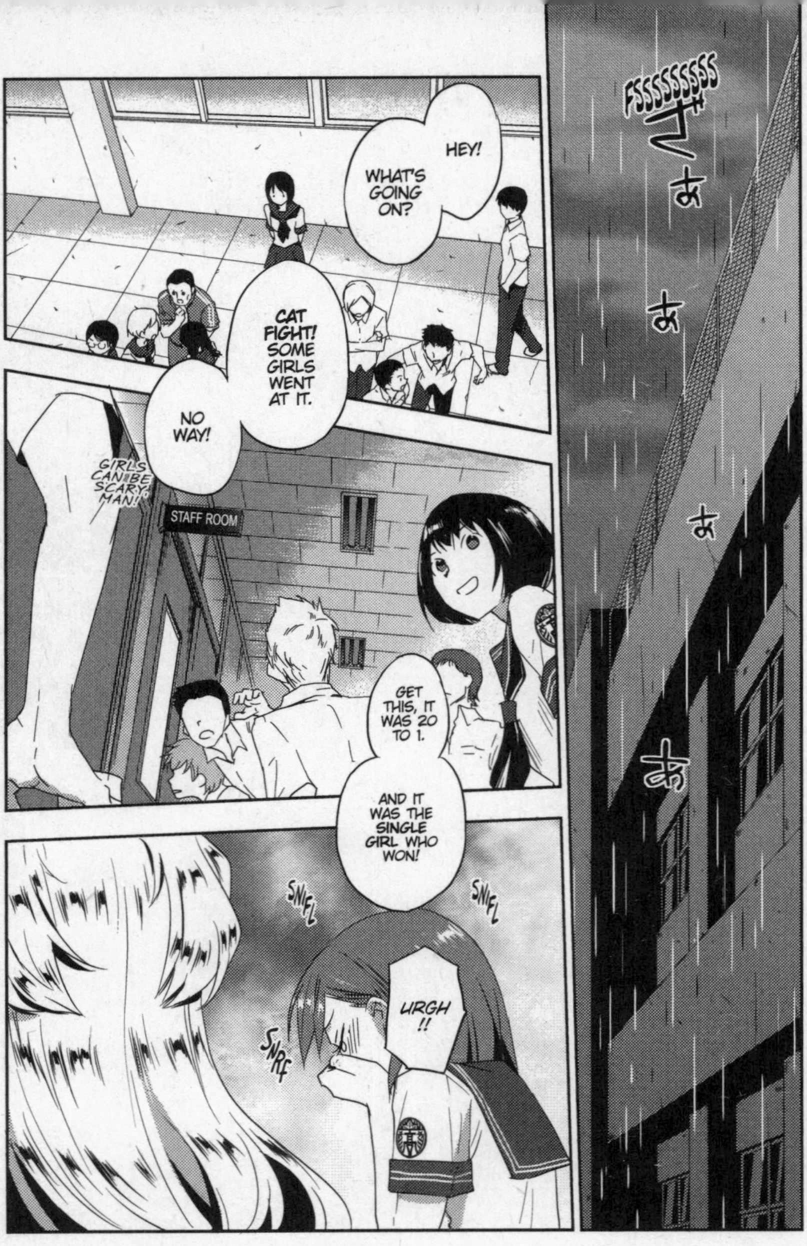
FSSSSSSSSSS
ざあああ
HEY! WHAT'S GOING ON?
CAT FIGHT! SOME GIRLS WENT AT IT.
NO WAY!
GIRLS CAN BE SCARY, MAN!
STAFF ROOM
GET THIS, IT WAS 20 TO 1.
AND IT WAS THE SINGLE GIRL WHO WON!
SNIFL
SNIFL
URGH !!
SNRF

## Chapter 6: I'm Always Watching

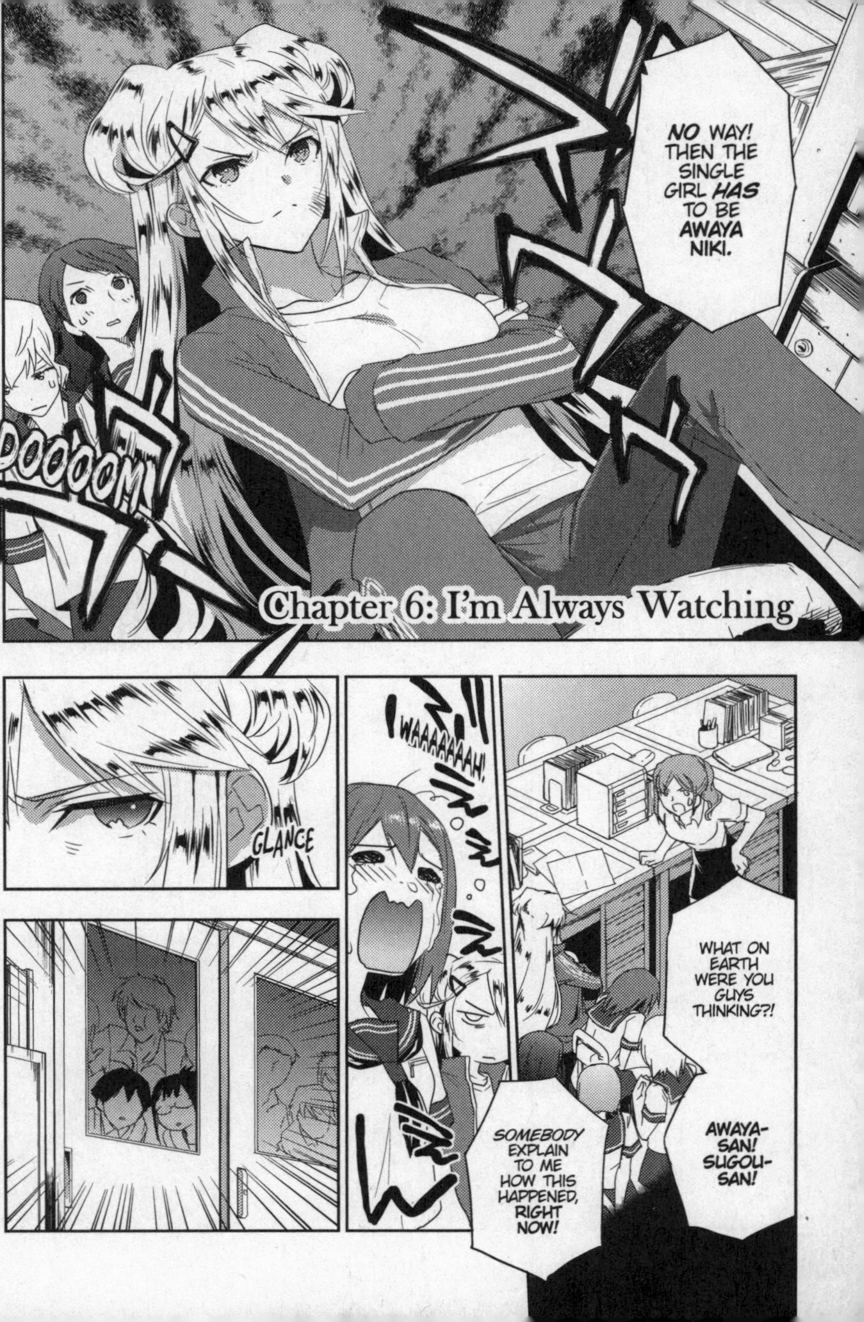
NO WAY! THEN THE SINGLE GIRL HAS TO BE AWAYA NIKI.
DOOOOM
Chapter 6: I'm Always Watching
WHAT ON EARTH WERE YOU GUYS THINKING?!
AWAYA-SAN! SUGOU-SAN!
SOMEBODY EXPLAIN TO ME HOW THIS HAPPENED, RIGHT NOW!
WAAAAAAAAH!
GLANCE

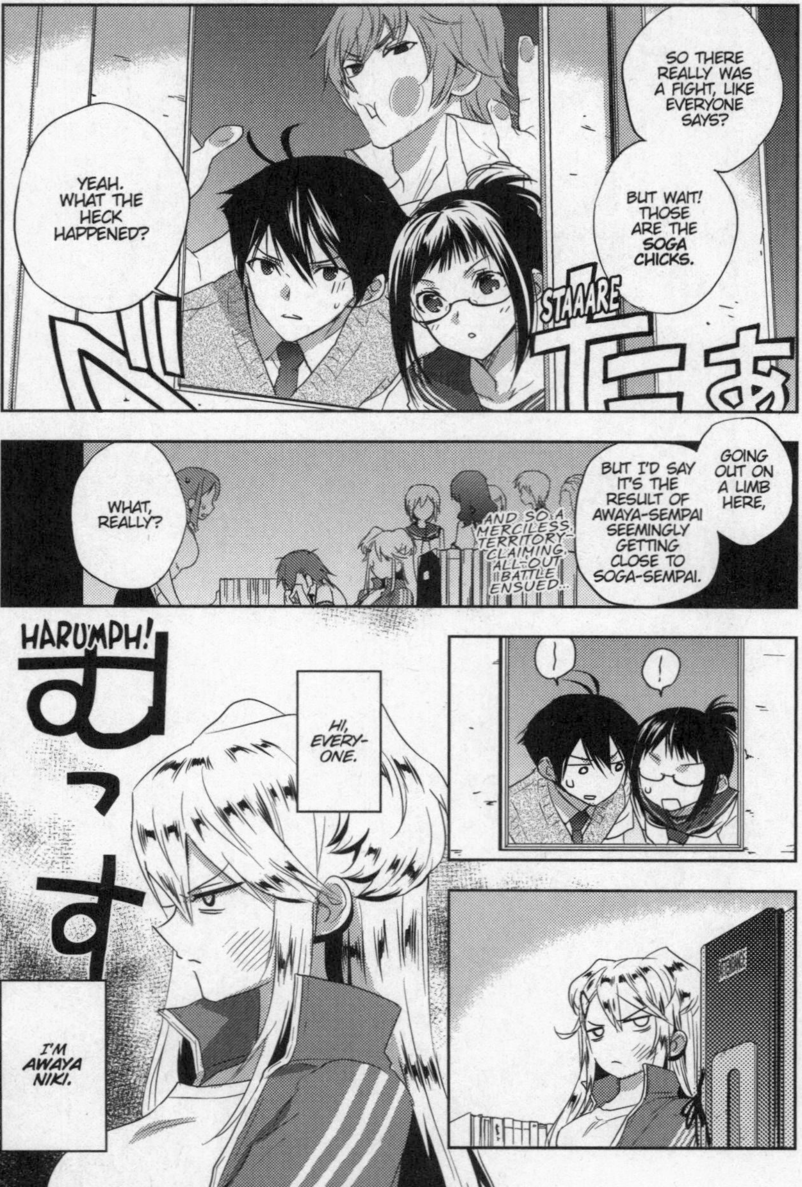
SO THERE REALLY WAS A FIGHT, LIKE EVERYONE SAYS?
BUT WAIT! THOSE ARE THE SOGA CHICKS.
STAAARE
YEAH. WHAT THE HECK HAPPENED?
GOING OUT ON A LIMB HERE,
BUT I'D SAY IT'S THE RESULT OF AWAYA-SEMPAI SEEMINGLY GETTING CLOSE TO SOGA-SEMPAI.
AND SO A MERCILESS, TERRITORY-CLAIMING, ALL-OUT BATTLE ENSUED...
WHAT, REALLY?
!
!
HARUMPH!
HI, EVERY-ONE.
I'M AWAYA NIKI.

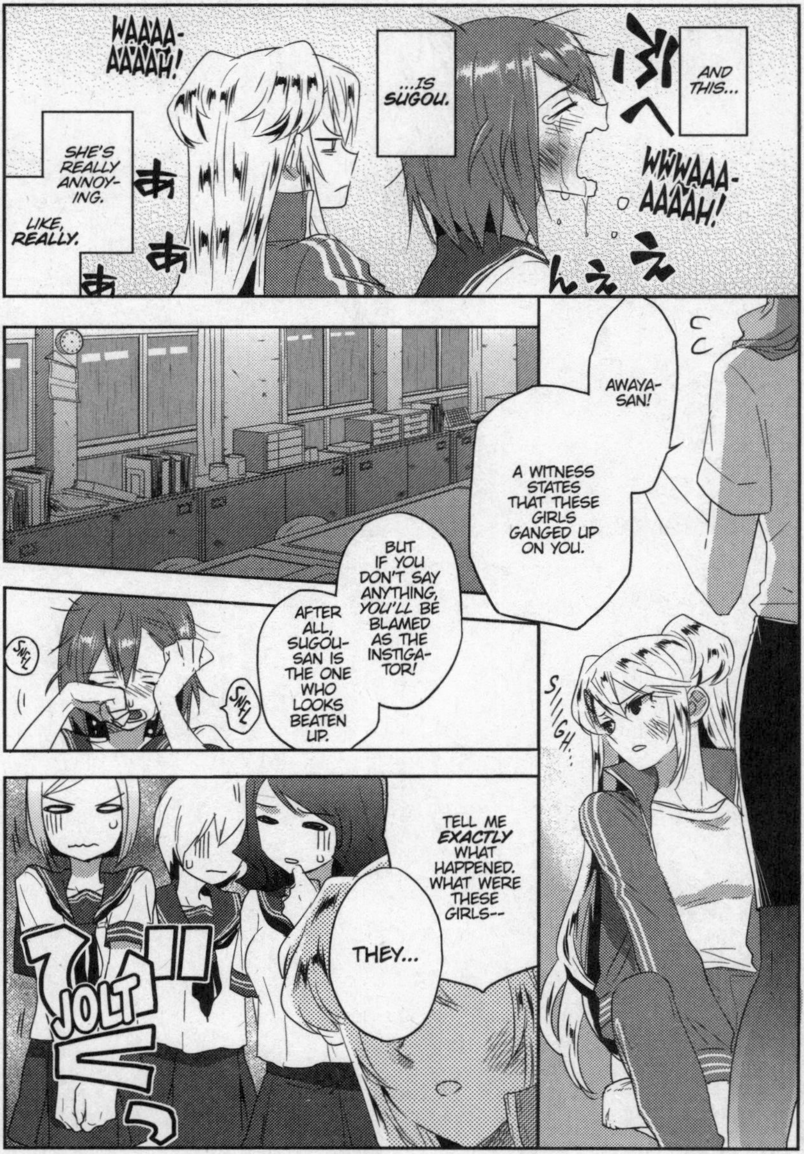
AND THIS...
WWWAAA-AAAAH!
...IS SUGOU.
WAAAA-AAAAH!
SHE'S REALLY ANNOY-ING.
LIKE, REALLY.
AWAYA-SAN!
A WITNESS STATES THAT THESE GIRLS GANGED UP ON YOU.
BUT IF YOU DON'T SAY ANYTHING, *YOU'LL* BE BLAMED AS THE INSTIGA-TOR!
AFTER ALL, SUGOU-SAN IS THE ONE WHO LOOKS BEATEN UP.
SNFL
SNFL
SIIIGH...
TELL ME ***EXACTLY*** WHAT HAPPENED. WHAT WERE THESE GIRLS--
THEY...
JOLT

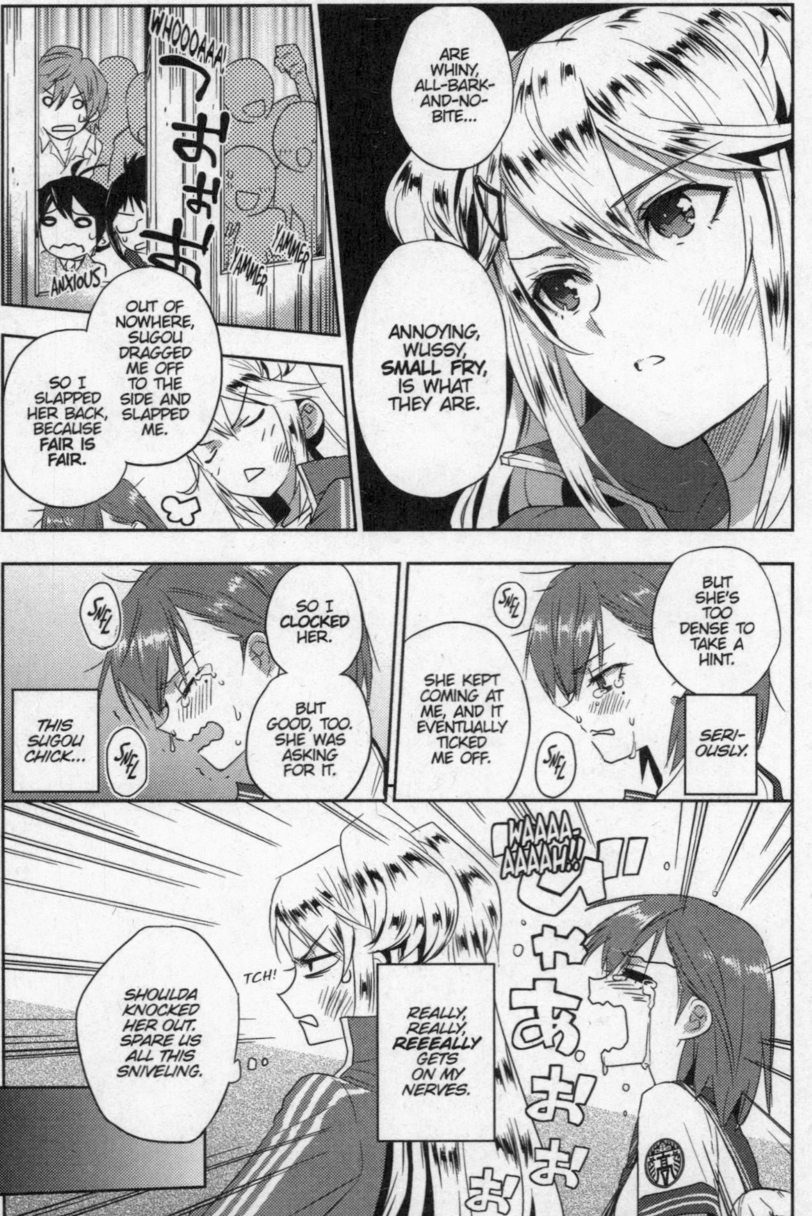
ARE WHINY, ALL-BARK-AND-NO-BITE...
ANNOYING, WUSSY, SMALL FRY, IS WHAT THEY ARE.
WHOOOAAA!
YAMMER
YAMMER
ANXIOUS
OUT OF NOWHERE, SUGOU DRAGGED ME OFF TO THE SIDE AND SLAPPED ME.
SO I SLAPPED HER BACK, BECAUSE FAIR IS FAIR.
BUT SHE'S TOO DENSE TO TAKE A HINT.
SERI-OUSLY.
SNFL
SHE KEPT COMING AT ME, AND IT EVENTUALLY TICKED ME OFF.
SNFL
SO I CLOCKED HER.
BUT GOOD, TOO. SHE WAS ASKING FOR IT.
SNFL
SNFL
THIS SUGOU CHICK...
WAAAA-AAAAH!!
REALLY, REALLY, REEEALLY GETS ON MY NERVES.
TCH!
SHOULDA KNOCKED HER OUT. SPARE US ALL THIS SNIVELING.

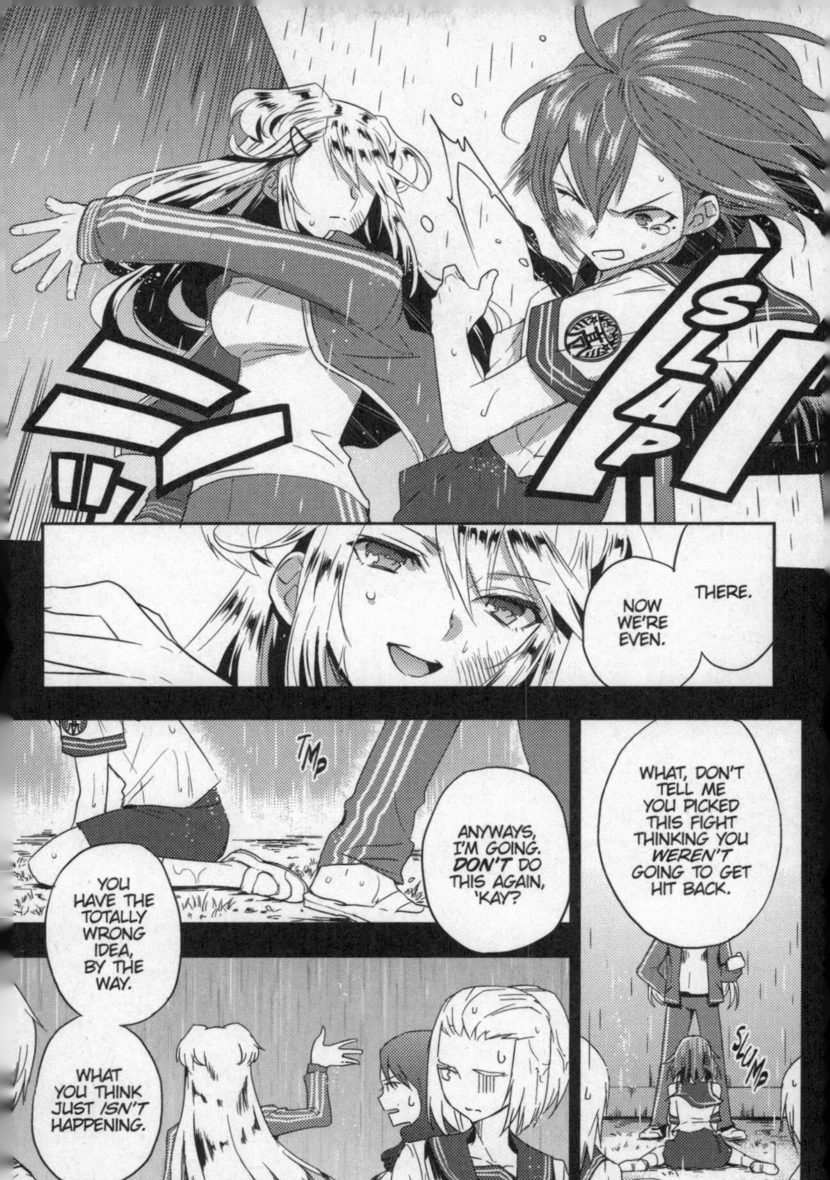
SLAP
!!
THERE.
NOW WE'RE EVEN.
WHAT, DON'T TELL ME YOU PICKED THIS FIGHT THINKING YOU *WEREN'T* GOING TO GET HIT BACK.
SLUMP
TMP
ANYWAYS, I'M GOING. ***DON'T*** DO THIS AGAIN, 'KAY?
YOU HAVE THE TOTALLY WRONG IDEA, BY THE WAY.
WHAT YOU THINK JUST *ISN'T* HAPPENING.

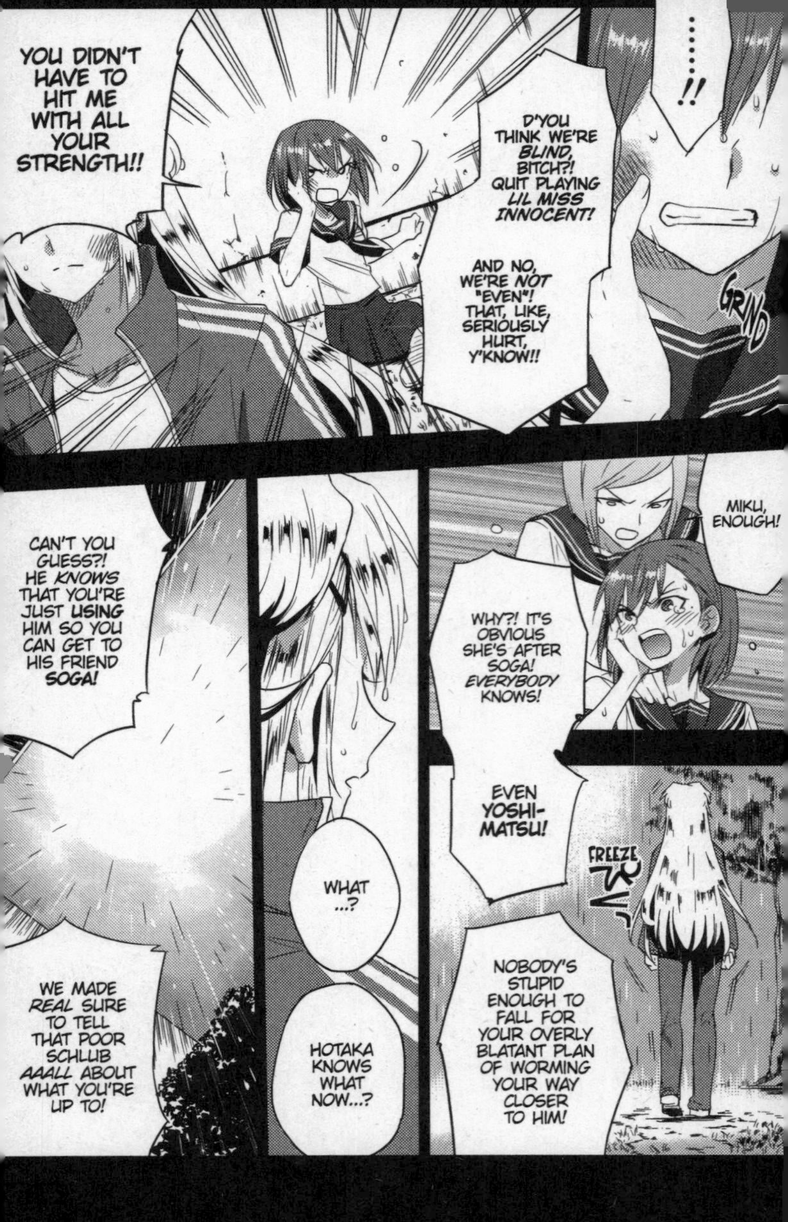
……!!
GRIND
YOU DIDN'T HAVE TO HIT ME WITH ALL YOUR STRENGTH!!
D'YOU THINK WE'RE *BLIND*, BITCH?! QUIT PLAYING *LIL MISS INNOCENT!*
AND NO, WE'RE *NOT* "EVEN"! THAT, LIKE, SERIOUSLY HURT, Y'KNOW!!
MIKU, ENOUGH!
WHY?! IT'S OBVIOUS SHE'S AFTER SOGA! *EVERYBODY* KNOWS!
EVEN YOSHI-MATSU!
FREEZE
NOBODY'S STUPID ENOUGH TO FALL FOR YOUR OVERLY BLATANT PLAN OF WORMING YOUR WAY CLOSER TO HIM!
WHAT ...?
HOTAKA KNOWS WHAT NOW...?
CAN'T YOU GUESS?! HE *KNOWS* THAT YOU'RE JUST USING HIM SO YOU CAN GET TO HIS FRIEND SOGA!
WE MADE *REAL* SURE TO TELL THAT POOR SCHLUB *AAALL* ABOUT WHAT YOU'RE UP TO!

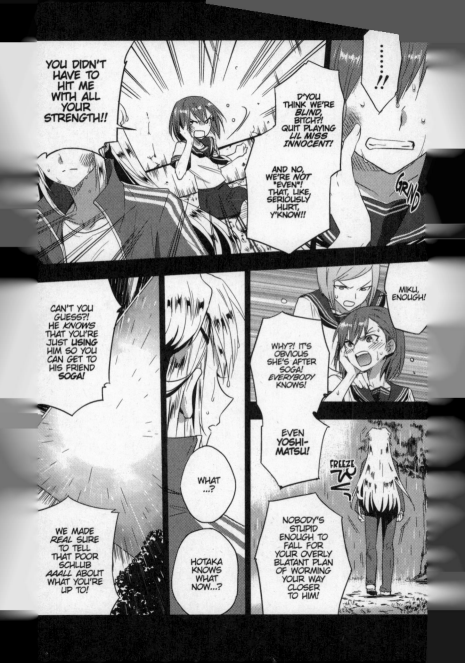

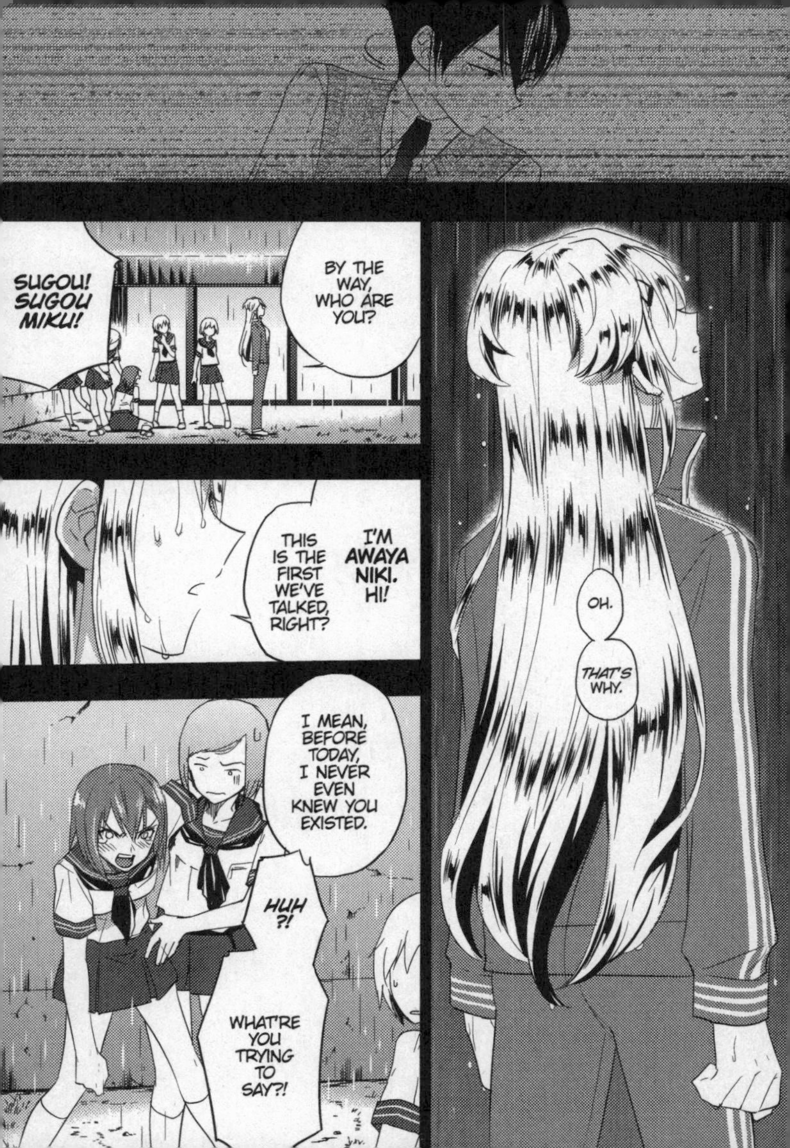
OH.
THAT'S WHY.
BY THE WAY, WHO ARE YOU?
SUGOU! SUGOU MIKU!
I'M AWAYA NIKI. HI!
THIS IS THE FIRST WE'VE TALKED, RIGHT?
I MEAN, BEFORE TODAY, I NEVER EVEN KNEW YOU EXISTED.
HUH?!
WHAT'RE YOU TRYING TO SAY?!

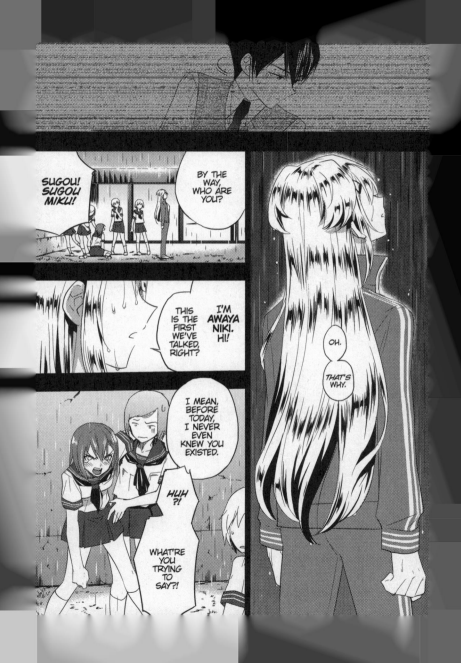

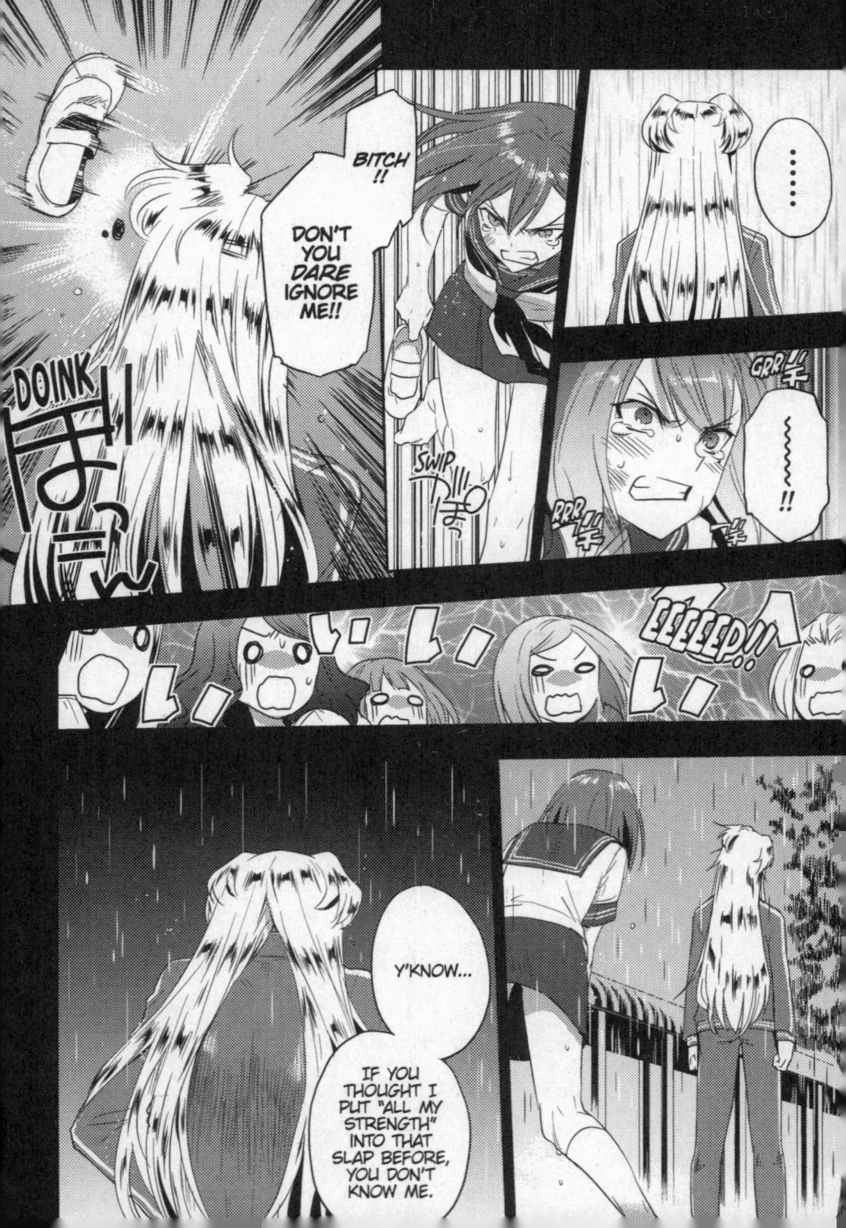
......
GRR
~~~~!!
RRR
BITCH!!
DON'T YOU DARE IGNORE ME!!
SWIP
DOINK
EEEEEP!!
Y'KNOW...
IF YOU THOUGHT I PUT "ALL MY STRENGTH" INTO THAT SLAP BEFORE, YOU DON'T KNOW ME.
~~~~

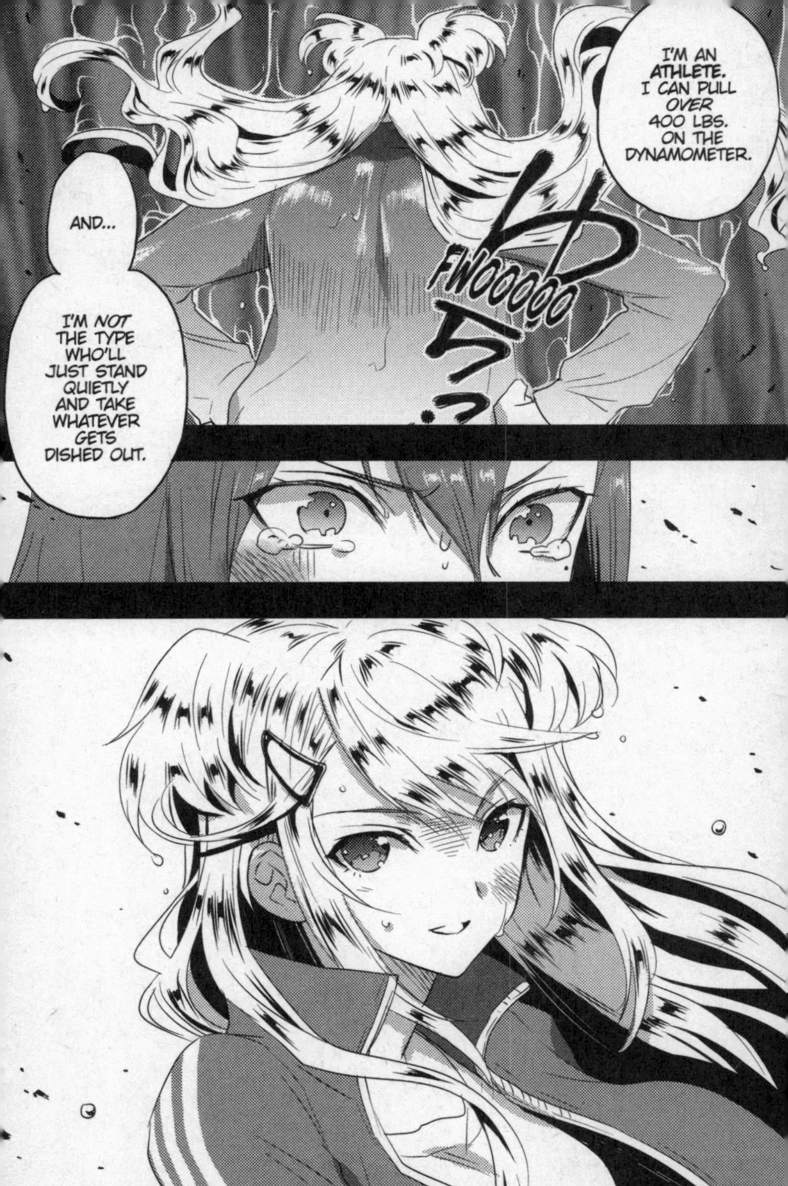
I'M AN ATHLETE. I CAN PULL OVER 400 LBS. ON THE DYNAMOMETER.
AND...
FWOOOOO
I'M NOT THE TYPE WHO'LL JUST STAND QUIETLY AND TAKE WHATEVER GETS DISHED OUT.

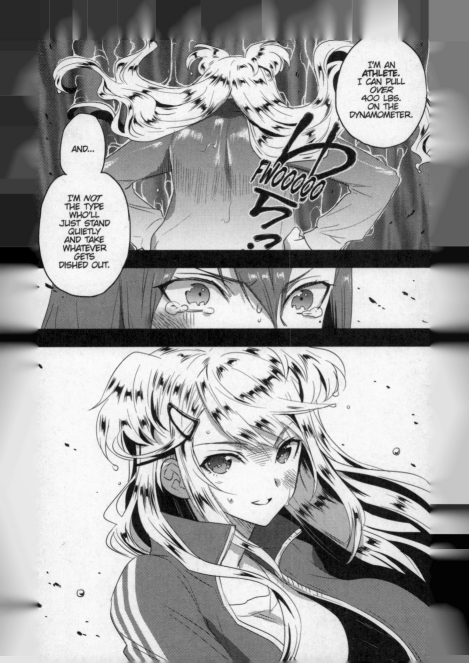

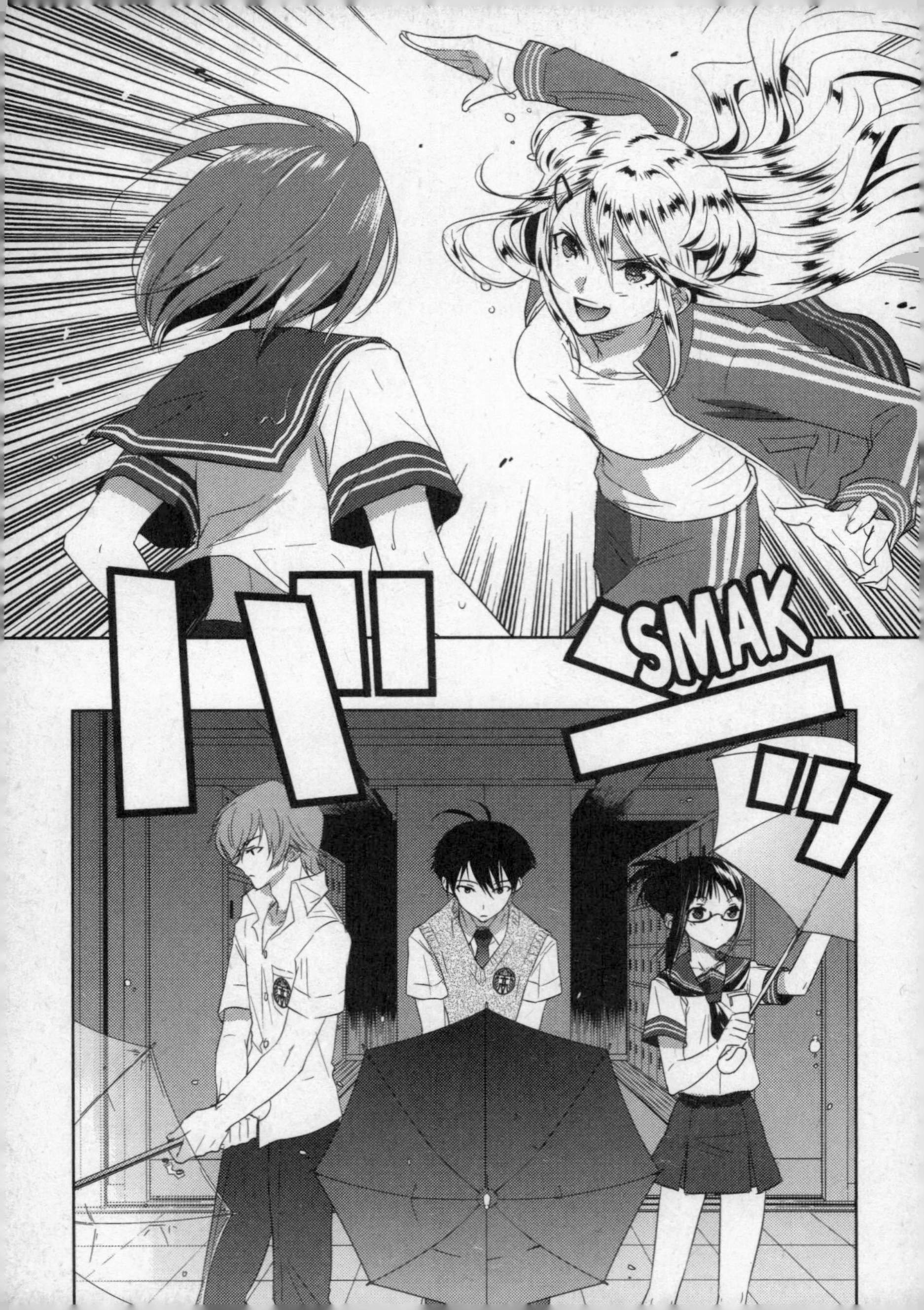
SMAK

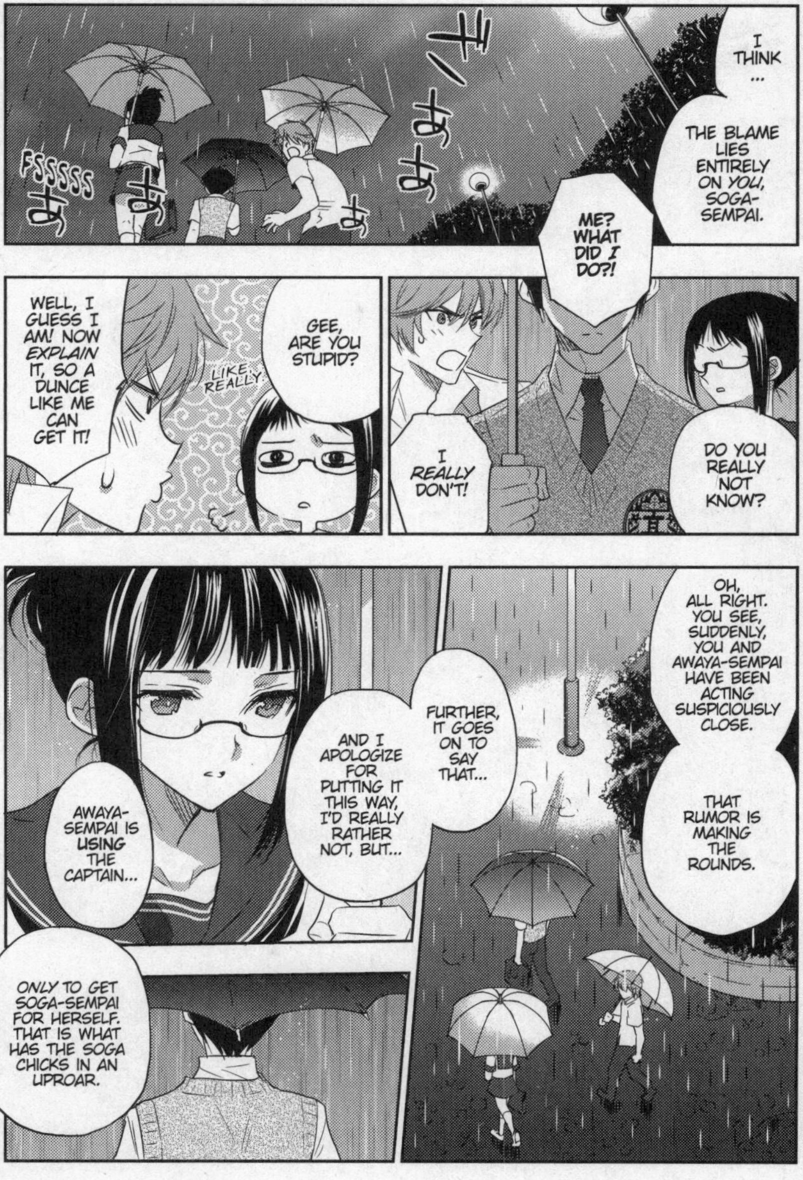
I THINK ...
THE BLAME LIES ENTIRELY ON *YOU*, SOGA-SEMPAI.
ME? WHAT DID *I* DO?!
ザーあああ
FSSSSS
DO YOU REALLY NOT KNOW?
I *REALLY* DON'T!
GEE, ARE YOU STUPID?
LIKE, REALLY.
WELL, I GUESS I AM! NOW *EXPLAIN* IT, SO A DUNCE LIKE ME CAN GET IT!
OH, ALL RIGHT. YOU SEE, SUDDENLY, YOU AND AWAYA-SEMPAI HAVE BEEN ACTING SUSPICIOUSLY CLOSE.
THAT RUMOR IS MAKING THE ROUNDS.
FURTHER, IT GOES ON TO SAY THAT...
AND I APOLOGIZE FOR PUTTING IT THIS WAY, I'D REALLY RATHER NOT, BUT...
AWAYA-SEMPAI IS USING THE CAPTAIN...
*ONLY* TO GET SOGA-SEMPAI FOR HERSELF. THAT IS WHAT HAS THE SOGA CHICKS IN AN UPROAR.

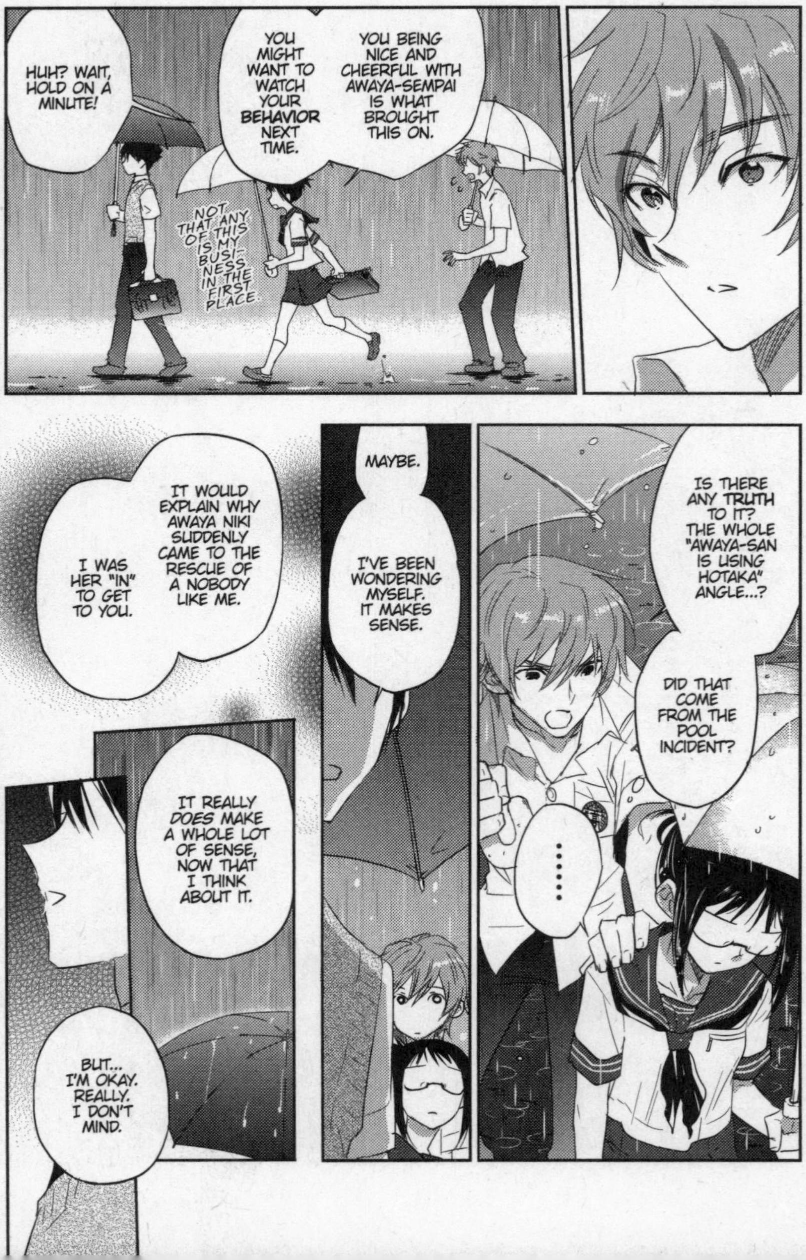
YOU BEING NICE AND CHEERFUL WITH AWAYA-SEMPAI IS WHAT BROUGHT THIS ON.
YOU MIGHT WANT TO WATCH YOUR BEHAVIOR NEXT TIME.
HUH? WAIT, HOLD ON A MINUTE!
NOT THAT ANY OF THIS IS MY BUSINESS IN THE FIRST PLACE.
IS THERE ANY TRUTH TO IT? THE WHOLE "AWAYA-SAN IS USING HOTAKA" ANGLE...?
DID THAT COME FROM THE POOL INCIDENT?
......
MAYBE.
I'VE BEEN WONDERING MYSELF. IT MAKES SENSE.
IT WOULD EXPLAIN WHY AWAYA NIKI SUDDENLY CAME TO THE RESCUE OF A NOBODY LIKE ME.
I WAS HER "IN" TO GET TO YOU.
IT REALLY DOES MAKE A WHOLE LOT OF SENSE, NOW THAT I THINK ABOUT IT.
BUT... I'M OKAY. REALLY. I DON'T MIND.

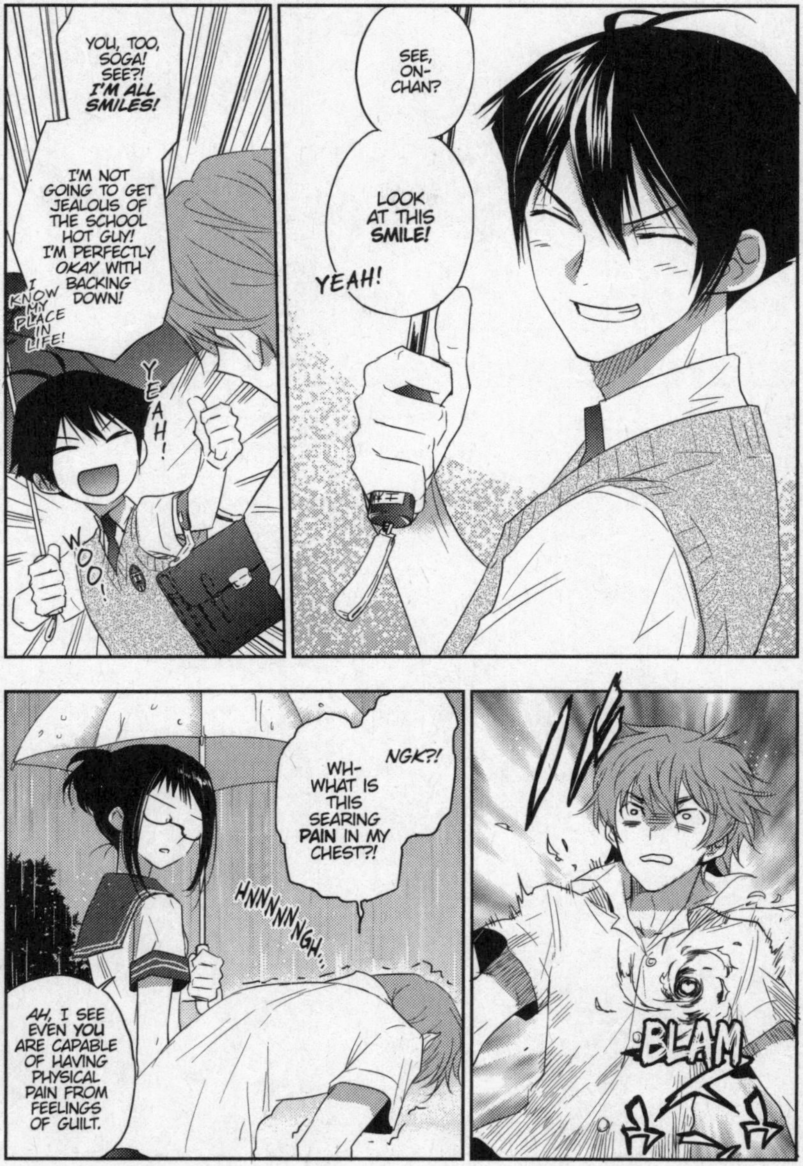
SEE, ON-CHAN?
LOOK AT THIS SMILE!
YEAH!
YOU, TOO, SOGA! SEE?! I'M ALL SMILES!
I'M NOT GOING TO GET JEALOUS OF THE SCHOOL HOT GUY! I'M PERFECTLY OKAY WITH BACKING DOWN!
I KNOW MY PLACE IN LIFE!
YEAH!
WOO!
BLAM
NGK?!
WH-WHAT IS THIS SEARING PAIN IN MY CHEST?!
HNNNNNNGH...
AH, I SEE EVEN YOU ARE CAPABLE OF HAVING PHYSICAL PAIN FROM FEELINGS OF GUILT.

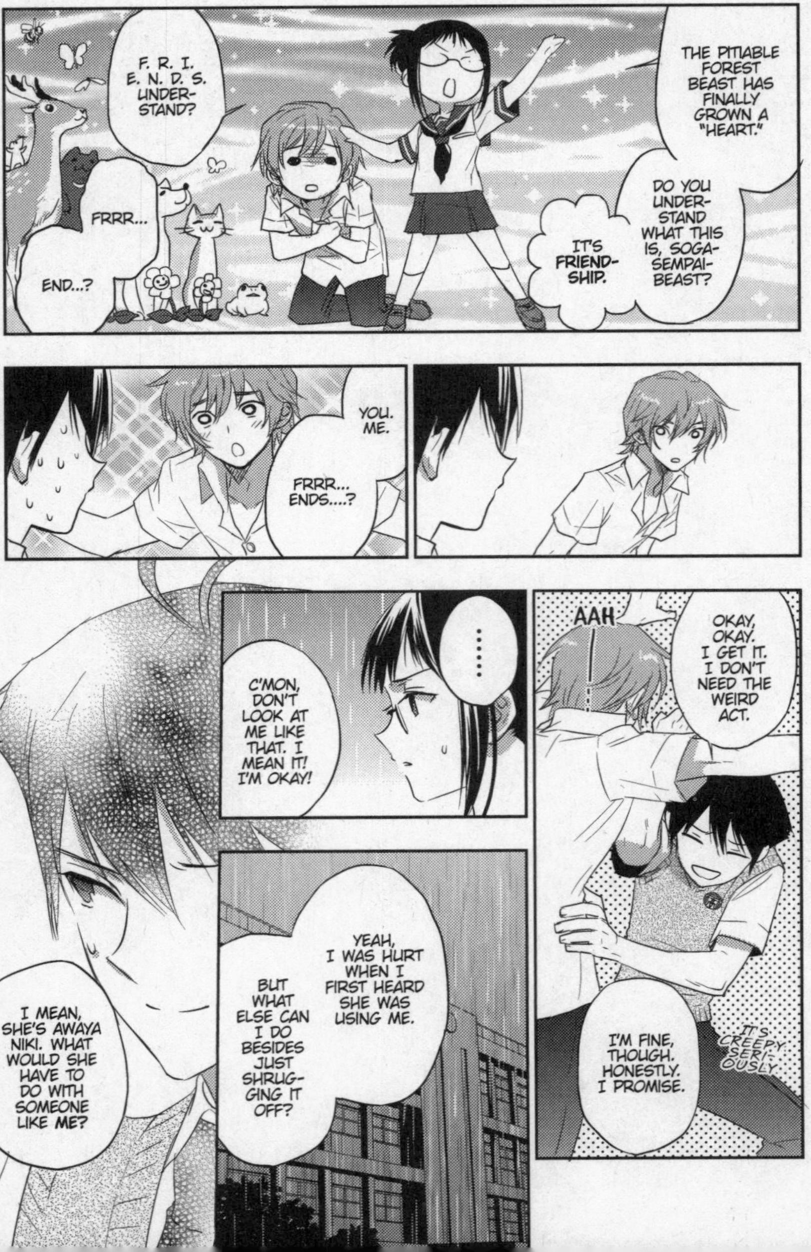
THE PITIABLE FOREST BEAST HAS FINALLY GROWN A "HEART."
DO YOU UNDERSTAND WHAT THIS IS, SOGA-SEMPAI-BEAST?
IT'S FRIENDSHIP.
F. R. I. E. N. D. S. UNDERSTAND?
FRRR... END...?
YOU. ME.
FRRR... ENDS....?
AAH
OKAY, OKAY. I GET IT. I DON'T NEED THE WEIRD ACT.
I'M FINE, THOUGH. HONESTLY. I PROMISE.
IT'S CREEPY. SERIOUSLY.
......
C'MON, DON'T LOOK AT ME LIKE THAT. I MEAN IT! I'M OKAY!
YEAH, I WAS HURT WHEN I FIRST HEARD SHE WAS USING ME.
BUT WHAT ELSE CAN I DO BESIDES JUST SHRUGGING IT OFF?
I MEAN, SHE'S AWAYA NIKI. WHAT WOULD SHE HAVE TO DO WITH SOMEONE LIKE ME?

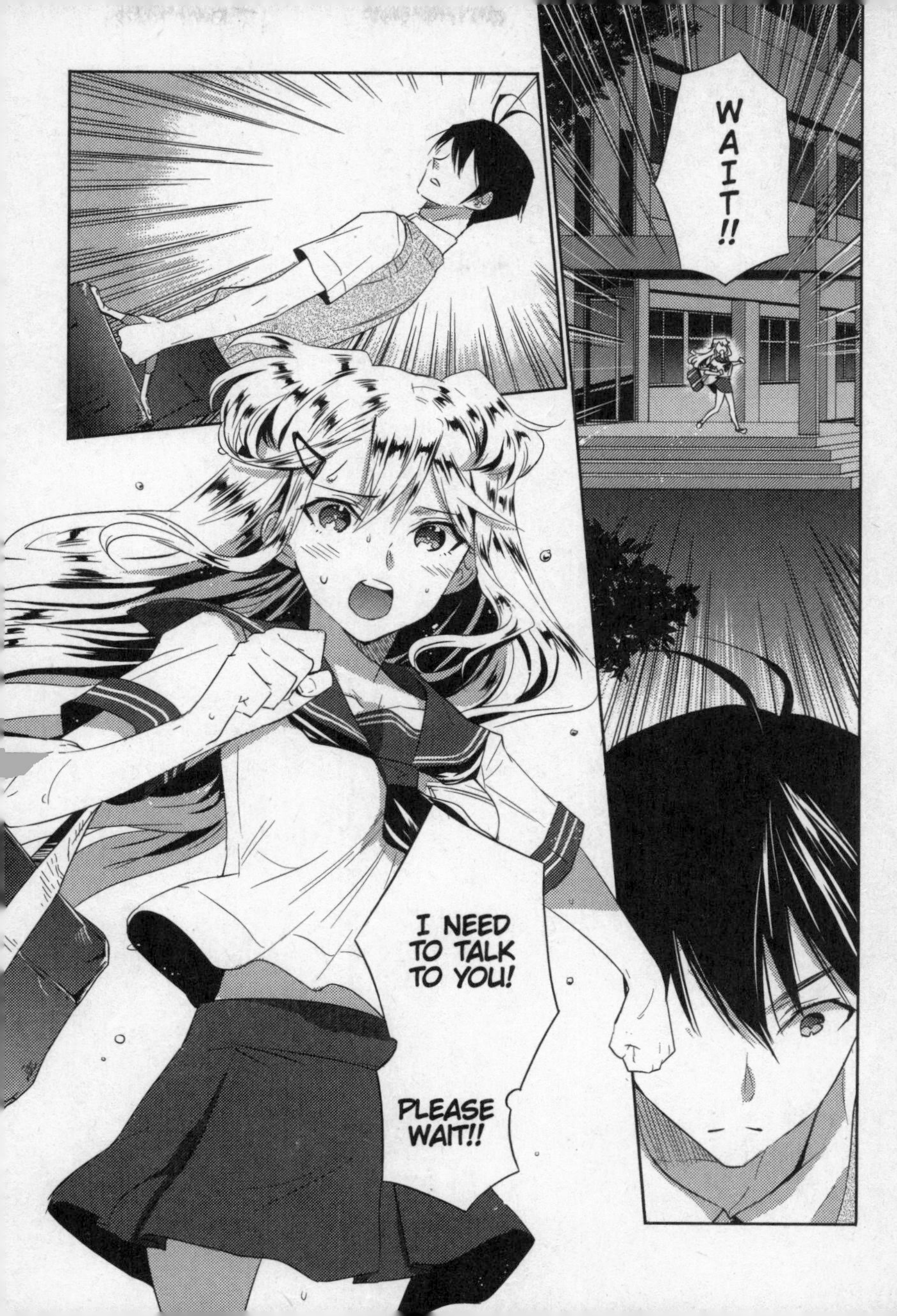
WAIT!!
I NEED TO TALK TO YOU!
PLEASE WAIT!!

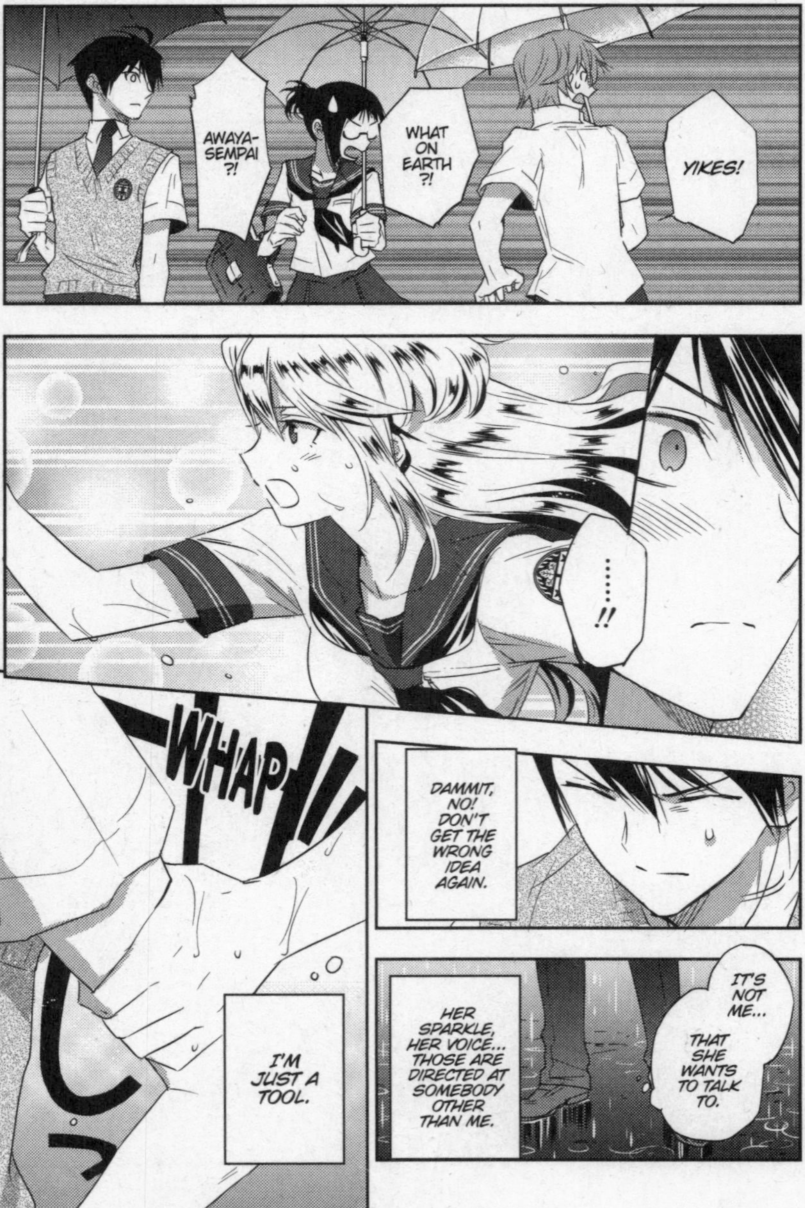
YIKES!
WHAT ON EARTH ?!
AWAYA-SEMPAI ?!
......!!
DAMMIT, NO! DON'T GET THE WRONG IDEA AGAIN.
IT'S NOT ME...
THAT SHE WANTS TO TALK TO.
HER SPARKLE, HER VOICE... THOSE ARE DIRECTED AT SOMEBODY OTHER THAN ME.
WHAP
I'M JUST A TOOL.

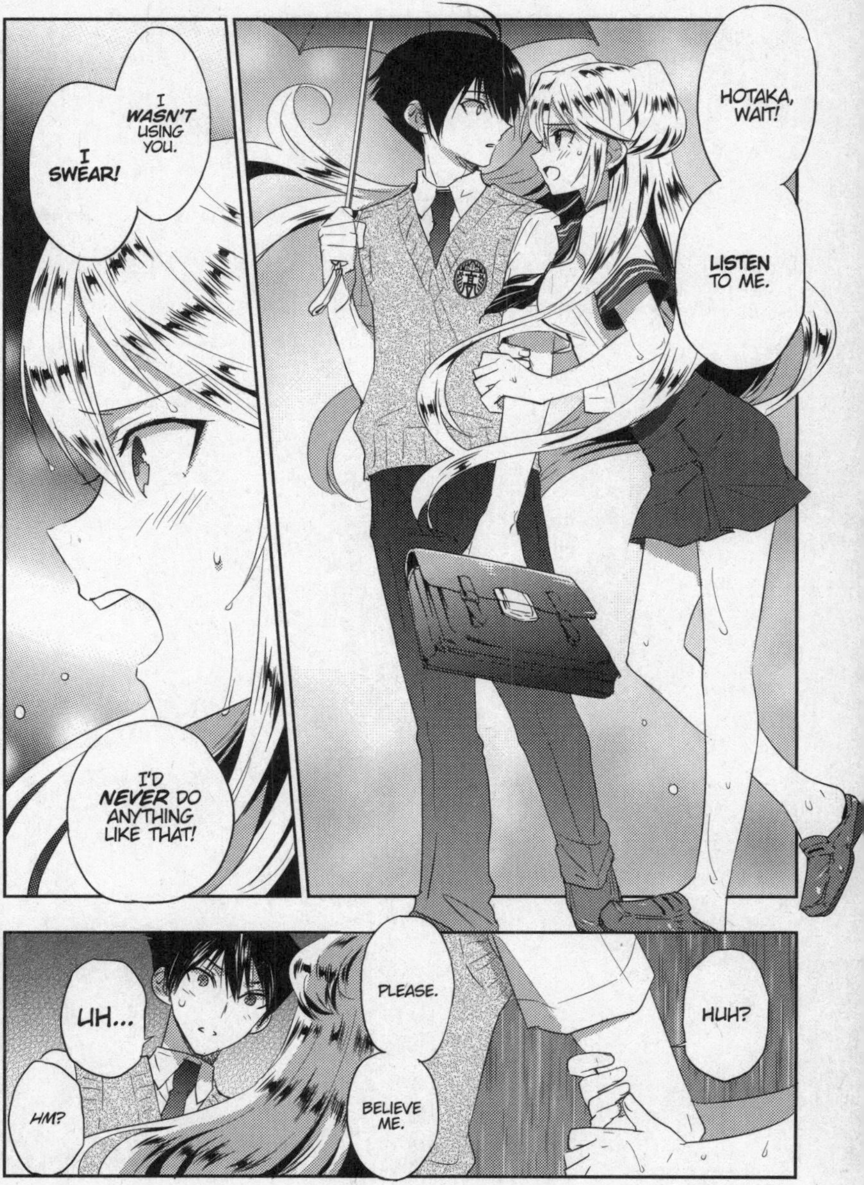
HOTAKA, WAIT!
LISTEN TO ME.
I WASN'T USING YOU.
I SWEAR!
I'D NEVER DO ANYTHING LIKE THAT!
HUH?
PLEASE.
BELIEVE ME.
UH...
HM?

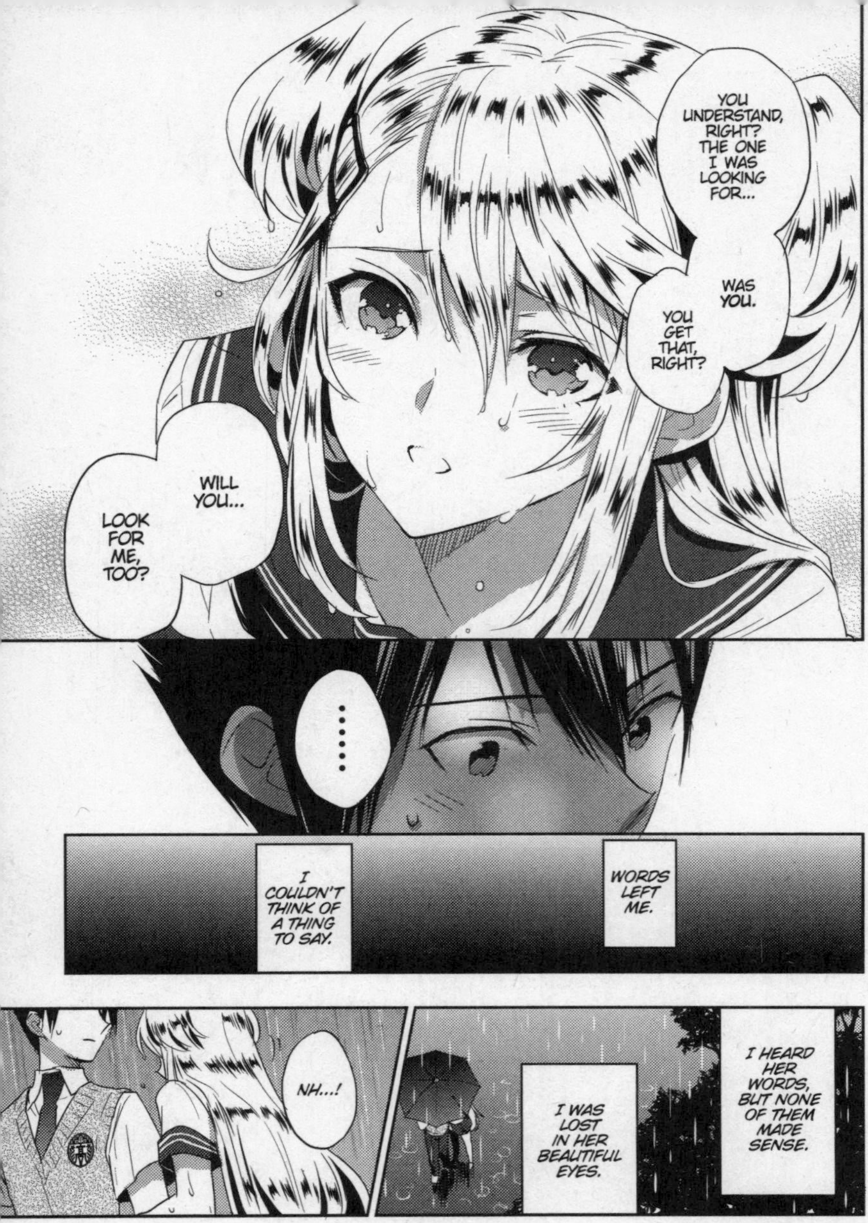
YOU UNDERSTAND, RIGHT? THE ONE I WAS LOOKING FOR...
WAS YOU.
YOU GET THAT, RIGHT?
WILL YOU...
LOOK FOR ME, TOO?
......
WORDS LEFT ME.
I COULDN'T THINK OF A THING TO SAY.
I HEARD HER WORDS, BUT NONE OF THEM MADE SENSE.
I WAS LOST IN HER BEAUTIFUL EYES.
NH...!

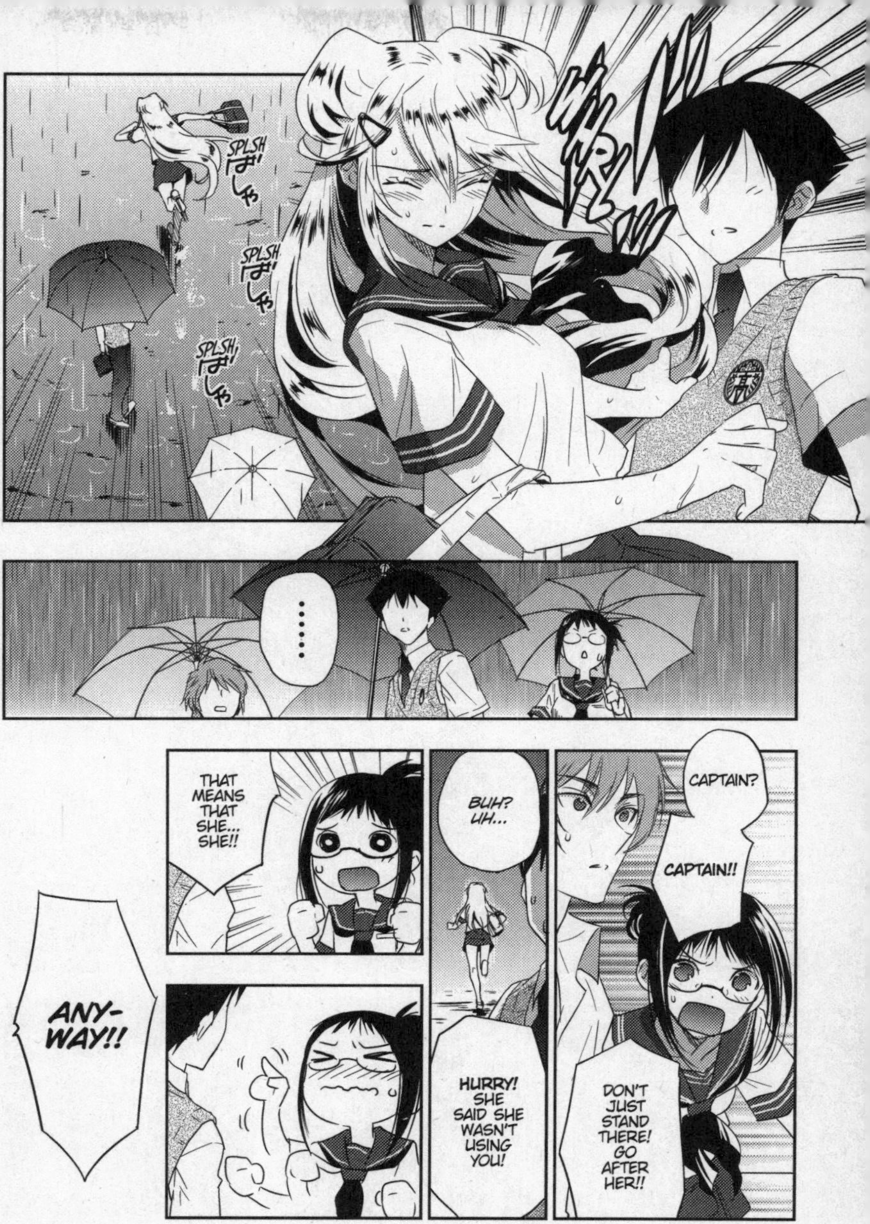
SPLSH
ぱしゃ
SPLSH
ぱしゃ
SPLSH
ぱしゃ
......
CAPTAIN?
CAPTAIN!!
DON'T JUST STAND THERE! GO AFTER HER!!
BUH? UH...
HURRY! SHE SAID SHE WASN'T USING YOU!
THAT MEANS THAT SHE... SHE!!
ANY-WAY!!

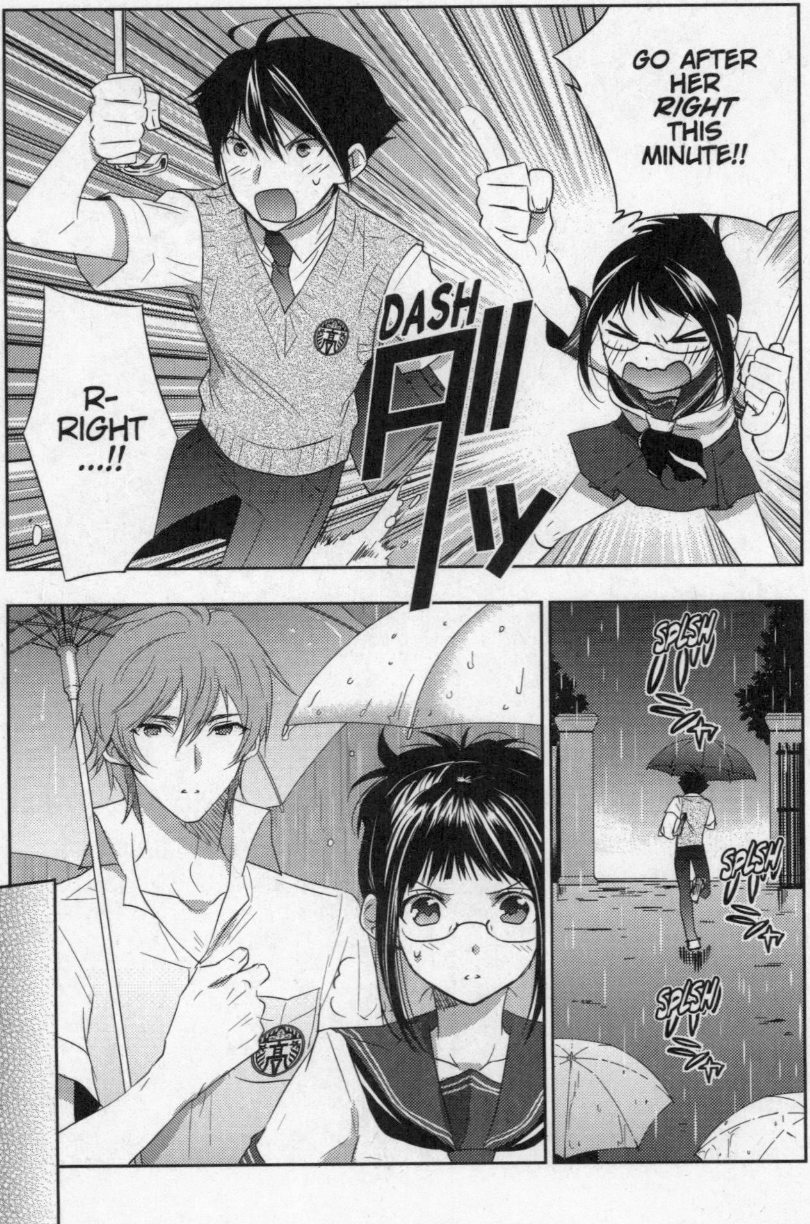
GO AFTER HER RIGHT THIS MINUTE!!
DASH
R-RIGHT ...!!
SPLSH
SPLSH
SPLSH

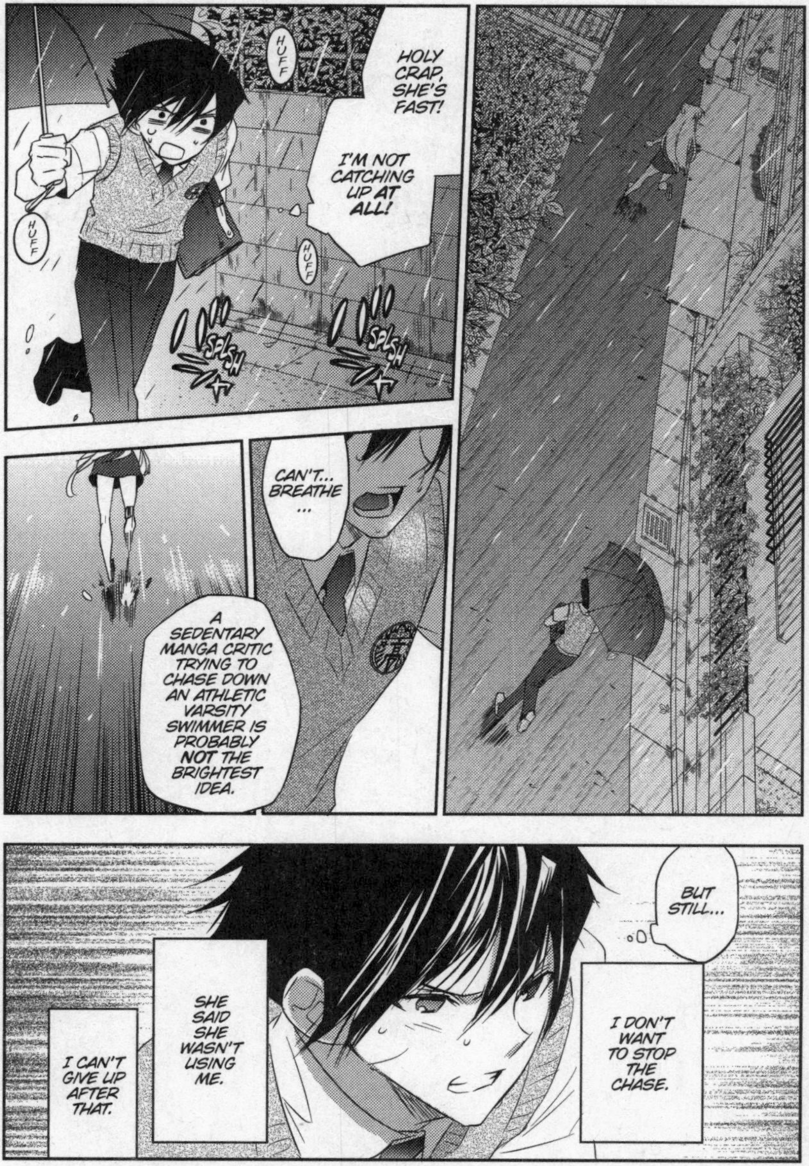
HOLY CRAP, SHE'S FAST!
I'M NOT CATCHING UP AT ALL!
HUFF
HUFF
HUFF
SPLSH
SPLSH
CAN'T... BREATHE ...
A SEDENTARY MANGA CRITIC TRYING TO CHASE DOWN AN ATHLETIC VARSITY SWIMMER IS PROBABLY NOT THE BRIGHTEST IDEA.
BUT STILL...
I DON'T WANT TO STOP THE CHASE.
SHE SAID SHE WASN'T USING ME.
I CAN'T GIVE UP AFTER THAT.

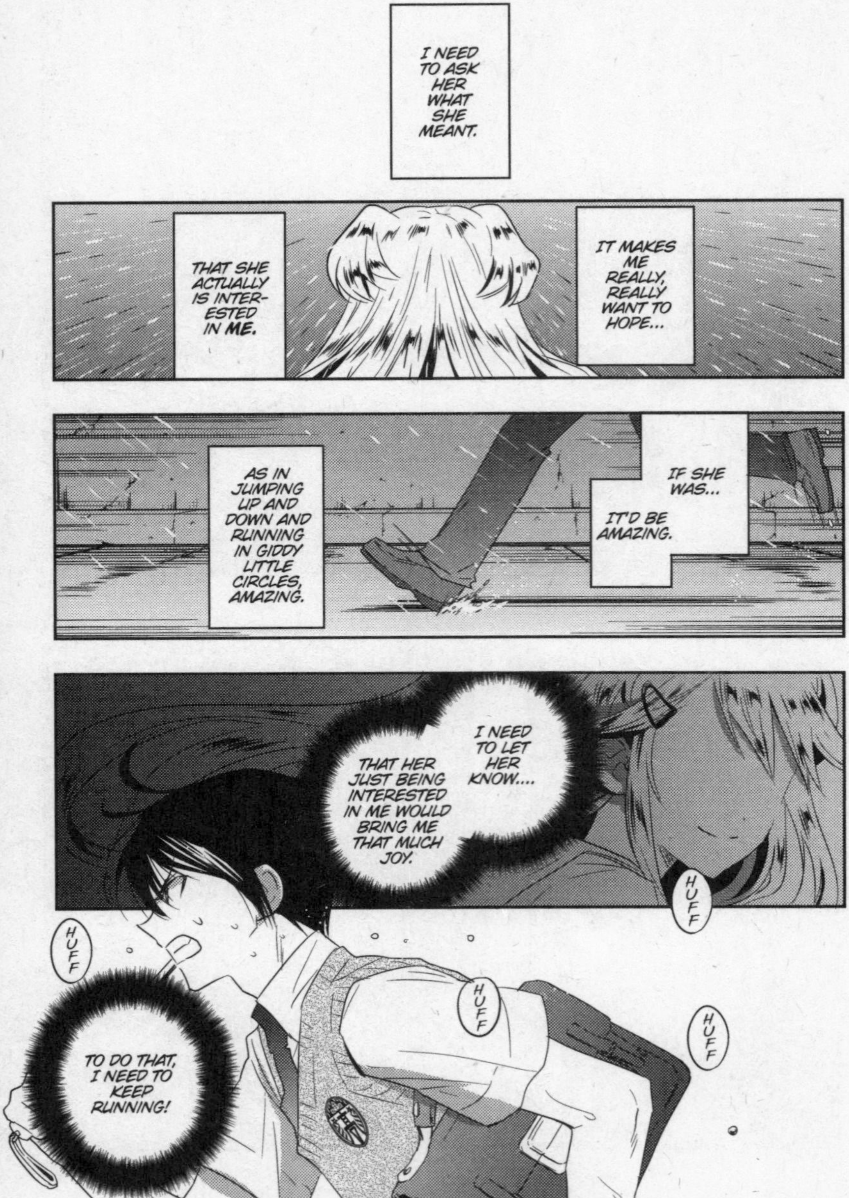
I NEED TO ASK HER WHAT SHE MEANT.
IT MAKES ME REALLY, REALLY WANT TO HOPE...
THAT SHE ACTUALLY IS INTER-ESTED IN ME.
IF SHE WAS...
IT'D BE AMAZING.
AS IN JUMPING UP AND DOWN AND RUNNING IN GIDDY LITTLE CIRCLES, AMAZING.
I NEED TO LET HER KNOW....
THAT HER JUST BEING INTERESTED IN ME WOULD BRING ME THAT MUCH JOY.
HUFF
HUFF
HUFF
HUFF
TO DO THAT, I NEED TO KEEP RUNNING!

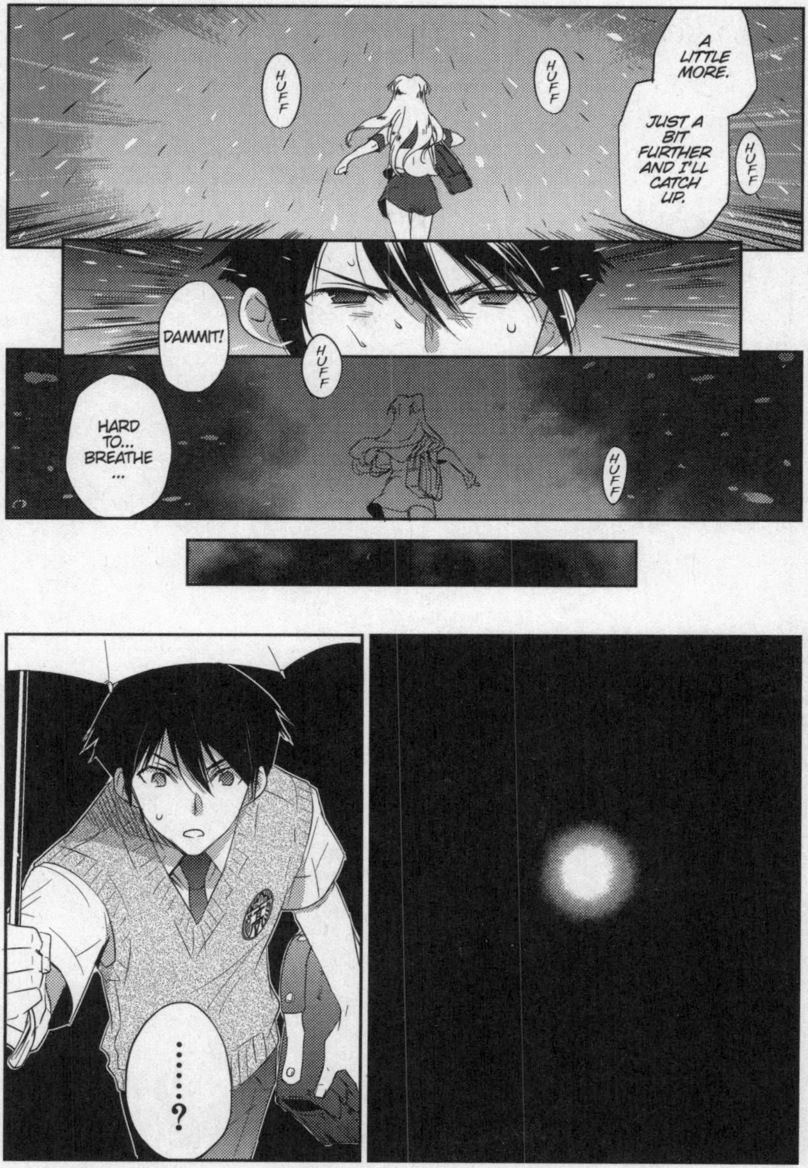
A LITTLE MORE.
JUST A BIT FURTHER AND I'LL CATCH UP.
HUFF
HUFF
HUFF
DAMMIT!
HUFF
HUFF
HARD TO... BREATHE ...
......?

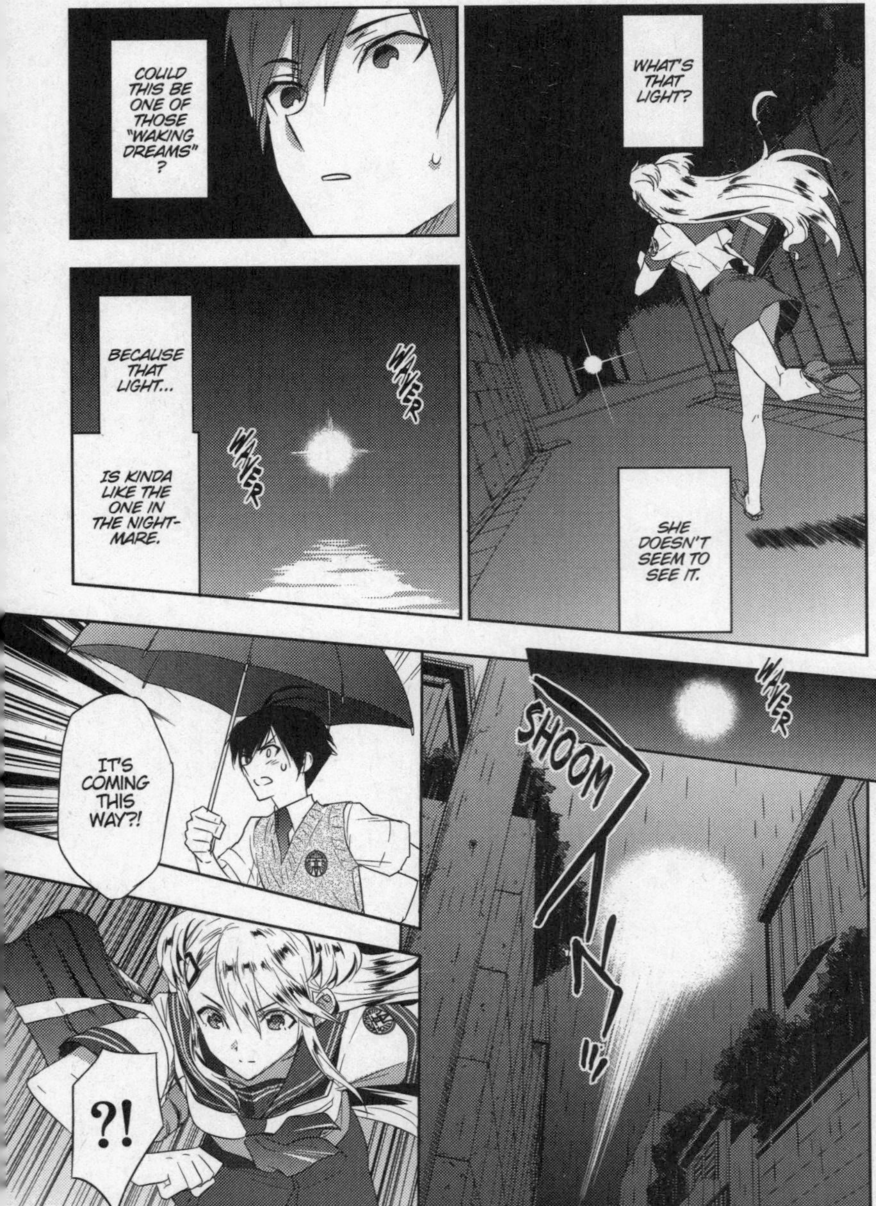
WHAT'S THAT LIGHT?
SHE DOESN'T SEEM TO SEE IT.
COULD THIS BE ONE OF THOSE "WAKING DREAMS"?
BECAUSE THAT LIGHT...
WAVER
WAVER
IS KINDA LIKE THE ONE IN THE NIGHT-MARE.
WAVER
SHOOM
IT'S COMING THIS WAY?!
?!

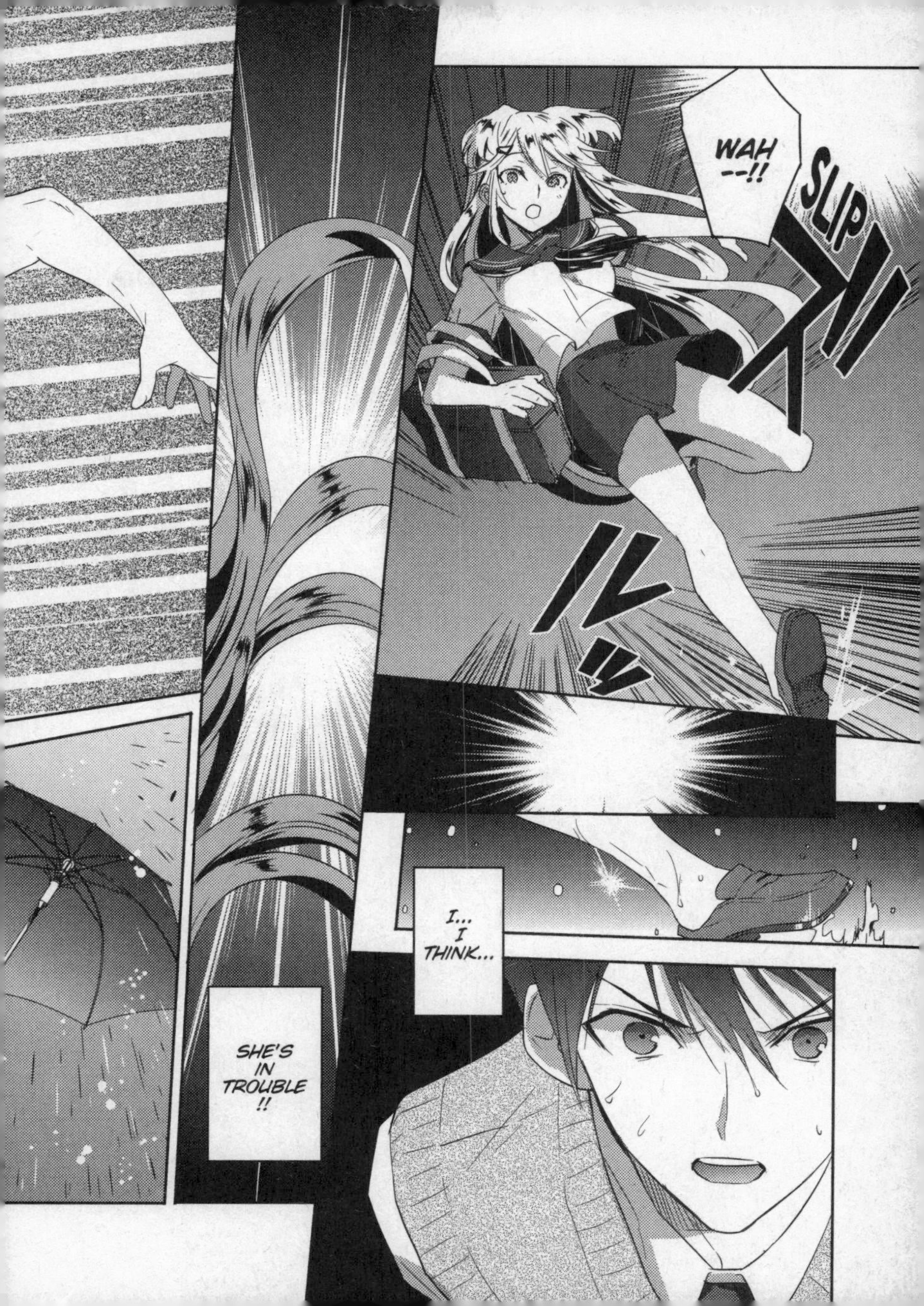
WAH --!!
SLIP
I... I THINK...
SHE'S IN TROUBLE !!

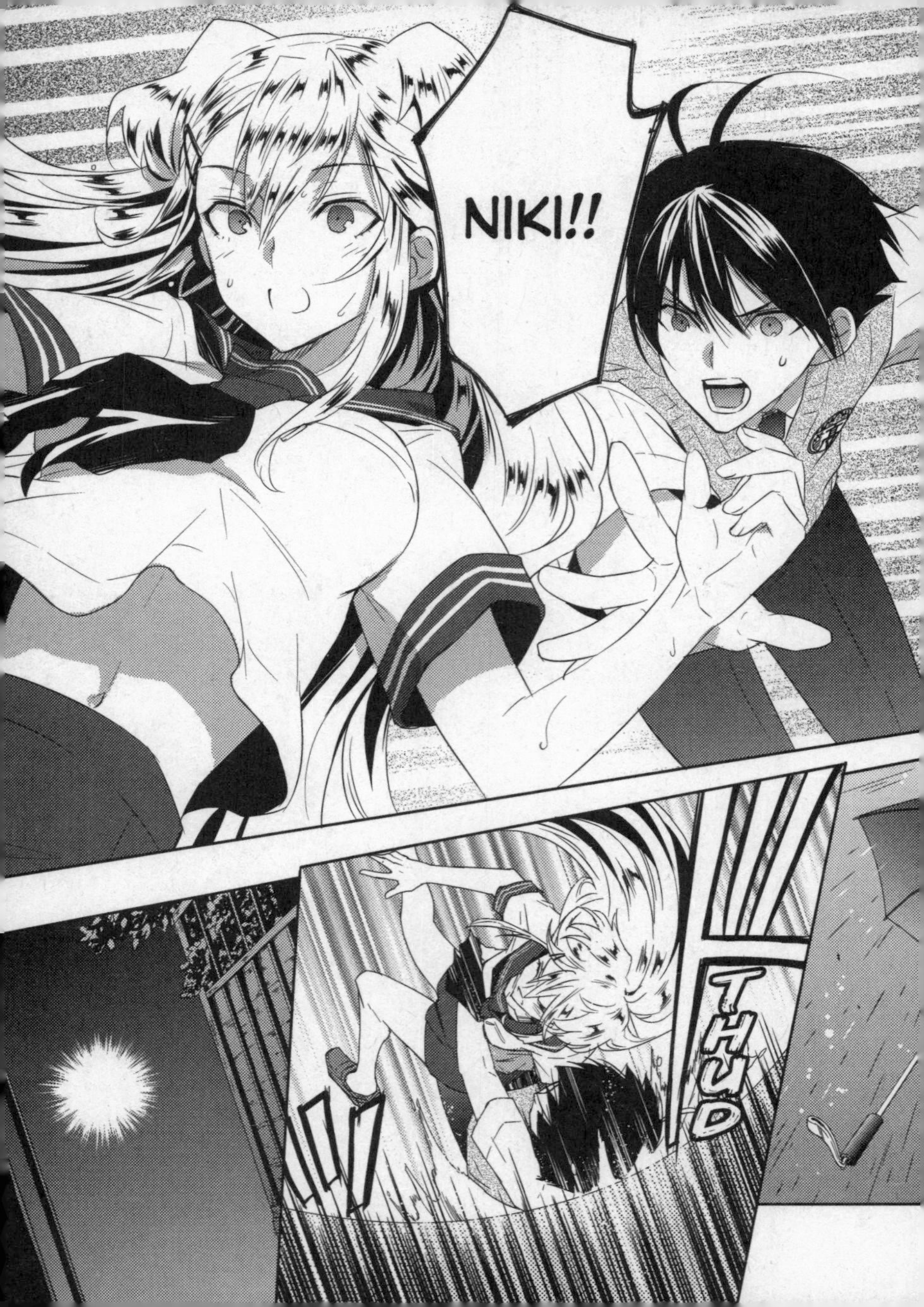
NIKI!!
THUD

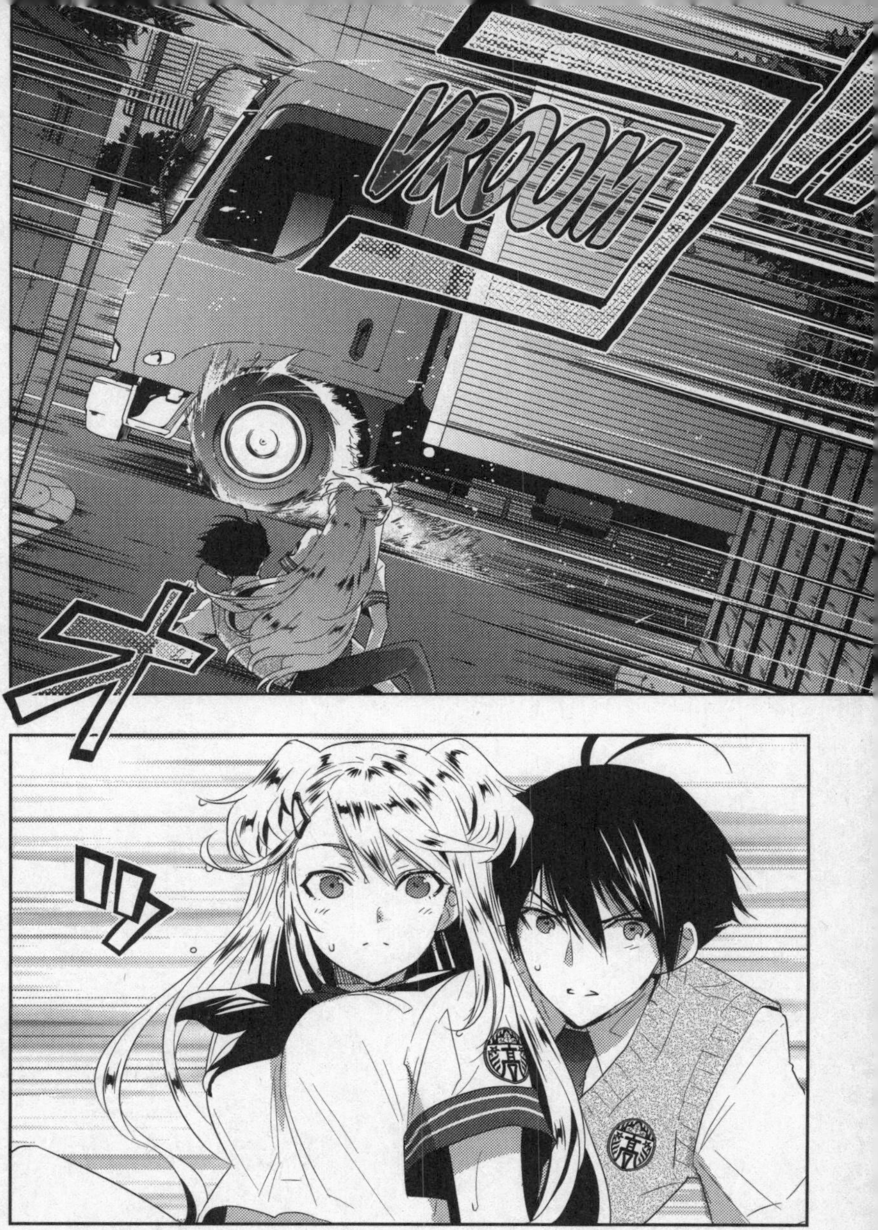
VROOM

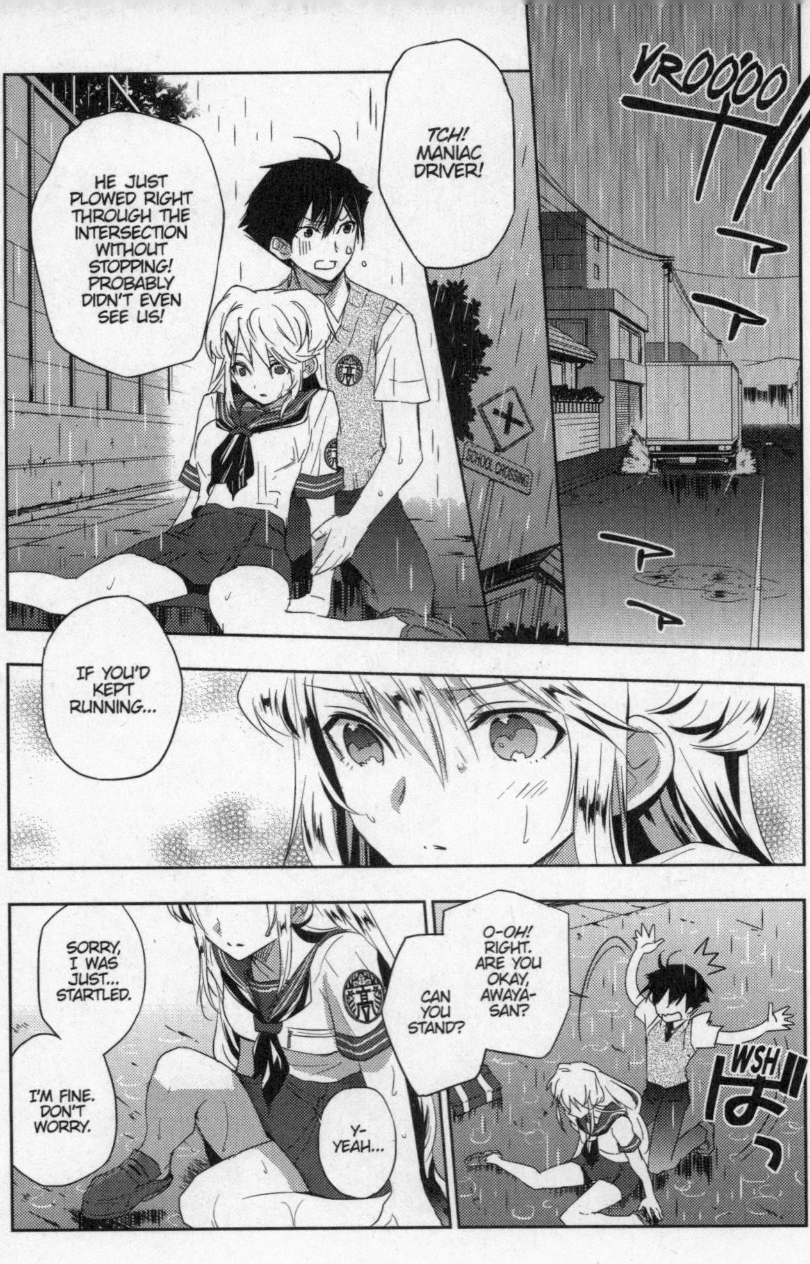
VROOOOO
TCH! MANIAC DRIVER!
HE JUST PLOWED RIGHT THROUGH THE INTERSECTION WITHOUT STOPPING! PROBABLY DIDN'T EVEN SEE US!
SCHOOL CROSSING
IF YOU'D KEPT RUNNING...
O-OH! RIGHT. ARE YOU OKAY, AWAYA-SAN?
CAN YOU STAND?
WSH
SORRY, I WAS JUST... STARTLED.
I'M FINE. DON'T WORRY.
Y-YEAH...

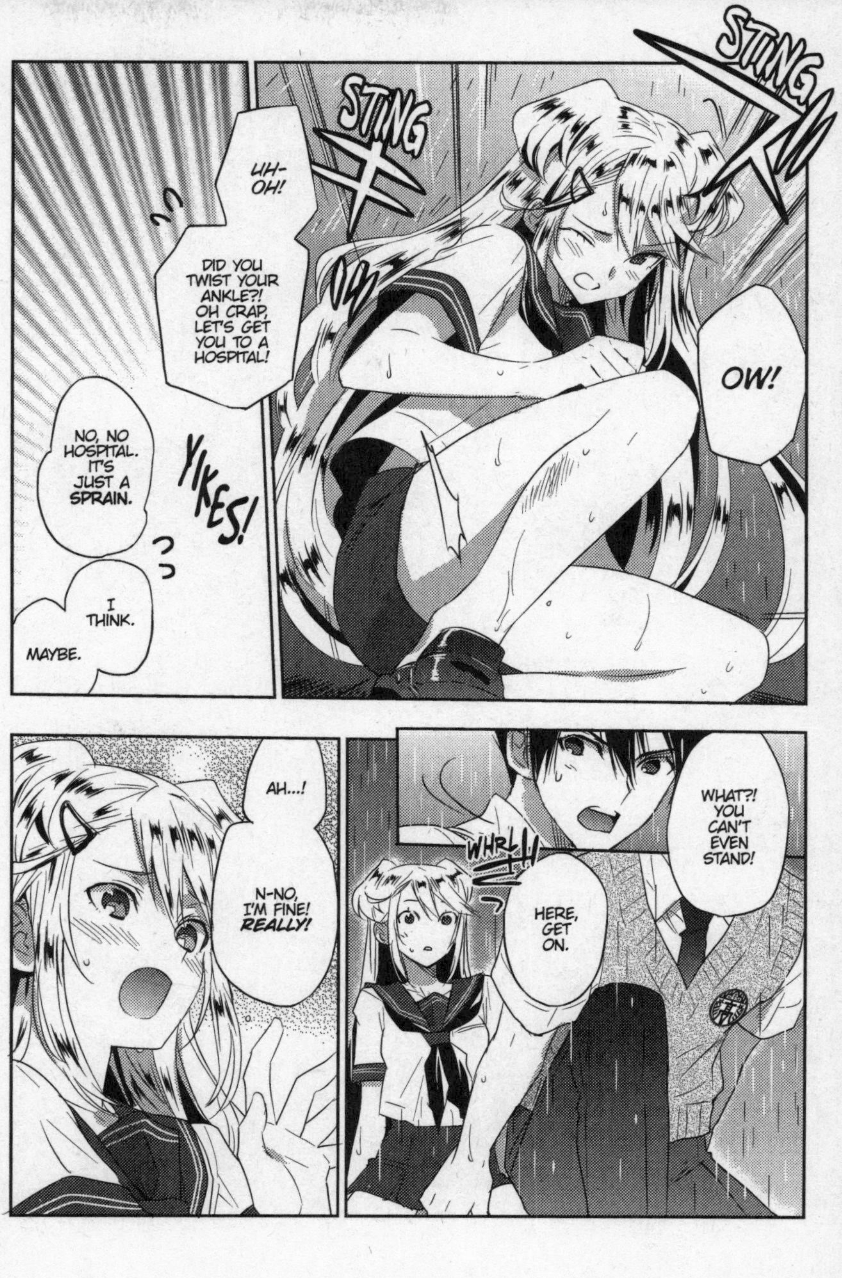
STING
STING
OW!
UH-OH!
DID YOU TWIST YOUR ANKLE?! OH CRAP, LET'S GET YOU TO A HOSPITAL!
YIKES!
NO, NO HOSPITAL. IT'S JUST A SPRAIN.
I THINK.
MAYBE.
WHAT?! YOU CAN'T EVEN STAND!
WHRL!!
HERE, GET ON.
AH...!
N-NO, I'M FINE! REALLY!

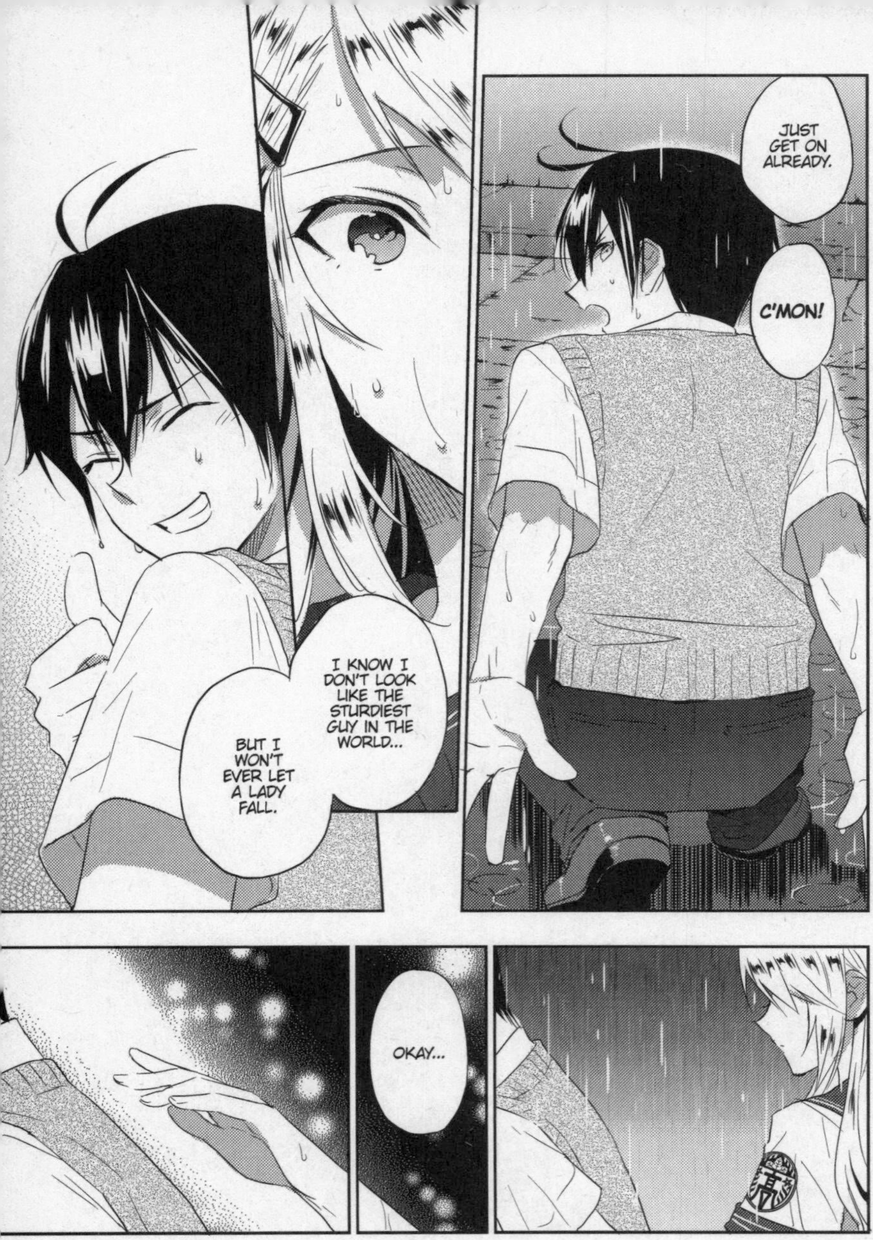
JUST GET ON ALREADY.
C'MON!
I KNOW I DON'T LOOK LIKE THE STURDIEST GUY IN THE WORLD...
BUT I WON'T EVER LET A LADY FALL.
OKAY...

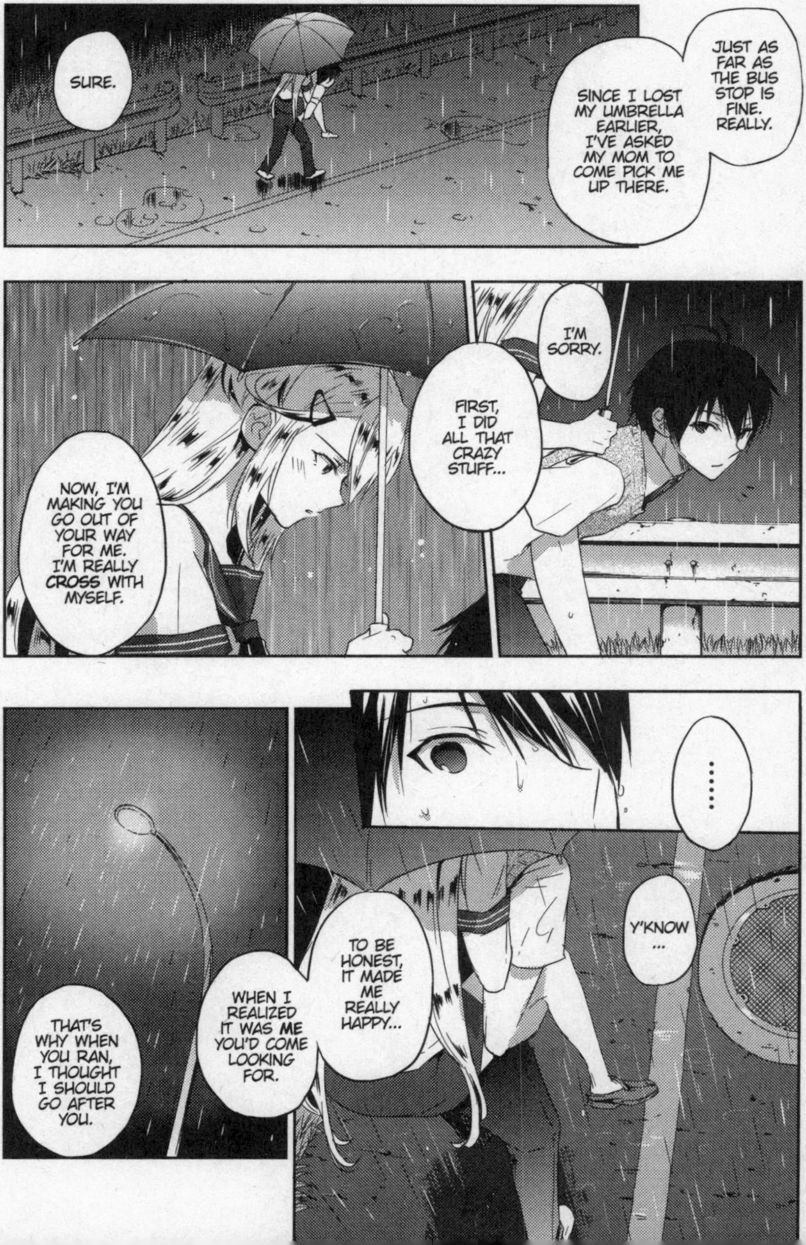
JUST AS FAR AS THE BUS STOP IS FINE. REALLY.
SINCE I LOST MY UMBRELLA EARLIER, I'VE ASKED MY MOM TO COME PICK ME UP THERE.
SURE.
I'M SORRY.
FIRST, I DID ALL THAT CRAZY STUFF...
NOW, I'M MAKING YOU GO OUT OF YOUR WAY FOR ME. I'M REALLY **CROSS** WITH MYSELF.
......
Y'KNOW ...
TO BE HONEST, IT MADE ME REALLY HAPPY...
WHEN I REALIZED IT WAS **ME** YOU'D COME LOOKING FOR.
THAT'S WHY WHEN YOU RAN, I THOUGHT I SHOULD GO AFTER YOU.

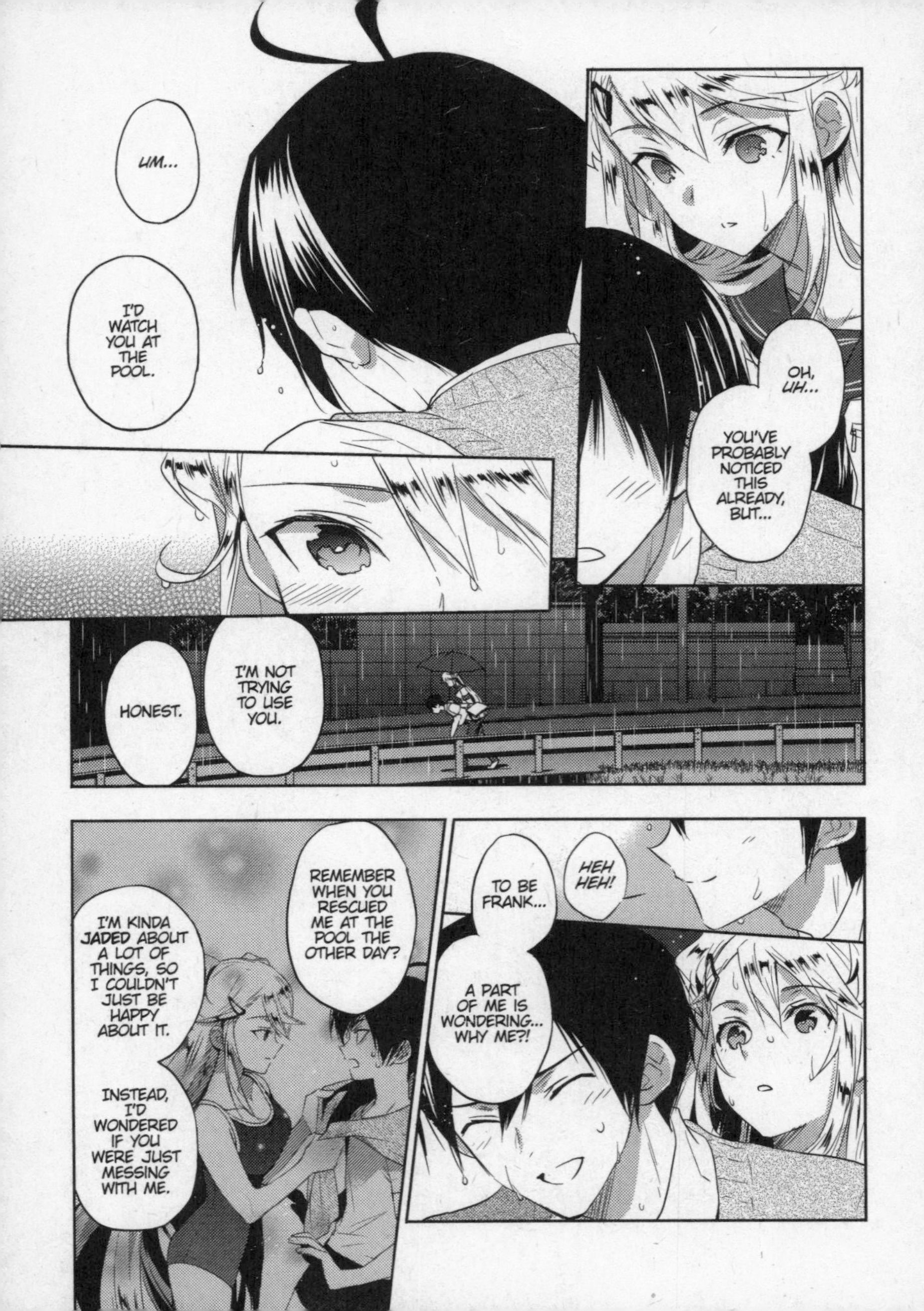
OH, UH...
YOU'VE PROBABLY NOTICED THIS ALREADY, BUT...
UM...
I'D WATCH YOU AT THE POOL.
I'M NOT TRYING TO USE YOU.
HONEST.
HEH HEH!
TO BE FRANK...
A PART OF ME IS WONDERING... WHY ME?!
REMEMBER WHEN YOU RESCUED ME AT THE POOL THE OTHER DAY?
I'M KINDA JADED ABOUT A LOT OF THINGS, SO I COULDN'T JUST BE HAPPY ABOUT IT.
INSTEAD, I'D WONDERED IF YOU WERE JUST MESSING WITH ME.

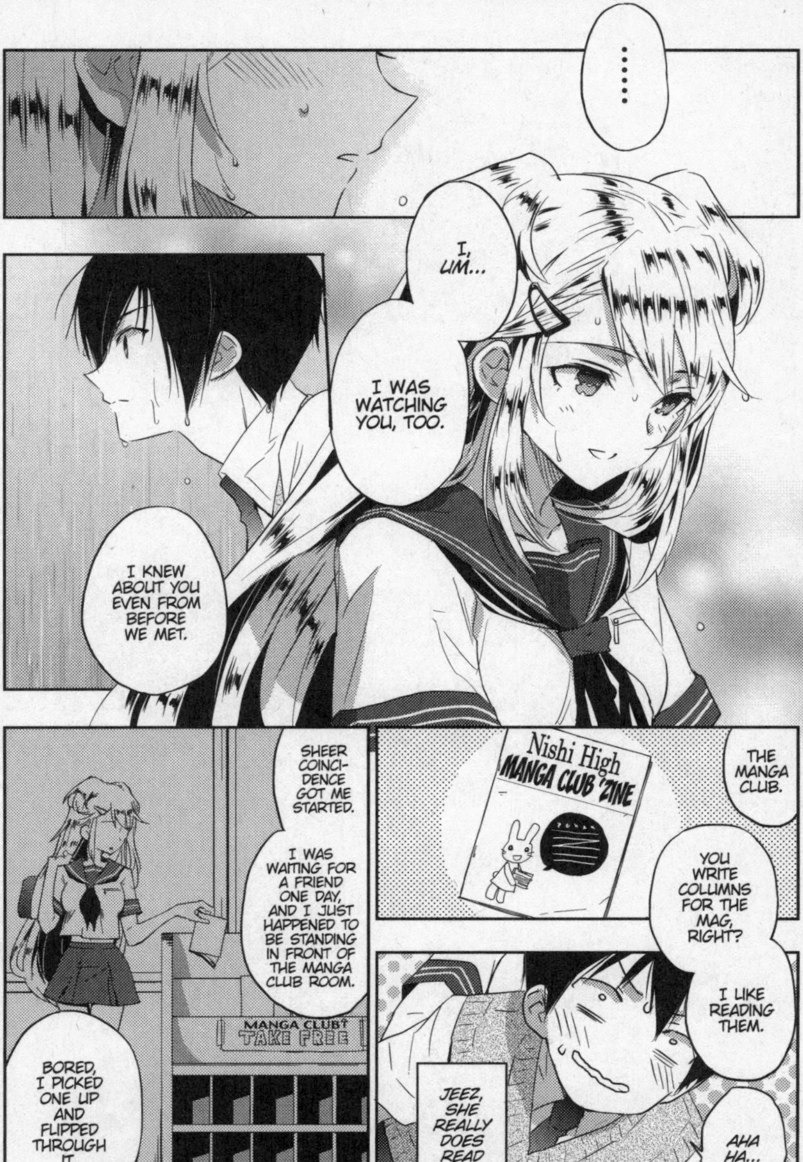
......
I, UM...
I WAS WATCHING YOU, TOO.
I KNEW ABOUT YOU EVEN FROM BEFORE WE MET.
Nishi High
MANGA CLUB 'ZINE
THE MANGA CLUB.
YOU WRITE COLUMNS FOR THE MAG, RIGHT?
I LIKE READING THEM.
AHA HA...
JEEZ, SHE REALLY DOES READ THEM?
SHEER COINCIDENCE GOT ME STARTED.
I WAS WAITING FOR A FRIEND ONE DAY, AND I JUST HAPPENED TO BE STANDING IN FRONT OF THE MANGA CLUB ROOM.
MANGA CLUB
TAKE FREE
BORED, I PICKED ONE UP AND FLIPPED THROUGH IT.

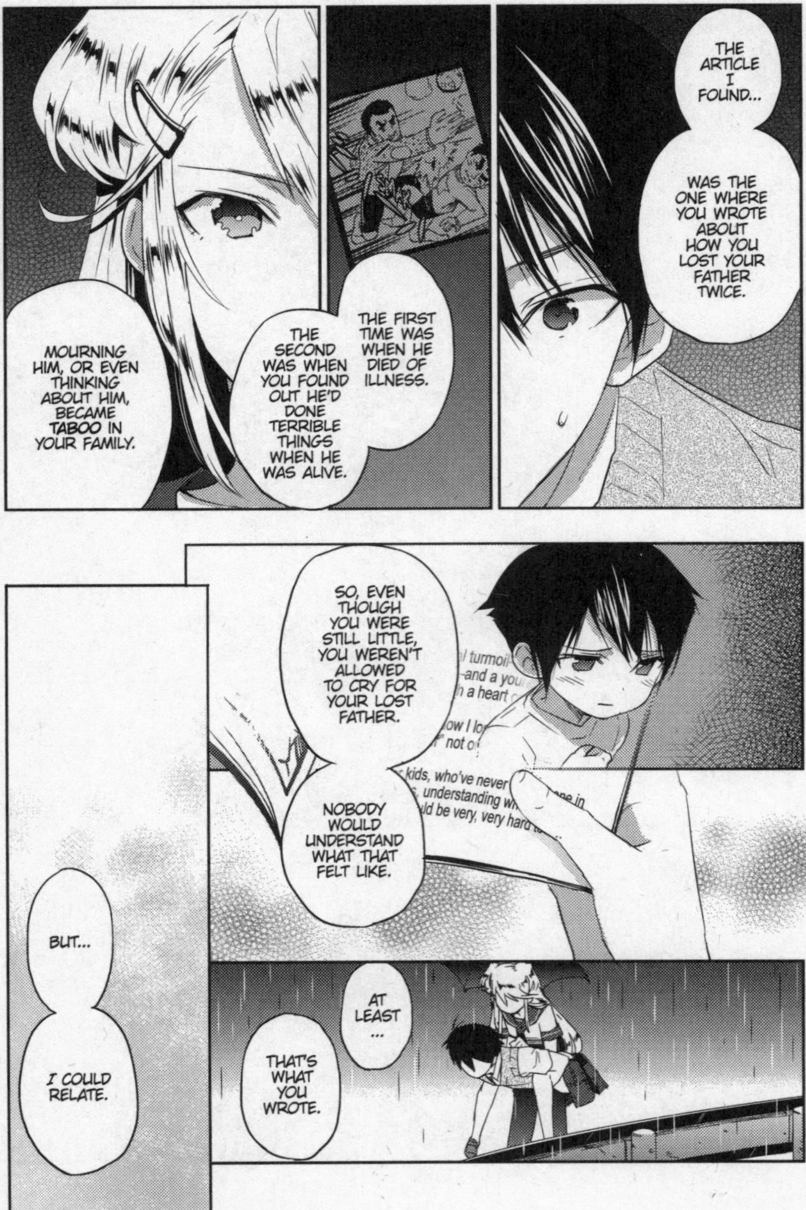
THE ARTICLE I FOUND...
WAS THE ONE WHERE YOU WROTE ABOUT HOW YOU LOST YOUR FATHER TWICE.
THE FIRST TIME WAS WHEN HE DIED OF ILLNESS.
THE SECOND WAS WHEN YOU FOUND OUT HE'D DONE TERRIBLE THINGS WHEN HE WAS ALIVE.
MOURNING HIM, OR EVEN THINKING ABOUT HIM, BECAME TABOO IN YOUR FAMILY.
SO, EVEN THOUGH YOU WERE STILL LITTLE, YOU WEREN'T ALLOWED TO CRY FOR YOUR LOST FATHER.
NOBODY WOULD UNDERSTAND WHAT THAT FELT LIKE.
AT LEAST ...
THAT'S WHAT YOU WROTE.
BUT...
I COULD RELATE.

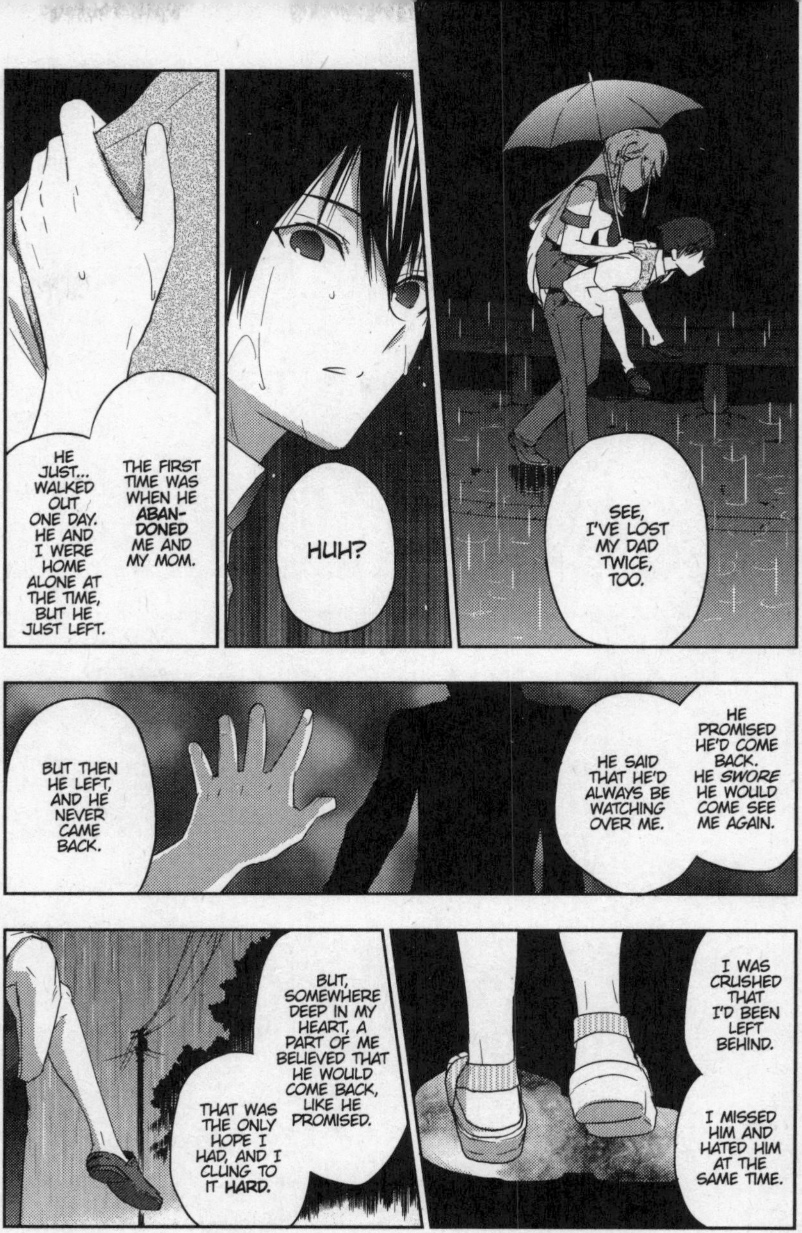
SEE, I'VE LOST MY DAD TWICE, TOO.
HUH?
THE FIRST TIME WAS WHEN HE ABANDONED ME AND MY MOM.
HE JUST... WALKED OUT ONE DAY. HE AND I WERE HOME ALONE AT THE TIME, BUT HE JUST LEFT.
HE PROMISED HE'D COME BACK. HE *SWORE* HE WOULD COME SEE ME AGAIN.
HE SAID THAT HE'D ALWAYS BE WATCHING OVER ME.
BUT THEN HE LEFT, AND HE NEVER CAME BACK.
I WAS CRUSHED THAT I'D BEEN LEFT BEHIND.
I MISSED HIM AND HATED HIM AT THE SAME TIME.
BUT, SOMEWHERE DEEP IN MY HEART, A PART OF ME BELIEVED THAT HE WOULD COME BACK, LIKE HE PROMISED.
THAT WAS THE ONLY HOPE I HAD, AND I CLUNG TO IT HARD.

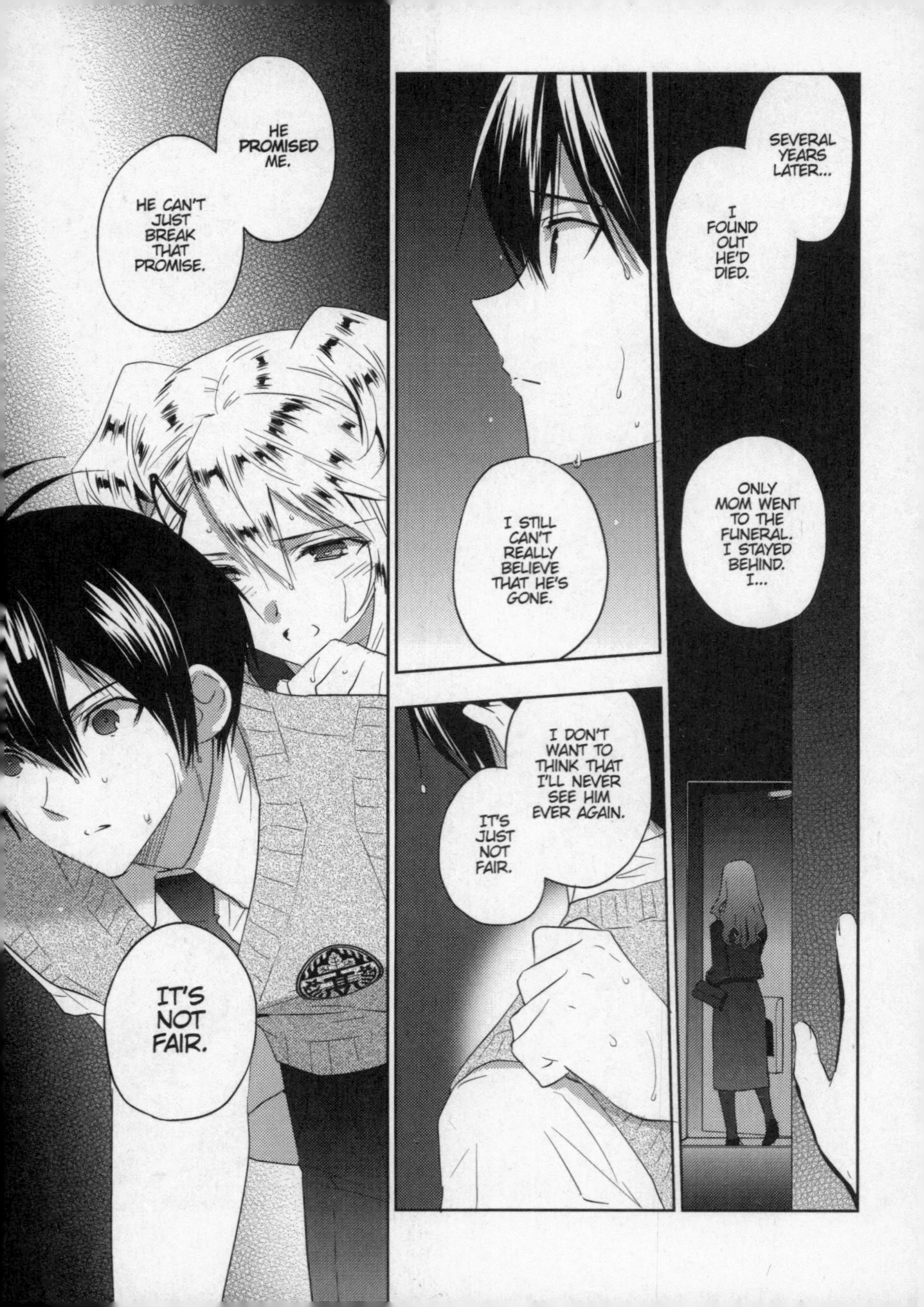
SEVERAL YEARS LATER...
I FOUND OUT HE'D DIED.
ONLY MOM WENT TO THE FUNERAL. I STAYED BEHIND. I...
I STILL CAN'T REALLY BELIEVE THAT HE'S GONE.
I DON'T WANT TO THINK THAT I'LL NEVER SEE HIM EVER AGAIN.
IT'S JUST NOT FAIR.
HE PROMISED ME.
HE CAN'T JUST BREAK THAT PROMISE.
IT'S NOT FAIR.

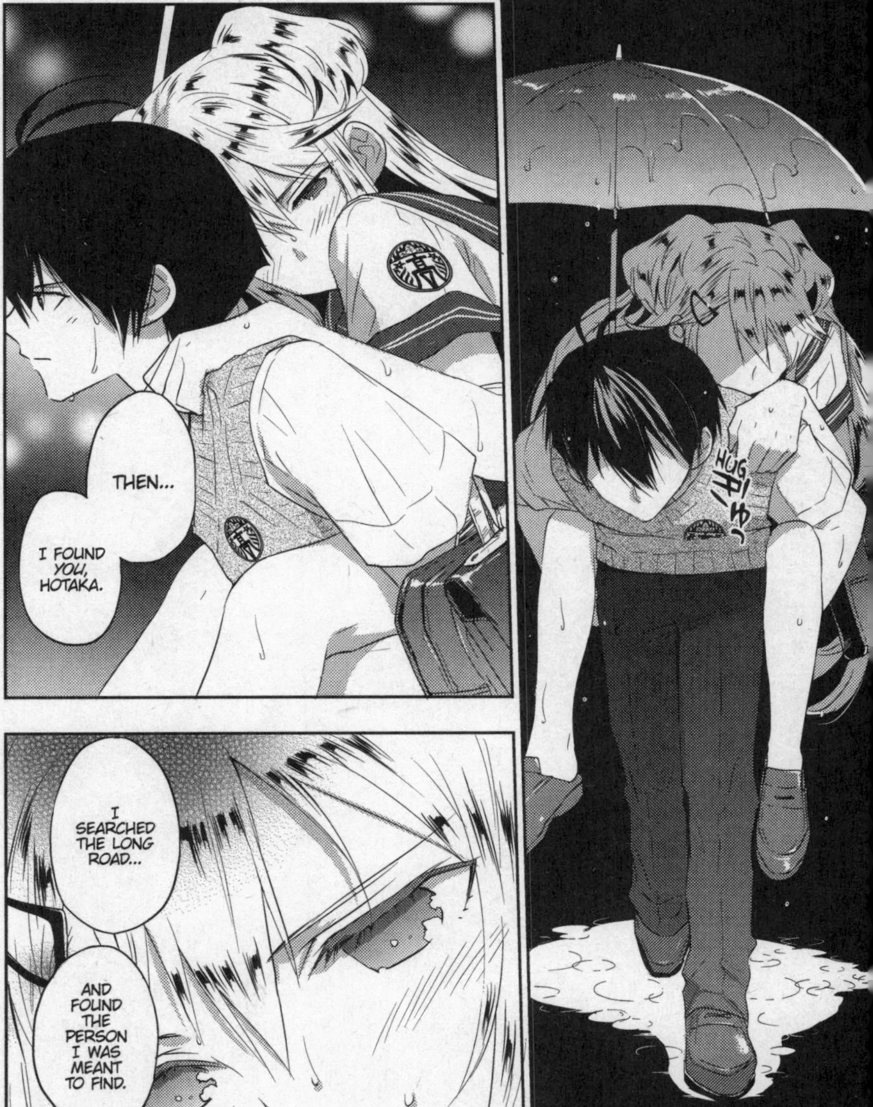
HUG
THEN...
I FOUND YOU, HOTAKA.
I SEARCHED THE LONG ROAD...
AND FOUND THE PERSON I WAS MEANT TO FIND.

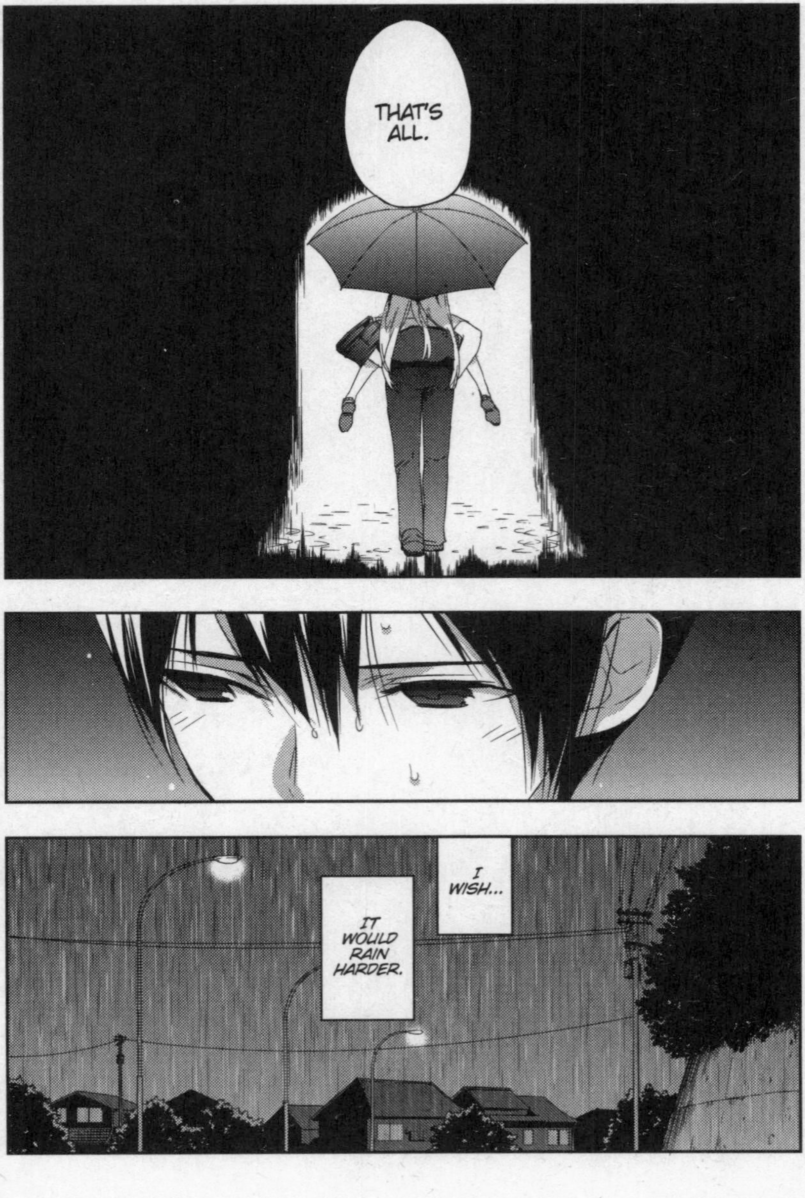
THAT'S ALL.
I WISH...
IT WOULD RAIN HARDER.

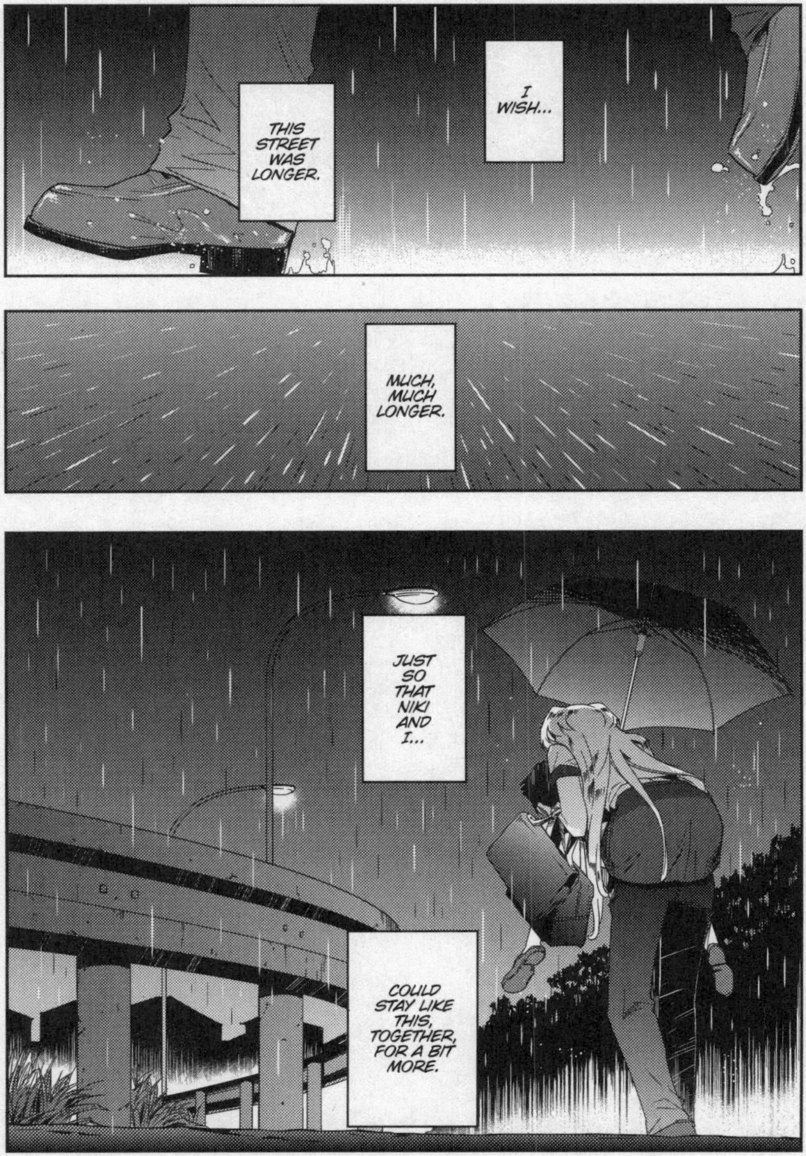
I WISH...
THIS STREET WAS LONGER.
MUCH, MUCH LONGER.
JUST SO THAT NIKI AND I...
COULD STAY LIKE THIS, TOGETHER, FOR A BIT MORE.

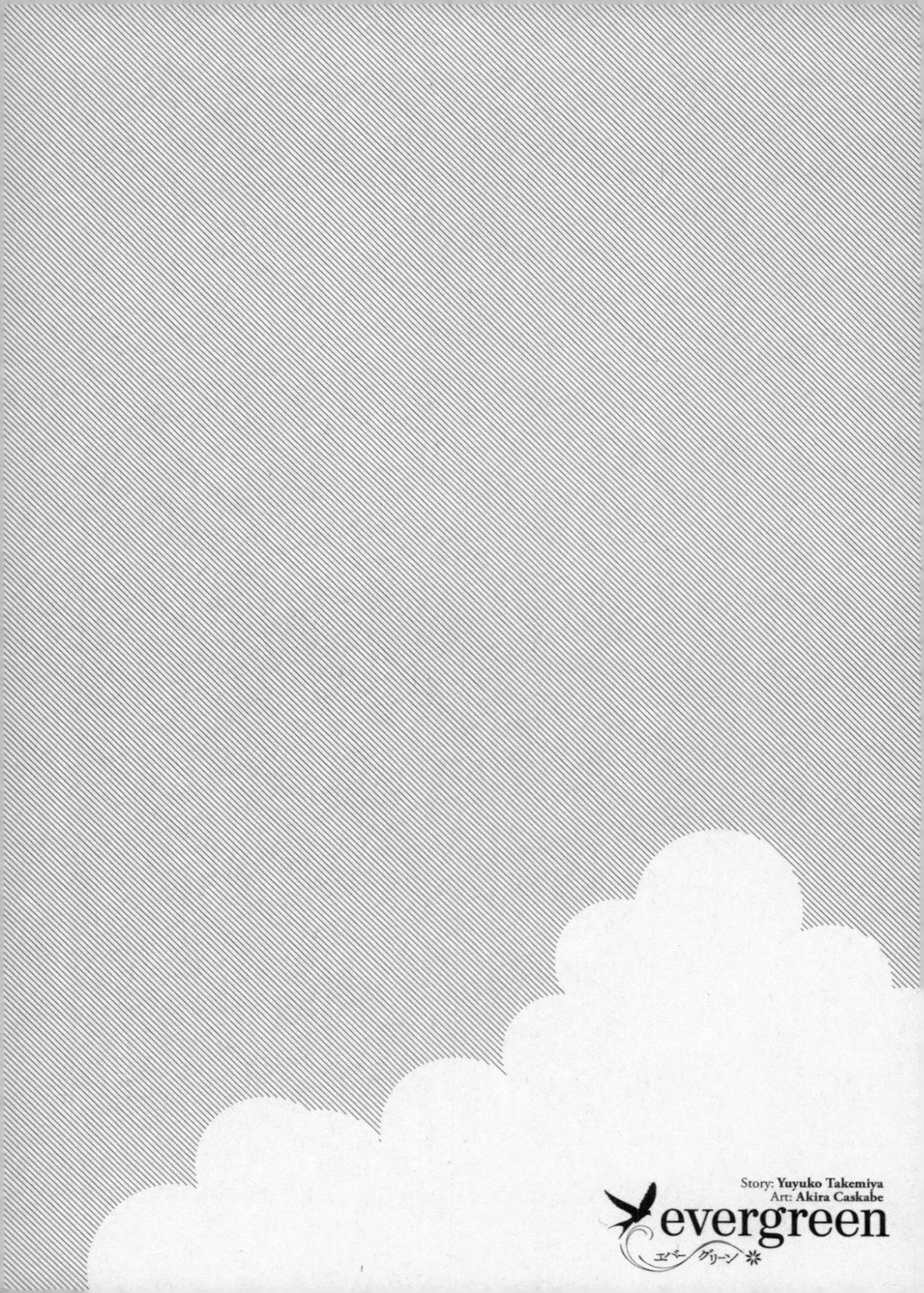
Story: Yuyuko Takemiya
Art: Akira Caskabe
evergreen
エバーグリーン

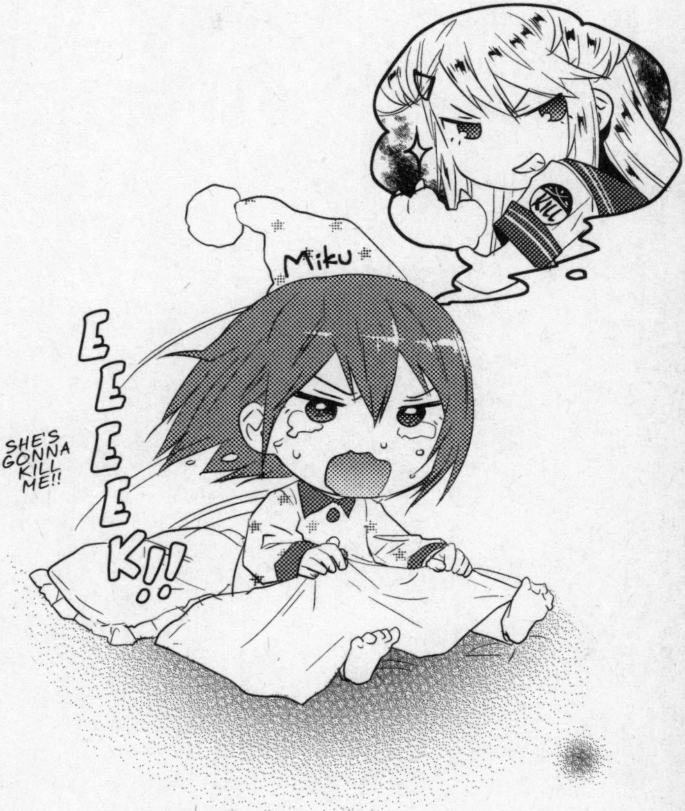
KILL
Miku
EEEEEK!!
SHE'S GONNA KILL ME!!

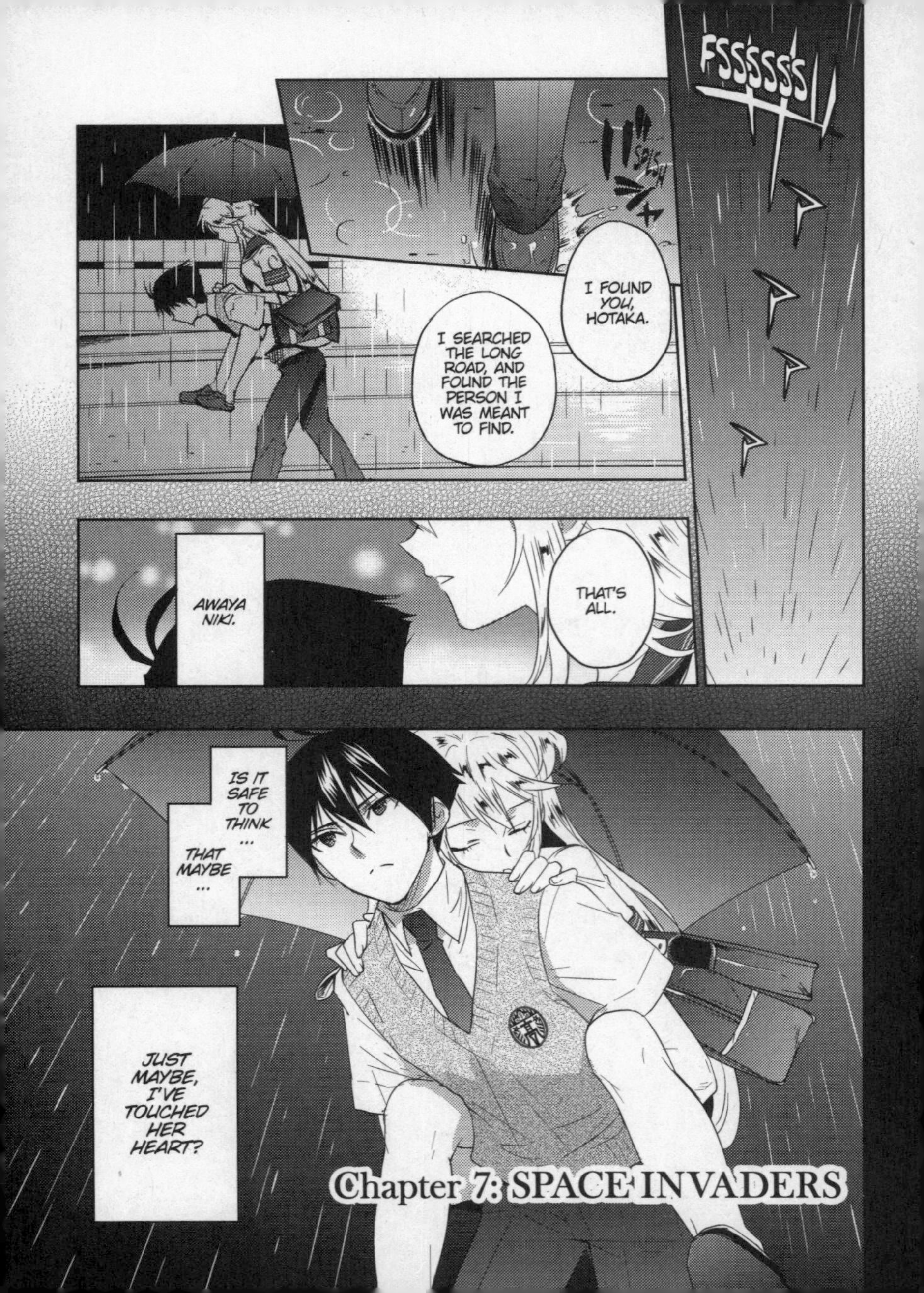
FSSSSSS
SPISH
I FOUND YOU, HOTAKA.
I SEARCHED THE LONG ROAD, AND FOUND THE PERSON I WAS MEANT TO FIND.
THAT'S ALL.
AWAYA NIKI.
IS IT SAFE TO THINK... THAT MAYBE...
JUST MAYBE, I'VE TOUCHED HER HEART?
Chapter 7: SPACE INVADERS

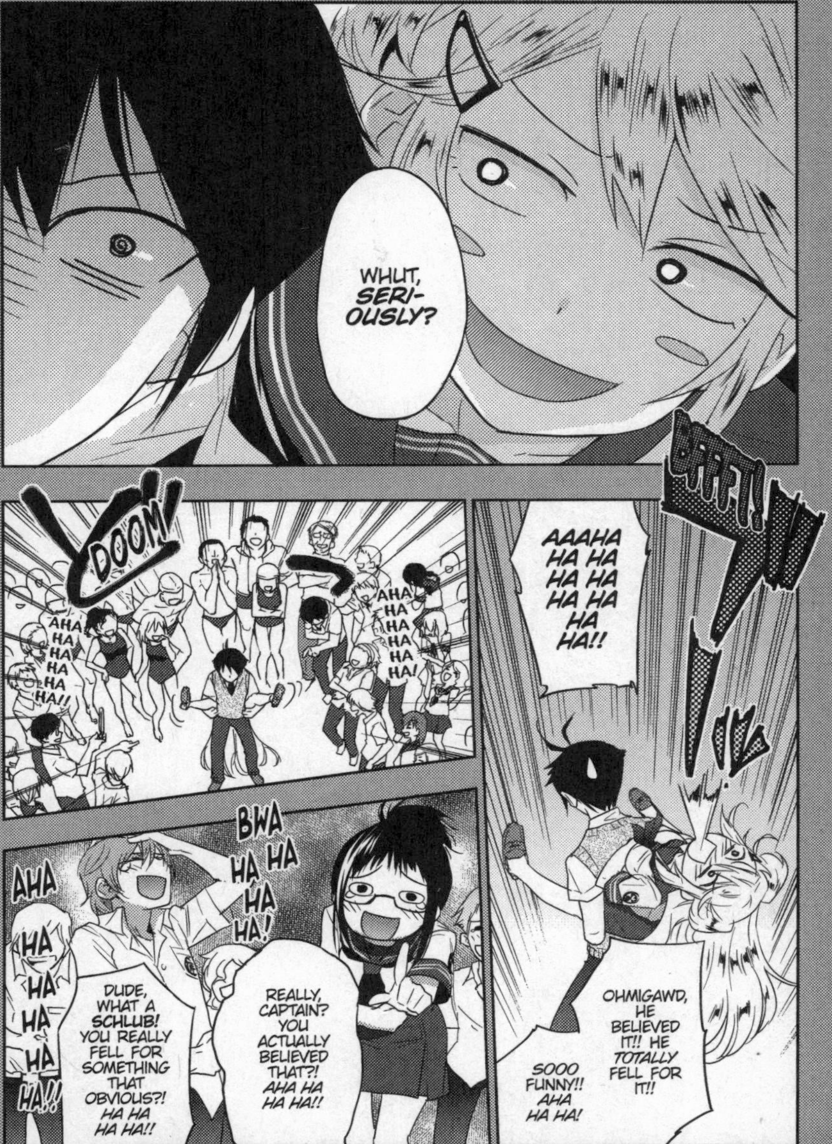
WHUT, SERIOUSLY?
AAAHA HA HA HA HA HA HA HA HA HA!!
OHMIGAWD, HE BELIEVED IT!! HE TOTALLY FELL FOR IT!!
SOOO FUNNY!! AHA HA HA!
DOOM
AHA HA HA HA HA HA HA!
AHA HA HA HA HA HA!!
BWA HA HA HA HA HA!
REALLY, CAPTAIN? YOU ACTUALLY BELIEVED THAT?! AHA HA HA HA!!
AHA HA HA HA HA HA!!
DUDE, WHAT A SCHLUB! YOU REALLY FELL FOR SOMETHING THAT OBVIOUS?! HA HA HA HA!!

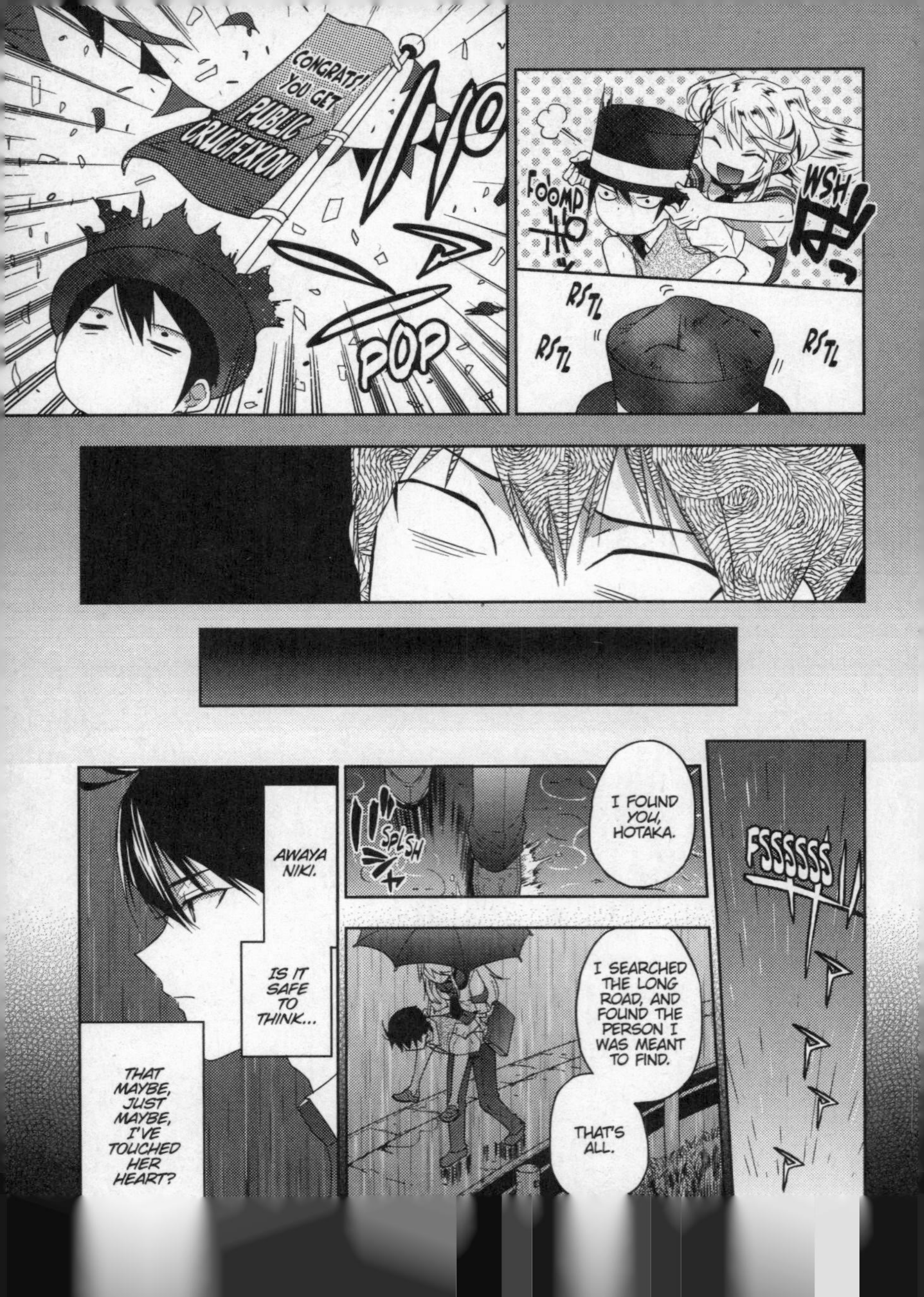
WSH
FOOMP
RSTL
RSTL
RSTL
CONGRATS! YOU GET PUBLIC CRUCIFIXION
NO
POP
FSSSSSS
I FOUND YOU, HOTAKA.
SPLSH
I SEARCHED THE LONG ROAD, AND FOUND THE PERSON I WAS MEANT TO FIND.
THAT'S ALL.
AWAYA NIKI.
IS IT SAFE TO THINK...
THAT MAYBE, JUST MAYBE, I'VE TOUCHED HER HEART?

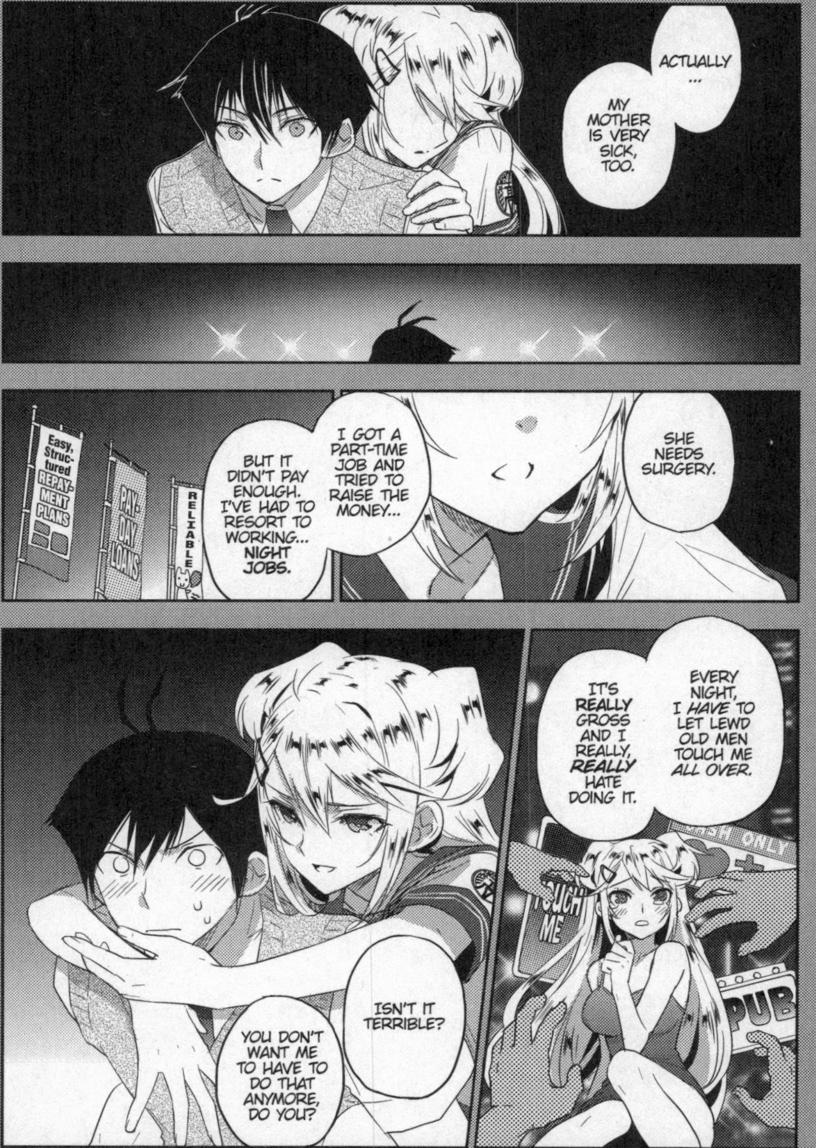
ACTUALLY ...
MY MOTHER IS VERY SICK, TOO.
SHE NEEDS SURGERY.
I GOT A PART-TIME JOB AND TRIED TO RAISE THE MONEY...
BUT IT DIDN'T PAY ENOUGH. I'VE HAD TO RESORT TO WORKING... NIGHT JOBS.
Easy, Structured REPAYMENT PLANS
PAY-DAY LOANS
RELIABLE
EVERY NIGHT, I *HAVE* TO LET LEWD OLD MEN TOUCH ME *ALL OVER.*
IT'S **REALLY** GROSS AND I REALLY, ***REALLY*** HATE DOING IT.
TOUCH ME
PUB
ISN'T IT TERRIBLE?
YOU DON'T WANT ME TO HAVE TO DO THAT ANYMORE, DO YOU?

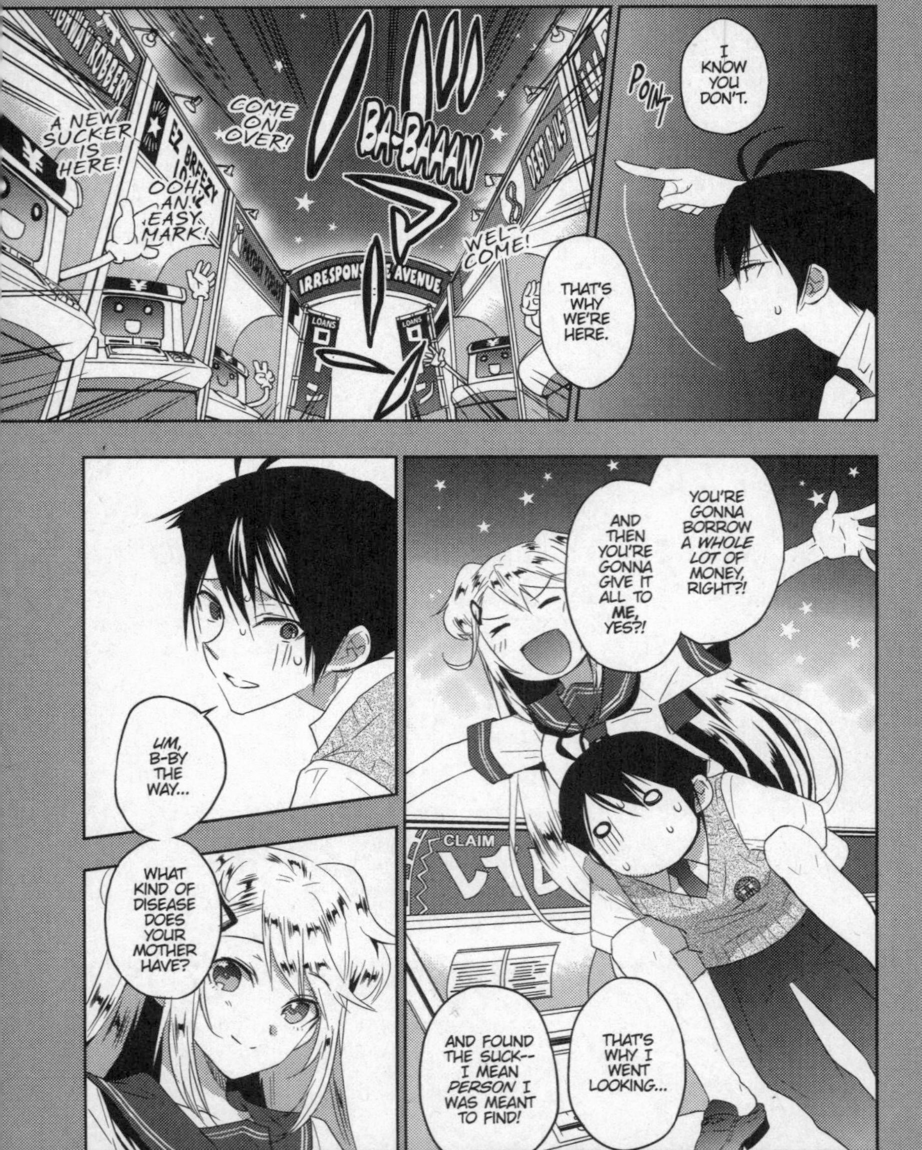
POINT
I KNOW YOU DON'T.
THAT'S WHY WE'RE HERE.
WEL-COME!
BA-BAAAN
COME ON OVER!
A NEW SUCKER IS HERE!
EZ BREEZY
OOH, AN EASY MARK!
LOANS
YOU'RE GONNA BORROW A *WHOLE LOT* OF MONEY, RIGHT?!
AND THEN YOU'RE GONNA GIVE IT ALL TO ME, YES?!
CLAIM
THAT'S WHY I WENT LOOKING...
AND FOUND THE SUCK-- I MEAN *PERSON* I WAS MEANT TO FIND!
UM, B-BY THE WAY...
WHAT KIND OF DISEASE DOES YOUR MOTHER HAVE?

Terminal Nostril Vibrissae Sensitivus Hemorrhagic Fever-itis.

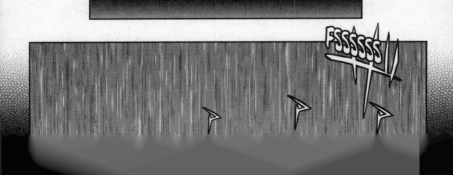

FSSSSSS

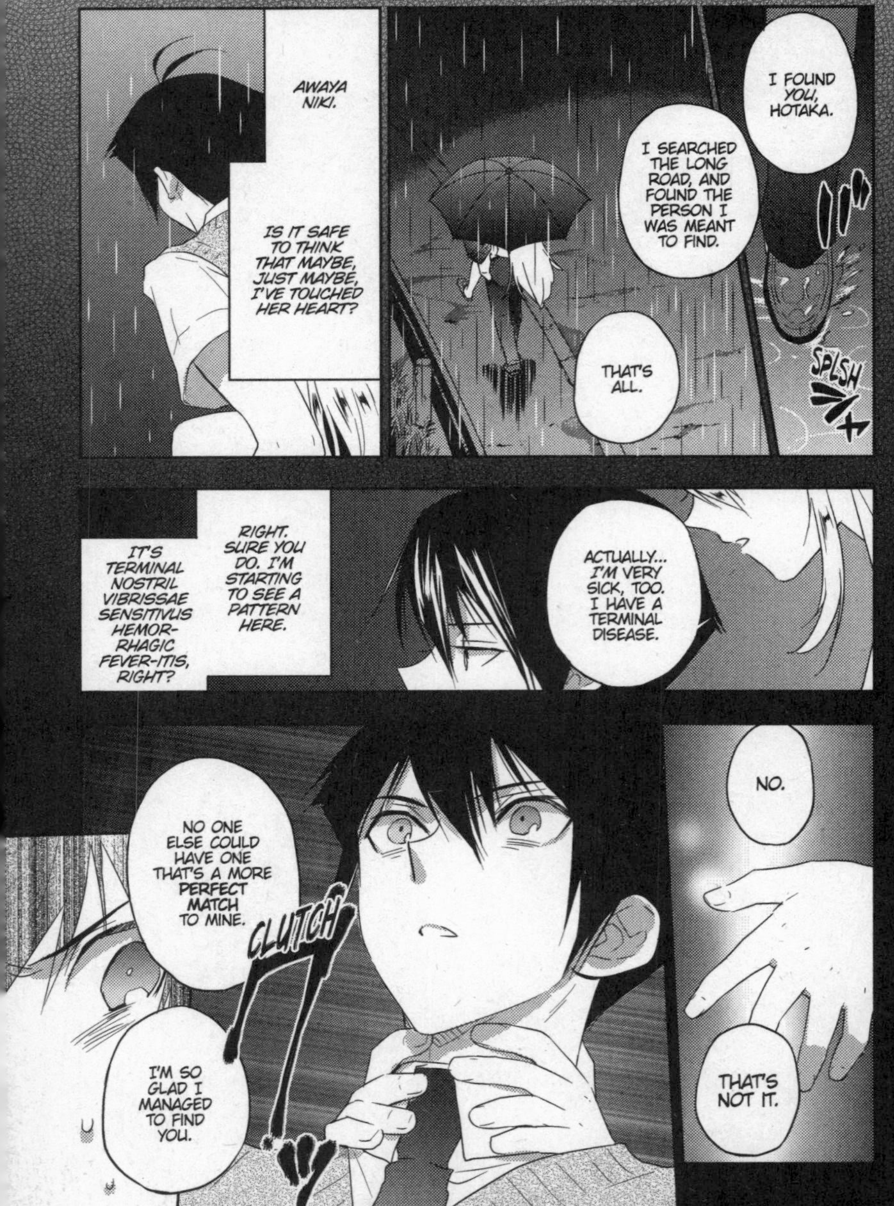
I FOUND YOU, HOTAKA.
I SEARCHED THE LONG ROAD, AND FOUND THE PERSON I WAS MEANT TO FIND.
THAT'S ALL.
SPLSH
AWAYA NIKI.
IS IT SAFE TO THINK THAT MAYBE, JUST MAYBE, I'VE TOUCHED HER HEART?
ACTUALLY... I'M VERY SICK, TOO. I HAVE A TERMINAL DISEASE.
RIGHT. SURE YOU DO. I'M STARTING TO SEE A PATTERN HERE.
IT'S TERMINAL NOSTRIL VIBRISSAE SENSITIVUS HEMORRHAGIC FEVER-ITIS, RIGHT?
NO.
THAT'S NOT IT.
NO ONE ELSE COULD HAVE ONE THAT'S A MORE PERFECT MATCH TO MINE.
CLUTCH
I'M SO GLAD I MANAGED TO FIND YOU.

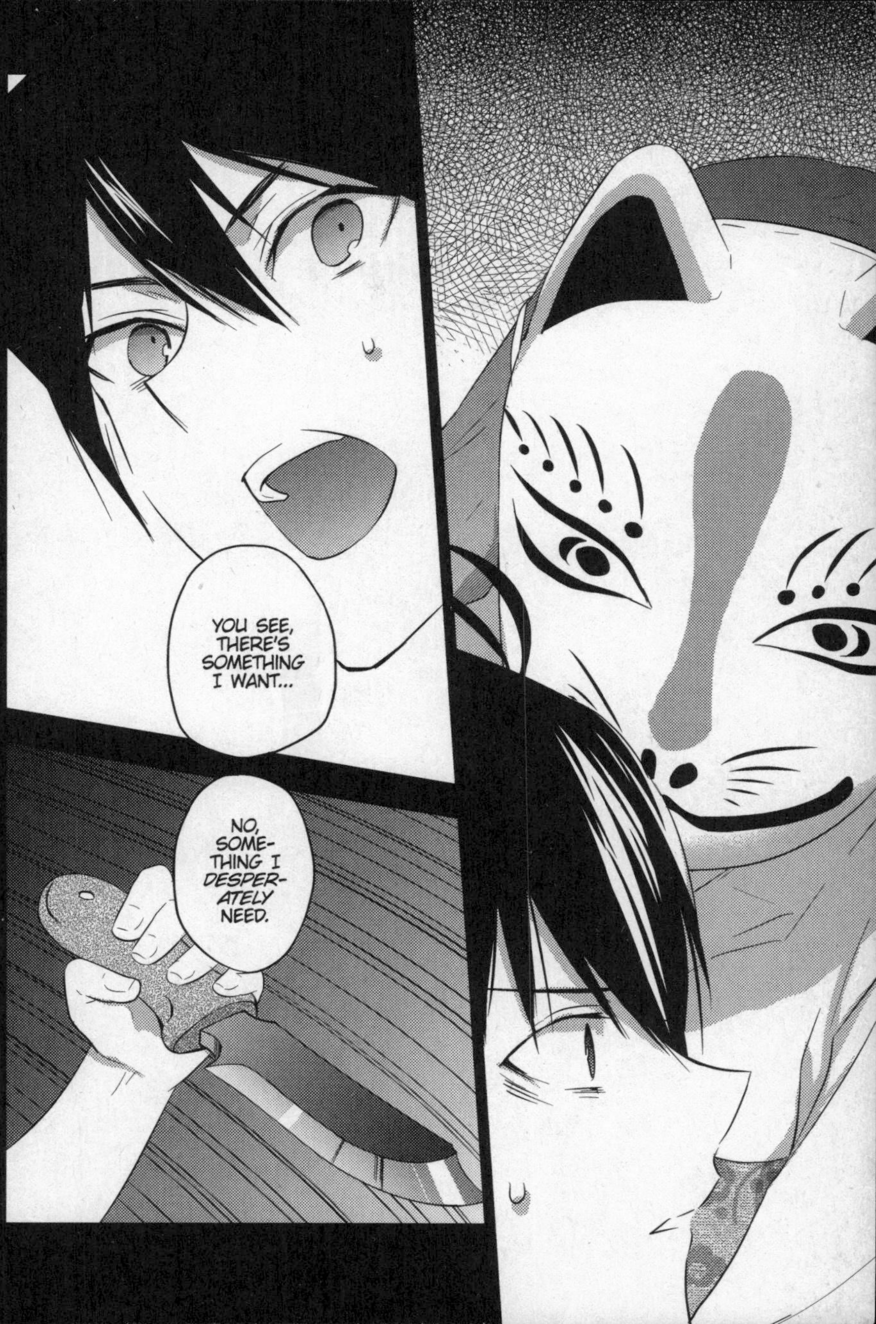
YOU SEE, THERE'S SOMETHING I WANT...
NO, SOME-THING I DESPER-ATELY NEED.

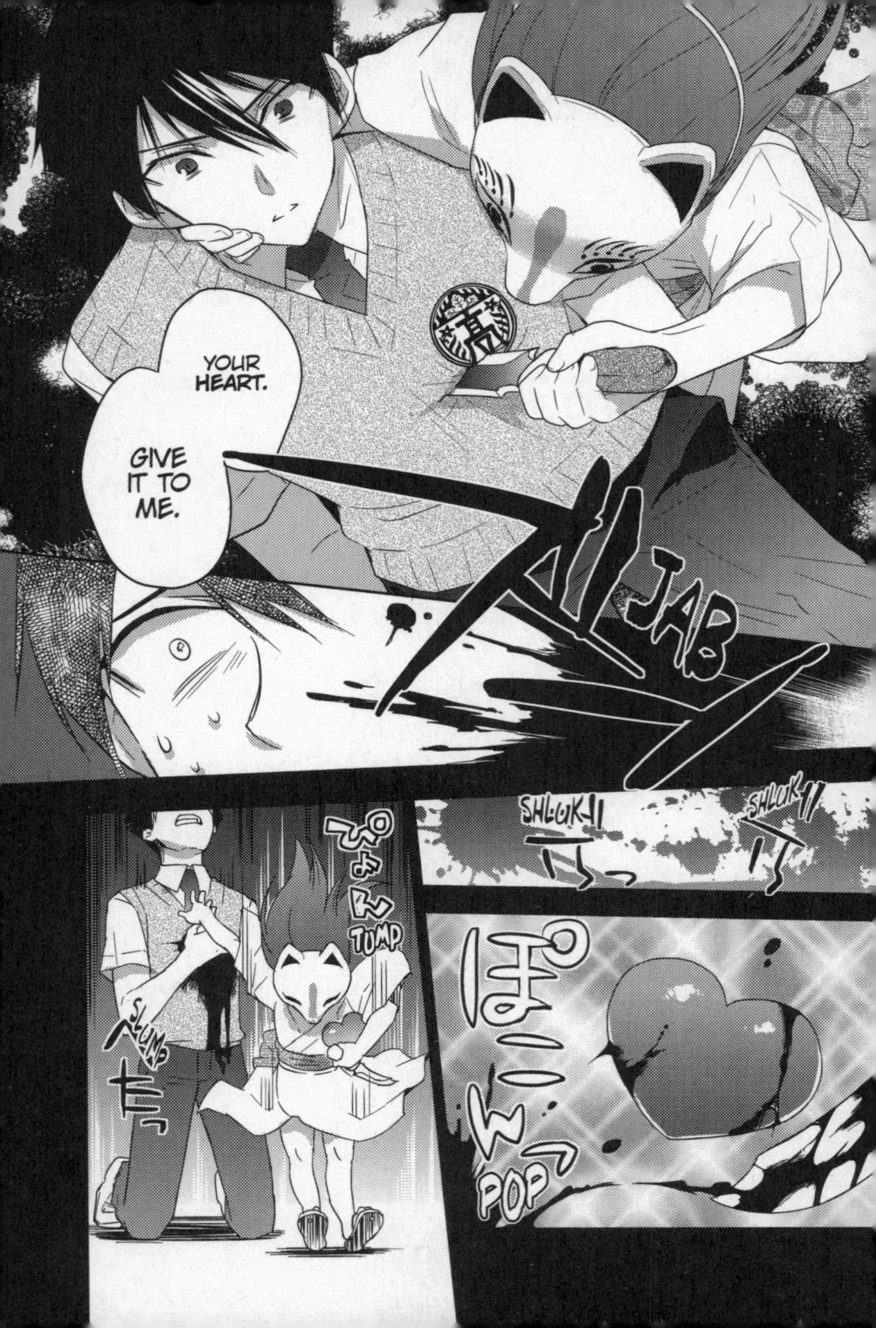
YOUR HEART.
GIVE IT TO ME.
JAB
SHLUK!!
SHLUK!!
ぽこんっ
POP
ぴょんっ
TUMP
SLUMP

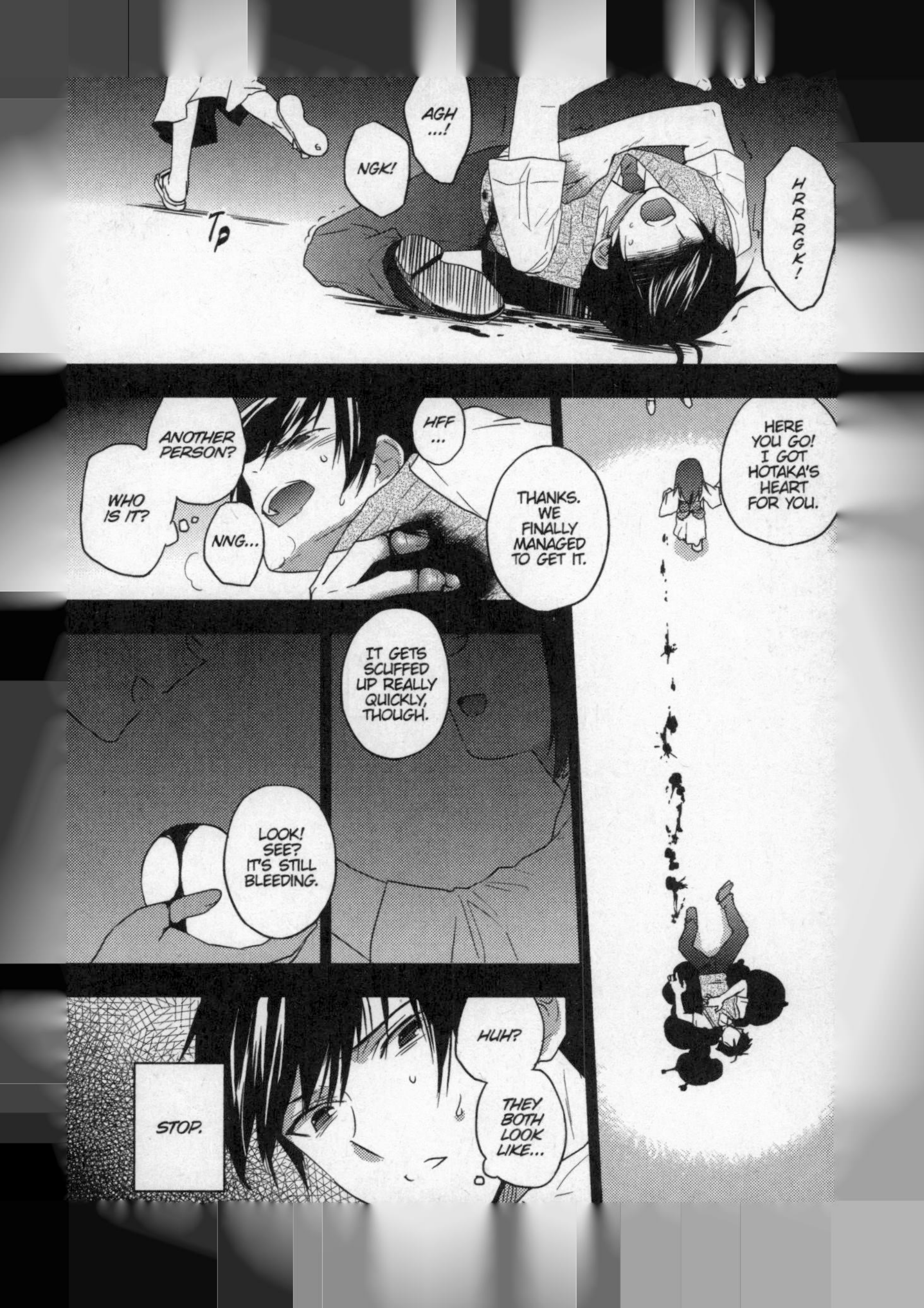
HRRRGK!
AGH ...!
NGK!
Tp
HERE YOU GO! I GOT HOTAKA'S HEART FOR YOU.
HFF ...
THANKS. WE FINALLY MANAGED TO GET IT.
ANOTHER PERSON?
WHO IS IT?
NNG...
IT GETS SCUFFED UP REALLY QUICKLY, THOUGH.
LOOK! SEE? IT'S STILL BLEEDING.
HUH?
THEY BOTH LOOK LIKE...
STOP.

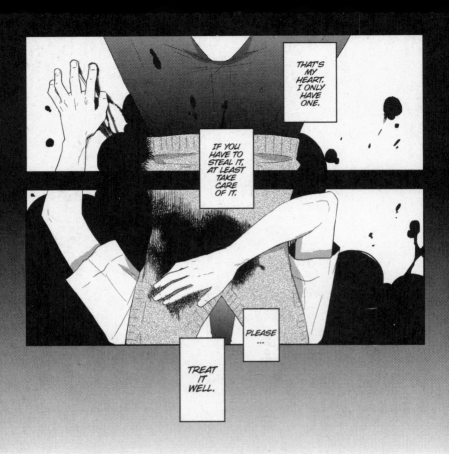

THAT'S MY HEART. I ONLY HAVE ONE.

IF YOU HAVE TO STEAL IT, AT LEAST TAKE CARE OF IT.

PLEASE ...

TREAT IT WELL.

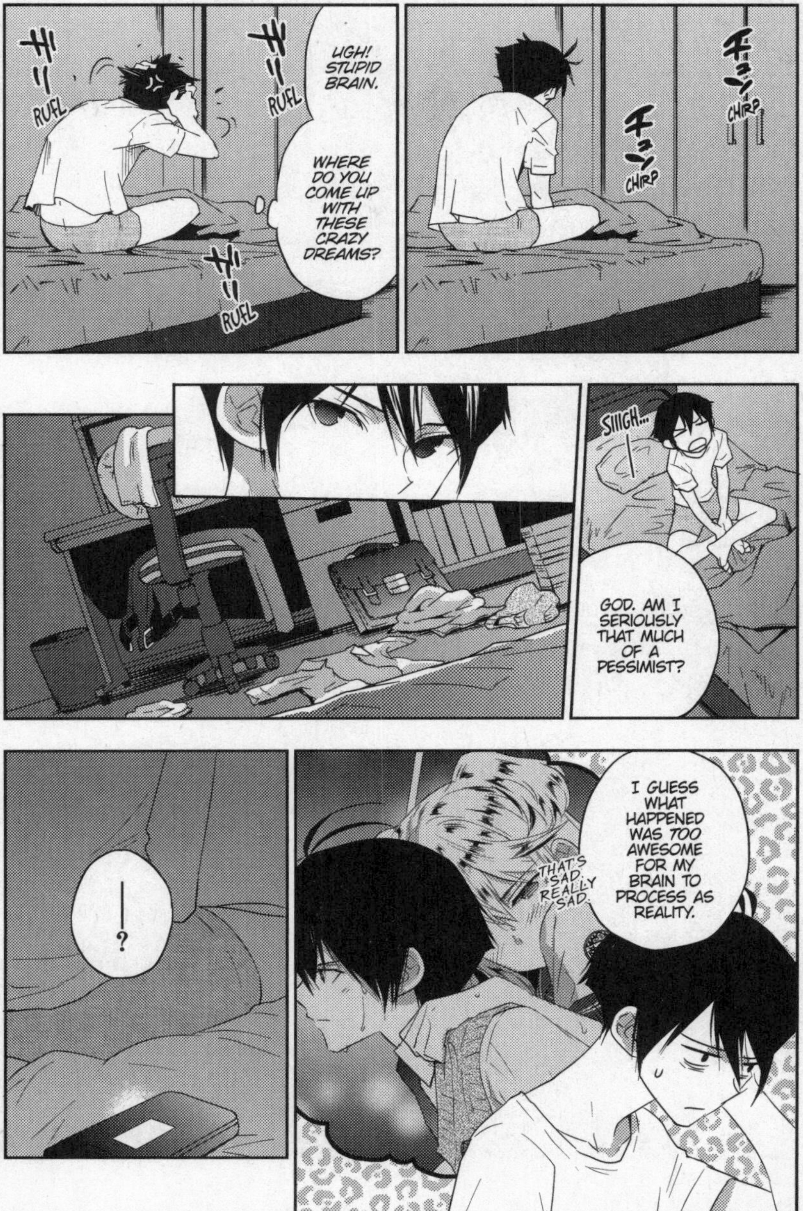

CHIRP
CHIRP
UGH! STUPID BRAIN.
RUFL
RUFL
WHERE DO YOU COME UP WITH THESE CRAZY DREAMS?
RUFL
SIIIGH...
GOD. AM I SERIOUSLY THAT MUCH OF A PESSIMIST?
I GUESS WHAT HAPPENED WAS *TOO* AWESOME FOR MY BRAIN TO PROCESS AS REALITY.
THAT'S SAD. REALLY SAD.
—?

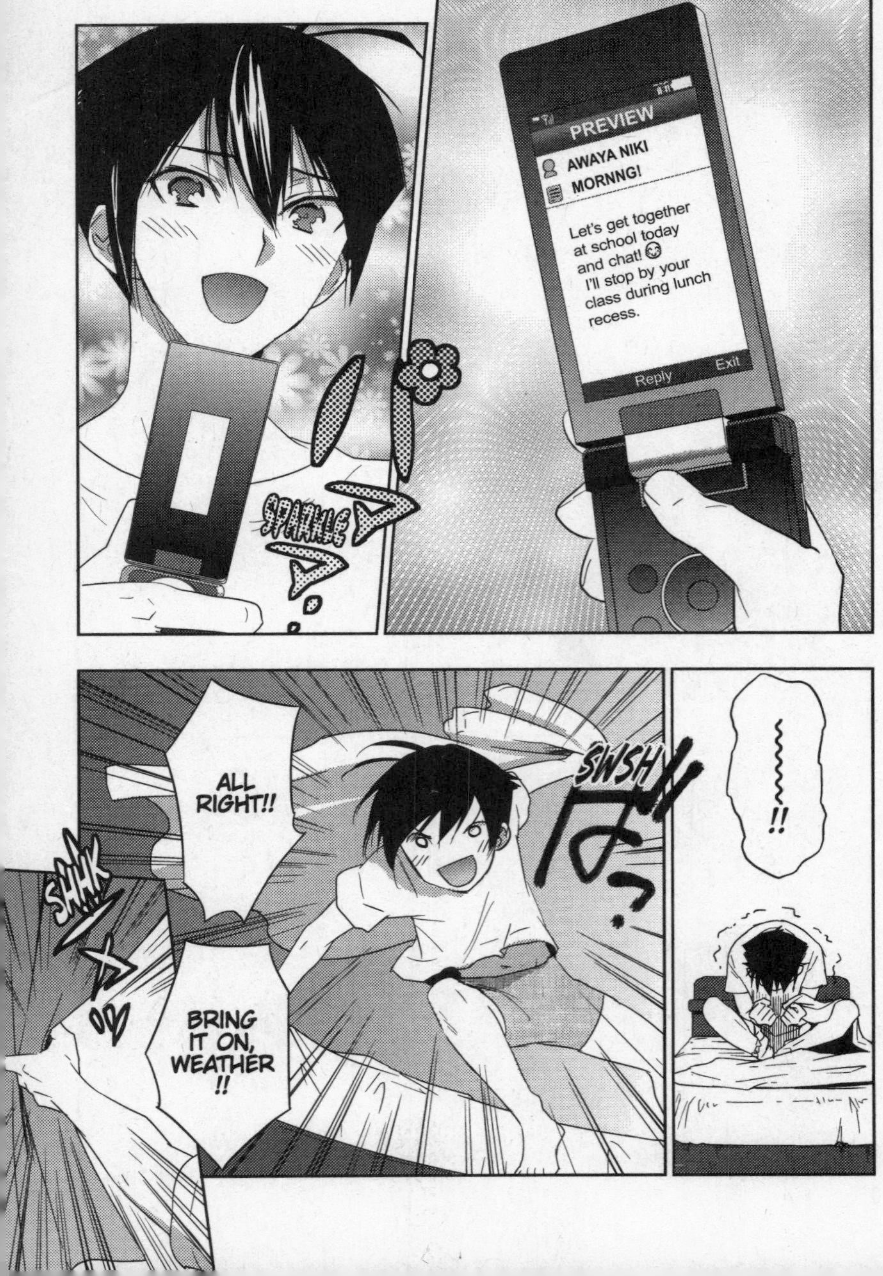
PREVIEW
AWAYA NIKI
MORNNG!
Let's get together at school today and chat! I'll stop by your class during lunch recess.
Reply
Exit
SPARKLE
......!!
SWSH
ALL RIGHT!!
BRING IT ON, WEATHER!!
SHHK

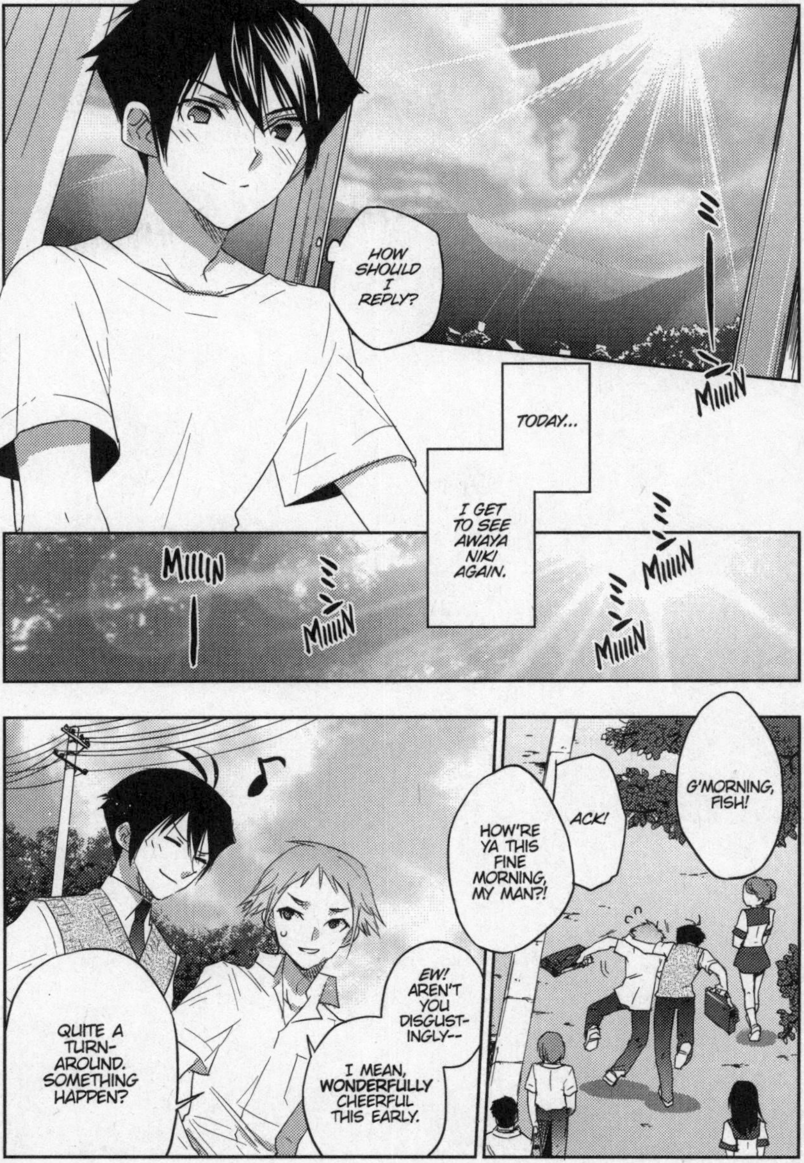
MIIIIN
HOW SHOULD I REPLY?
TODAY...
I GET TO SEE AWAYA NIKI AGAIN.
MIIIIN
MIIIIN
MIIIIN
MIIIIN
G'MORNING, FISH!
ACK!
HOW'RE YA THIS FINE MORNING, MY MAN?!
EW! AREN'T YOU DISGUST-INGLY--
I MEAN, WONDERFULLY CHEERFUL THIS EARLY.
QUITE A TURN-AROUND. SOMETHING HAPPEN?

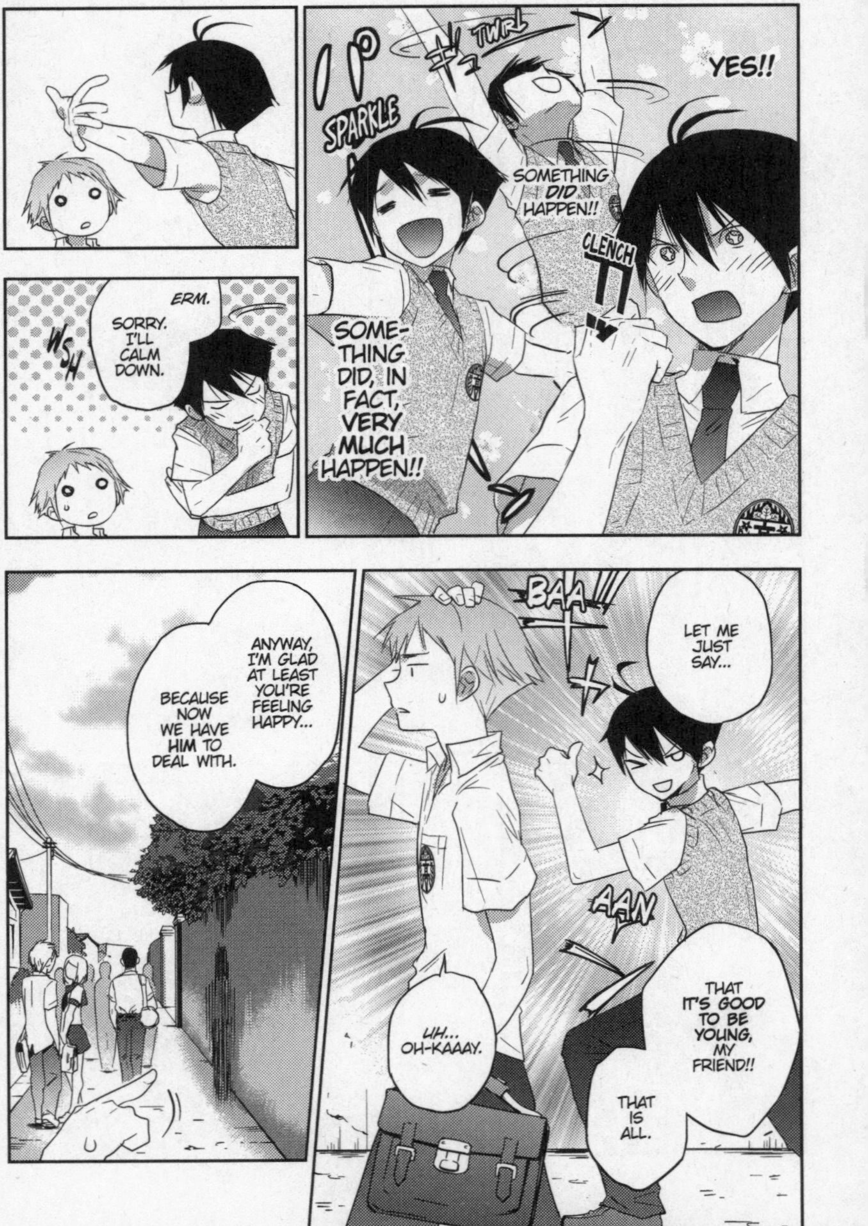
YES!!
TWRL
SPARKLE
SOMETHING DID HAPPEN!!
CLENCH
SOME-THING DID, IN FACT, VERY MUCH HAPPEN!!
ERM.
SORRY. I'LL CALM DOWN.
WSH
BAA!!
LET ME JUST SAY...
AAN
THAT IT'S GOOD TO BE YOUNG, MY FRIEND!!
THAT IS ALL.
UH... OH-KAAAY.
ANYWAY, I'M GLAD AT LEAST YOU'RE FEELING HAPPY...
BECAUSE NOW WE HAVE HIM TO DEAL WITH.

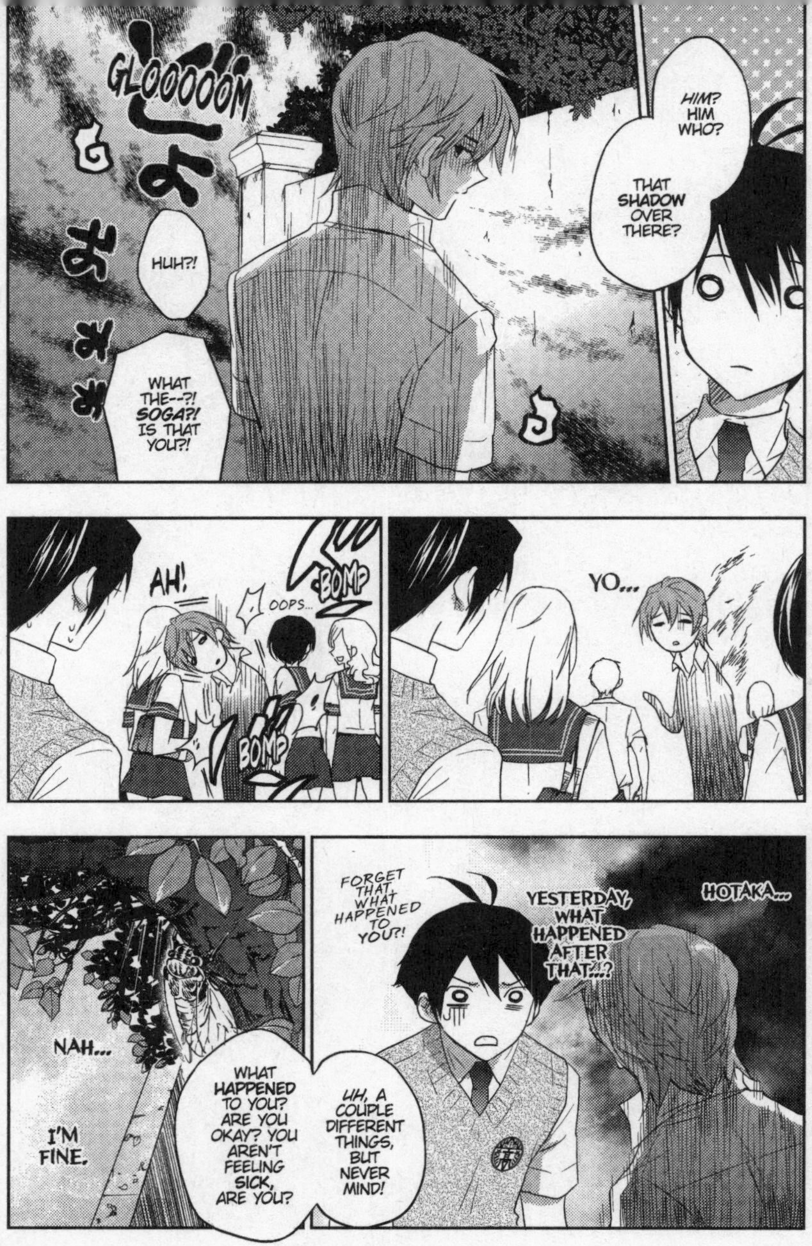
HIM? HIM WHO?
THAT SHADOW OVER THERE?
GLOOOOOM
HUH?!
WHAT THE--?! SOGA?! IS THAT YOU?!
YO...
AH!
OOPS...
BOMP
BOMP
HOTAKA...
YESTERDAY, WHAT HAPPENED AFTER THAT...?
FORGET THAT WHAT HAPPENED TO YOU?!
UH, A COUPLE DIFFERENT THINGS, BUT NEVER MIND!
WHAT HAPPENED TO YOU? ARE YOU OKAY? YOU AREN'T FEELING SICK, ARE YOU?
NAH...
I'M FINE.

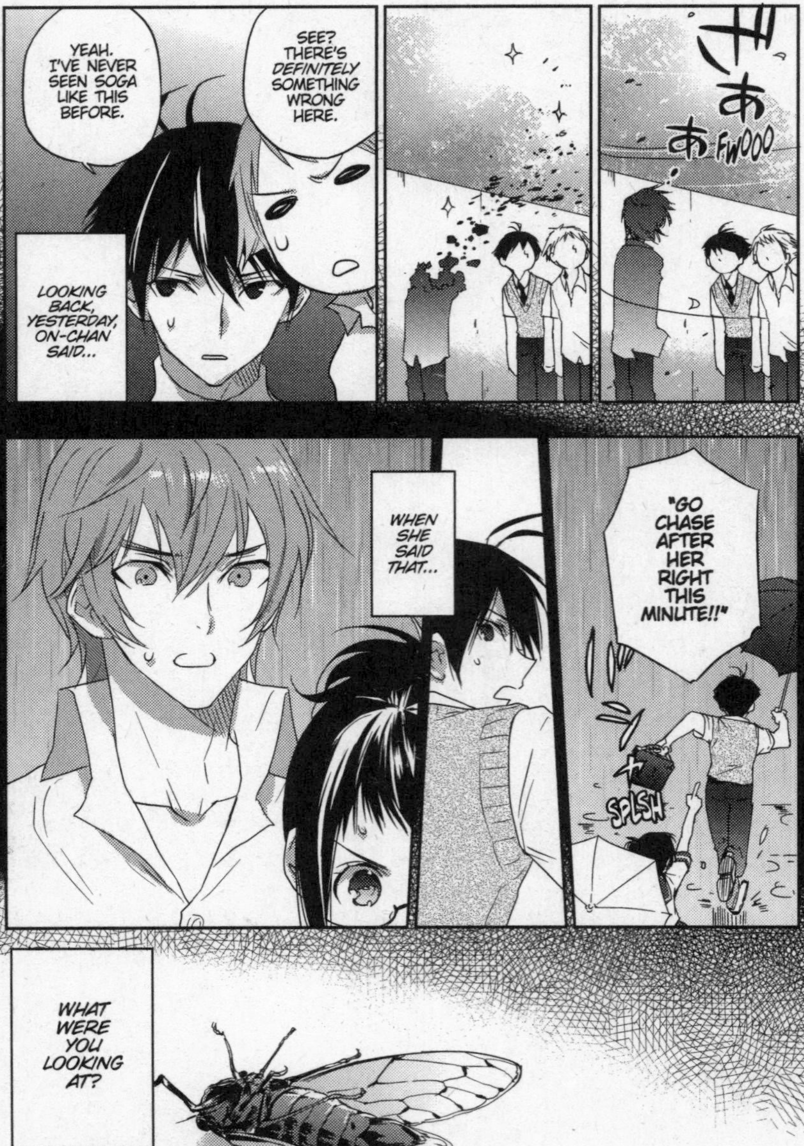
ざぁぁ FWOOO
SEE? THERE'S DEFINITELY SOMETHING WRONG HERE.
YEAH. I'VE NEVER SEEN SOGA LIKE THIS BEFORE.
LOOKING BACK, YESTERDAY, ON-CHAN SAID...
"GO CHASE AFTER HER RIGHT THIS MINUTE!!"
SPLSH
WHEN SHE SAID THAT...
WHAT WERE YOU LOOKING AT?

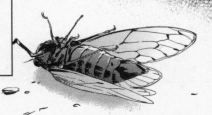

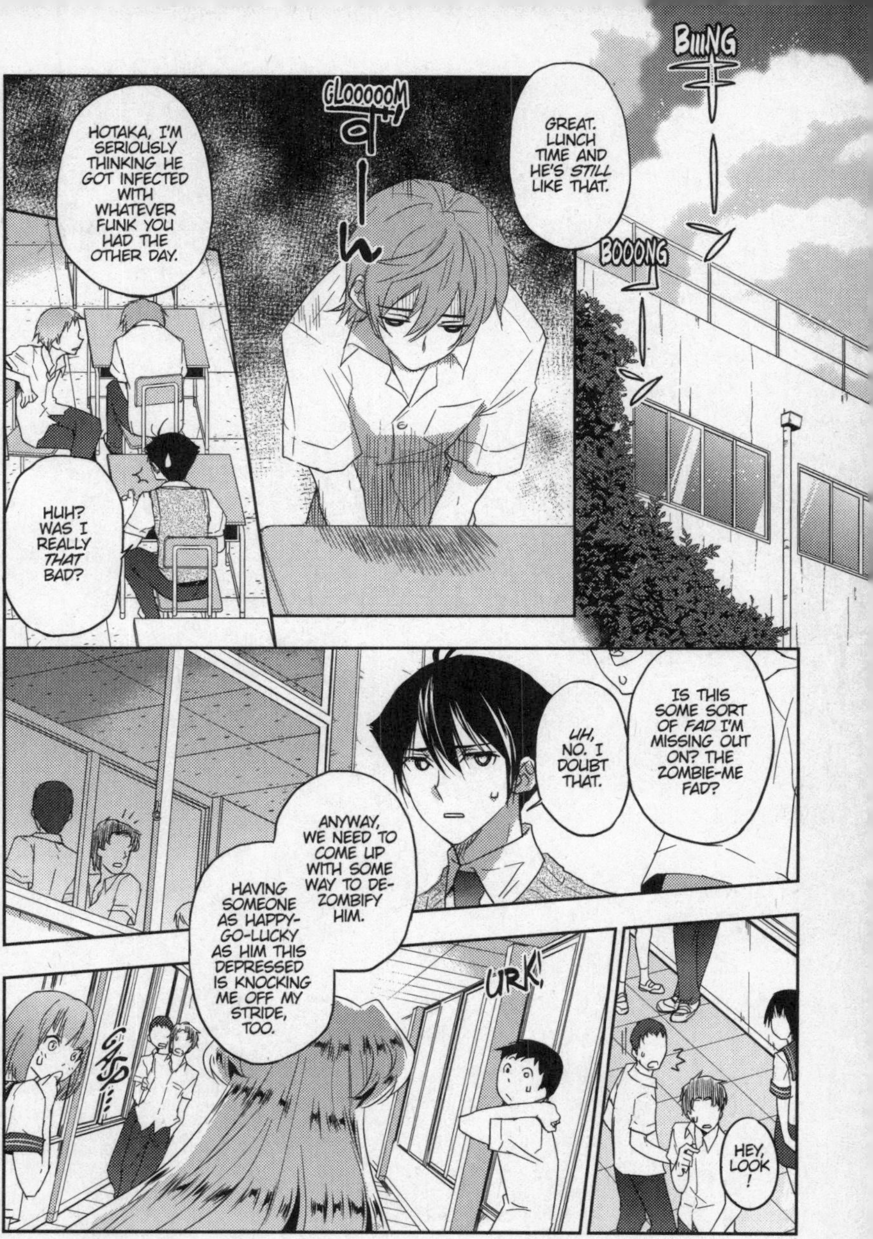
BIIING
BOOONG
GLOOOOOM
GREAT. LUNCH TIME AND HE'S *STILL* LIKE THAT.
HOTAKA, I'M SERIOUSLY THINKING HE GOT INFECTED WITH WHATEVER FUNK YOU HAD THE OTHER DAY.
HUH? WAS I REALLY *THAT* BAD?
IS THIS SOME SORT OF *FAD* I'M MISSING OUT ON? THE ZOMBIE-ME FAD?
*UH,* NO. I DOUBT THAT.
ANYWAY, WE NEED TO COME UP WITH SOME WAY TO DE-ZOMBIFY HIM.
HAVING SOMEONE AS HAPPY-GO-LUCKY AS HIM THIS DEPRESSED IS KNOCKING ME OFF MY STRIDE, TOO.
HEY, LOOK!
URK!
GASP...!

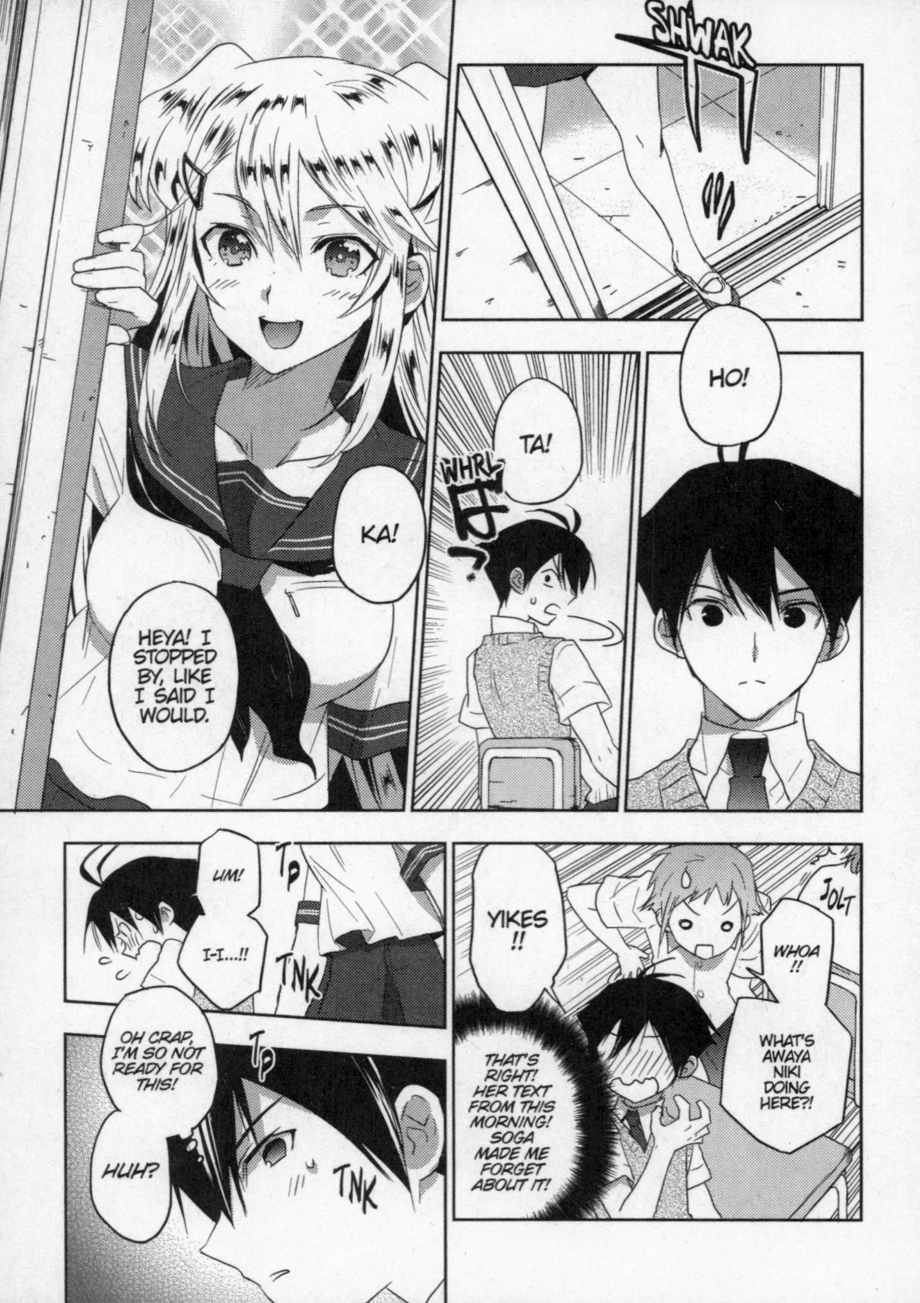
SHWAK
HO!
TA!
WHRL
KA!
HEYA! I STOPPED BY, LIKE I SAID I WOULD.
JOLT
WHOA !!
YIKES !!
WHAT'S AWAYA NIKI DOING HERE?!
THAT'S RIGHT! HER TEXT FROM THIS MORNING! SOGA MADE ME FORGET ABOUT IT!
UM!
TP
I-I...!!
TNK
OH CRAP, I'M SO NOT READY FOR THIS!
TP
HUH?
TNK

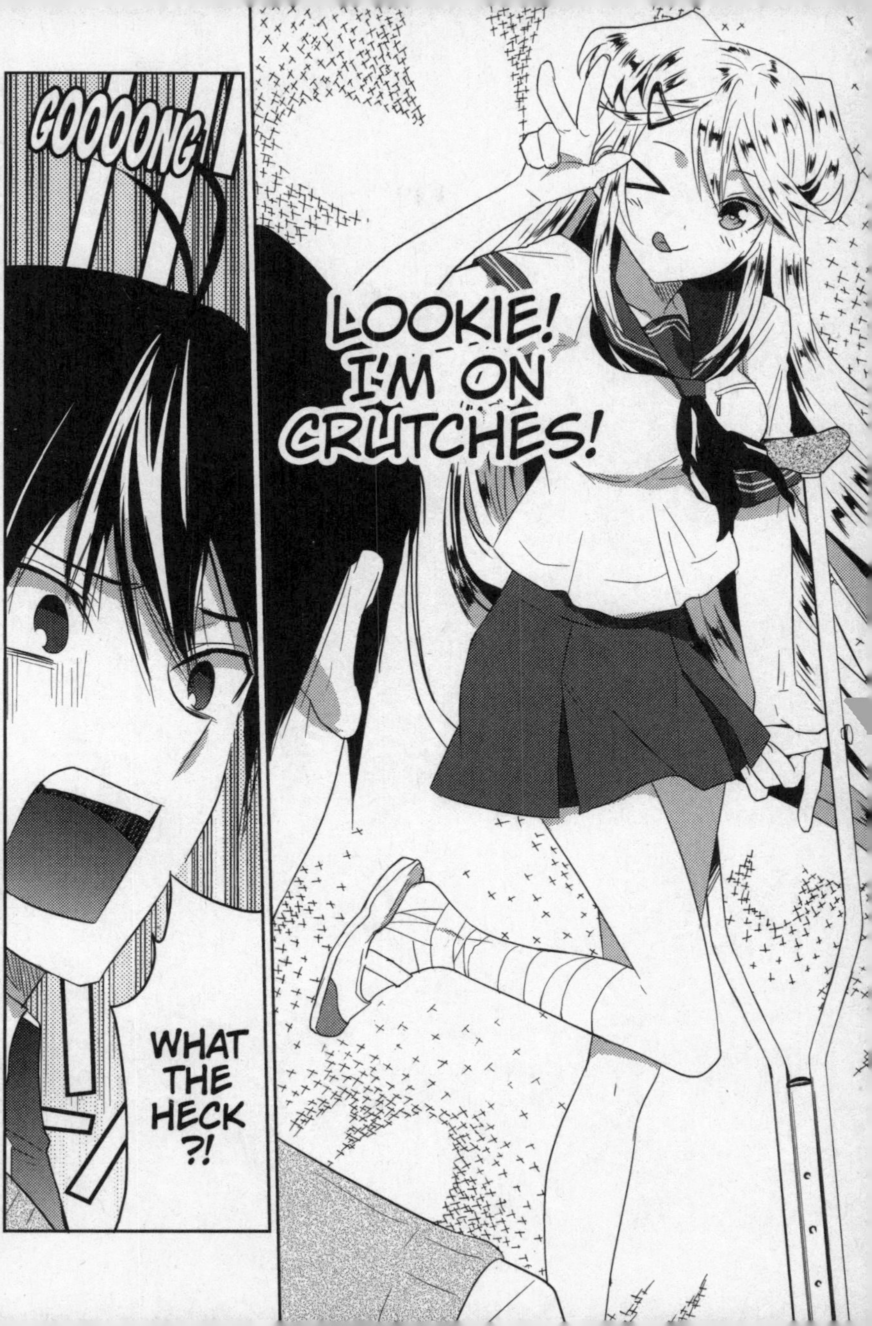
LOOKIE! I'M ON CRUTCHES!
GOOOONG!
WHAT THE HECK?!

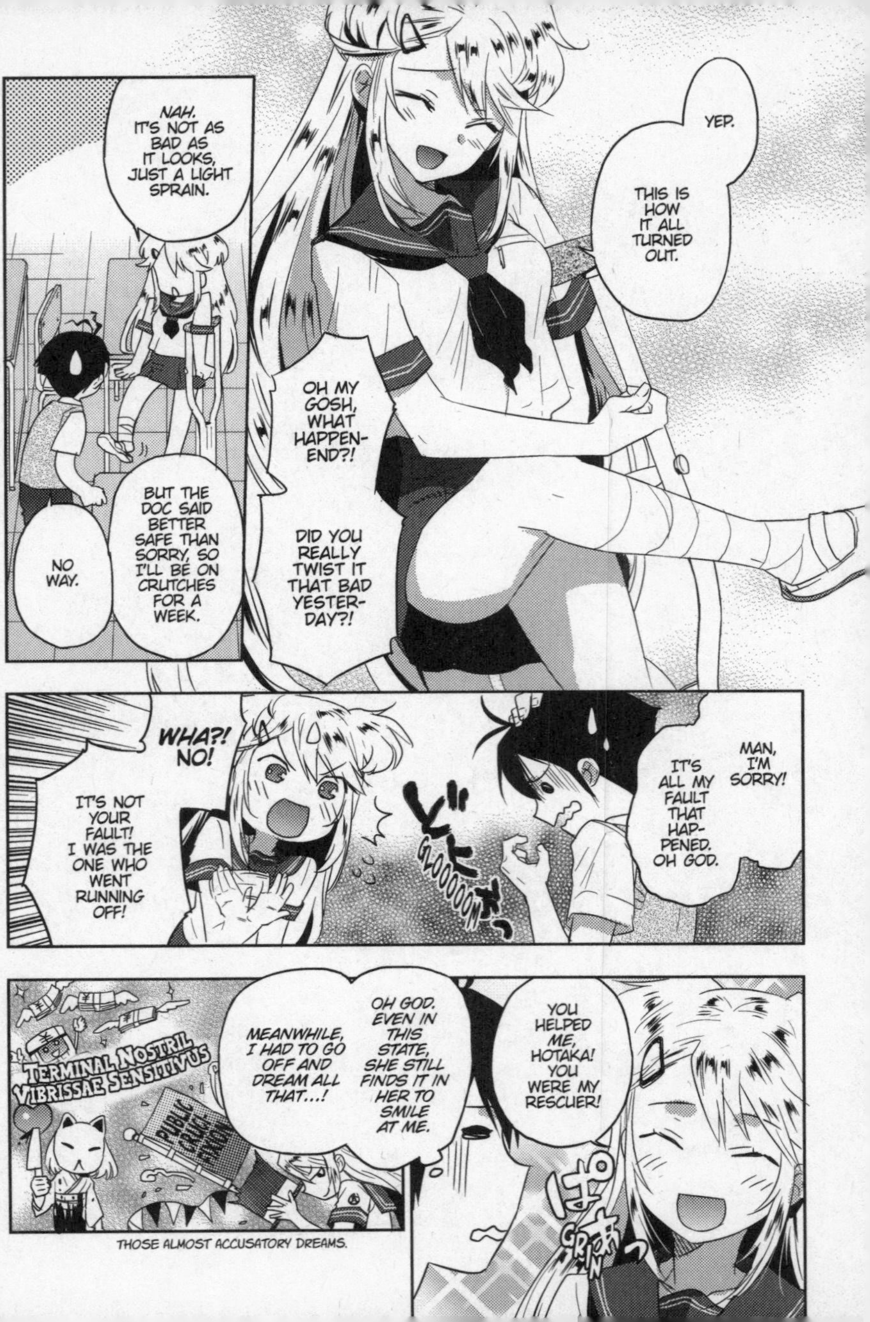
YEP.
THIS IS HOW IT ALL TURNED OUT.
OH MY GOSH, WHAT HAPPEN-END?!
DID YOU REALLY TWIST IT THAT BAD YESTER-DAY?!
NAH. IT'S NOT AS BAD AS IT LOOKS, JUST A LIGHT SPRAIN.
BUT THE DOC SAID BETTER SAFE THAN SORRY, SO I'LL BE ON CRUTCHES FOR A WEEK.
NO WAY.
MAN, I'M SORRY!
IT'S ALL MY FAULT THAT HAP-PENED. OH GOD.
GLOOOOOOM
WHA?! NO!
IT'S NOT YOUR FAULT! I WAS THE ONE WHO WENT RUNNING OFF!
YOU HELPED ME, HOTAKA! YOU WERE MY RESCUER!
OH GOD. EVEN IN THIS STATE, SHE STILL FINDS IT IN HER TO SMILE AT ME.
MEANWHILE, I HAD TO GO OFF AND DREAM ALL THAT...!
GRIN
TERMINAL NOSTRIL VIBRISSAE SENSITIVUS
PUBLIC CRUCI-FIXION
THOSE ALMOST ACCUSATORY DREAMS.

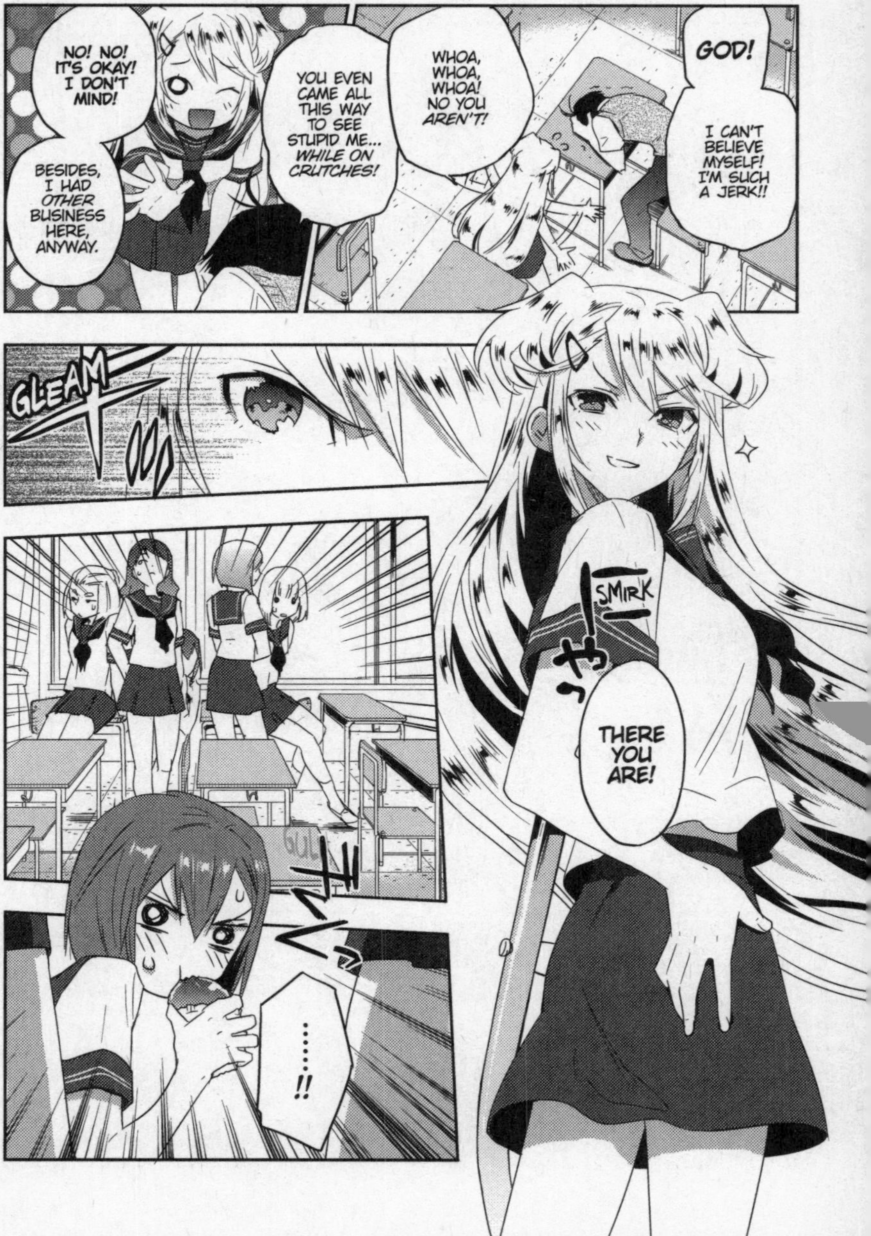
GOD!
I CAN'T BELIEVE MYSELF! I'M SUCH A JERK!!
WHOA, WHOA, WHOA! NO YOU AREN'T!
YOU EVEN CAME ALL THIS WAY TO SEE STUPID ME... *WHILE ON CRUTCHES!*
NO! NO! IT'S OKAY! I DON'T MIND!
BESIDES, I HAD *OTHER* BUSINESS HERE, ANYWAY.
GLEAM
SMIRK
THERE YOU ARE!
GULP
......!!

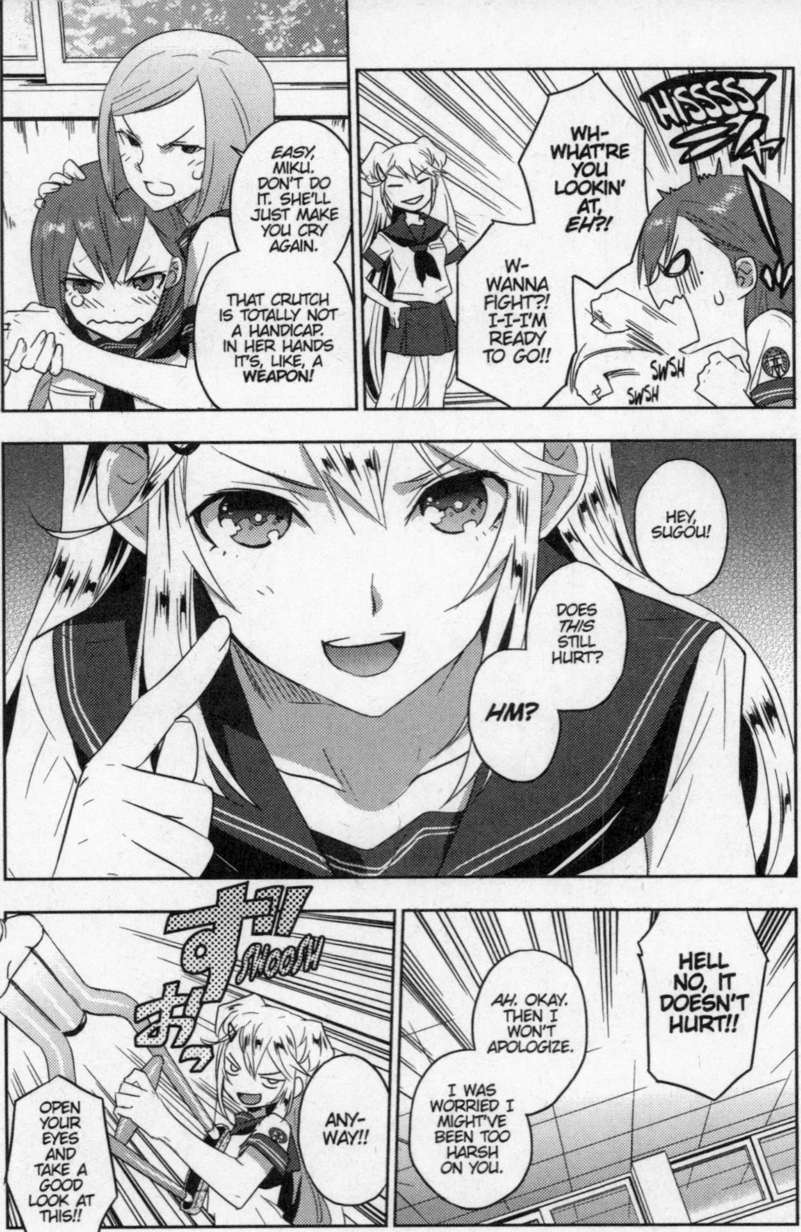
HSSSS
WH- WHAT'RE YOU LOOKIN' AT, EH?!
W- WANNA FIGHT?! I-I-I'M READY TO GO!!
SWSH
SWSH
EASY, MIKU. DON'T DO IT. SHE'LL JUST MAKE YOU CRY AGAIN.
THAT CRUTCH IS TOTALLY NOT A HANDICAP. IN HER HANDS IT'S, LIKE, A WEAPON!
HEY, SUGOU!
DOES THIS STILL HURT?
HM?
HELL NO, IT DOESN'T HURT!!
AH. OKAY. THEN I WON'T APOLOGIZE.
I WAS WORRIED I MIGHT'VE BEEN TOO HARSH ON YOU.
ANY-WAY!!
OPEN YOUR EYES AND TAKE A GOOD LOOK AT THIS!!

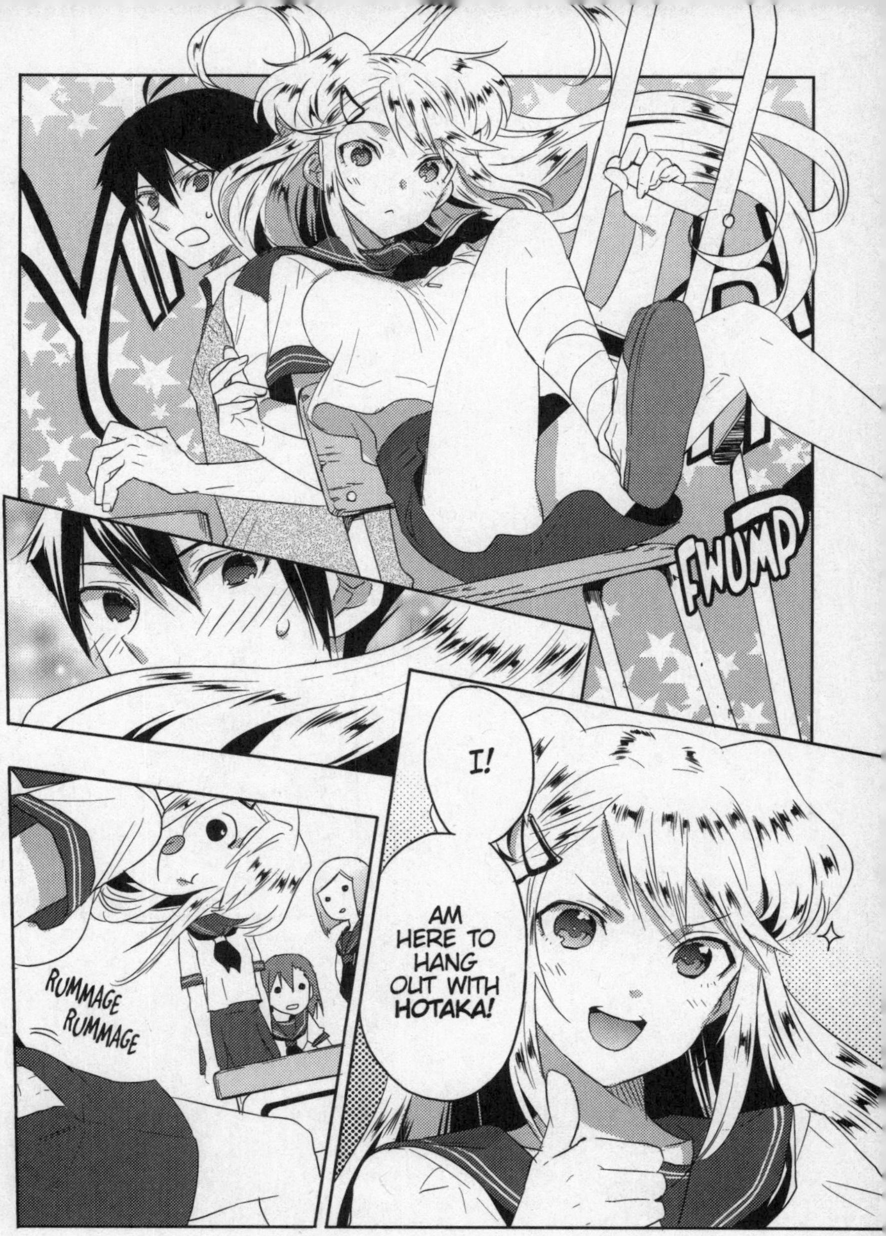
FWUMP
I!
AM HERE TO HANG OUT WITH HOTAKA!
RUMMAGE RUMMAGE

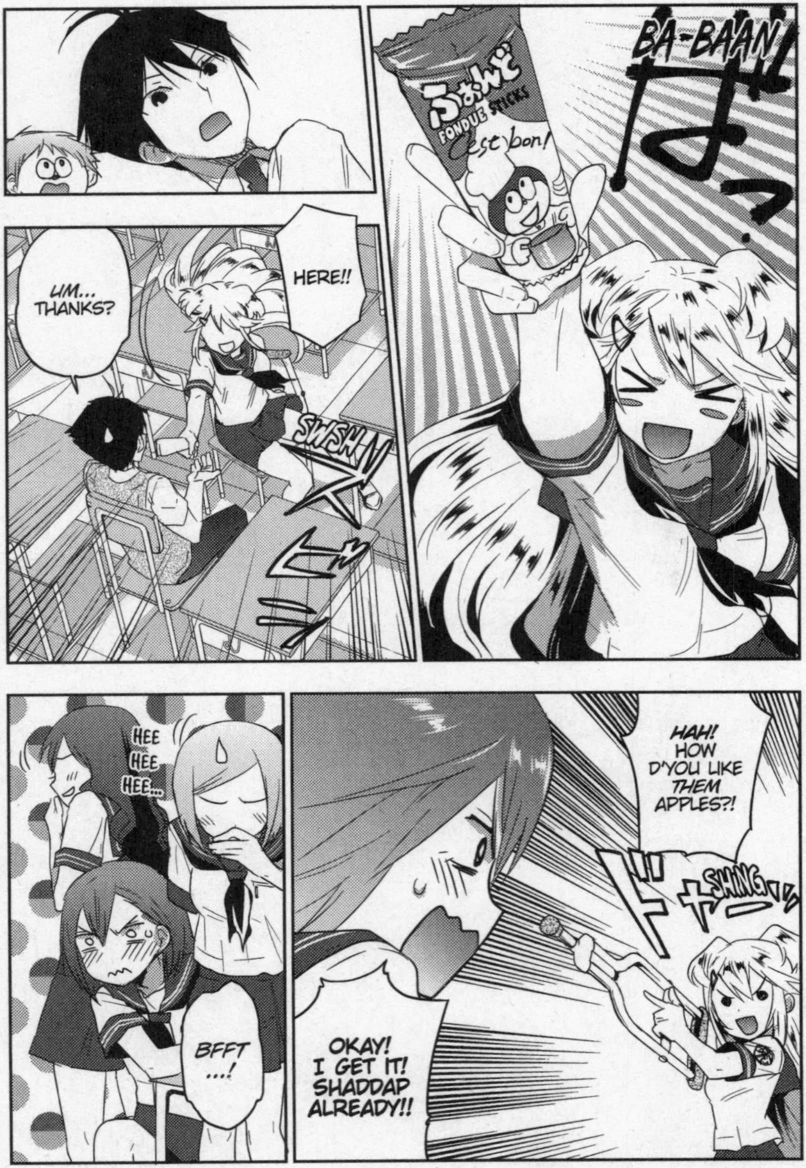
BA-BAAN!
FONDUE STICKS
C'est bon!
HERE!!
UM... THANKS?
SWSH
HAH! HOW D'YOU LIKE THEM APPLES?!
SHING
OKAY! I GET IT! SHADDAP ALREADY!!
HEE HEE HEE...
BFFT ...!

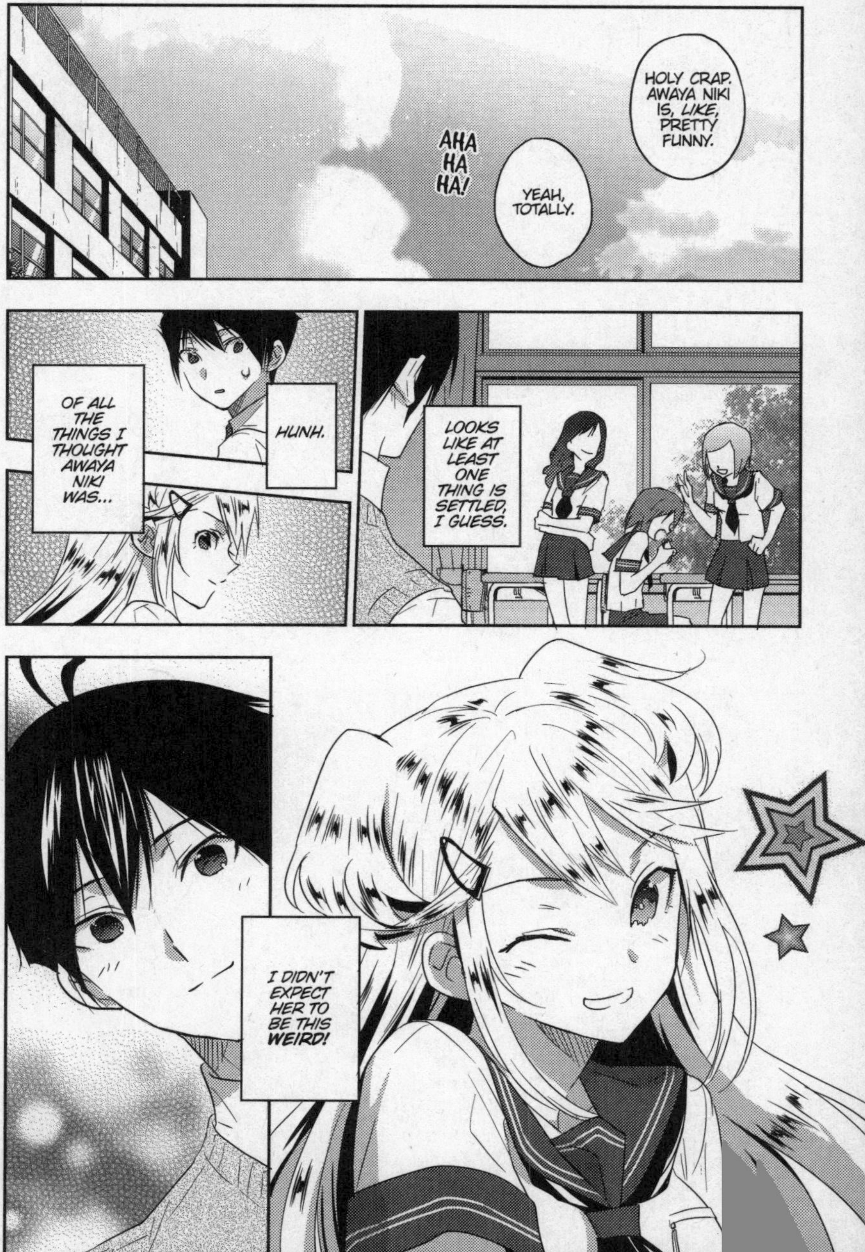
HOLY CRAP. AWAYA NIKI IS, *LIKE*, PRETTY FUNNY.
YEAH, TOTALLY.
AHA HA HA!
LOOKS LIKE AT LEAST ONE THING IS SETTLED, I GUESS.
HUNH.
OF ALL THE THINGS I THOUGHT AWAYA NIKI WAS...
I DIDN'T EXPECT HER TO BE THIS **WEIRD!**

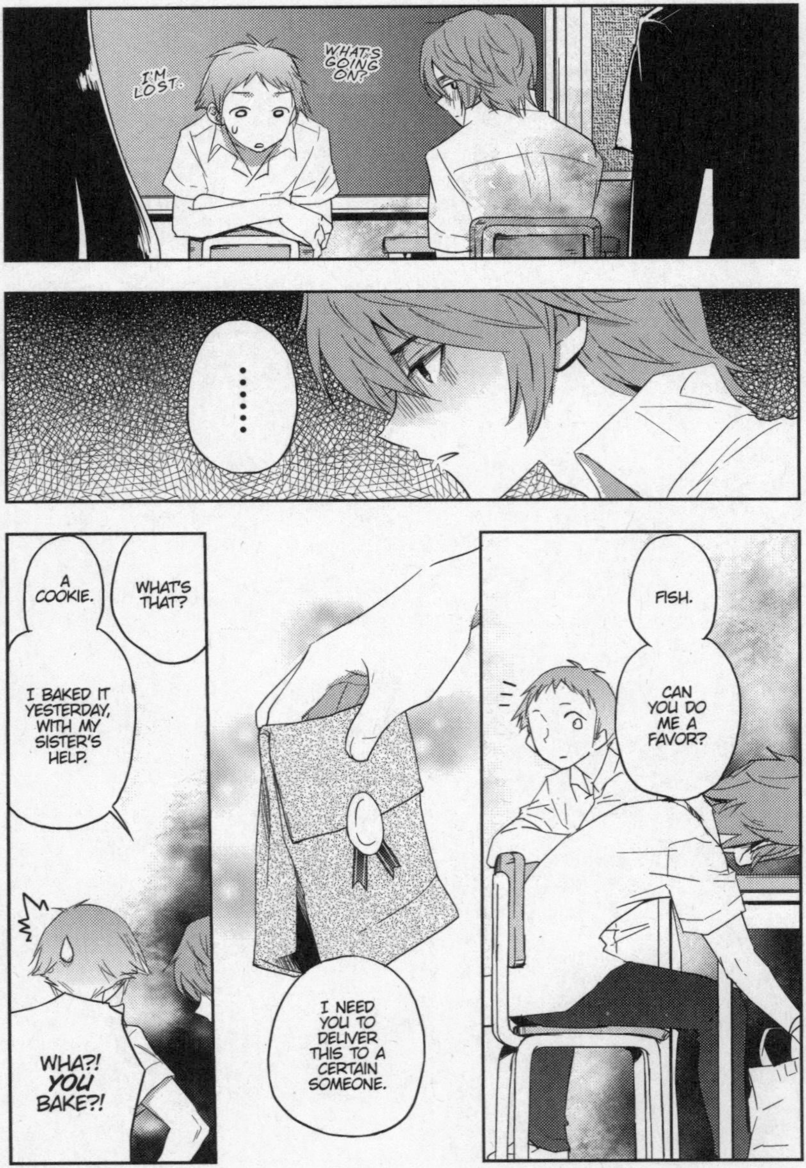

WHAT'S GOING ON?
I'M LOST.
......
FISH.
CAN YOU DO ME A FAVOR?
I NEED YOU TO DELIVER THIS TO A CERTAIN SOMEONE.
WHAT'S THAT?
A COOKIE.
I BAKED IT YESTERDAY, WITH MY SISTER'S HELP.
WHA?! *YOU* BAKE?!

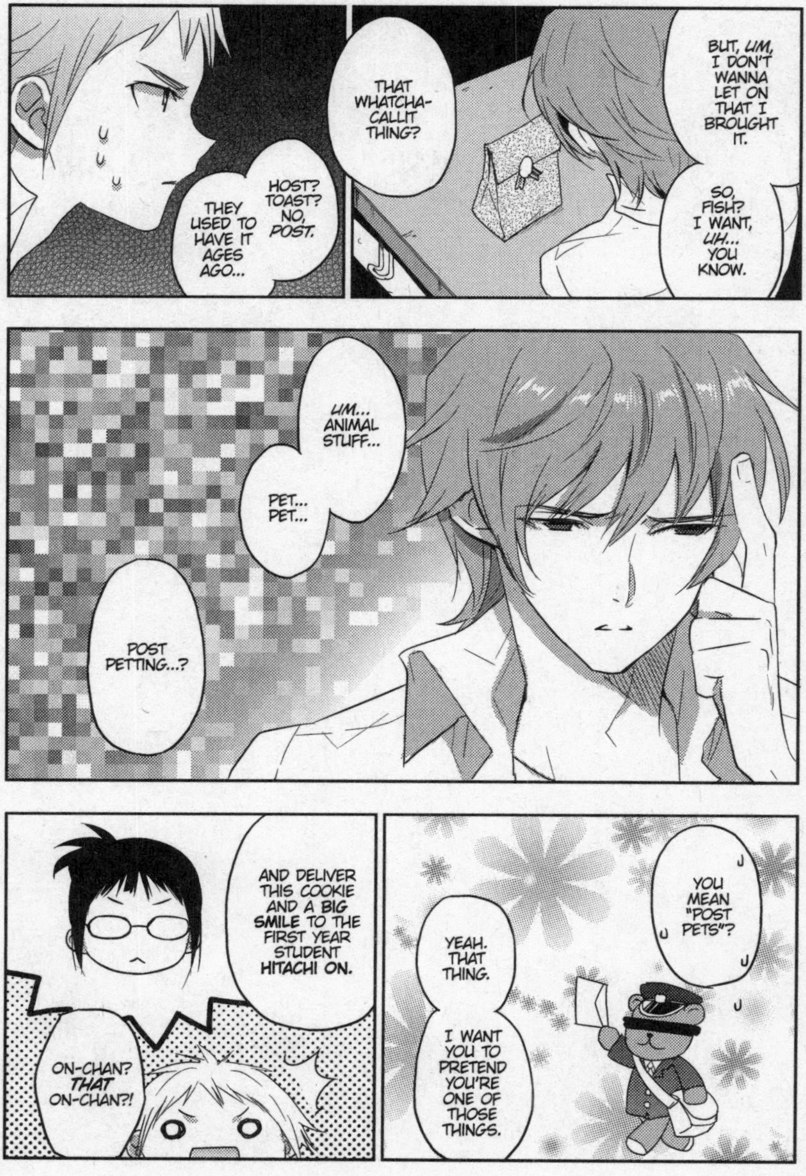
BUT, UM, I DON'T WANNA LET ON THAT I BROUGHT IT.
SO, FISH? I WANT, UH... YOU KNOW.
THAT WHATCHA-CALLIT THING?
HOST? TOAST? NO, POST.
THEY USED TO HAVE IT AGES AGO...
UM... ANIMAL STUFF...
PET... PET...
POST PETTING...?
YOU MEAN "POST PETS"?
YEAH. THAT THING.
I WANT YOU TO PRETEND YOU'RE ONE OF THOSE THINGS.
AND DELIVER THIS COOKIE AND A BIG SMILE TO THE FIRST YEAR STUDENT HITACHI ON.
ON-CHAN? THAT ON-CHAN?!

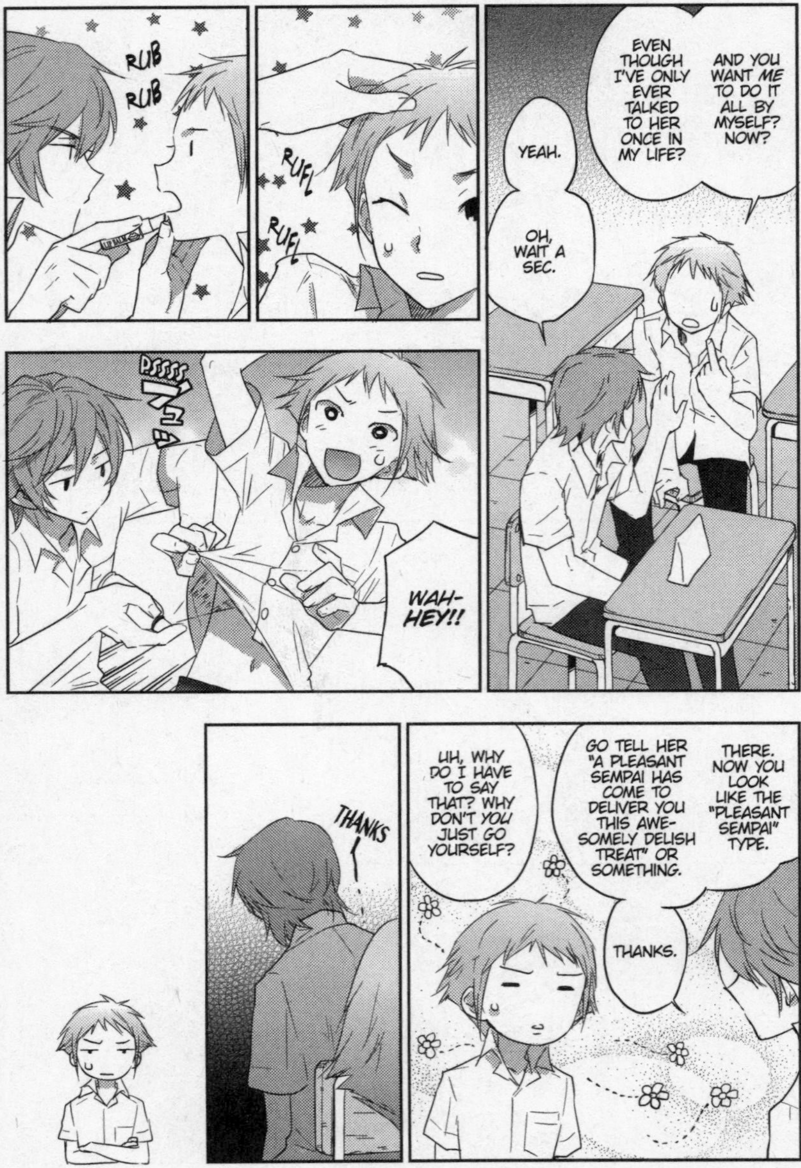
EVEN THOUGH I'VE ONLY EVER TALKED TO HER ONCE IN MY LIFE? AND YOU WANT *ME* TO DO IT ALL BY MYSELF? NOW?
YEAH.
OH, WAIT A SEC.
RUFL
RUFL
RUB
RUB
PSSSSS
WAH-HEY!!
THERE. NOW YOU LOOK LIKE THE "PLEASANT SEMPAI" TYPE.
GO TELL HER "A PLEASANT SEMPAI HAS COME TO DELIVER YOU THIS AWESOMELY DELISH TREAT" OR SOMETHING.
UH, WHY DO I HAVE TO SAY THAT? WHY DON'T *YOU* JUST GO YOURSELF?
THANKS.
THANKS

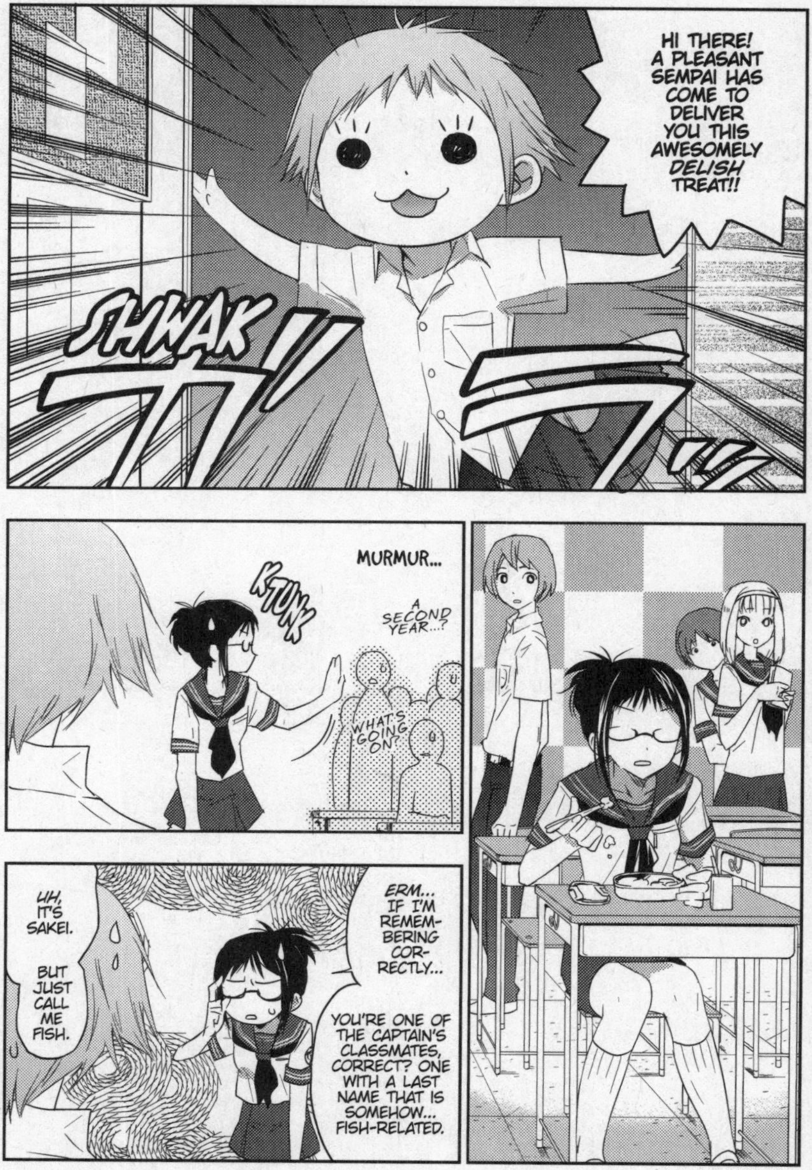
HI THERE! A PLEASANT SEMPAI HAS COME TO DELIVER YOU THIS AWESOMELY *DELISH* TREAT!!
SHWAK
MURMUR...
A SECOND YEAR...?
K-TUNK
WHAT'S GOING ON?
ERM... IF I'M REMEMBERING CORRECTLY...
YOU'RE ONE OF THE CAPTAIN'S CLASSMATES, CORRECT? ONE WITH A LAST NAME THAT IS SOMEHOW... FISH-RELATED.
UH, IT'S SAKEI.
BUT JUST CALL ME FISH.
WHAT'S WITH THAT LOOK?

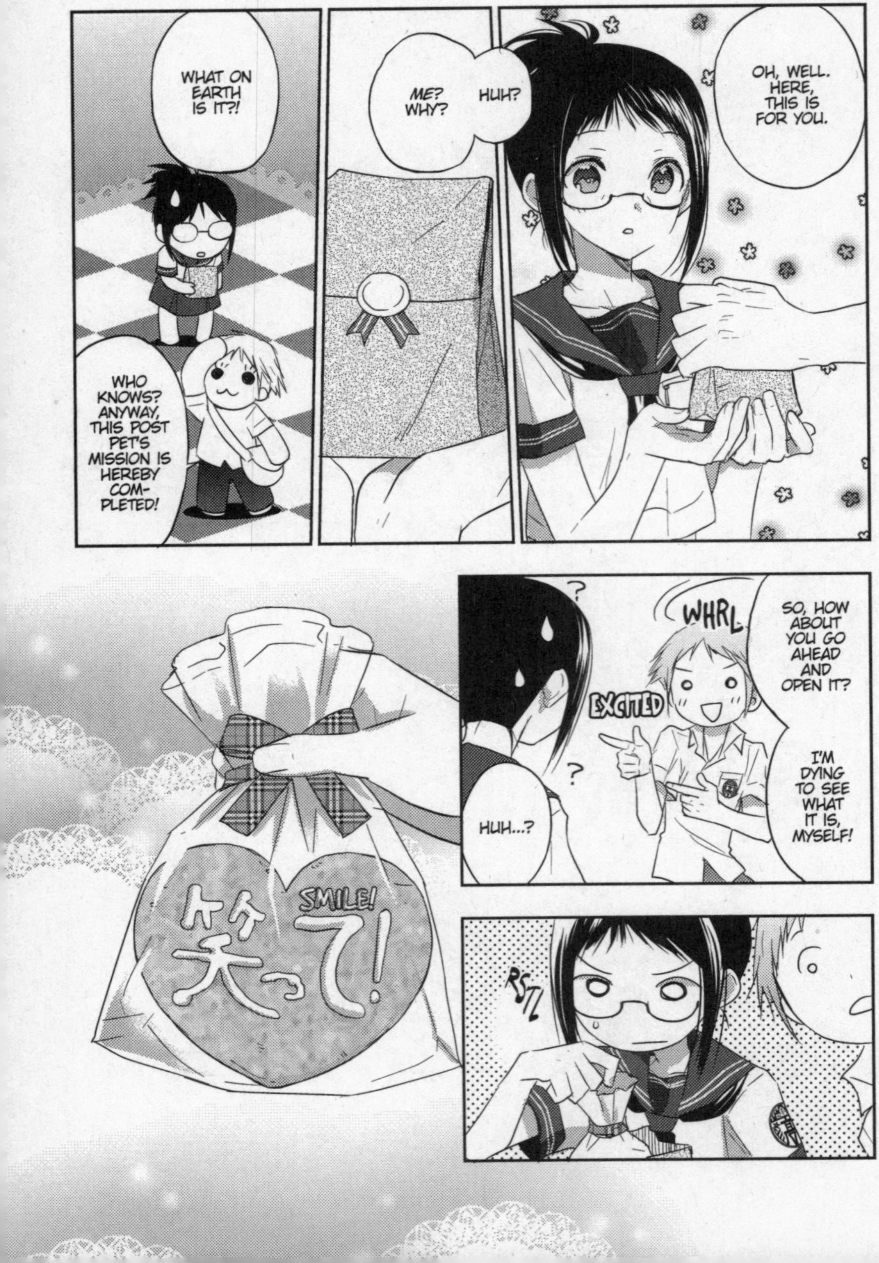
OH, WELL. HERE, THIS IS FOR YOU.
HUH?
ME? WHY?
WHAT ON EARTH IS IT?!
WHO KNOWS? ANYWAY, THIS POST PET'S MISSION IS HEREBY COMPLETED!
SO, HOW ABOUT YOU GO AHEAD AND OPEN IT?
WHRL
EXCITED
I'M DYING TO SEE WHAT IT IS, MYSELF!
HUH...?
RSTL
笑って!
SMILE!

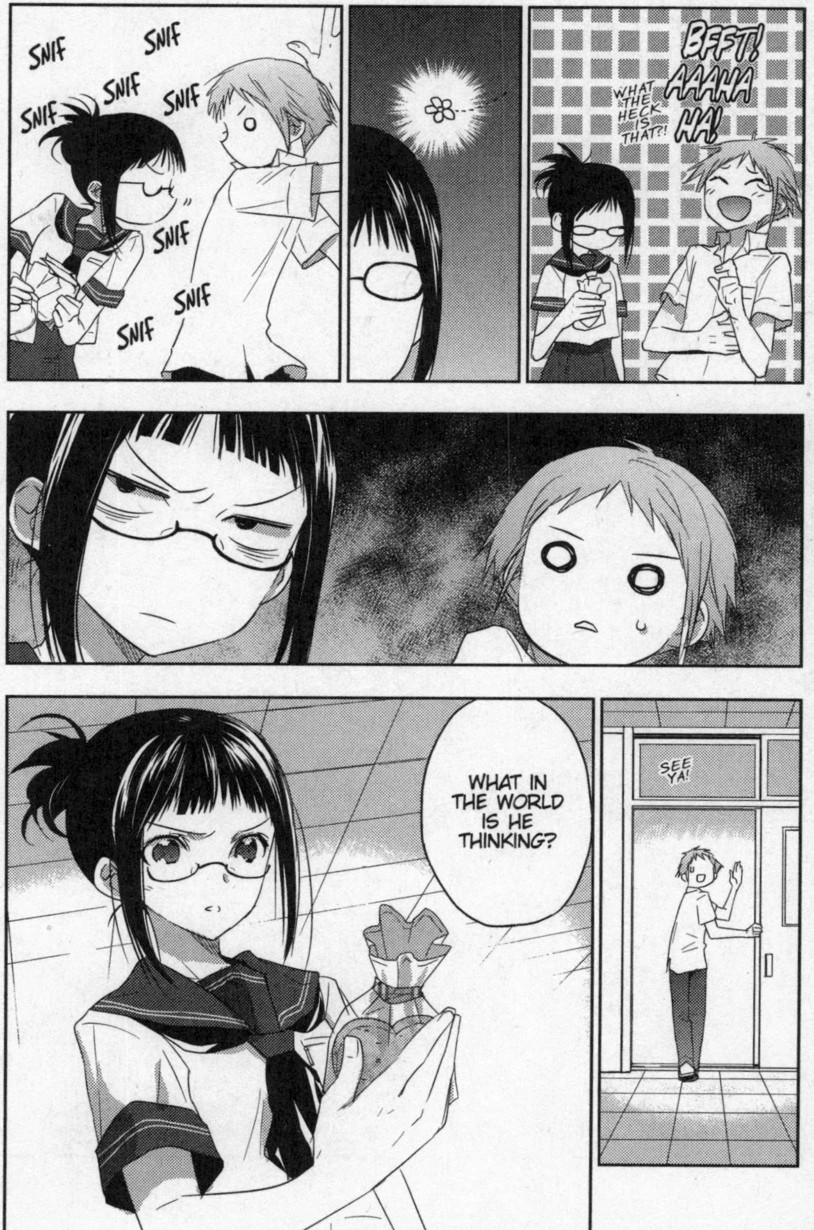
BFFT! AAAHA HA!
WHAT THE HECK IS THAT?!
SNIF
SNIF
SNIF
SNIF
SNIF
SNIF
SNIF
SNIF
SEE YA!
WHAT IN THE WORLD IS HE THINKING?

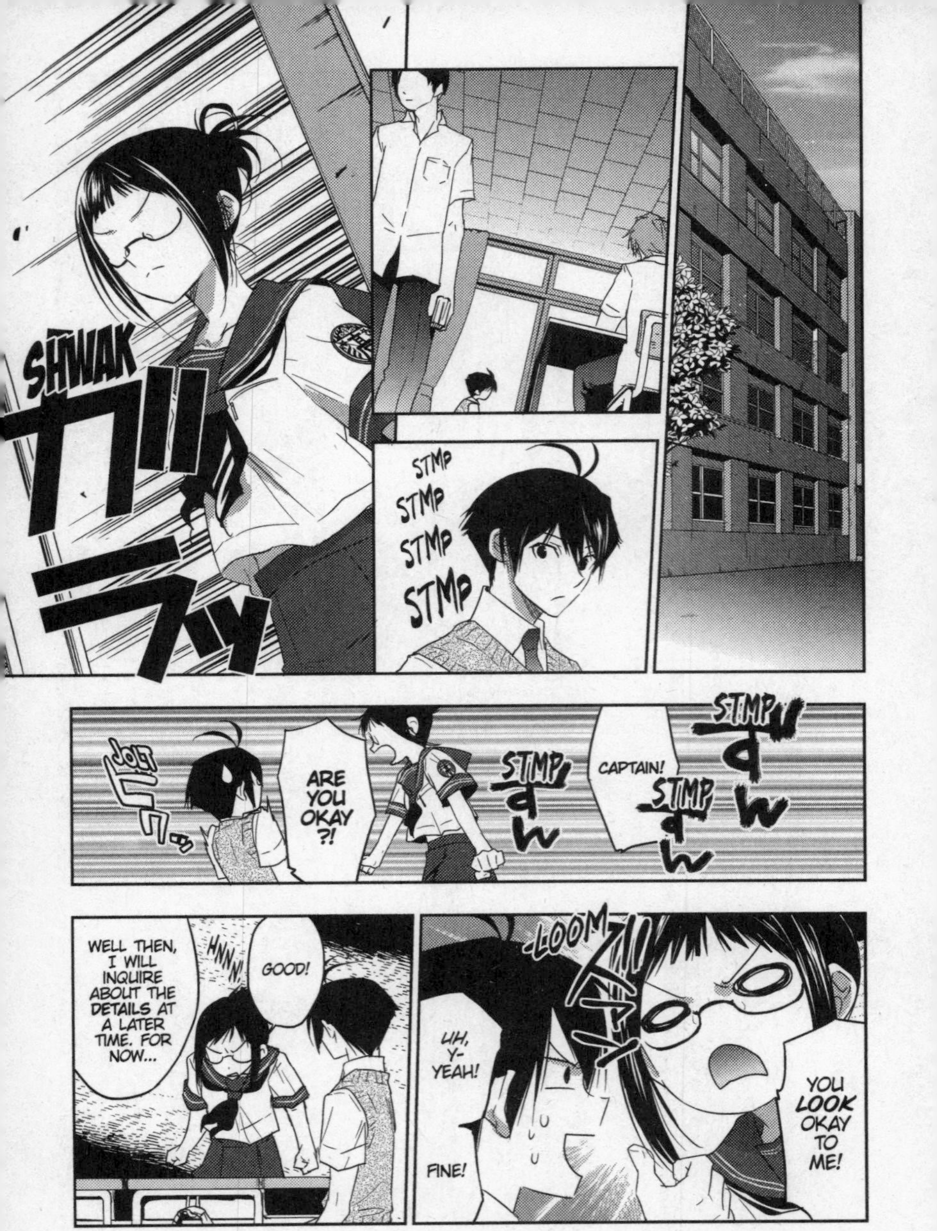
STMP
STMP
STMP
STMP
SHWAK
STMP
CAPTAIN!
STMP
STMP
ARE YOU OKAY?!
JOLT
LOOM
YOU LOOK OKAY TO ME!
UH, Y-YEAH!
FINE!
GOOD!
HNNN!
WELL THEN, I WILL INQUIRE ABOUT THE DETAILS AT A LATER TIME. FOR NOW...

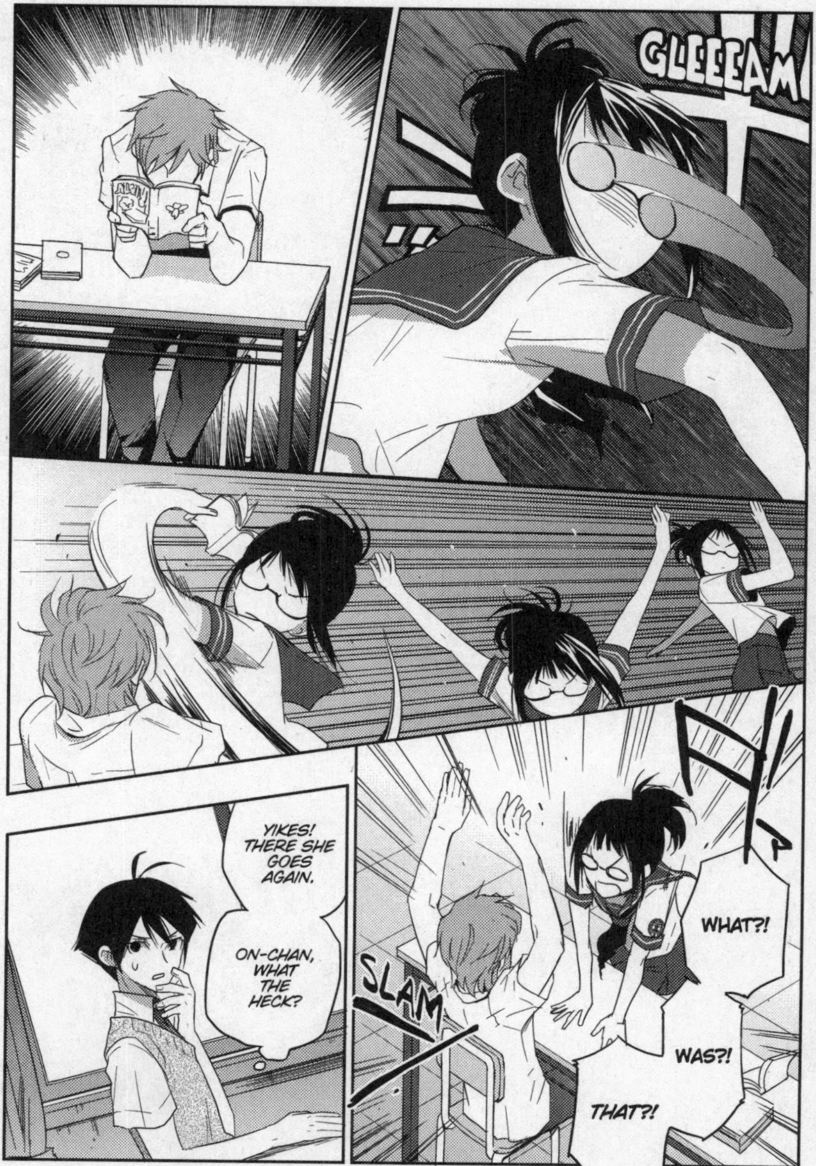
GLEEEAM!
WHAT?!
WAS?!
THAT?!
SLAM
YIKES! THERE SHE GOES AGAIN.
ON-CHAN, WHAT THE HECK?

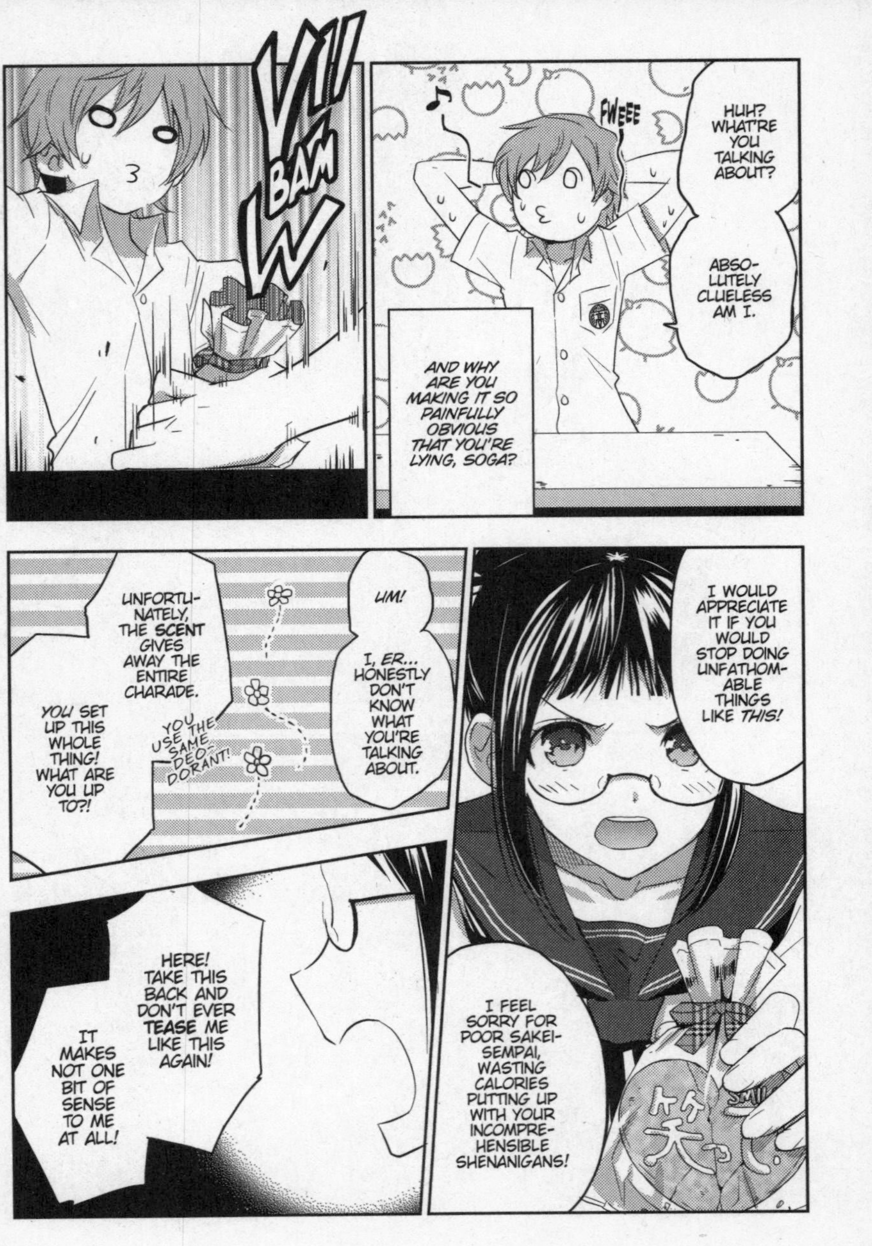
HUH? WHAT'RE YOU TALKING ABOUT?
ABSOLUTELY CLUELESS AM I.
FWEEE
AND WHY ARE YOU MAKING IT SO PAINFULLY OBVIOUS THAT YOU'RE LYING, SOGA?
BAM
I WOULD APPRECIATE IT IF YOU WOULD STOP DOING UNFATHOMABLE THINGS LIKE *THIS!*
*UM!*
I, *ER...* HONESTLY DON'T KNOW WHAT YOU'RE TALKING ABOUT.
UNFORTUNATELY, THE SCENT GIVES AWAY THE ENTIRE CHARADE.
YOU USE THE SAME DEODORANT!
*YOU* SET UP THIS WHOLE THING! WHAT ARE YOU UP TO?!
I FEEL SORRY FOR POOR SAKEI-SEMPAI, WASTING CALORIES PUTTING UP WITH YOUR INCOMPREHENSIBLE SHENANIGANS!
HERE! TAKE THIS BACK AND DON'T EVER TEASE ME LIKE THIS AGAIN!
IT MAKES NOT ONE BIT OF SENSE TO ME AT ALL!

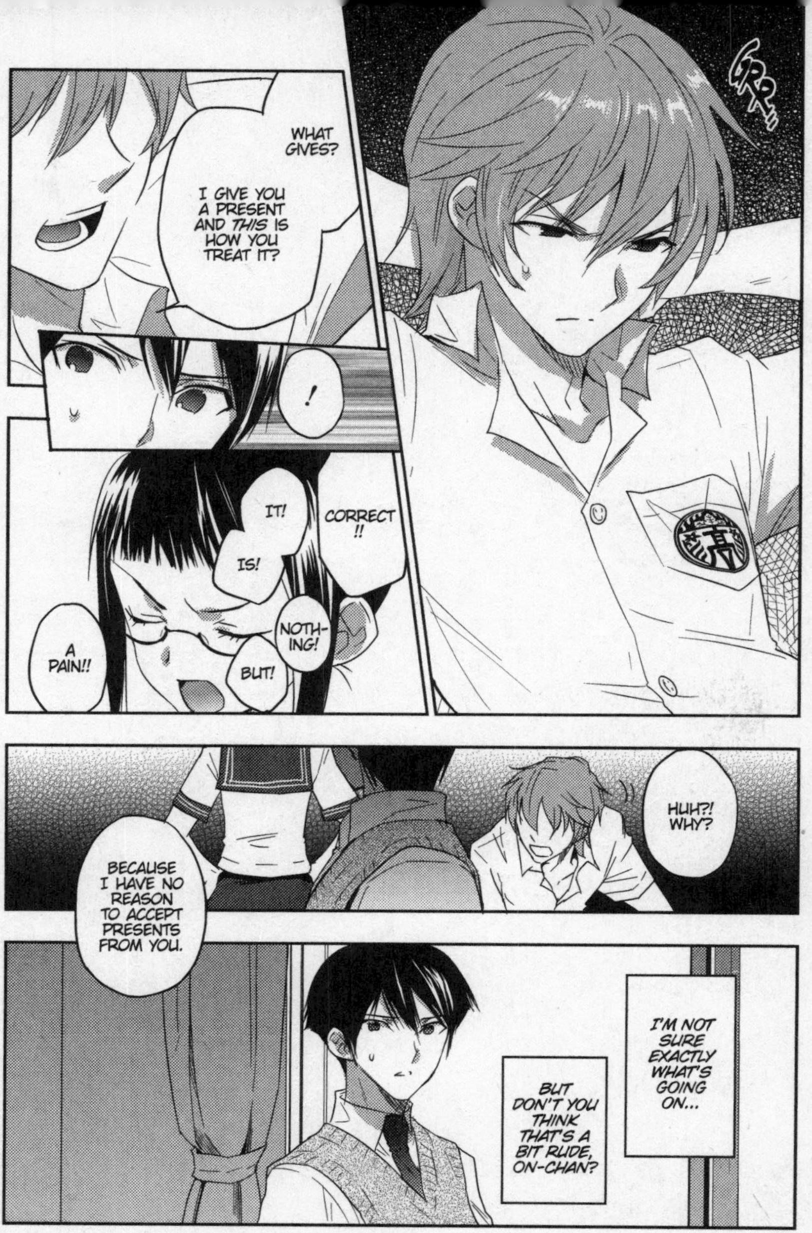
GRR...
WHAT GIVES?
I GIVE YOU A PRESENT AND *THIS* IS HOW YOU TREAT IT?
!
CORRECT!!
IT!
IS!
NOTHING!
BUT!
A PAIN!!
HUH?! WHY?
BECAUSE I HAVE NO REASON TO ACCEPT PRESENTS FROM YOU.
I'M NOT SURE EXACTLY WHAT'S GOING ON...
BUT DON'T YOU THINK THAT'S A BIT RUDE, ON-CHAN?

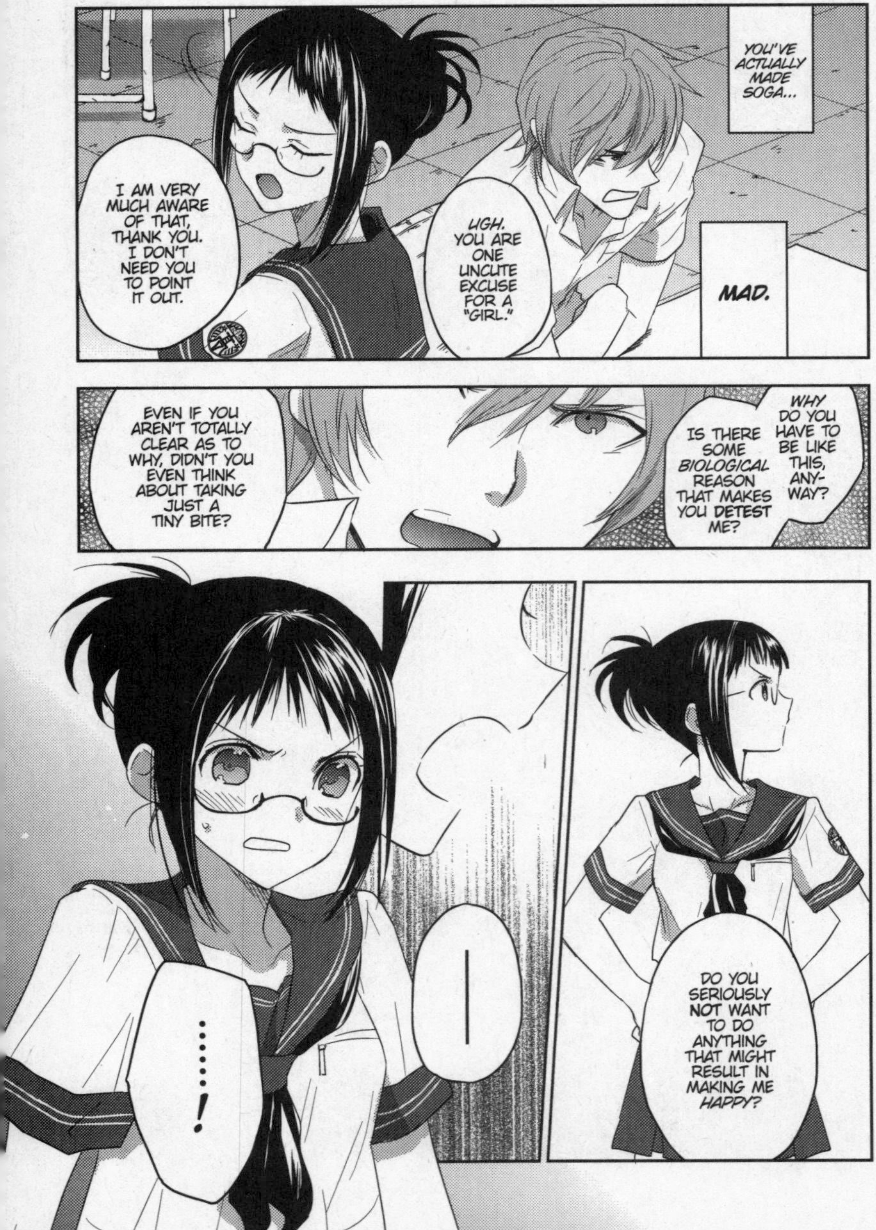
YOU'VE ACTUALLY MADE SOGA...
MAD.
UGH. YOU ARE ONE UNCUTE EXCUSE FOR A "GIRL."
I AM VERY MUCH AWARE OF THAT, THANK YOU. I DON'T NEED YOU TO POINT IT OUT.
WHY DO YOU HAVE TO BE LIKE THIS, ANY-WAY?
IS THERE SOME *BIOLOGICAL* REASON THAT MAKES YOU DETEST ME?
EVEN IF YOU AREN'T TOTALLY CLEAR AS TO WHY, DIDN'T YOU EVEN THINK ABOUT TAKING JUST A TINY BITE?
DO YOU SERIOUSLY NOT WANT TO DO ANYTHING THAT MIGHT RESULT IN MAKING ME *HAPPY*?
—
......!

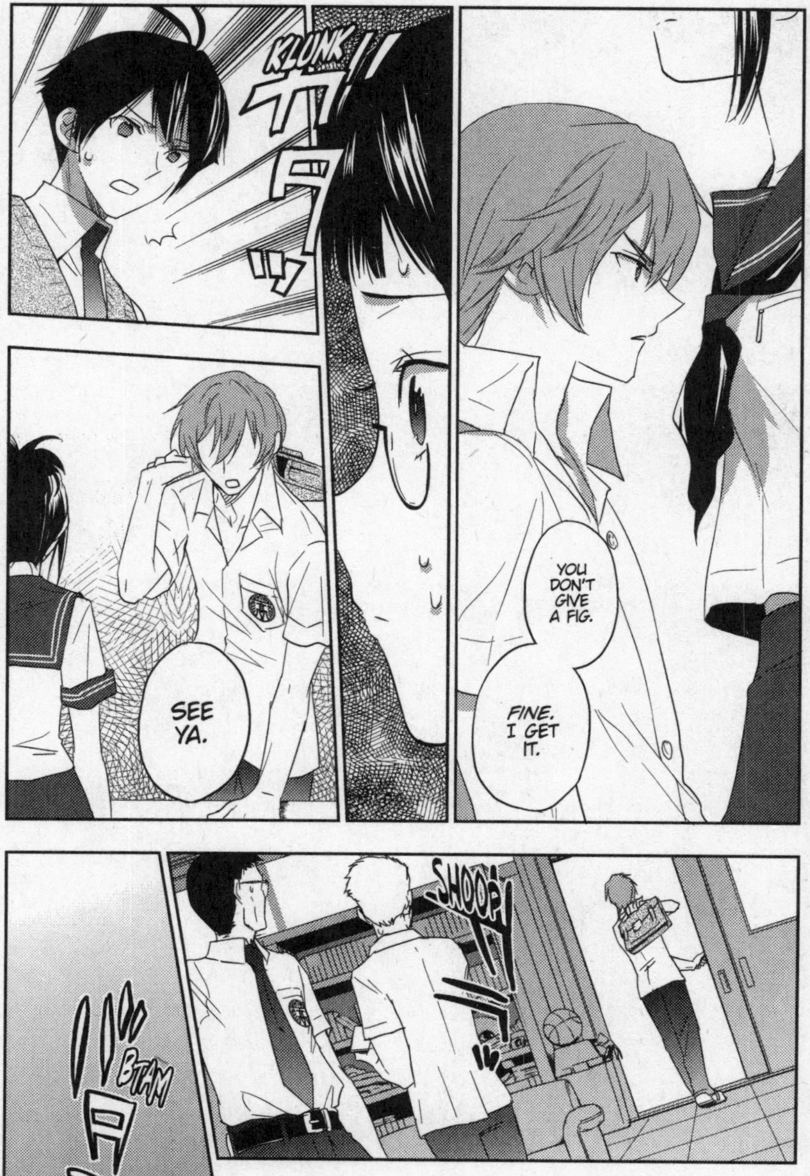
YOU DON'T GIVE A FIG.
FINE. I GET IT.
KLUNK
SEE YA.
SHOOP
BTAM

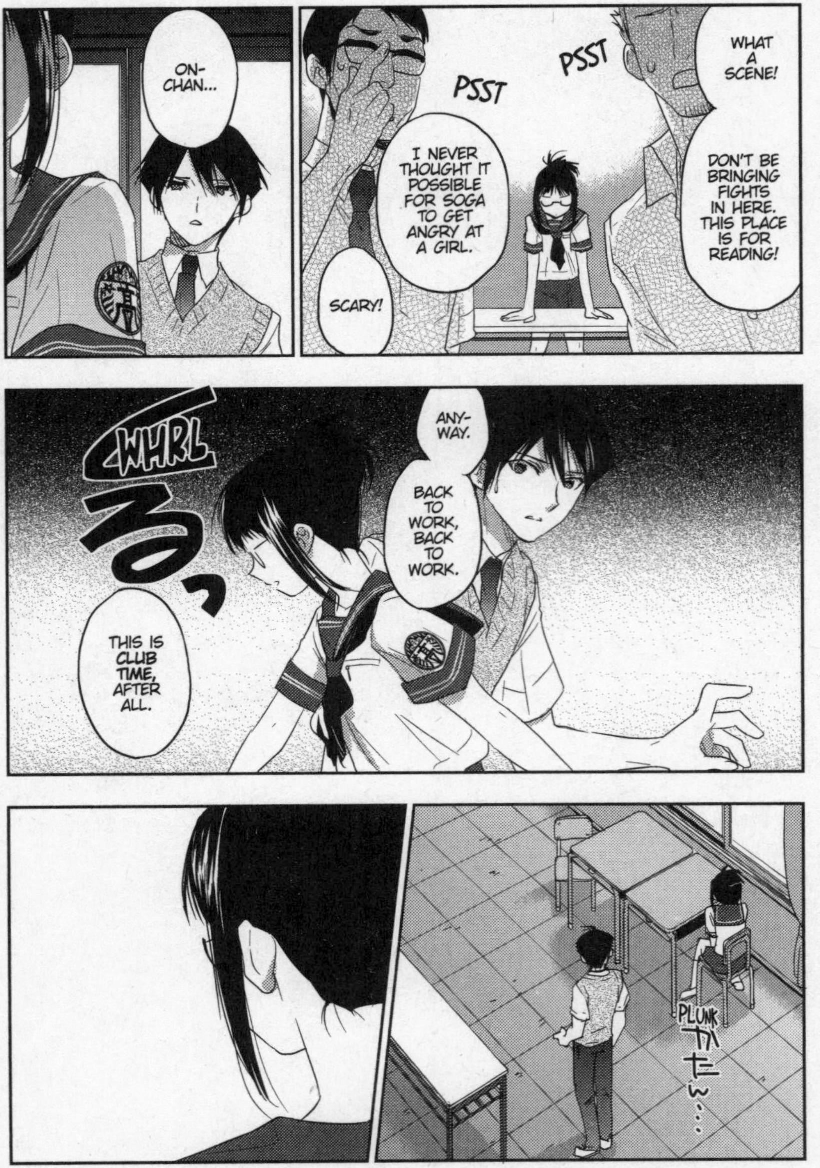
WHAT A SCENE!
PSST
DON'T BE BRINGING FIGHTS IN HERE. THIS PLACE IS FOR READING!
PSST
I NEVER THOUGHT IT POSSIBLE FOR SOGA TO GET ANGRY AT A GIRL.
SCARY!
ON-CHAN...
ANY-WAY.
BACK TO WORK, BACK TO WORK.
WHRL
THIS IS CLUB TIME, AFTER ALL.
PLUNK

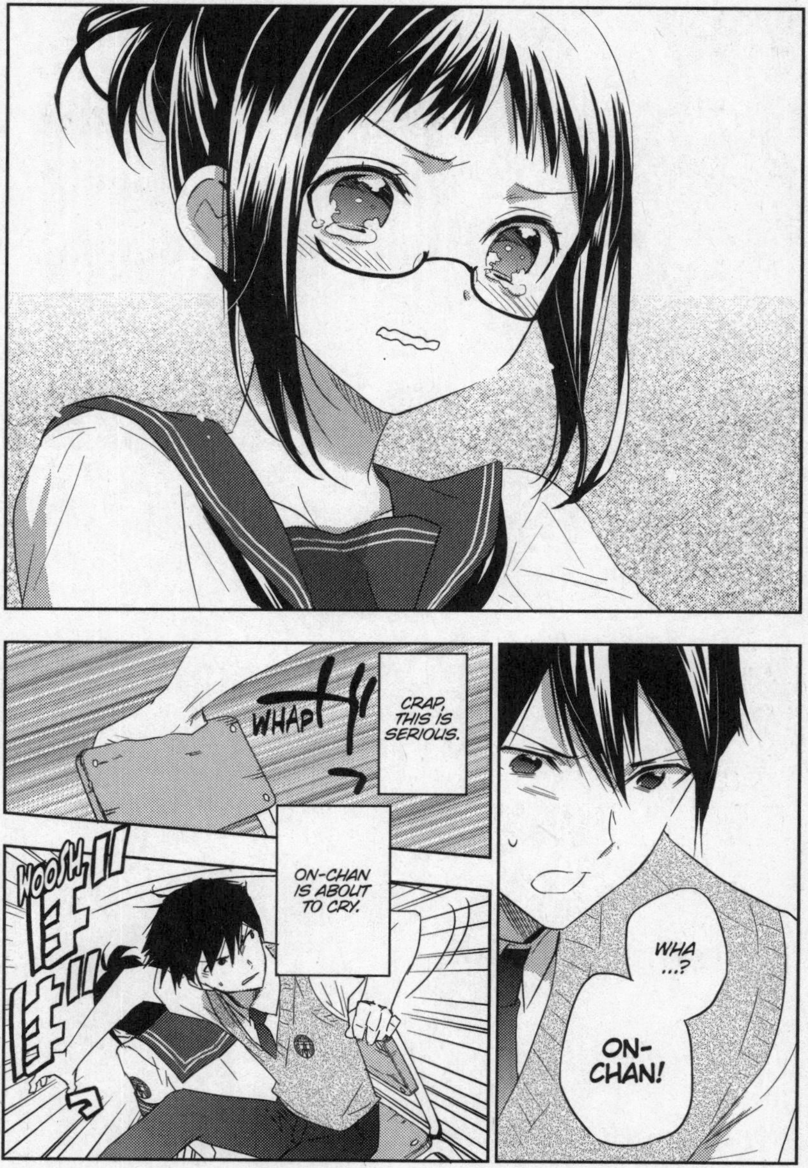
WHA ...?
ON-CHAN!
WHAP
CRAP, THIS IS SERIOUS.
ON-CHAN IS ABOUT TO CRY.
WOOSH

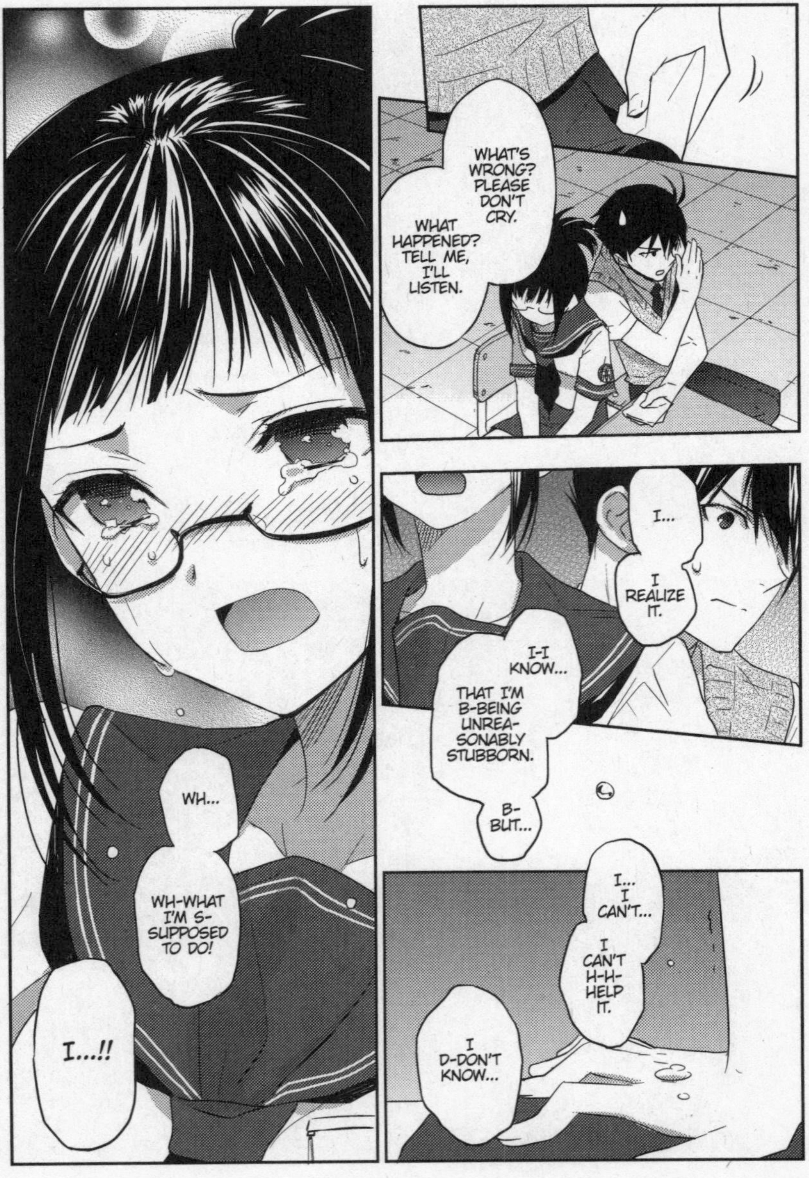
WHAT'S WRONG? PLEASE DON'T CRY.
WHAT HAPPENED? TELL ME, I'LL LISTEN.
I...
I REALIZE IT.
I-I KNOW...
THAT I'M B-BEING UNREASONABLY STUBBORN.
B-BUT...
I... I CAN'T...
I CAN'T H-H-HELP IT.
I D-DON'T KNOW...
WH...
WH-WHAT I'M S-SUPPOSED TO DO!
I...!!

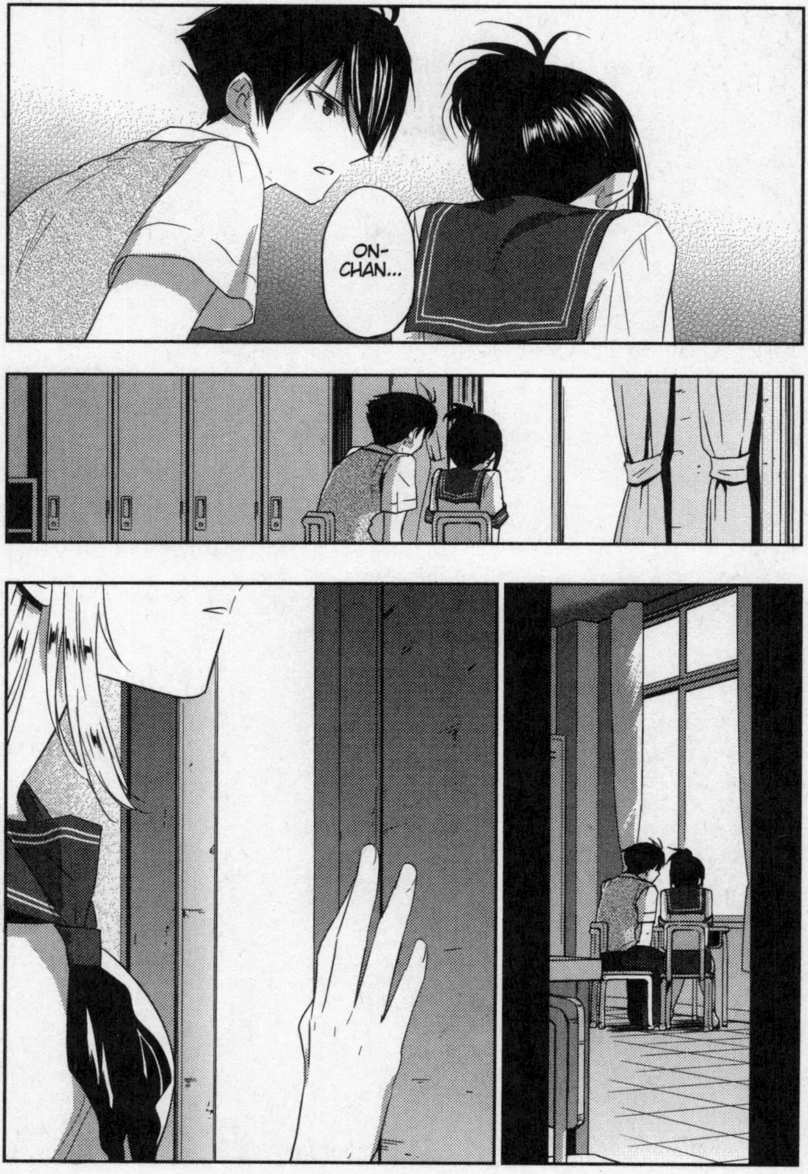
ON-
CHAN...

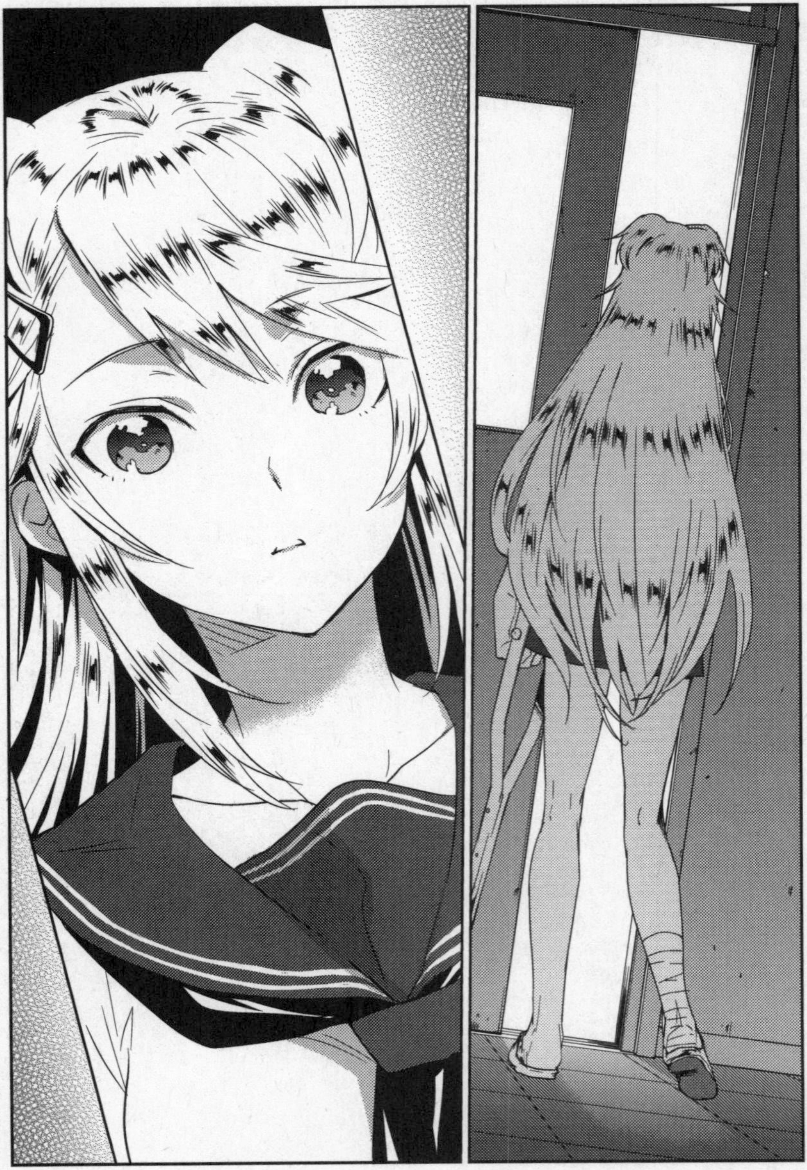

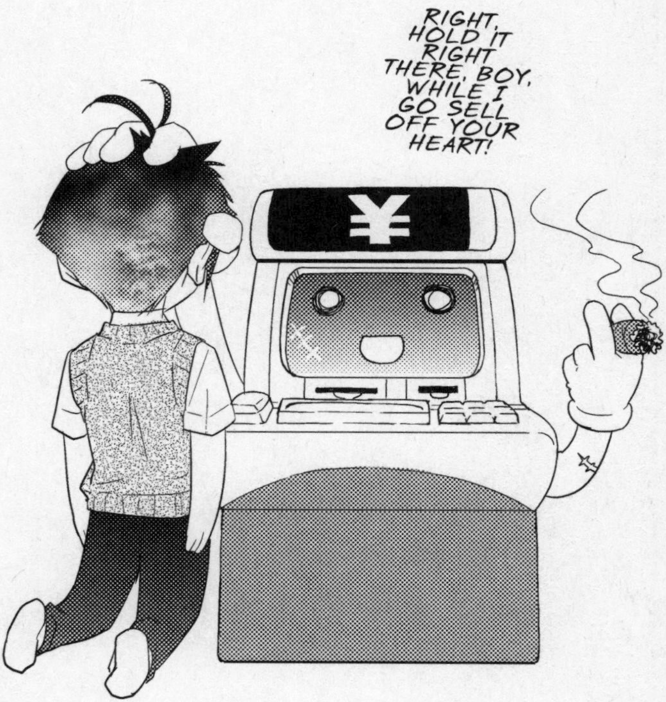
RIGHT, HOLD IT RIGHT THERE, BOY, WHILE I GO SELL OFF YOUR HEART!

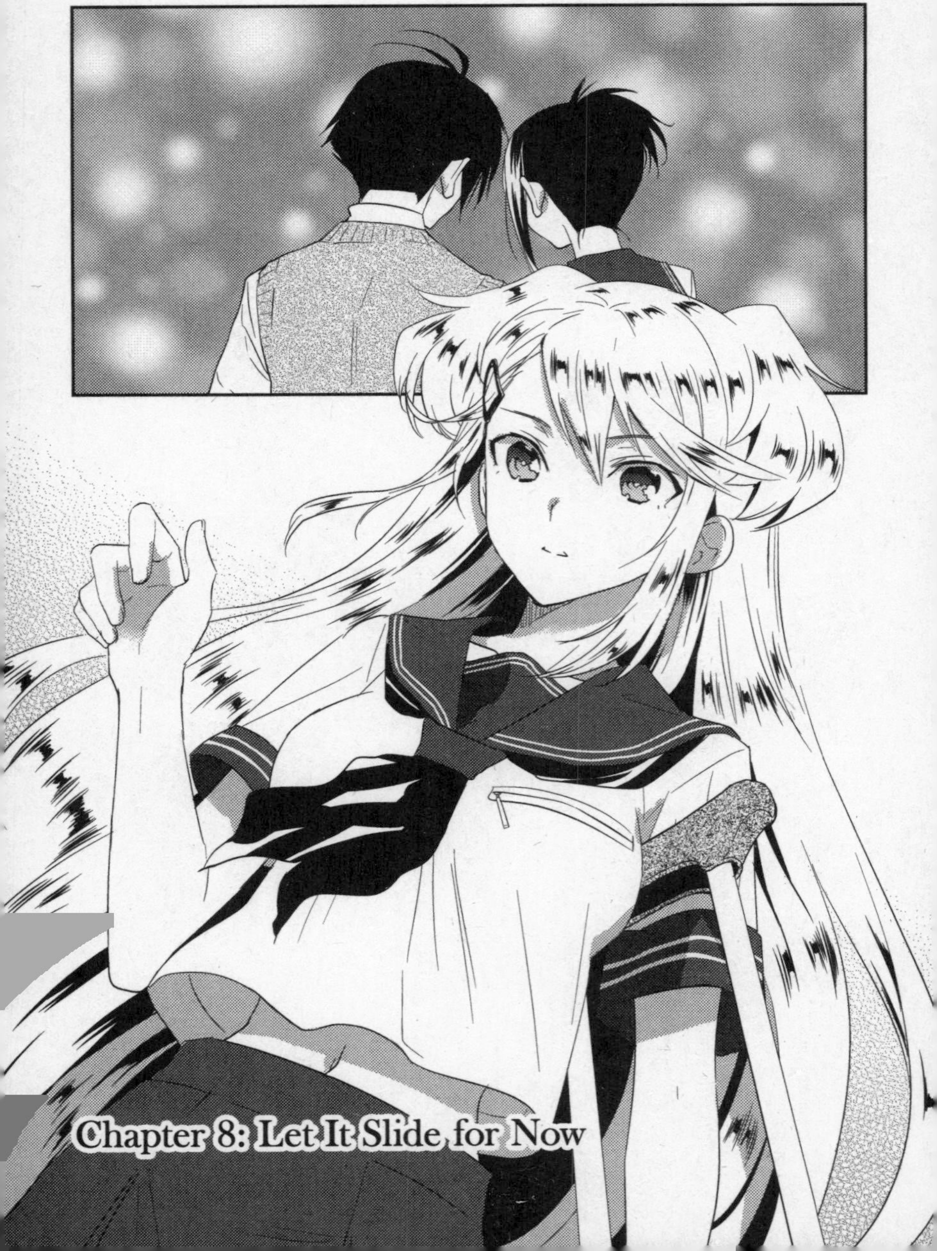
Chapter 8: Let It Slide for Now

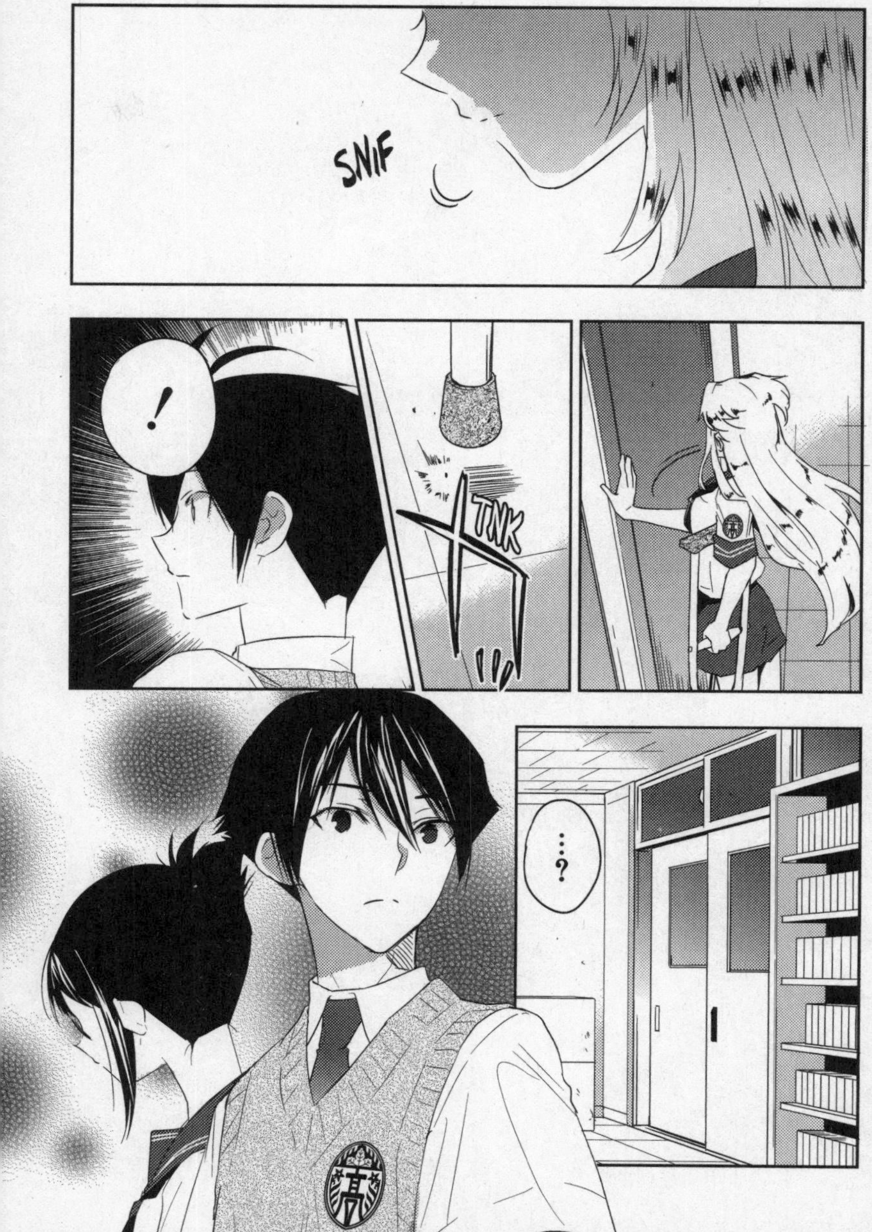
SNIF
TNK
!
...?

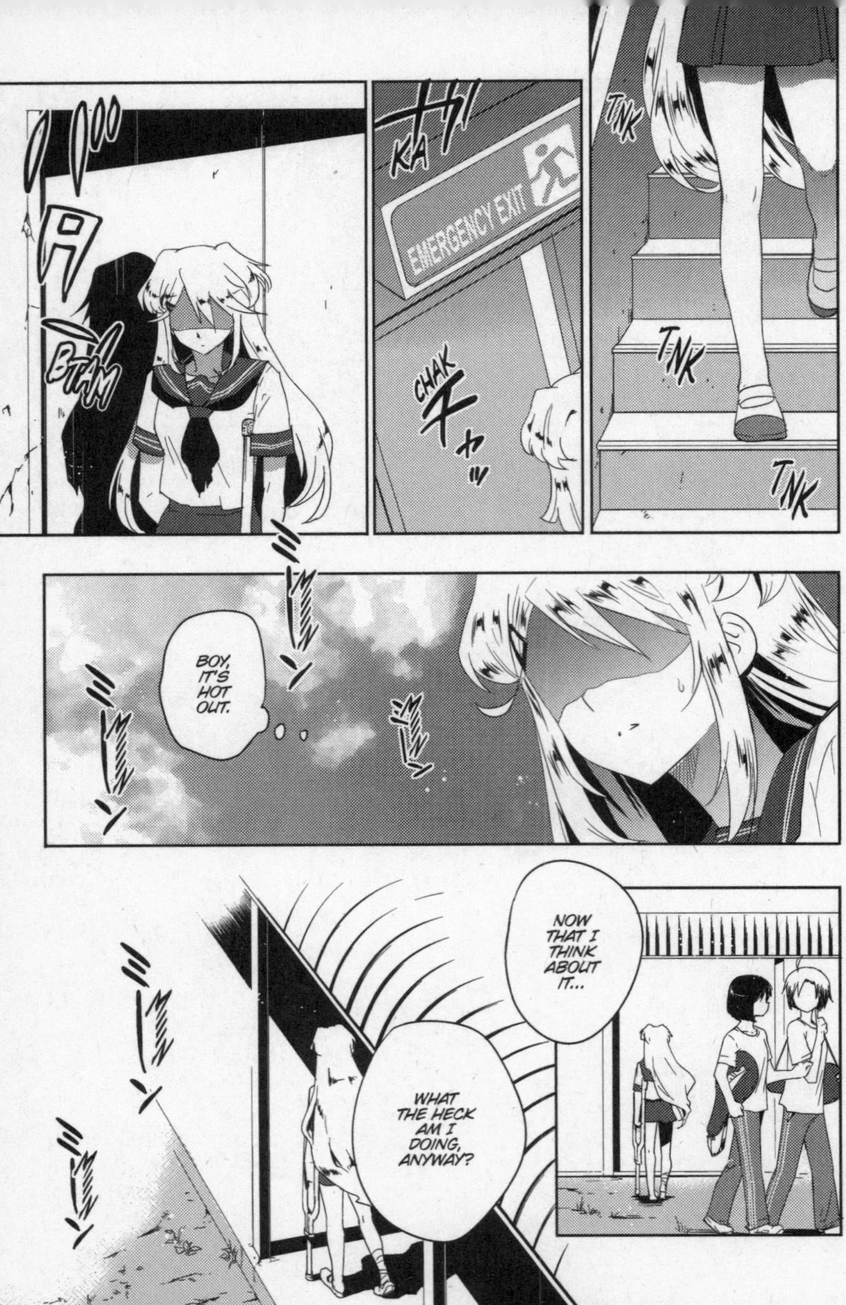
TNK
TNK
TNK
KA CHI
EMERGENCY EXIT
CHAK
BTAM
BOY, IT'S HOT OUT.
NOW THAT I THINK ABOUT IT...
WHAT THE HECK AM I DOING, ANYWAY?

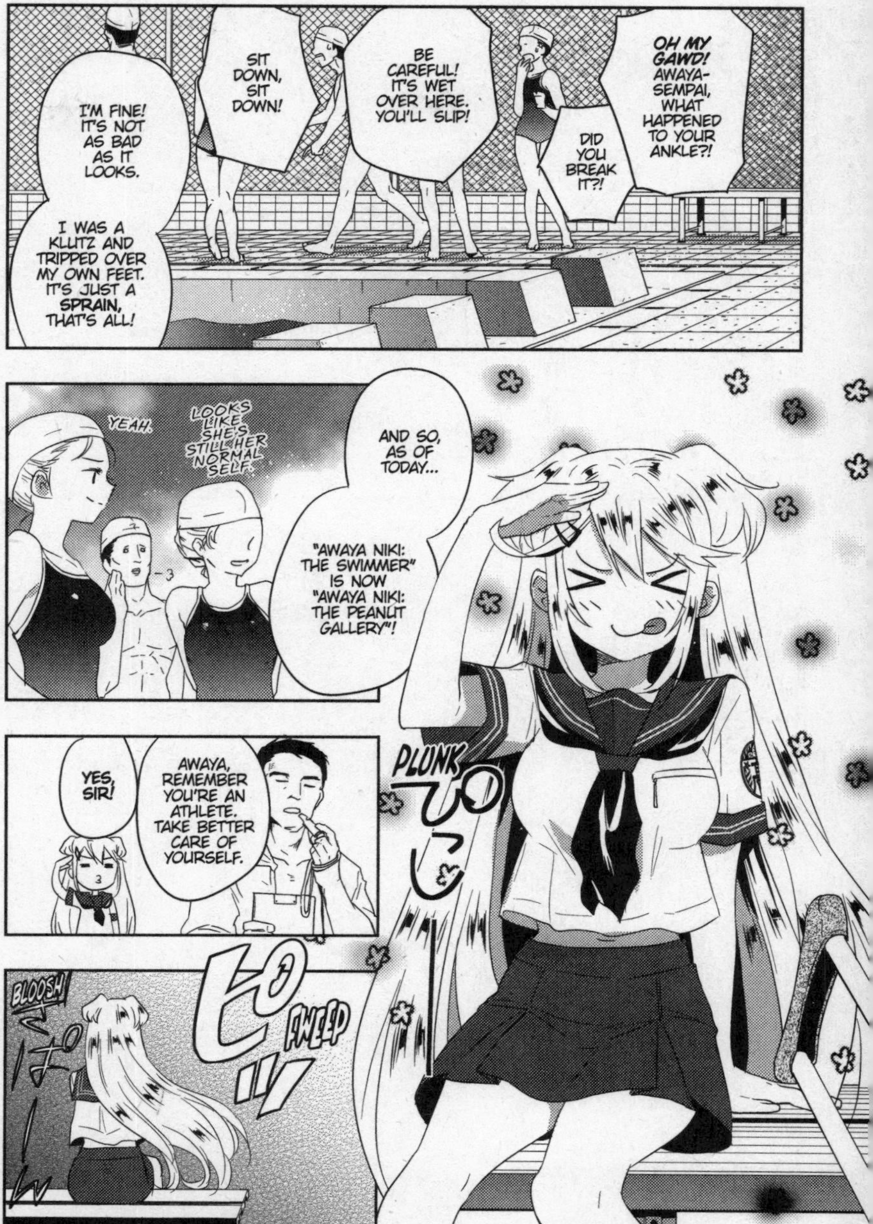
OH MY GAWD! AWAYA-SEMPAI, WHAT HAPPENED TO YOUR ANKLE?!
DID YOU BREAK IT?!
BE CAREFUL! IT'S WET OVER HERE. YOU'LL SLIP!
SIT DOWN, SIT DOWN!
I'M FINE! IT'S NOT AS BAD AS IT LOOKS.
I WAS A KLUTZ AND TRIPPED OVER MY OWN FEET. IT'S JUST A SPRAIN, THAT'S ALL!
AND SO, AS OF TODAY...
"AWAYA NIKI: THE SWIMMER" IS NOW "AWAYA NIKI: THE PEANUT GALLERY"!
PLUNK
FWEEP
LOOKS LIKE SHE'S STILL HER NORMAL SELF.
YEAH.
AWAYA, REMEMBER YOU'RE AN ATHLETE. TAKE BETTER CARE OF YOURSELF.
YES, SIR!
BLOOSH

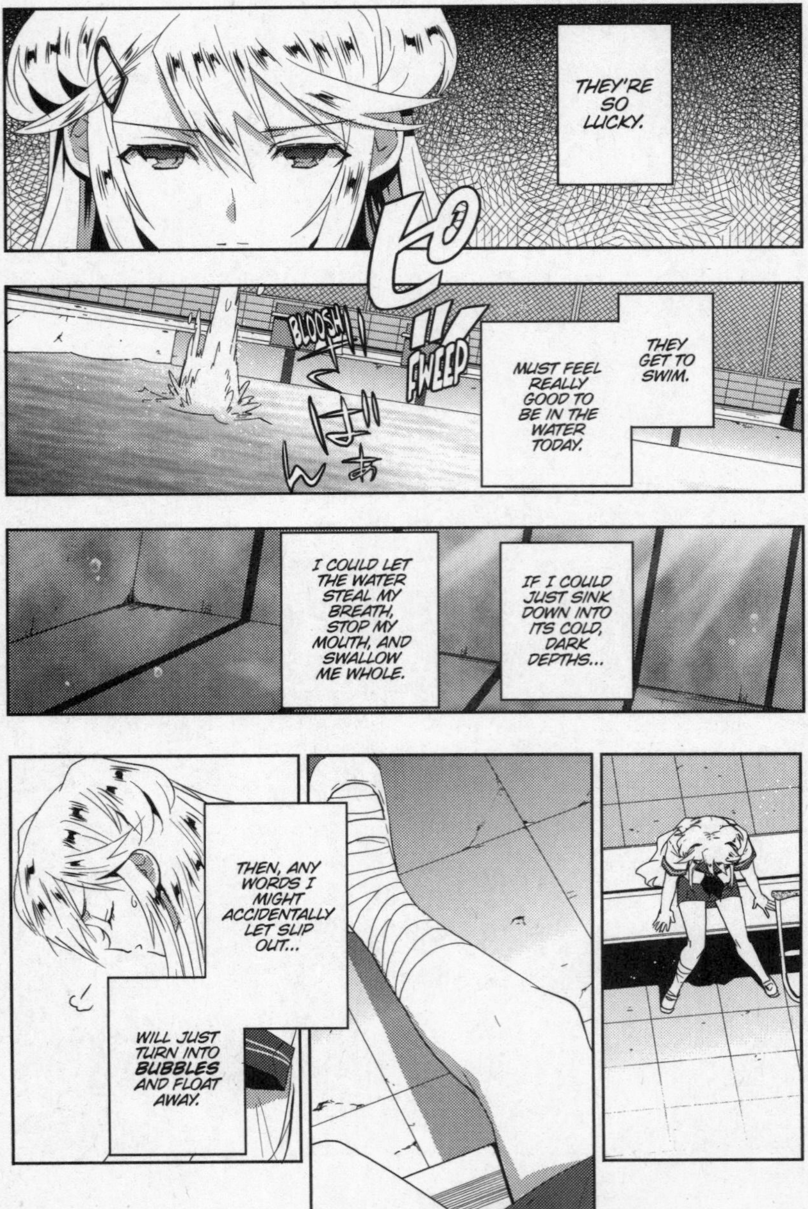
THEY'RE SO LUCKY.
THEY GET TO SWIM.
MUST FEEL REALLY GOOD TO BE IN THE WATER TODAY.
FWEEP
BLOOSH
IF I COULD JUST SINK DOWN INTO ITS COLD, DARK DEPTHS...
I COULD LET THE WATER STEAL MY BREATH, STOP MY MOUTH, AND SWALLOW ME WHOLE.
THEN, ANY WORDS I MIGHT ACCIDENTALLY LET SLIP OUT...
WILL JUST TURN INTO **BUBBLES** AND FLOAT AWAY.

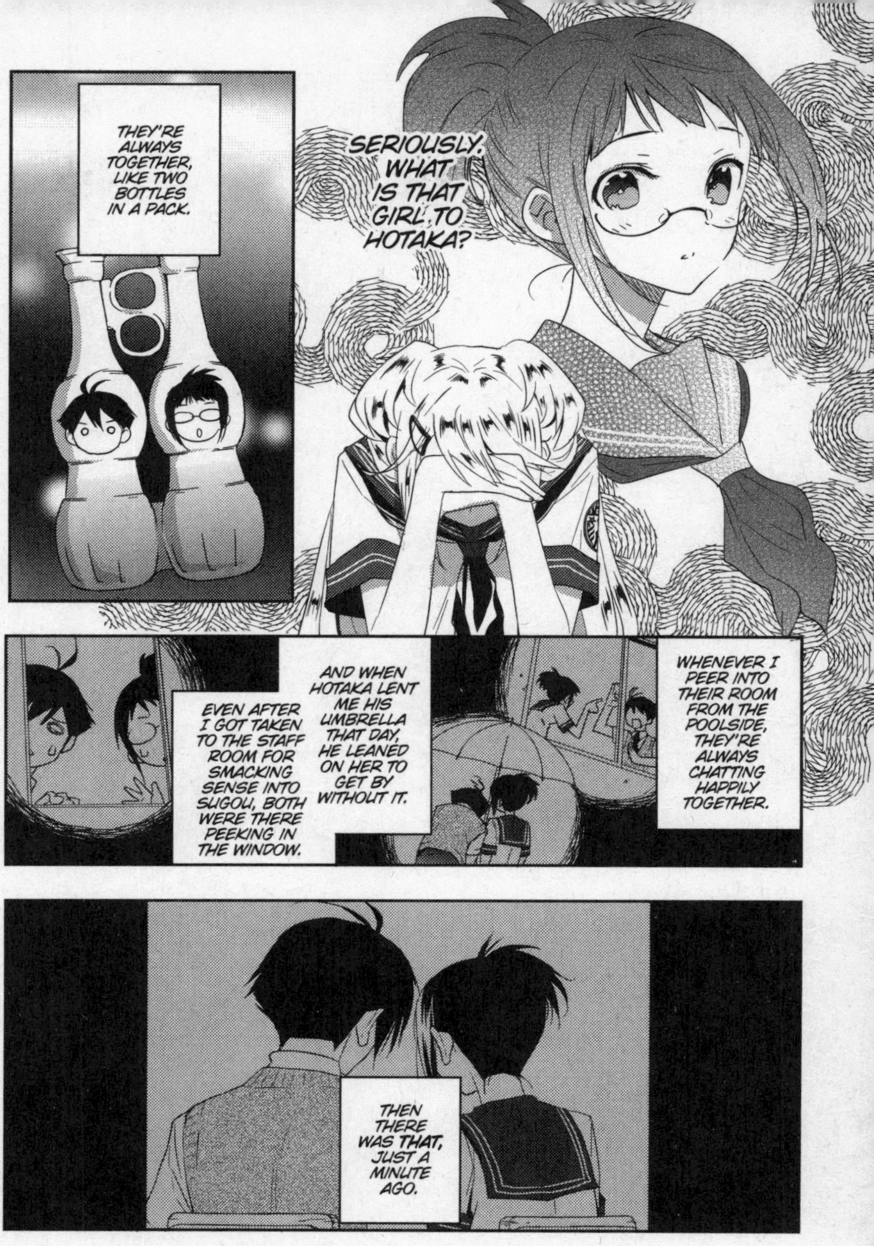
SERIOUSLY. WHAT IS THAT GIRL TO HOTAKA?
THEY'RE ALWAYS TOGETHER, LIKE TWO BOTTLES IN A PACK.
WHENEVER I PEER INTO THEIR ROOM FROM THE POOLSIDE, THEY'RE ALWAYS CHATTING HAPPILY TOGETHER.
AND WHEN HOTAKA LENT ME HIS UMBRELLA THAT DAY, HE LEANED ON HER TO GET BY WITHOUT IT.
EVEN AFTER I GOT TAKEN TO THE STAFF ROOM FOR SMACKING SENSE INTO SUGOU, BOTH WERE THERE PEEKING IN THE WINDOW.
THEN THERE WAS THAT, JUST A MINUTE AGO.

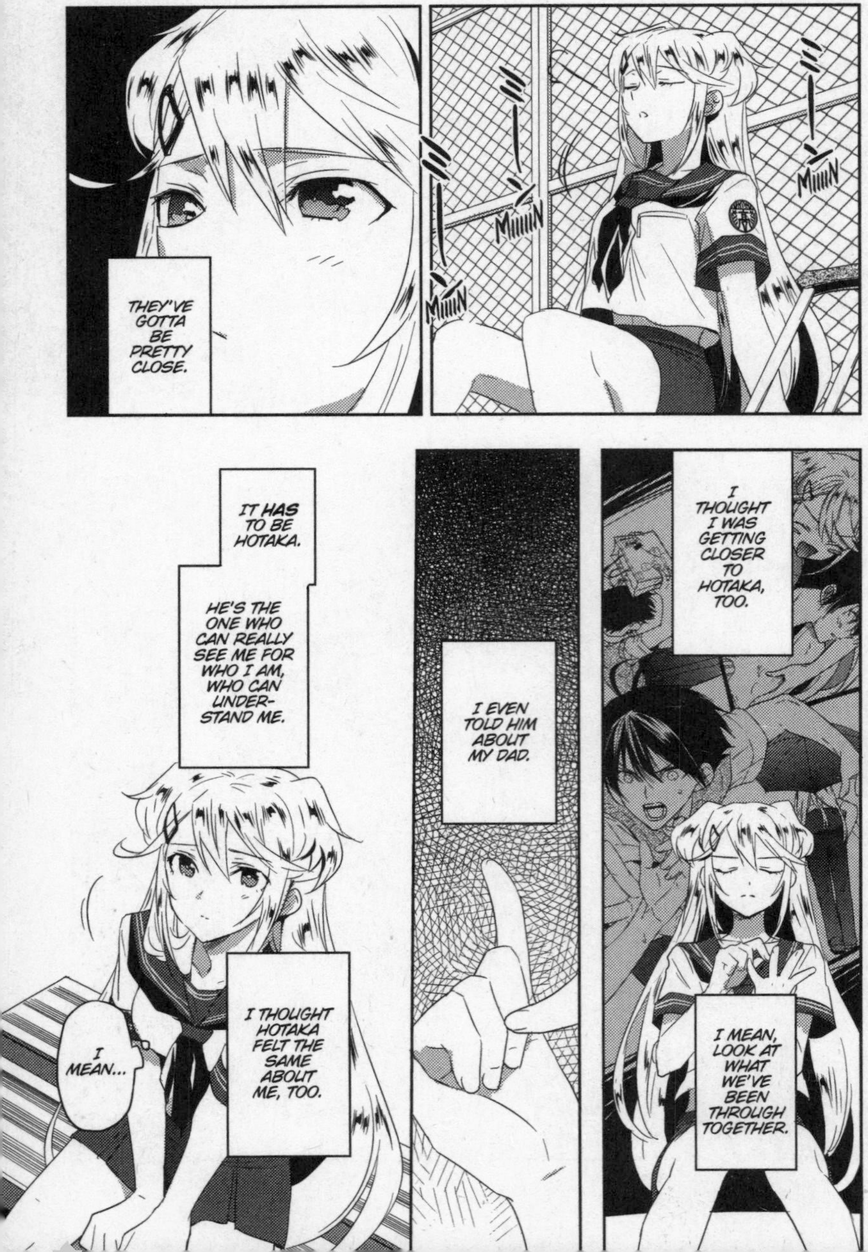
MiiiN
MiiiN
MiiiN
THEY'VE GOTTA BE PRETTY CLOSE.
I THOUGHT I WAS GETTING CLOSER TO HOTAKA, TOO.
I MEAN, LOOK AT WHAT WE'VE BEEN THROUGH TOGETHER.
I EVEN TOLD HIM ABOUT MY DAD.
IT HAS TO BE HOTAKA.
HE'S THE ONE WHO CAN REALLY SEE ME FOR WHO I AM, WHO CAN UNDER-STAND ME.
I THOUGHT HOTAKA FELT THE SAME ABOUT ME, TOO.
I MEAN...

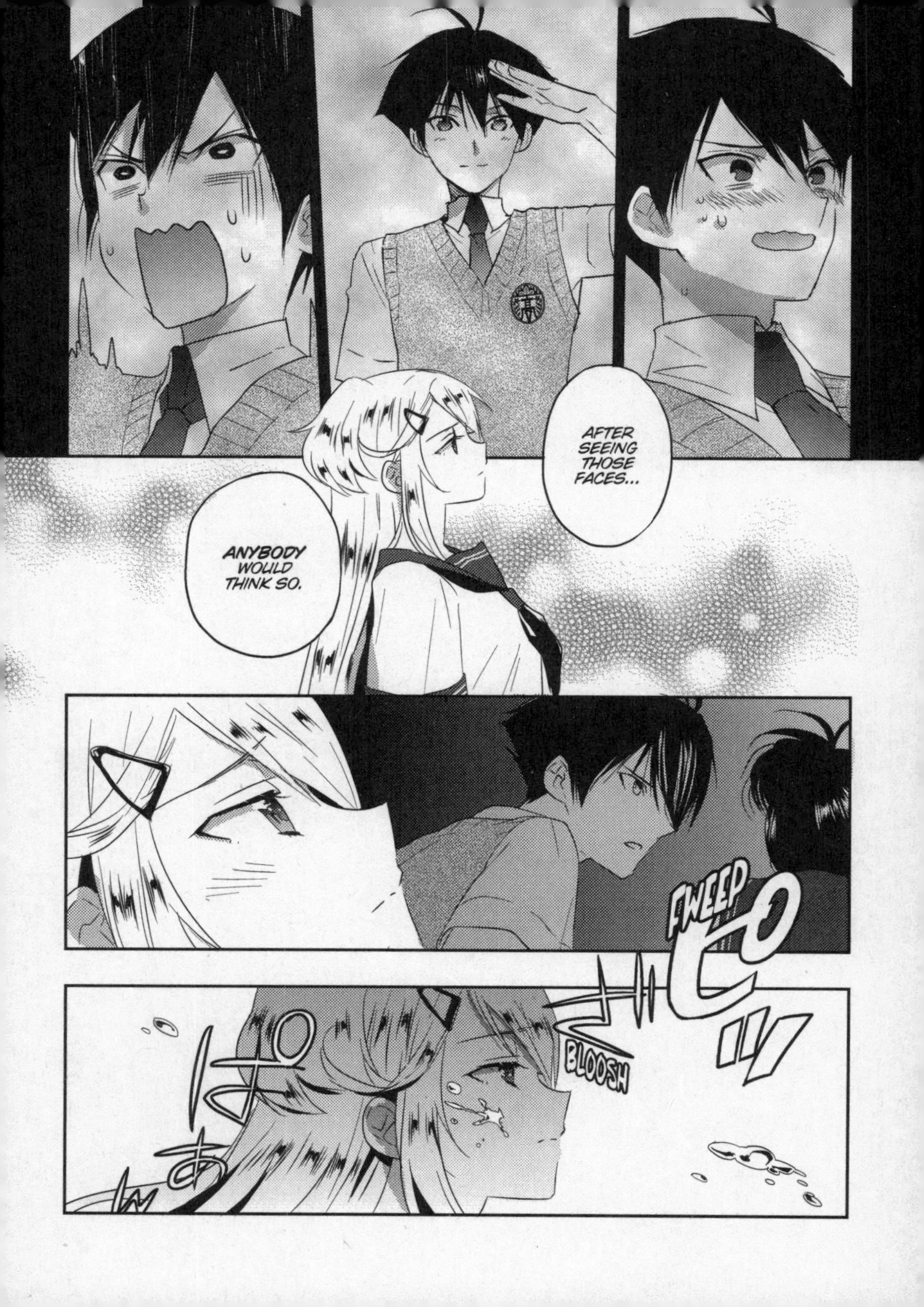
AFTER SEEING THOSE FACES...
ANYBODY WOULD THINK SO.
FWEEP
BLOOSH

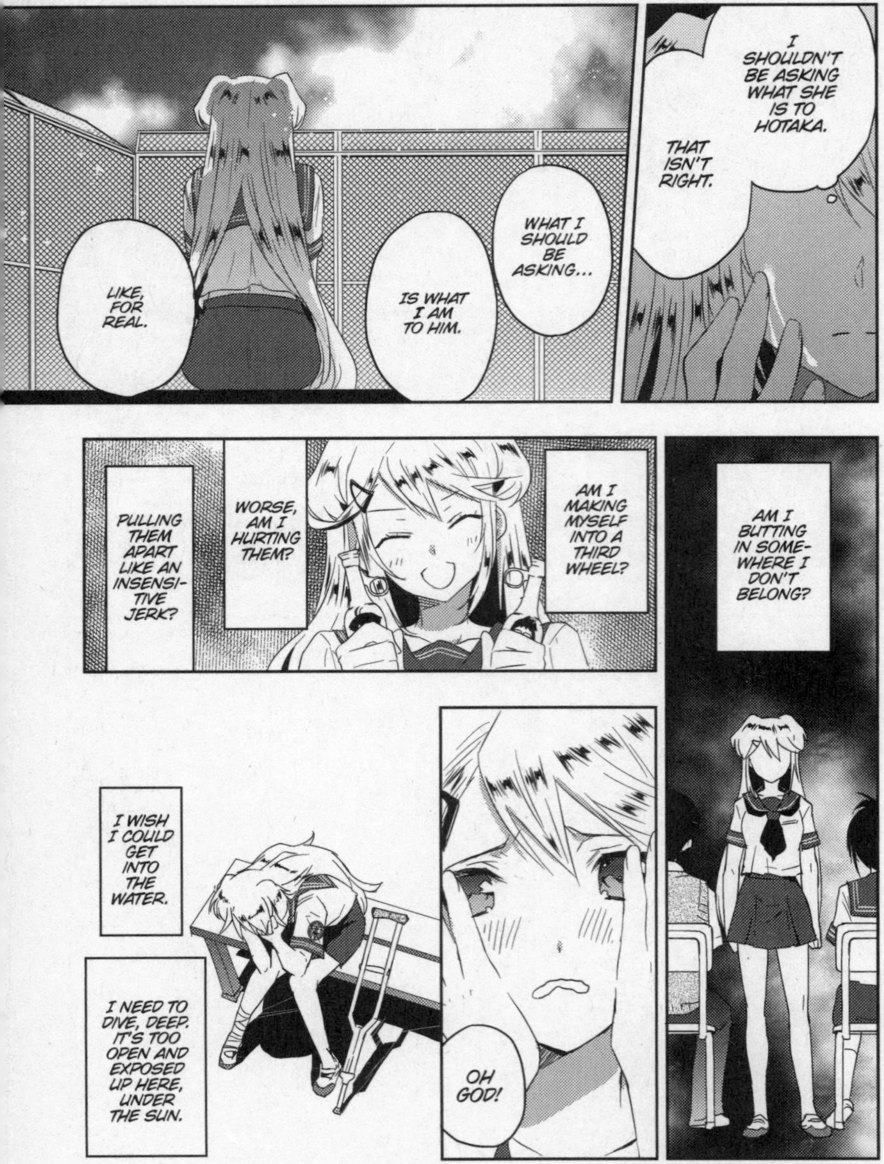
I SHOULDN'T BE ASKING WHAT SHE IS TO HOTAKA.
THAT ISN'T RIGHT.
WHAT I SHOULD BE ASKING...
IS WHAT I AM TO HIM.
LIKE, FOR REAL.
AM I BUTTING IN SOME-WHERE I DON'T BELONG?
AM I MAKING MYSELF INTO A THIRD WHEEL?
WORSE, AM I HURTING THEM?
PULLING THEM APART LIKE AN INSENSI-TIVE JERK?
OH GOD!
I WISH I COULD GET INTO THE WATER.
I NEED TO DIVE, DEEP. IT'S TOO OPEN AND EXPOSED UP HERE, UNDER THE SUN.

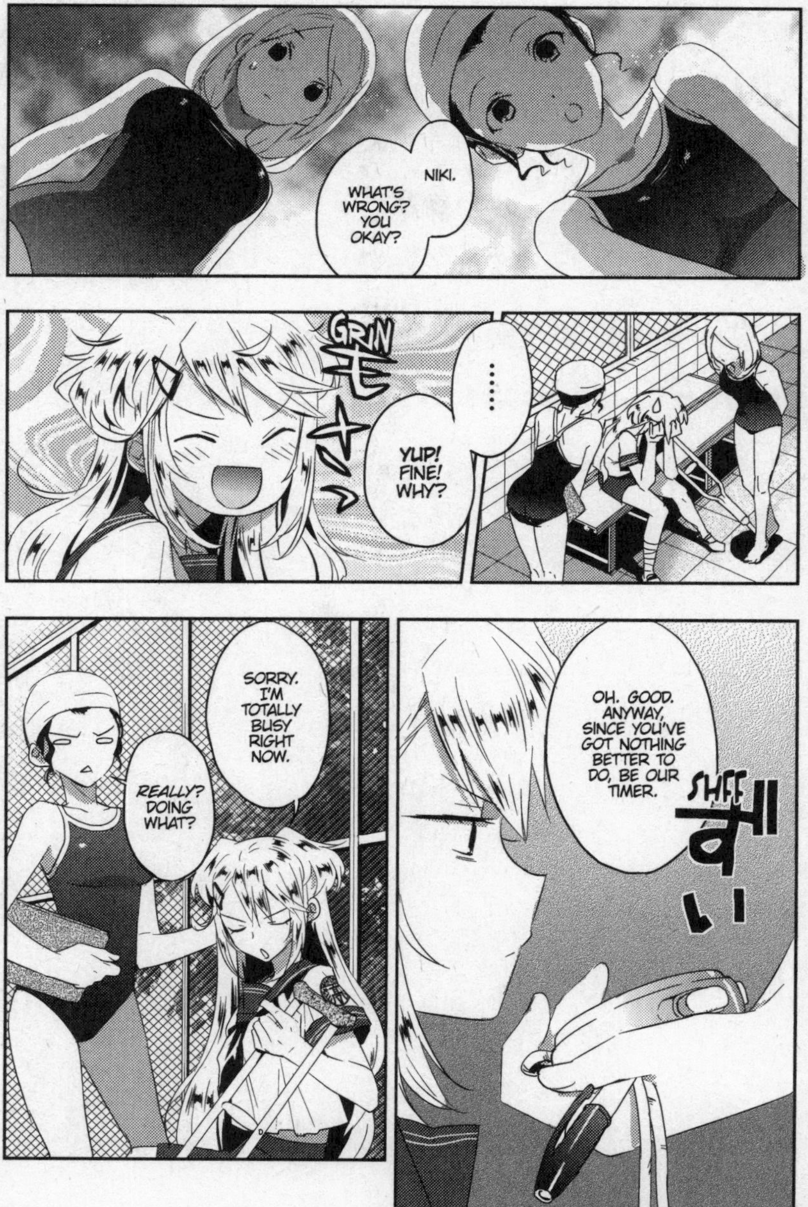
NIKI.
WHAT'S WRONG? YOU OKAY?
......
GRIN
YUP! FINE! WHY?
OH. GOOD. ANYWAY, SINCE YOU'VE GOT NOTHING BETTER TO DO, BE OUR TIMER.
SHFF
SORRY. I'M TOTALLY BUSY RIGHT NOW.
*REALLY?* DOING WHAT?

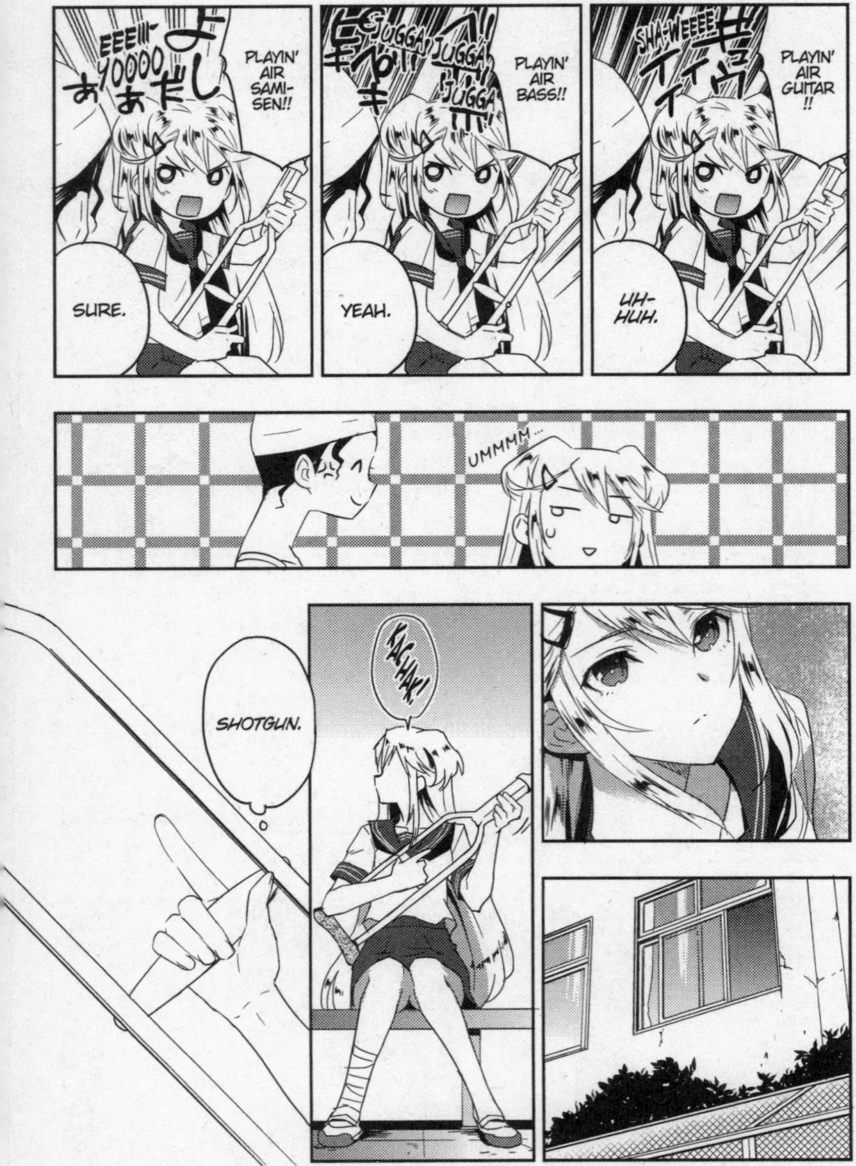

PLAYIN' AIR GUITAR !!
SHA-WEEEE
UH-HUH.
PLAYIN' AIR BASS!!
JUGGA JUGGA JUGGA
YEAH.
PLAYIN' AIR SAMI-SEN!!
EEEIIII- YOOOO
SURE.
UMMMM...
KACHAK!
SHOTGUN.

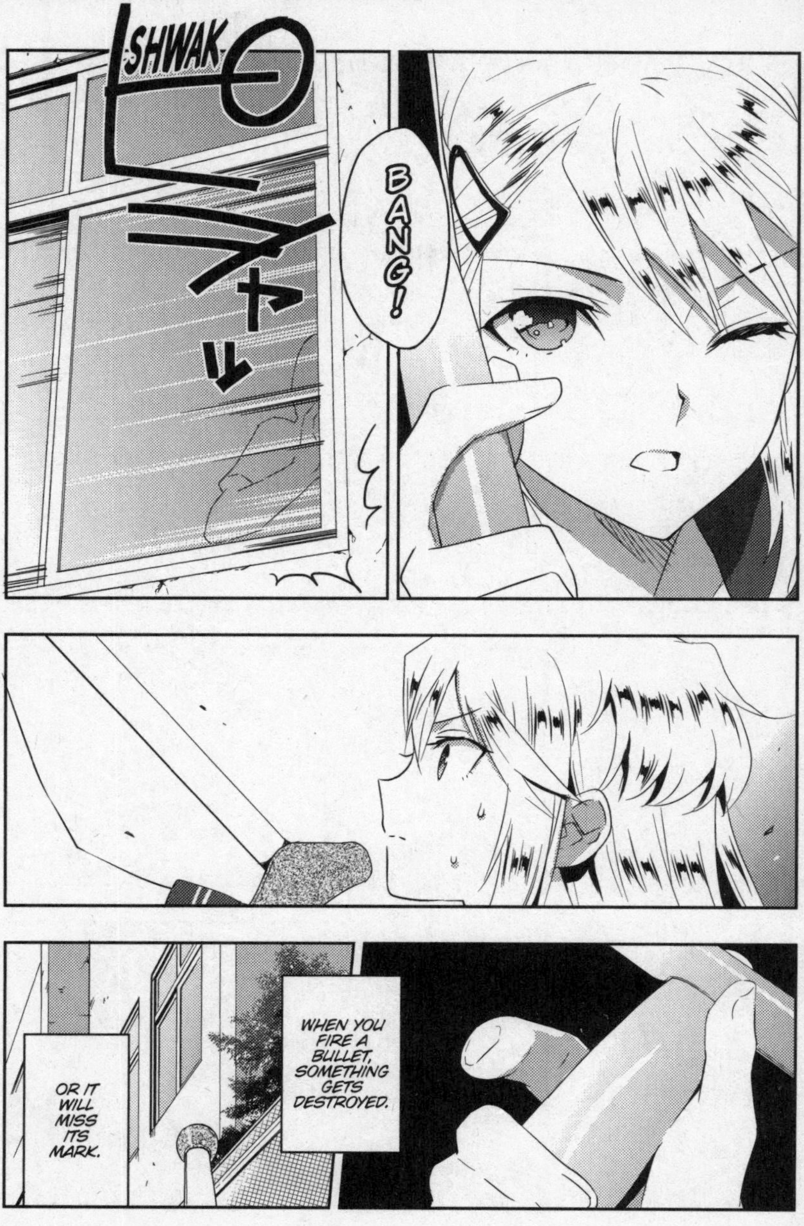
BANG!
SHWAK
WHEN YOU FIRE A BULLET, SOMETHING GETS DESTROYED.
OR IT WILL MISS ITS MARK.

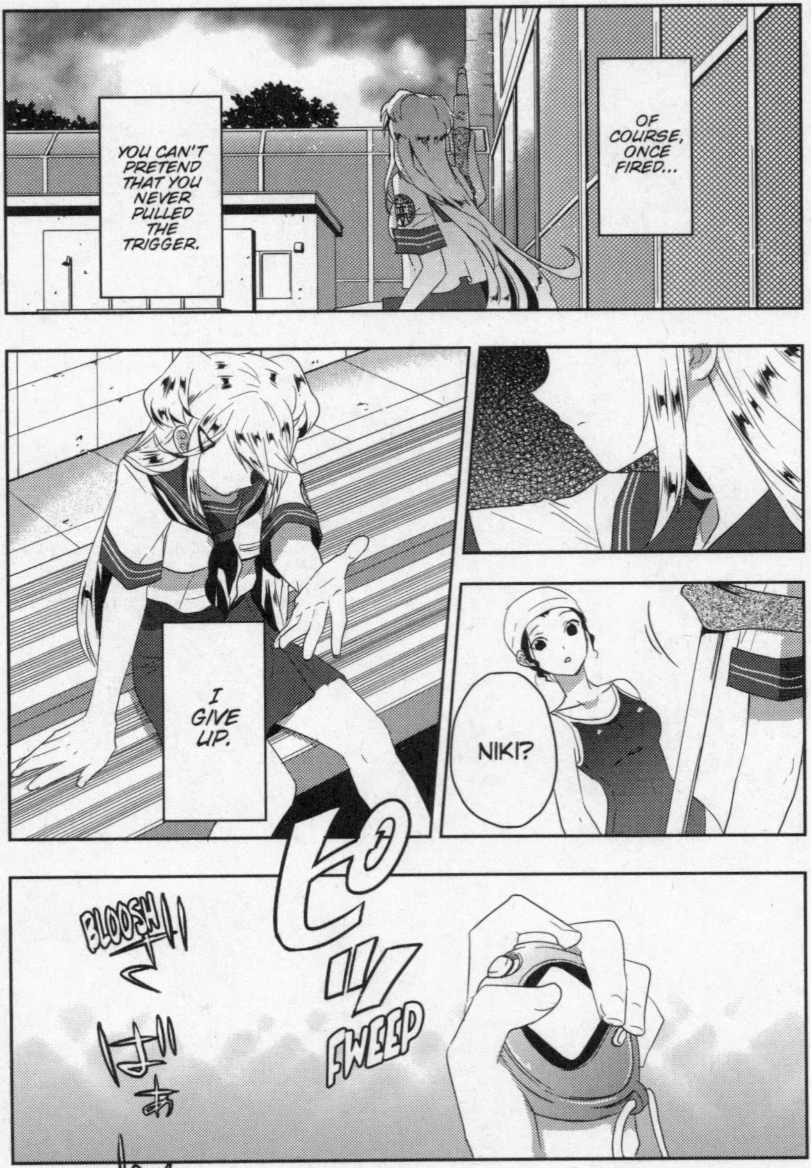
OF COURSE, ONCE FIRED...
YOU CAN'T PRETEND THAT YOU NEVER PULLED THE TRIGGER.
NIKI?
I GIVE UP.
ピーッ
FWEEP
BLOOSH
ざばぁん

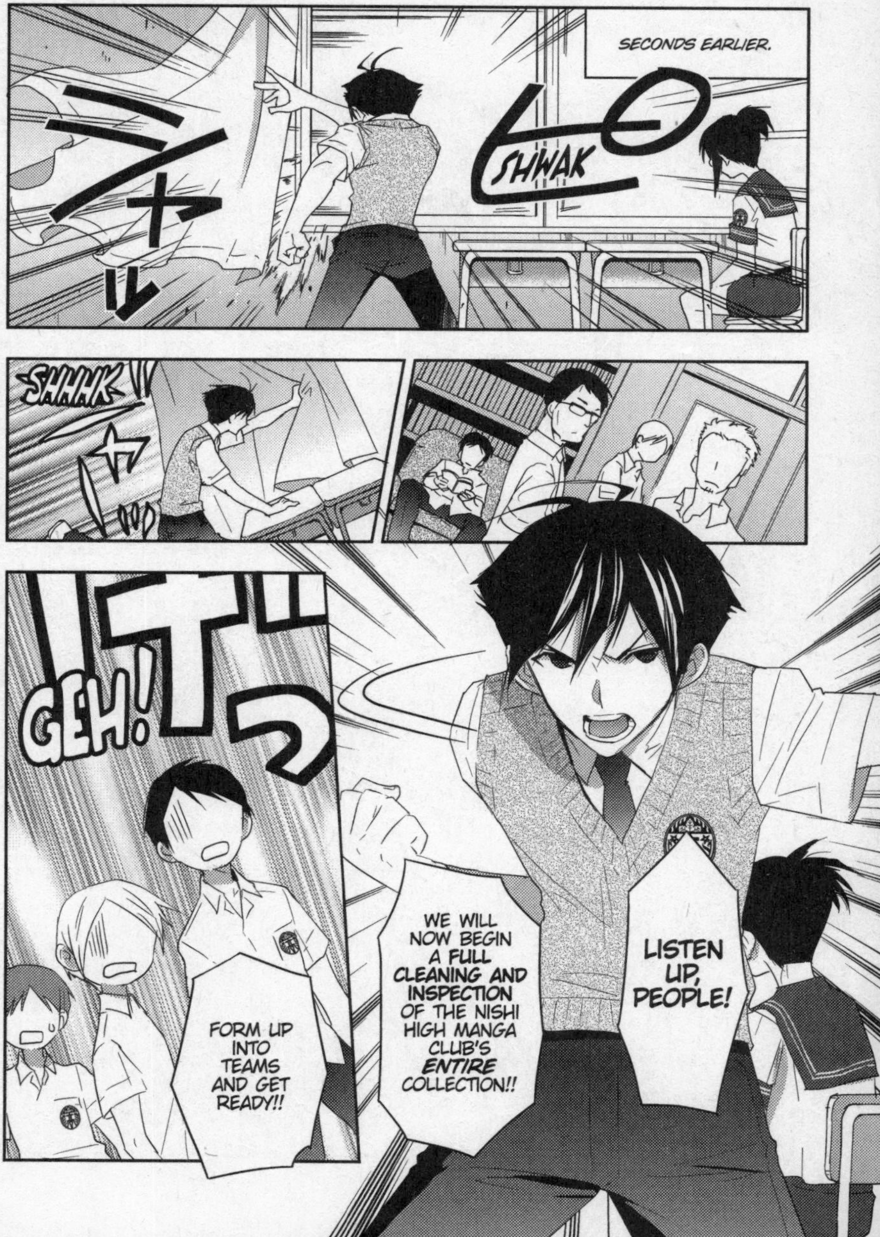
SECONDS EARLIER.
SHWAK
SHHHK
LISTEN UP, PEOPLE!
WE WILL NOW BEGIN A FULL CLEANING AND INSPECTION OF THE NISHI HIGH MANGA CLUB'S *ENTIRE* COLLECTION!!
FORM UP INTO TEAMS AND GET READY!!
GEH!

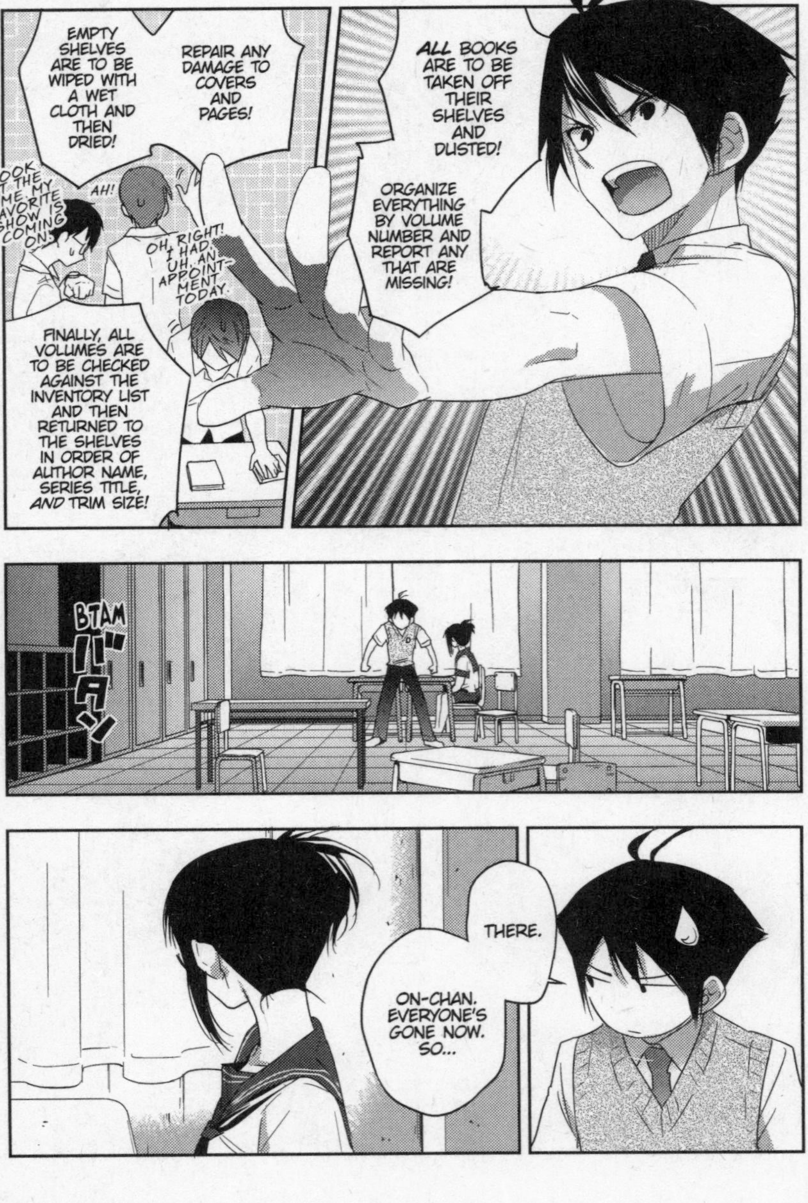
ALL BOOKS ARE TO BE TAKEN OFF THEIR SHELVES AND DUSTED!
ORGANIZE EVERYTHING BY VOLUME NUMBER AND REPORT ANY THAT ARE MISSING!
REPAIR ANY DAMAGE TO COVERS AND PAGES!
EMPTY SHELVES ARE TO BE WIPED WITH A WET CLOTH AND THEN DRIED!
AH!
LOOK AT THE TIME. MY FAVORITE SHOW IS COMING ON.
OH, RIGHT! I HAD, UH, AN APPOINTMENT TODAY.
FINALLY, ALL VOLUMES ARE TO BE CHECKED AGAINST THE INVENTORY LIST AND THEN RETURNED TO THE SHELVES IN ORDER OF AUTHOR NAME, SERIES TITLE, AND TRIM SIZE!
BTAM
THERE.
ON-CHAN. EVERYONE'S GONE NOW. SO...

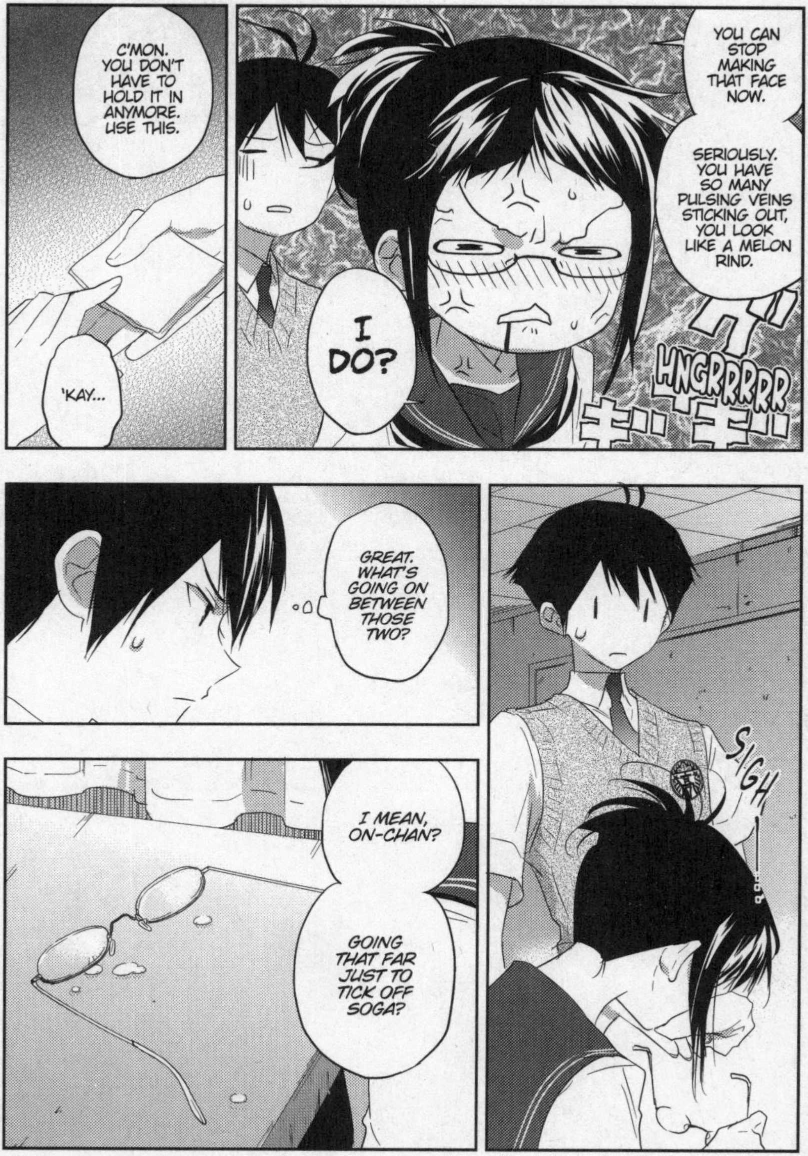

YOU CAN STOP MAKING THAT FACE NOW.
SERIOUSLY. YOU HAVE SO MANY PULSING VEINS STICKING OUT, YOU LOOK LIKE A MELON RIND.
HNGRRRRR
I DO?
C'MON. YOU DON'T HAVE TO HOLD IT IN ANYMORE. USE THIS.
'KAY...
SIGH
GREAT. WHAT'S GOING ON BETWEEN THOSE TWO?
I MEAN, ON-CHAN?
GOING THAT FAR JUST TO TICK OFF SOGA?

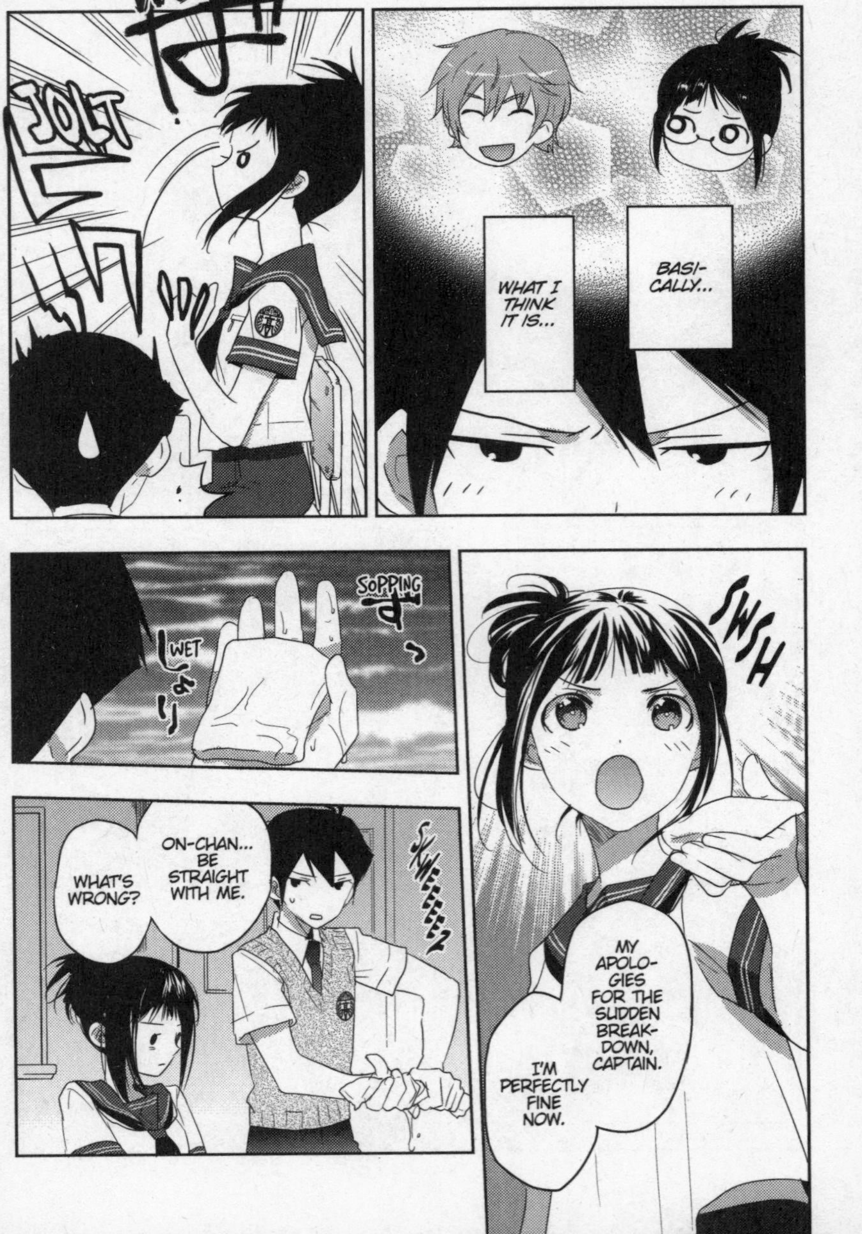

BASI-CALLY...
WHAT I THINK IT IS...
WSH
JOLT
SWSH
MY APOLOGIES FOR THE SUDDEN BREAK-DOWN, CAPTAIN.
I'M PERFECTLY FINE NOW.
SOPPING
WET
ON-CHAN... BE STRAIGHT WITH ME.
WHAT'S WRONG?
SKWEEEEZ

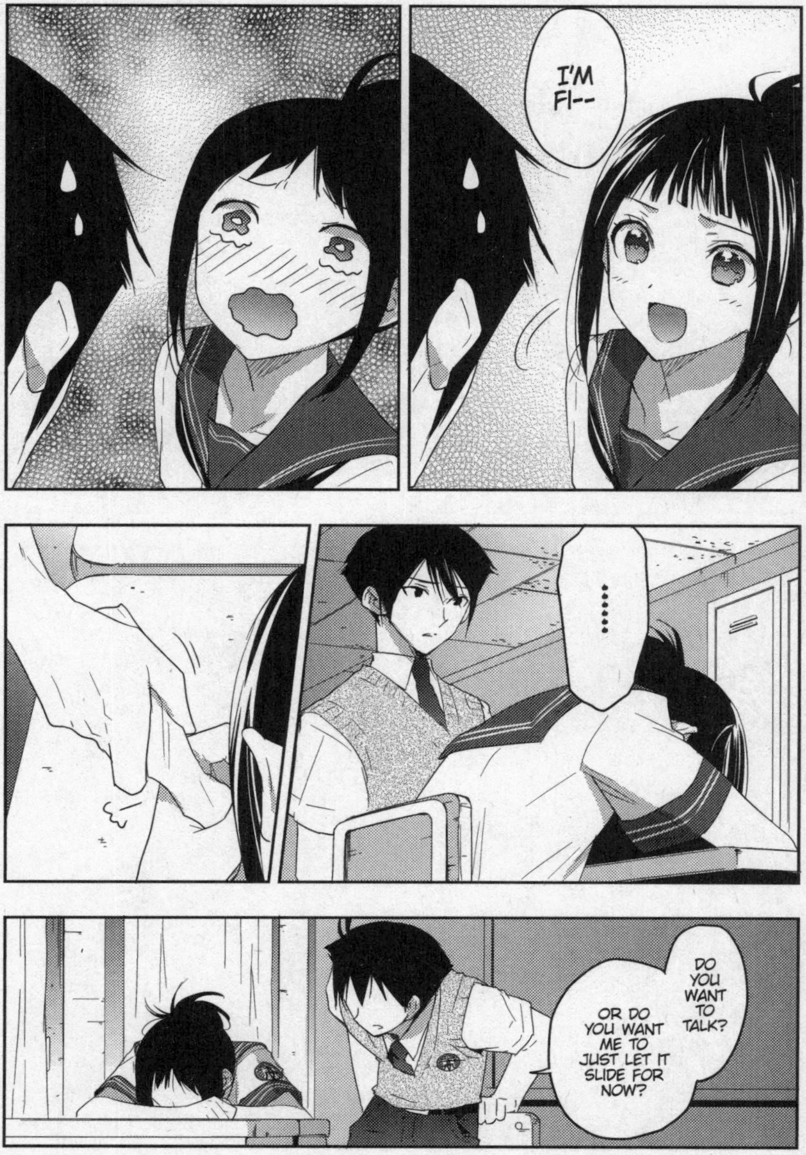
I'M FI--
......
DO YOU WANT TO TALK?
OR DO YOU WANT ME TO JUST LET IT SLIDE FOR NOW?

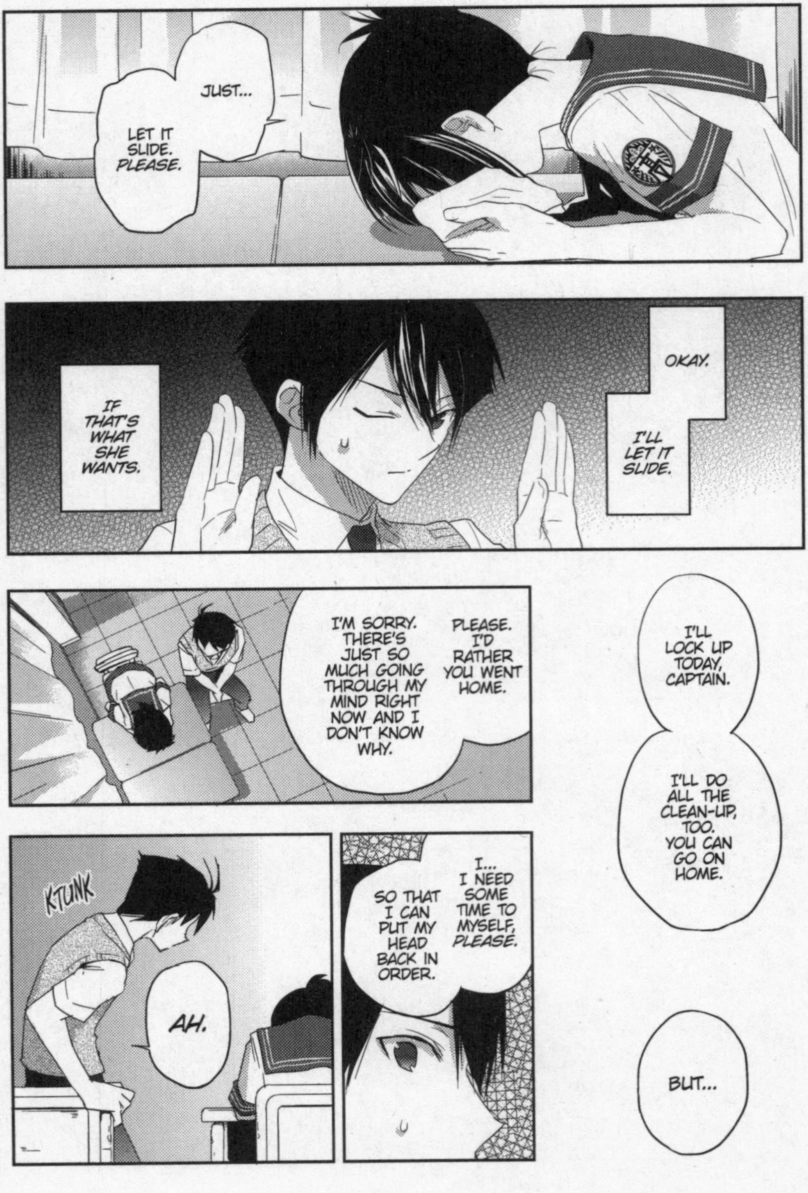
JUST...
LET IT SLIDE. PLEASE.
OKAY.
I'LL LET IT SLIDE.
IF THAT'S WHAT SHE WANTS.
I'LL LOCK UP TODAY, CAPTAIN.
I'LL DO ALL THE CLEAN-UP, TOO. YOU CAN GO ON HOME.
PLEASE. I'D RATHER YOU WENT HOME.
I'M SORRY. THERE'S JUST SO MUCH GOING THROUGH MY MIND RIGHT NOW AND I DON'T KNOW WHY.
BUT...
I... I NEED SOME TIME TO MYSELF, PLEASE.
SO THAT I CAN PUT MY HEAD BACK IN ORDER.
K-TUNK
AH.

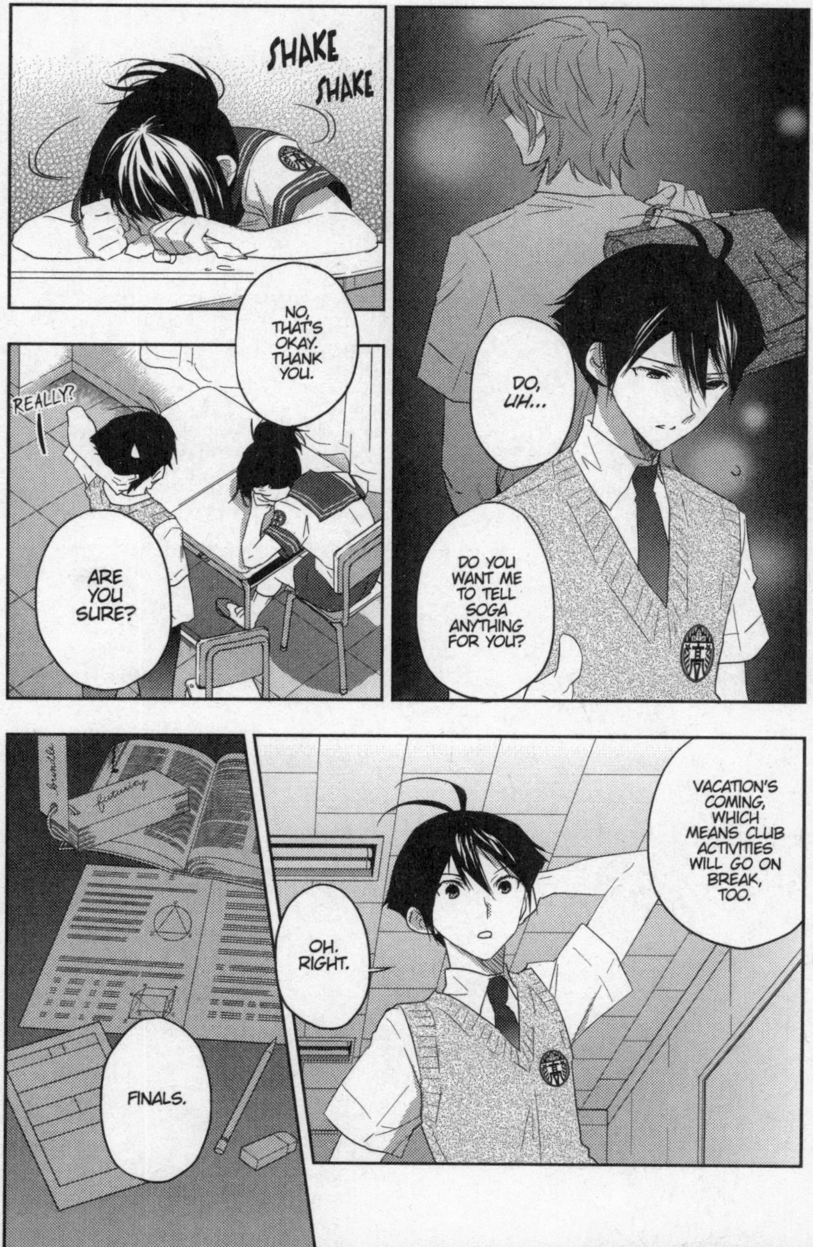
DO, UH...
DO YOU WANT ME TO TELL SOGA ANYTHING FOR YOU?
SHAKE
SHAKE
NO, THAT'S OKAY. THANK YOU.
REALLY?
ARE YOU SURE?
VACATION'S COMING, WHICH MEANS CLUB ACTIVITIES WILL GO ON BREAK, TOO.
OH. RIGHT.
FINALS.

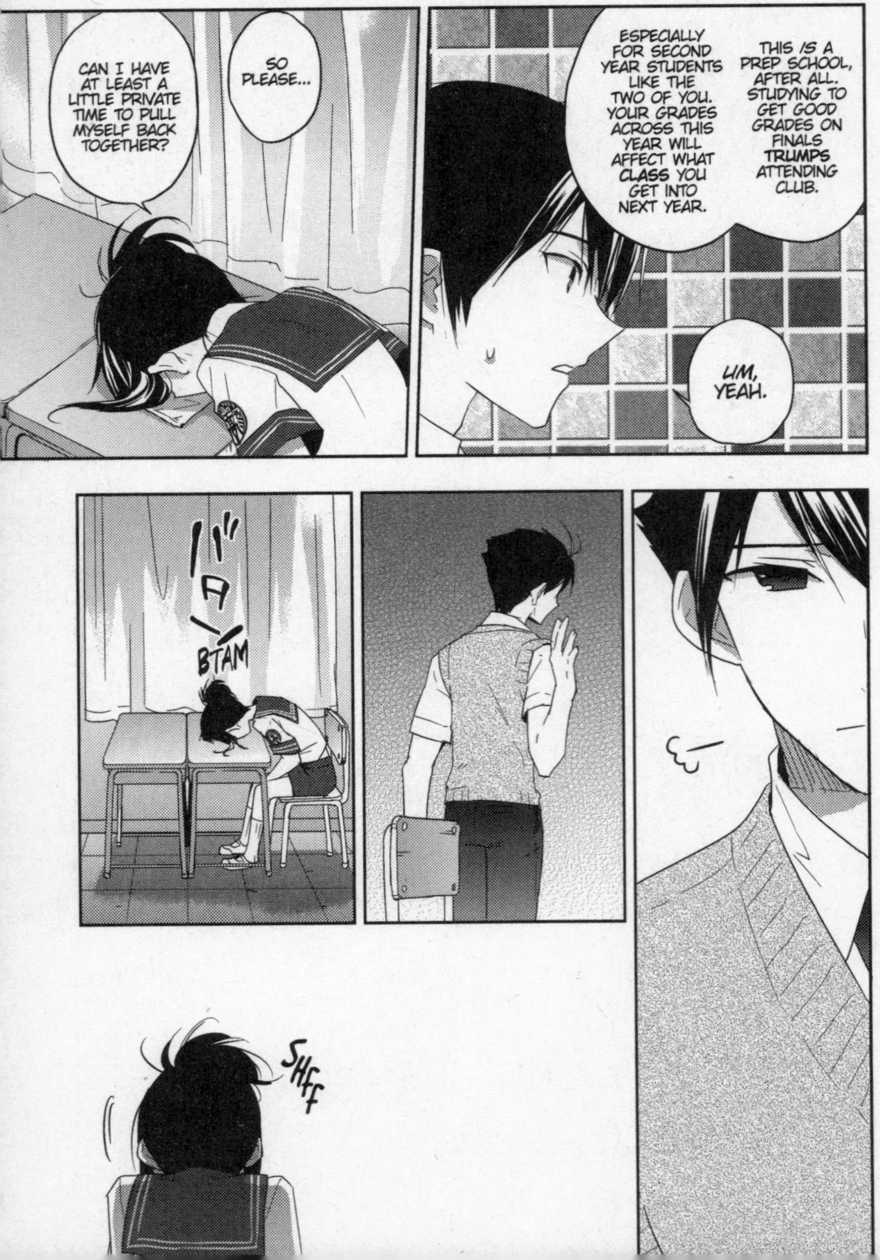
THIS IS A PREP SCHOOL, AFTER ALL. STUDYING TO GET GOOD GRADES ON FINALS TRUMPS ATTENDING CLUB.
ESPECIALLY FOR SECOND YEAR STUDENTS LIKE THE TWO OF YOU. YOUR GRADES ACROSS THIS YEAR WILL AFFECT WHAT CLASS YOU GET INTO NEXT YEAR.
UM, YEAH.
SO PLEASE...
CAN I HAVE AT LEAST A LITTLE PRIVATE TIME TO PULL MYSELF BACK TOGETHER?
BTAM
SHFF

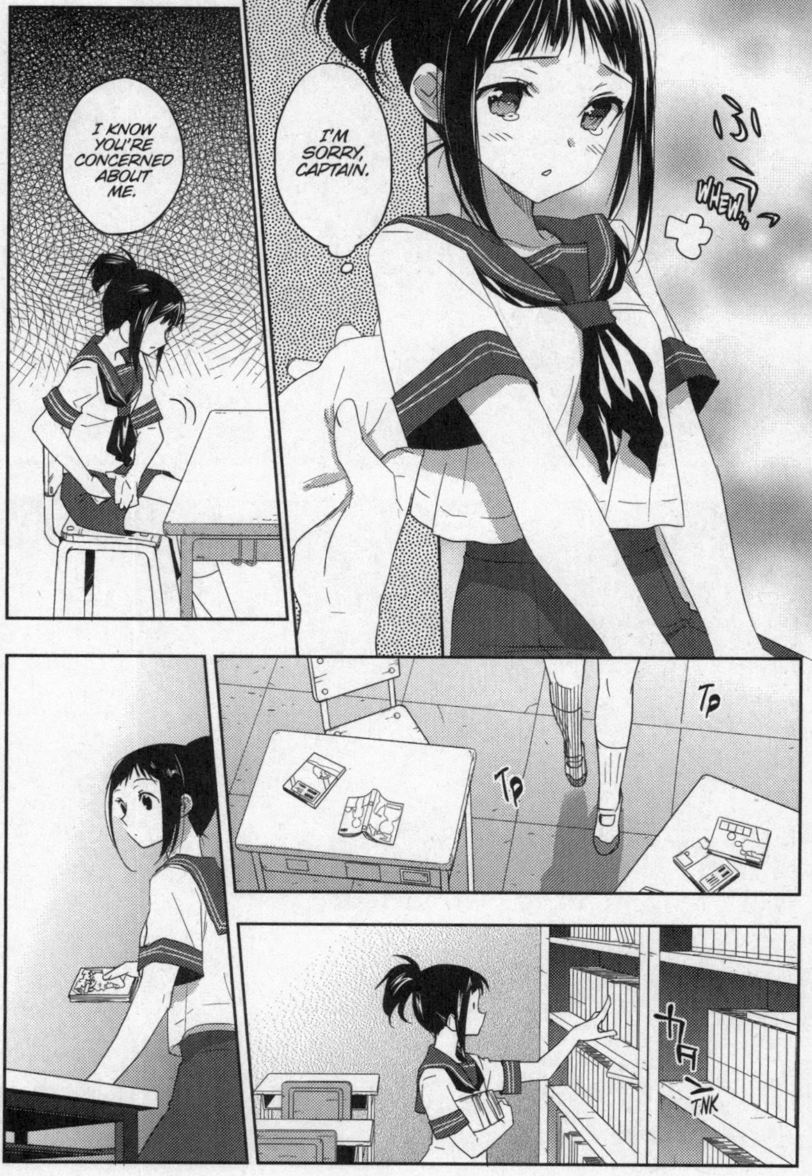
ふぅ
WHEW...
I'M SORRY, CAPTAIN.
I KNOW YOU'RE CONCERNED ABOUT ME.
Tp
Tp
カタ
TNK

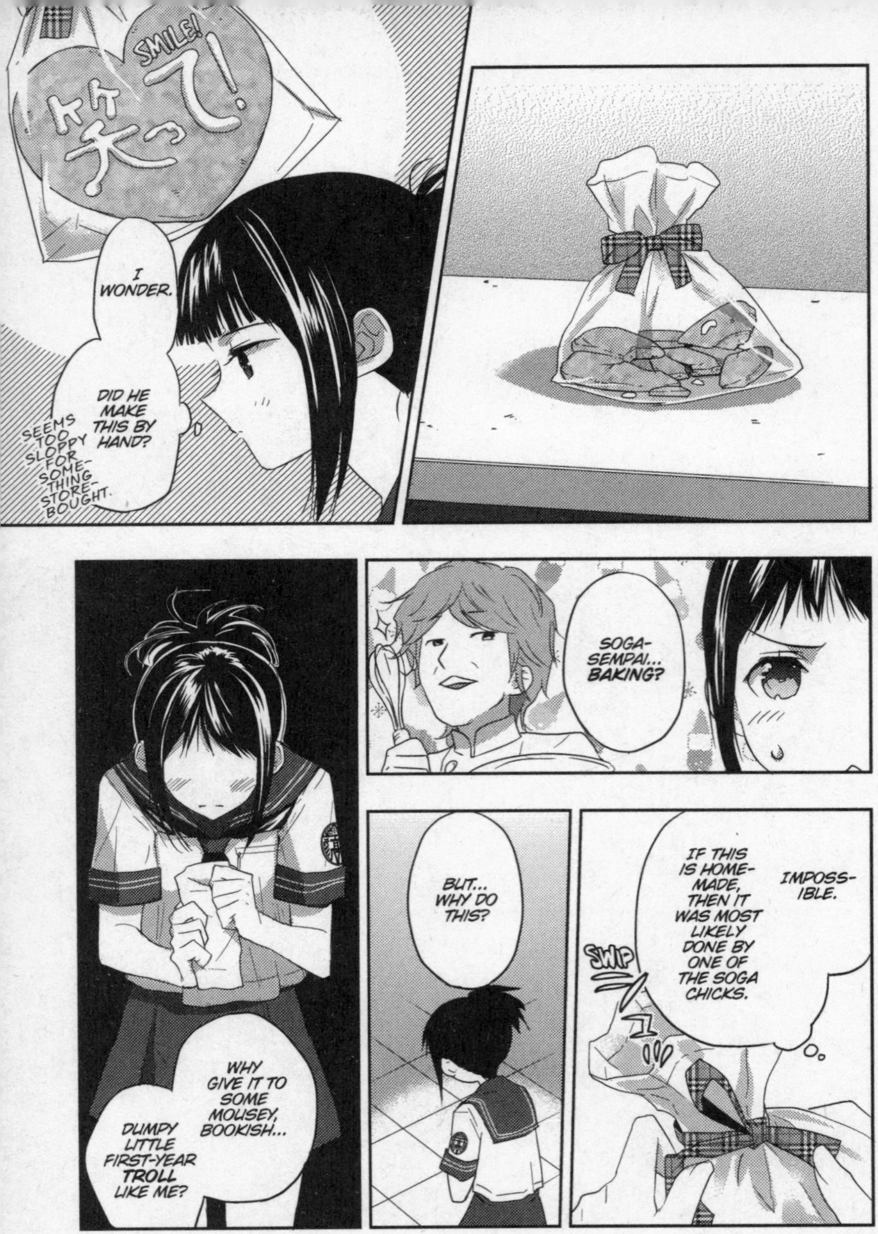
SMILE!
I WONDER.
DID HE MAKE THIS BY HAND?
SEEMS TOO SLOPPY FOR SOME-THING STORE-BOUGHT.
SOGA-SEMPAI... BAKING?
IMPOSS-IBLE.
IF THIS IS HOME-MADE, THEN IT WAS MOST LIKELY DONE BY ONE OF THE SOGA CHICKS.
SWIP
BUT... WHY DO THIS?
WHY GIVE IT TO SOME MOUSEY, BOOKISH...
DUMPY LITTLE FIRST-YEAR TROLL LIKE ME?

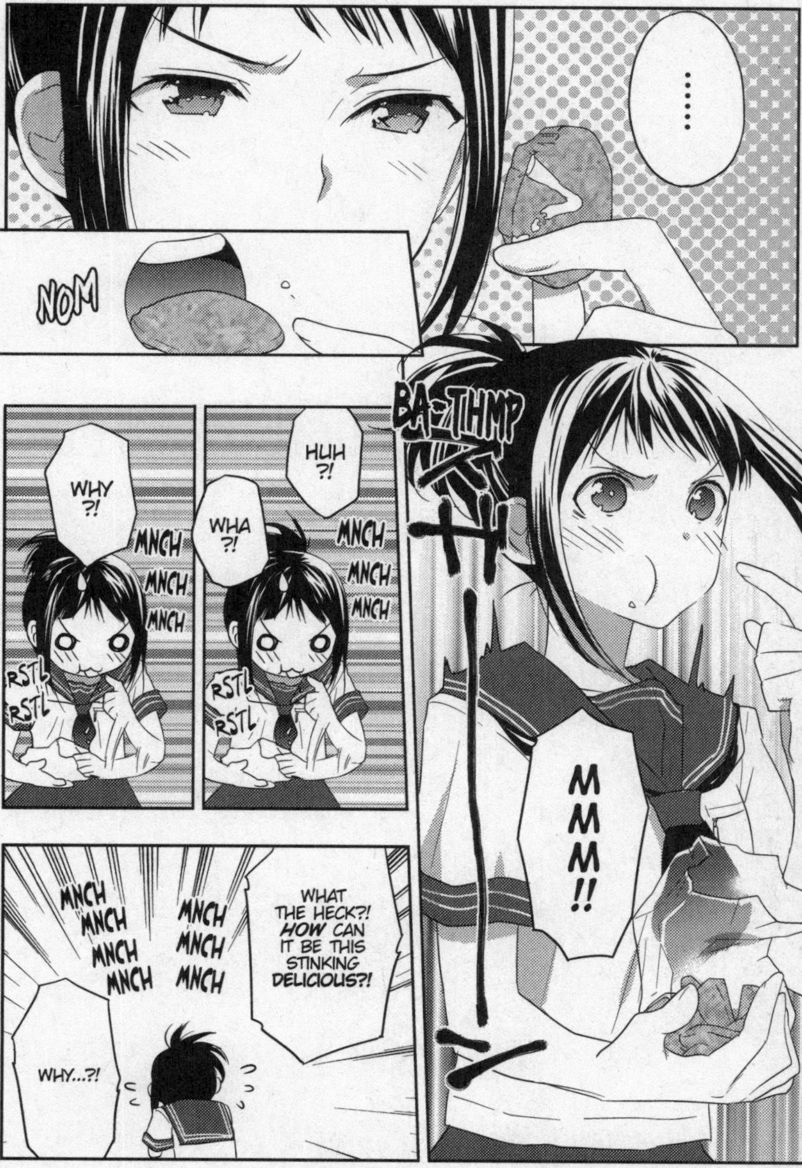
......
NOM
BA-THMP
MMM!!
HUH?!
WHA?!
MNCH MNCH MNCH
RSTL RSTL
WHY?!
MNCH MNCH MNCH
RSTL RSTL
WHAT THE HECK?! *HOW* CAN IT BE THIS STINKING **DELICIOUS**?!
MNCH MNCH MNCH
MNCH MNCH MNCH MNCH
WHY...?!

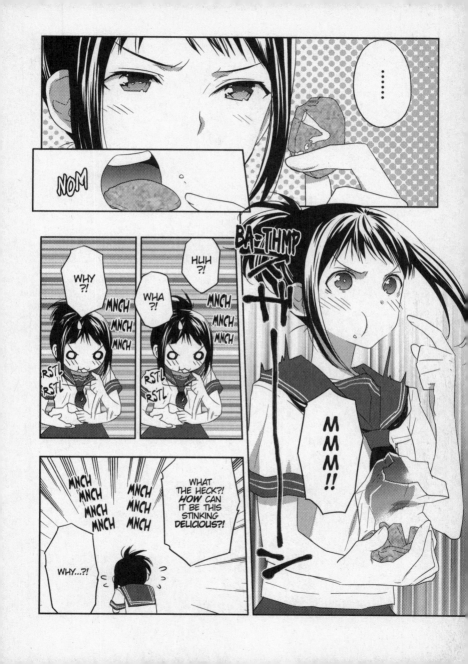

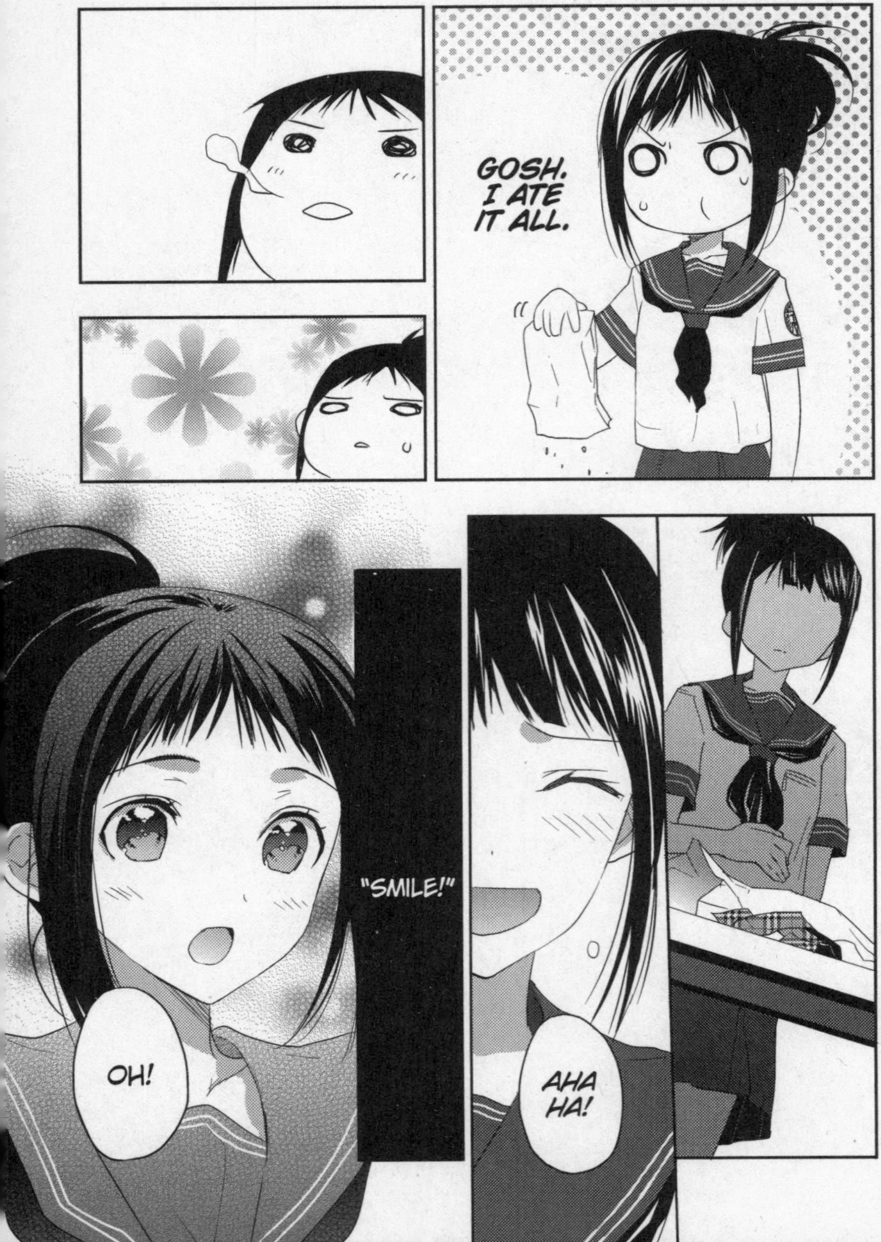
GOSH. I ATE IT ALL.
AHA HA!
"SMILE!"
OH!

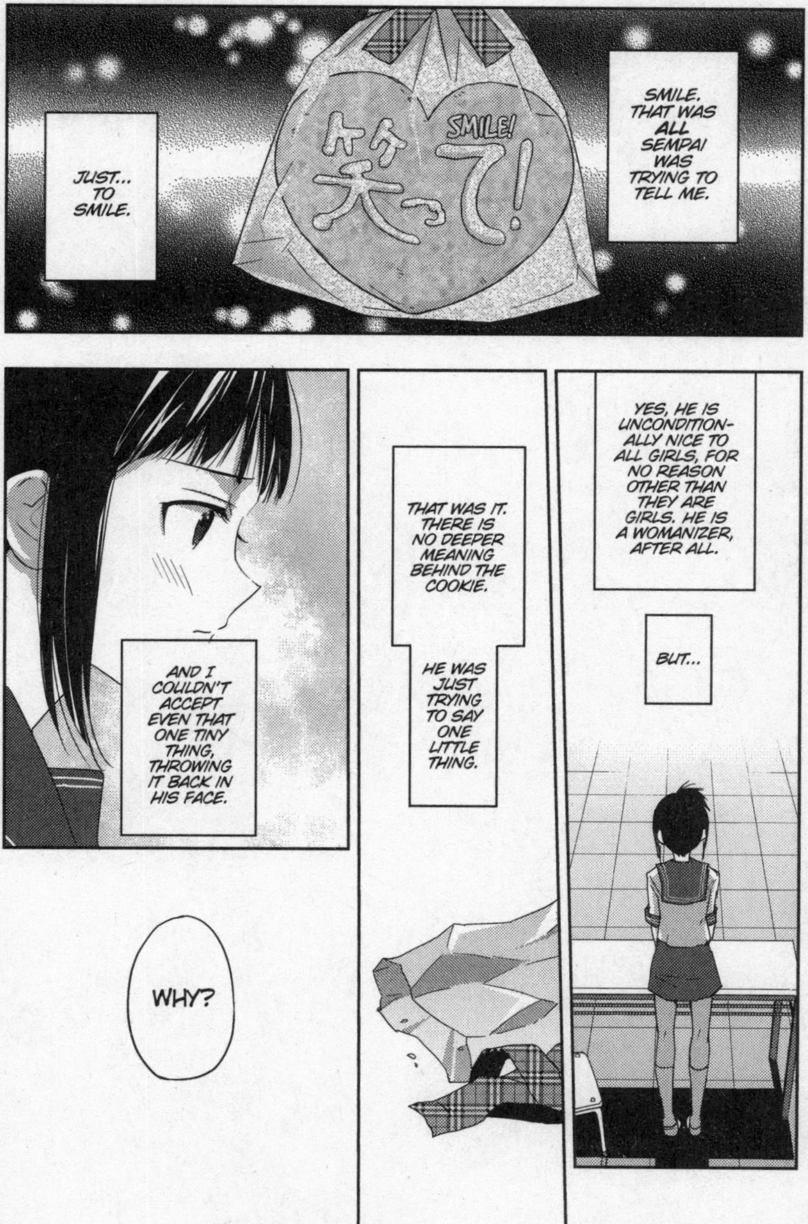

SMILE. THAT WAS ALL SEMPAI WAS TRYING TO TELL ME.
SMILE!
笑って!
JUST... TO SMILE.
YES, HE IS UNCONDITION-ALLY NICE TO ALL GIRLS, FOR NO REASON OTHER THAN THEY ARE GIRLS. HE IS A WOMANIZER, AFTER ALL.
BUT...
THAT WAS IT. THERE IS NO DEEPER MEANING BEHIND THE COOKIE.
HE WAS JUST TRYING TO SAY ONE LITTLE THING.
AND I COULDN'T ACCEPT EVEN THAT ONE TINY THING, THROWING IT BACK IN HIS FACE.
WHY?

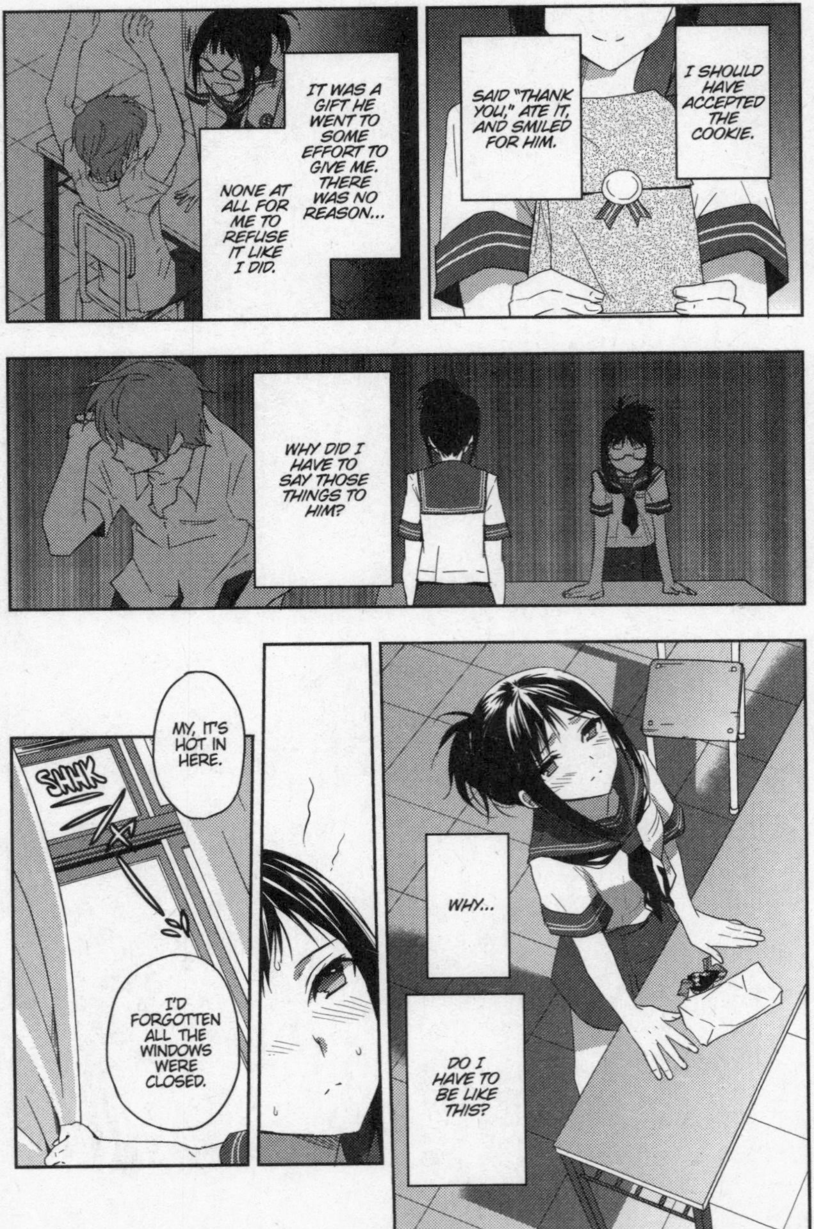
I SHOULD HAVE ACCEPTED THE COOKIE.
SAID "THANK YOU," ATE IT, AND SMILED FOR HIM.
IT WAS A GIFT HE WENT TO SOME EFFORT TO GIVE ME. THERE WAS NO REASON...
NONE AT ALL FOR ME TO REFUSE IT LIKE I DID.
WHY DID I HAVE TO SAY THOSE THINGS TO HIM?
WHY...
DO I HAVE TO BE LIKE THIS?
MY, IT'S HOT IN HERE.
SHHK
I'D FORGOTTEN ALL THE WINDOWS WERE CLOSED.

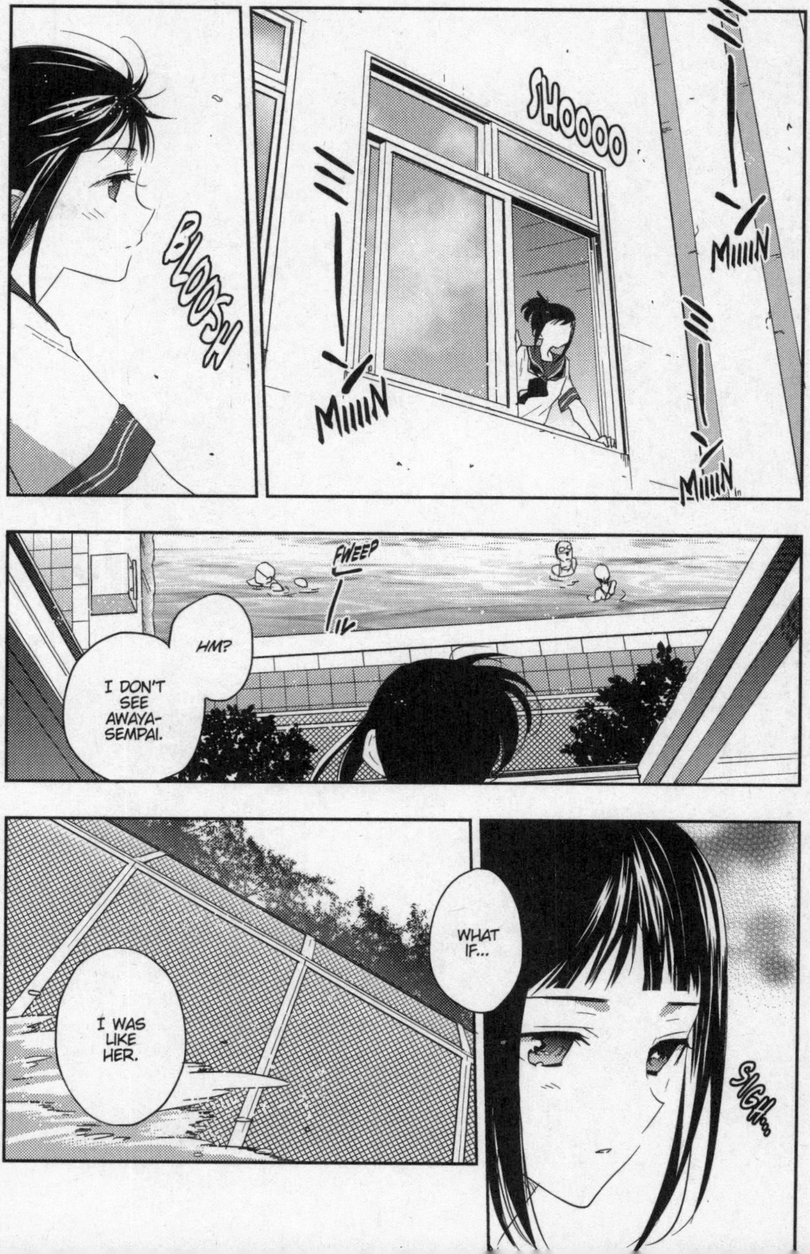
MiiiiN
SHOOOO
MiiiiN
MiiiiN
BLOOSH
FWEEP
HM?
I DON'T SEE AWAYA-SEMPAI.
WHAT IF...
SIGH...
I WAS LIKE HER.

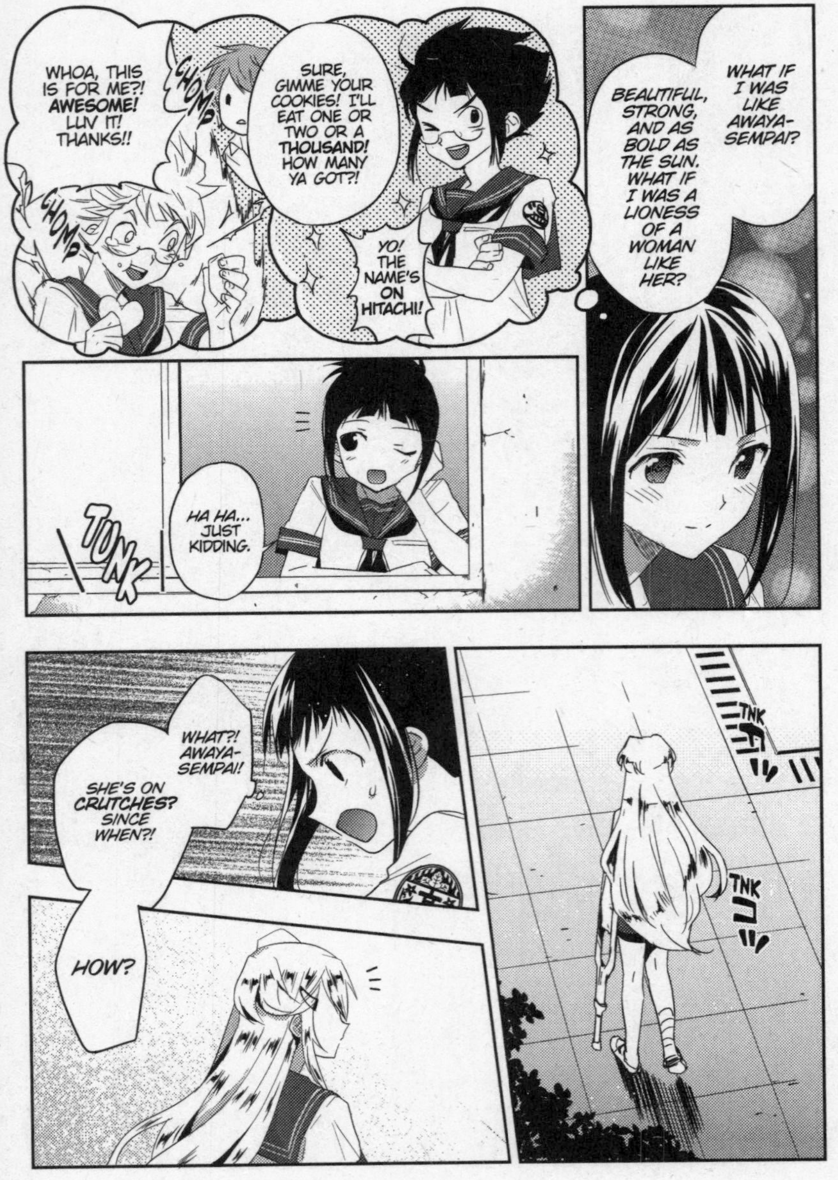
WHAT IF I WAS LIKE AWAYA-SEMPAI?
BEAUTIFUL, STRONG, AND AS BOLD AS THE SUN. WHAT IF I WAS A LIONESS OF A WOMAN LIKE HER?
YO! THE NAME'S ON HITACHI!
SURE, GIMME YOUR COOKIES! I'LL EAT ONE OR TWO OR A THOUSAND! HOW MANY YA GOT?!
CHOMP
WHOA, THIS IS FOR ME?! AWESOME! LUV IT! THANKS!!
CHOMP
HA HA... JUST KIDDING.
TUNK
TNK
TNK
WHAT?! AWAYA-SEMPAI!
SHE'S ON CRUTCHES? SINCE WHEN?!
HOW?

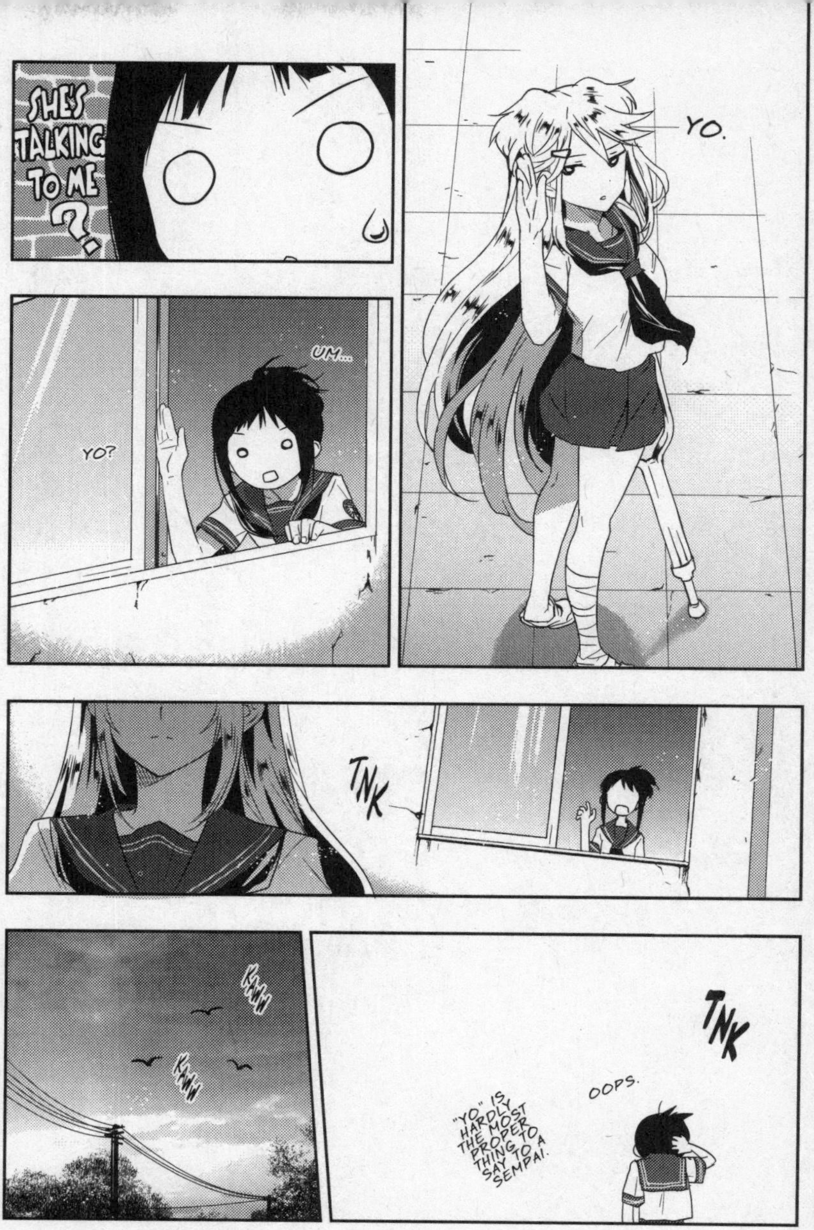
YO.
SHE'S TALKING TO ME?
UM...
YO?
TNK
TNK
OOPS.
"YO" IS HARDLY THE MOST PROPER THING TO SAY TO A SEMPAI.
KAWW
KAWW

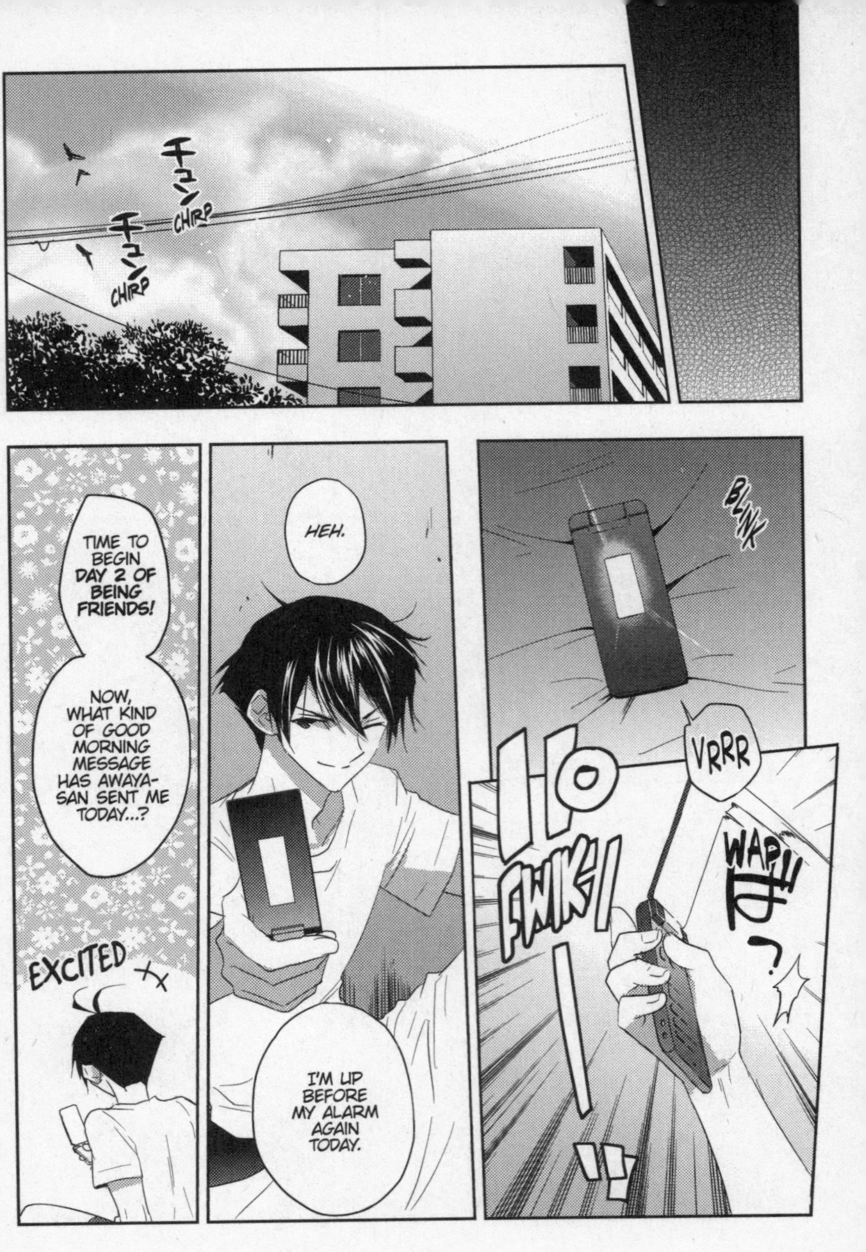
チュン
CHIRP
チュン
CHIRP
BLINK
VRRR
FWIK!
WAP!!!
HEH.
I'M UP BEFORE MY ALARM AGAIN TODAY.
TIME TO BEGIN DAY 2 OF BEING FRIENDS!
NOW, WHAT KIND OF GOOD MORNING MESSAGE HAS AWAYA-SAN SENT ME TODAY...?
EXCITED

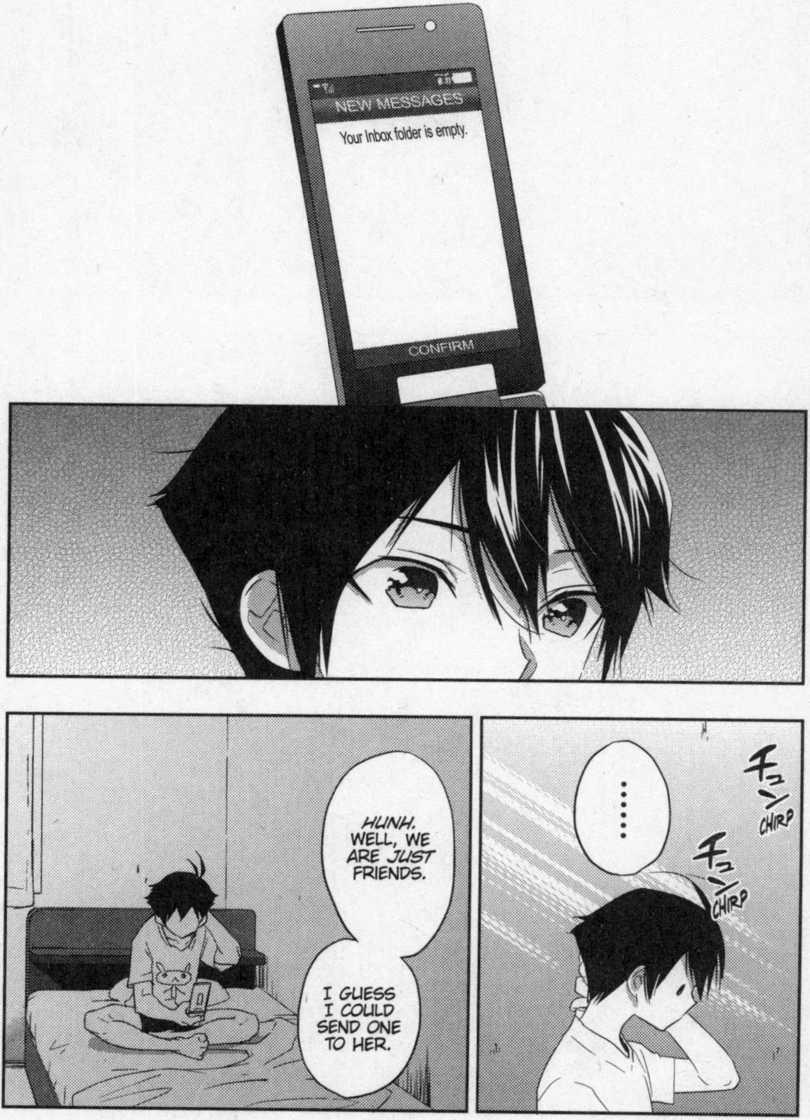
NEW MESSAGES
Your Inbox folder is empty.
CONFIRM
......
チュン CHIRP
チュン CHIRP
HUNH. WELL, WE ARE JUST FRIENDS.
I GUESS I COULD SEND ONE TO HER.

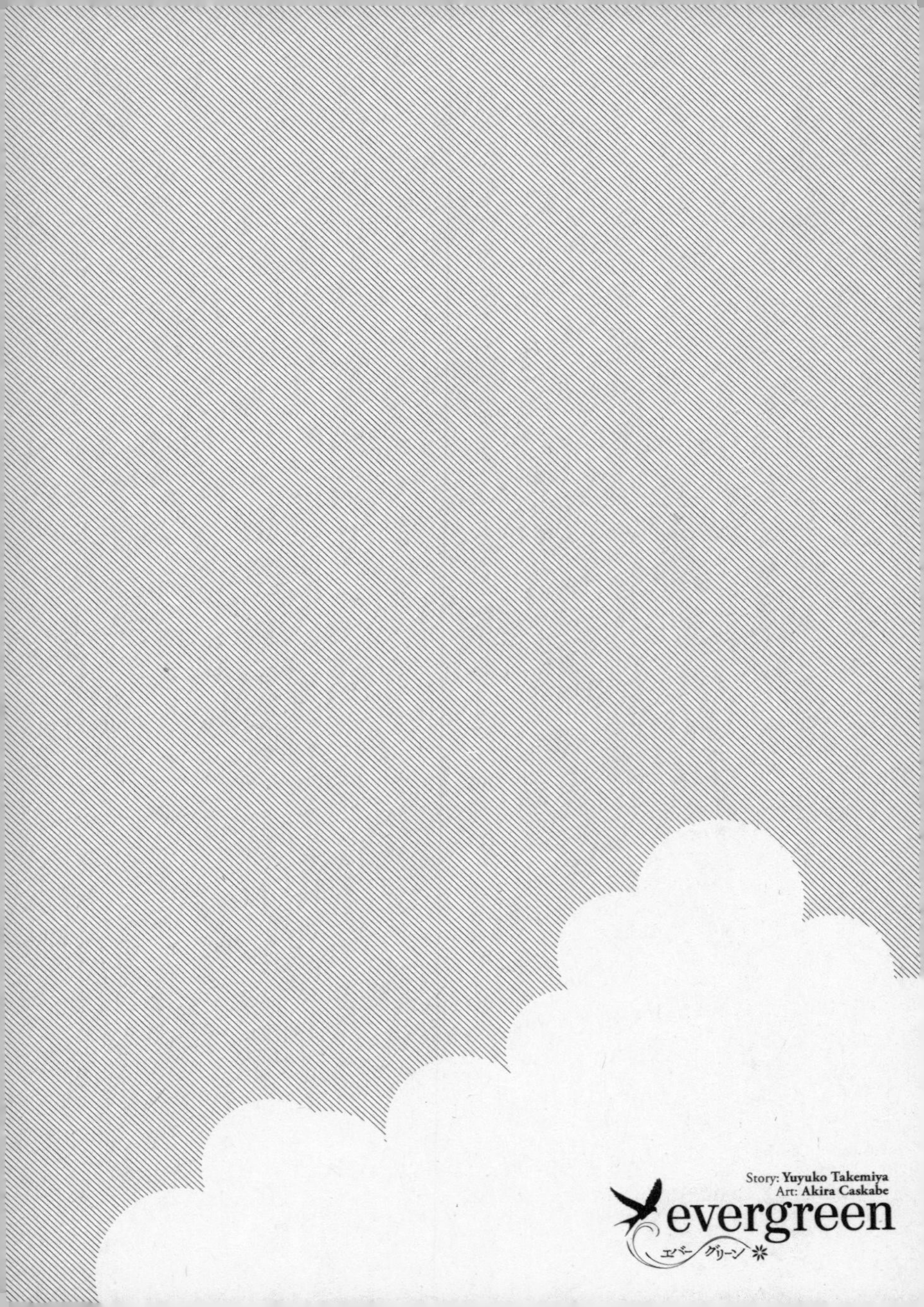
Story: Yuyuko Takemiya
Art: Akira Caskabe
evergreen
エバーグリーン

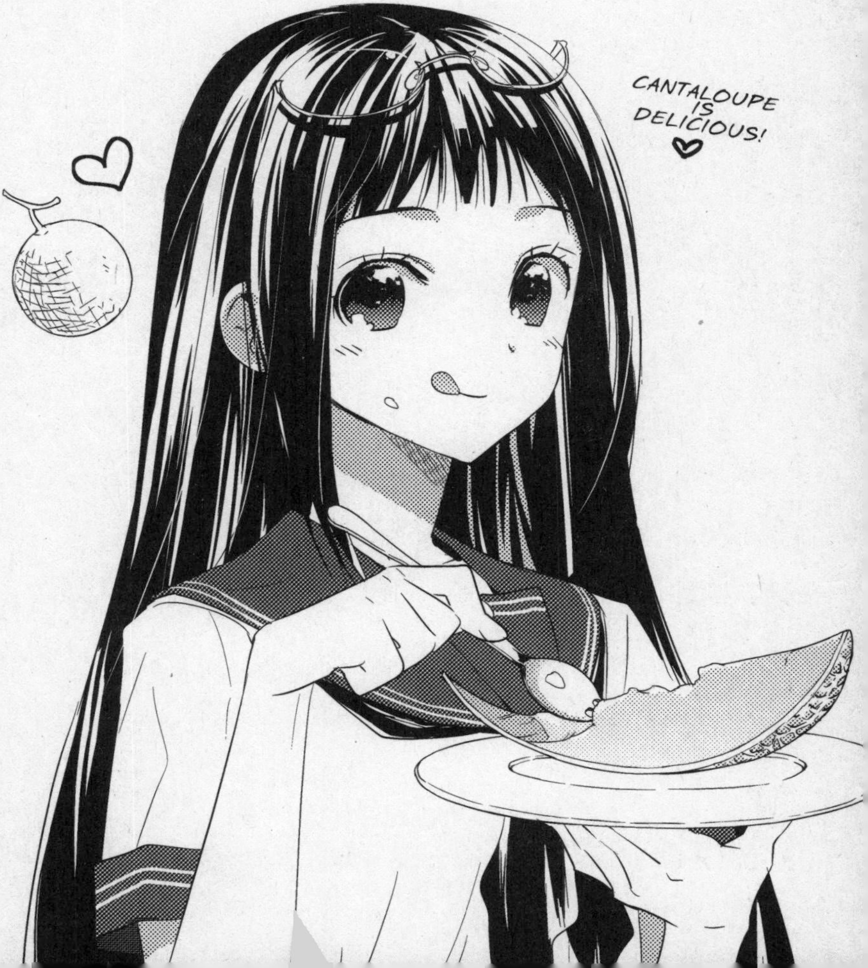
CANTALOUPE IS DELICIOUS!

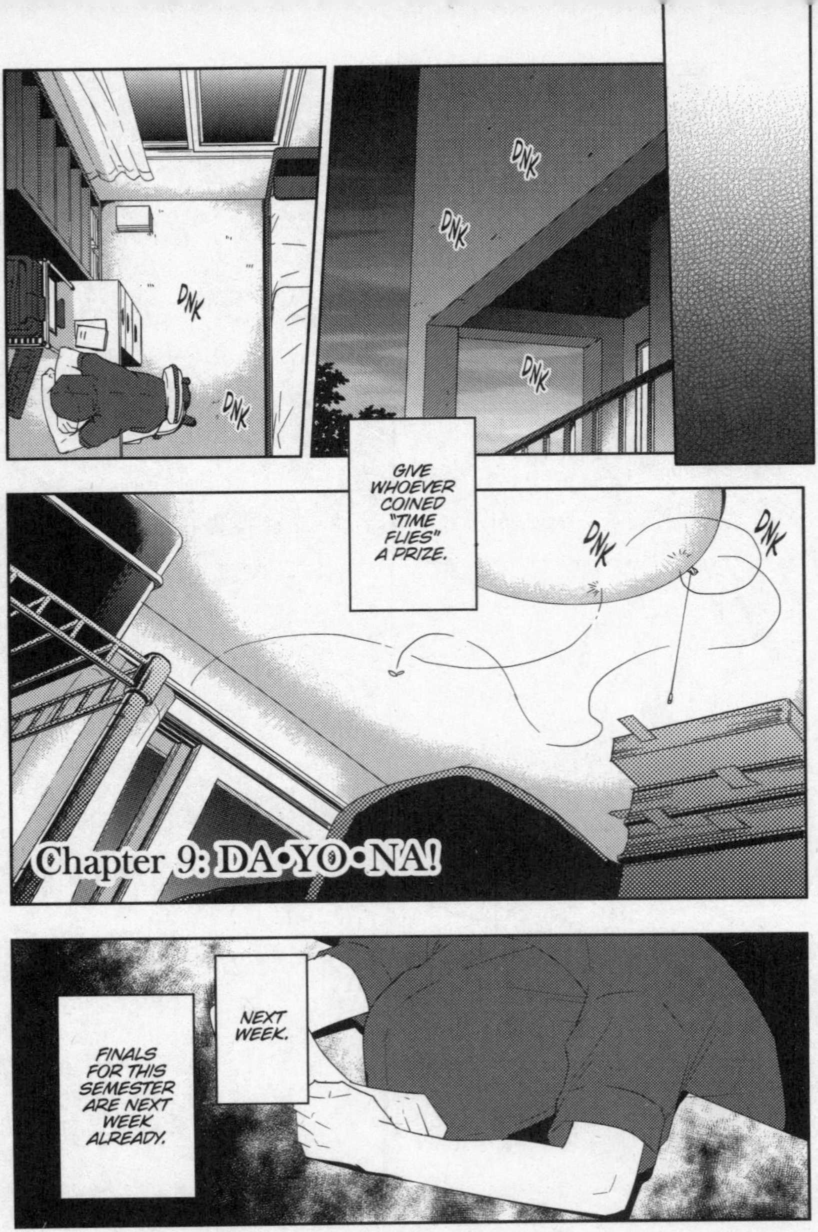
DNK
DNK
DNK
DNK
DNK
GIVE WHOEVER COINED "TIME FLIES" A PRIZE.
DNK
DNK
Chapter 9: DA•YO•NA!
NEXT WEEK.
FINALS FOR THIS SEMESTER ARE NEXT WEEK ALREADY.

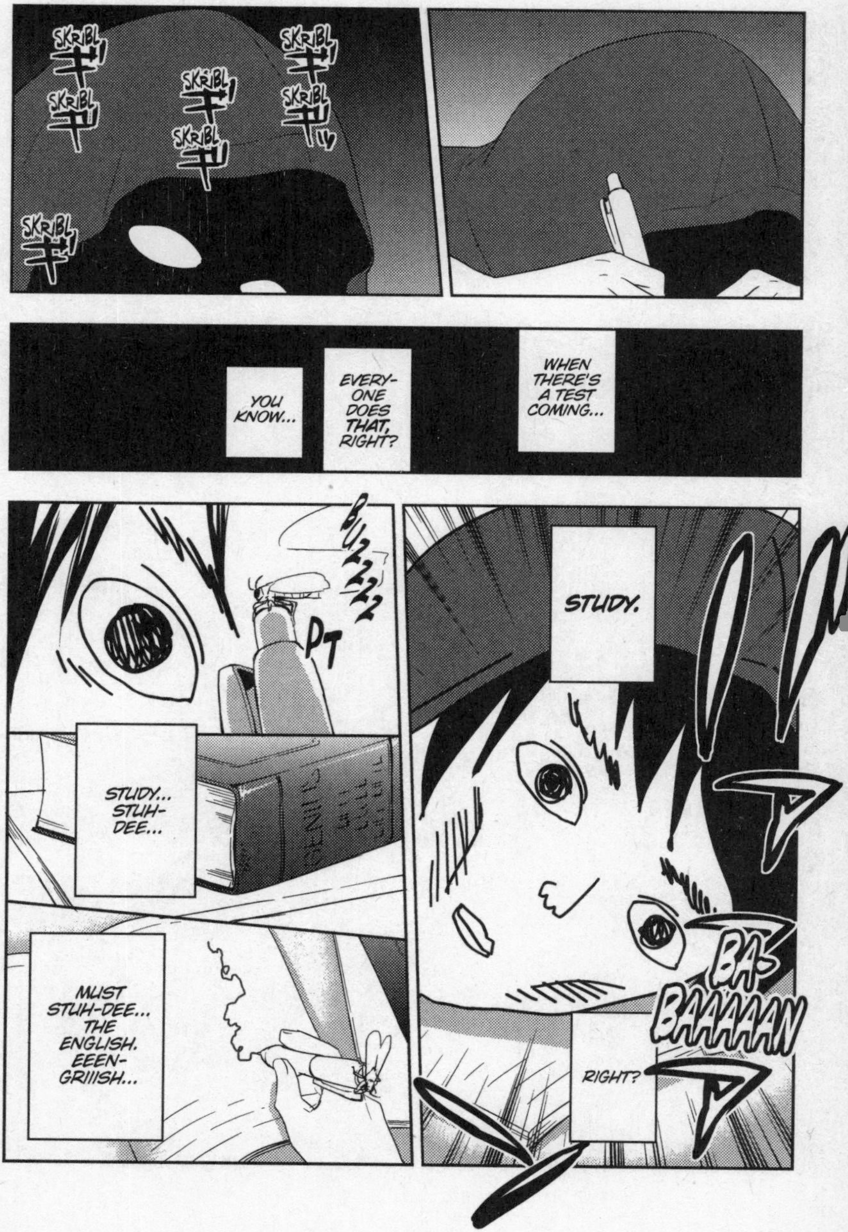
SKRIBL
SKRIBL
SKRIBL
SKRIBL
SKRIBL
SKRIBL
WHEN THERE'S A TEST COMING...
EVERY-ONE DOES THAT, RIGHT?
YOU KNOW...
STUDY.
BA-BAAAAAN
RIGHT?
BUZZZZZ
PT
STUDY... STUH-DEE...
MUST STUH-DEE... THE ENGLISH. EEEN-GRIIISH...

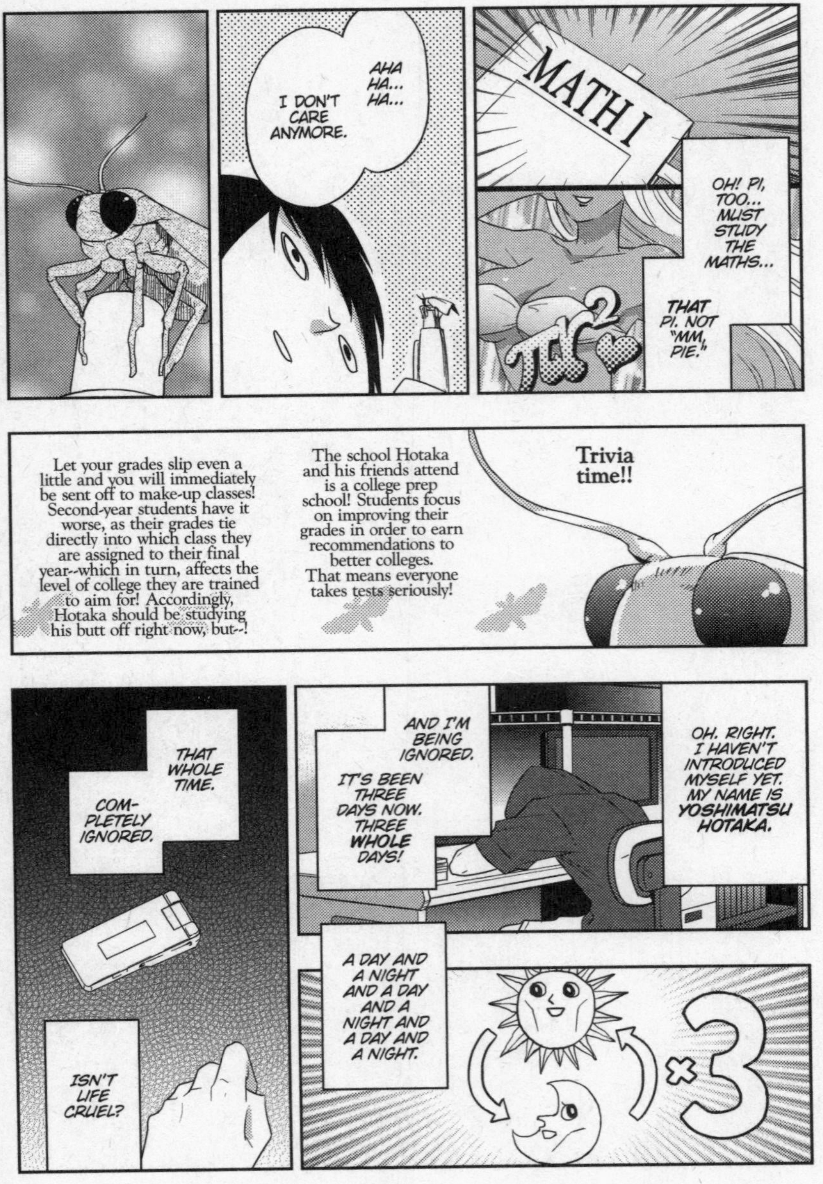
MATH I
OH! PI, TOO... MUST STUDY THE MATHS...
THAT PI. NOT "MM, PIE."
π²
AHA HA... HA...
I DON'T CARE ANYMORE.
Trivia time!!
The school Hotaka and his friends attend is a college prep school! Students focus on improving their grades in order to earn recommendations to better colleges. That means everyone takes tests seriously!
Let your grades slip even a little and you will immediately be sent off to make-up classes! Second-year students have it worse, as their grades tie directly into which class they are assigned to their final year--which in turn, affects the level of college they are trained to aim for! Accordingly, Hotaka should be studying his butt off right now, but--!
OH. RIGHT. I HAVEN'T INTRODUCED MYSELF YET. MY NAME IS YOSHIMATSU HOTAKA.
AND I'M BEING IGNORED.
IT'S BEEN THREE DAYS NOW. THREE WHOLE DAYS!
A DAY AND A NIGHT AND A DAY AND A NIGHT AND A DAY AND A NIGHT.
×3
THAT WHOLE TIME.
COM-PLETELY IGNORED.
ISN'T LIFE CRUEL?

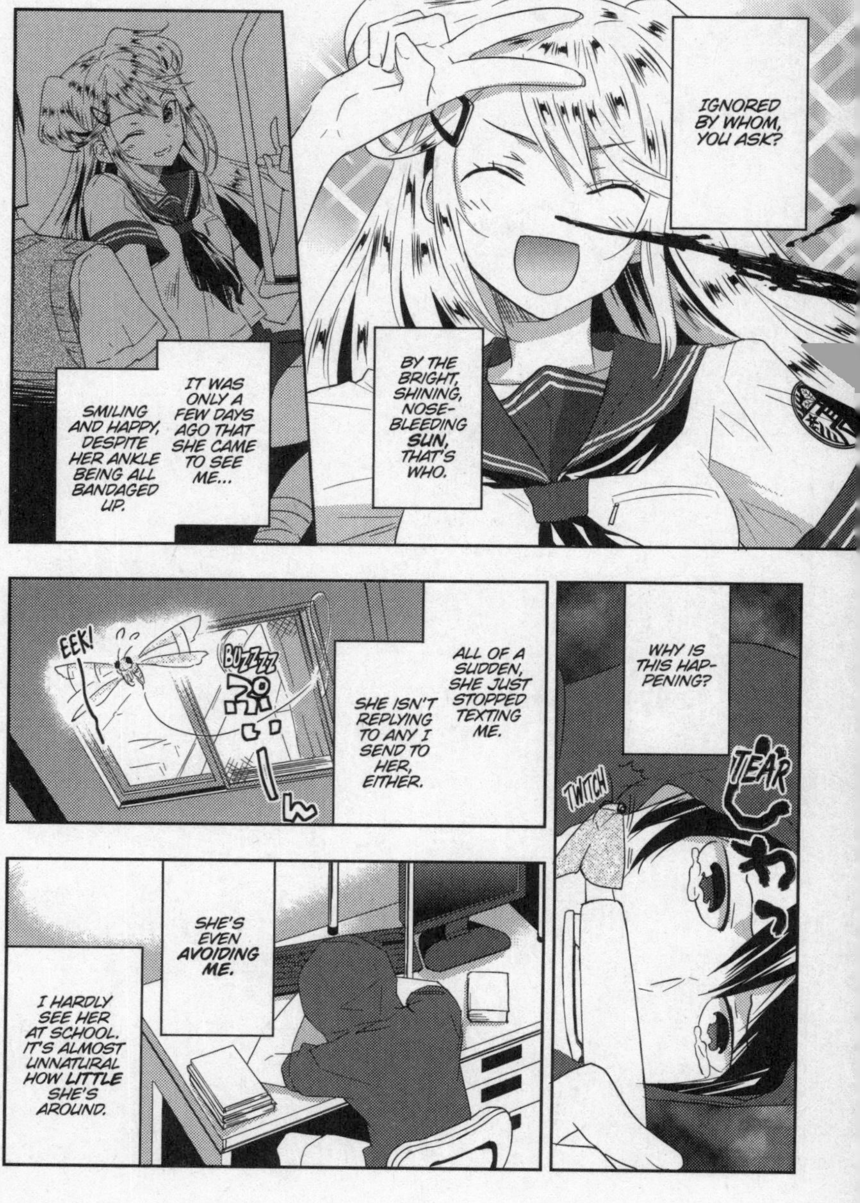
IGNORED BY WHOM, YOU ASK?
BY THE BRIGHT, SHINING, NOSE-BLEEDING SUN, THAT'S WHO.
IT WAS ONLY A FEW DAYS AGO THAT SHE CAME TO SEE ME...
SMILING AND HAPPY, DESPITE HER ANKLE BEING ALL BANDAGED UP.
WHY IS THIS HAP-PENING?
TEAR
TWITCH
ALL OF A SUDDEN, SHE JUST STOPPED TEXTING ME.
SHE ISN'T REPLYING TO ANY I SEND TO HER, EITHER.
BUZZZZ
EEK!
SHE'S EVEN AVOIDING ME.
I HARDLY SEE HER AT SCHOOL. IT'S ALMOST UNNATURAL HOW LITTLE SHE'S AROUND.

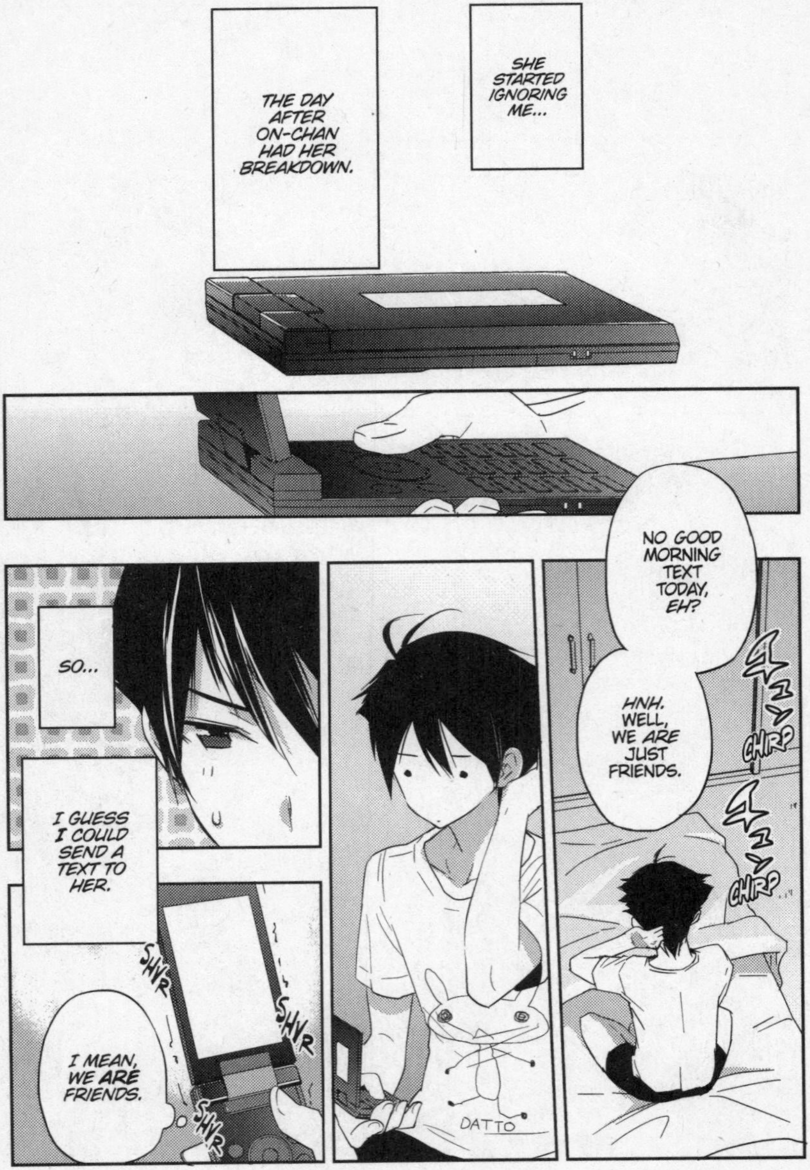
SHE STARTED IGNORING ME...
THE DAY AFTER ON-CHAN HAD HER BREAKDOWN.
NO GOOD MORNING TEXT TODAY, EH?
HNH. WELL, WE ARE JUST FRIENDS.
CHIRP
CHIRP
DATTO
SO...
I GUESS I COULD SEND A TEXT TO HER.
SHVR
SHVR
SHVR
I MEAN, WE ARE FRIENDS.

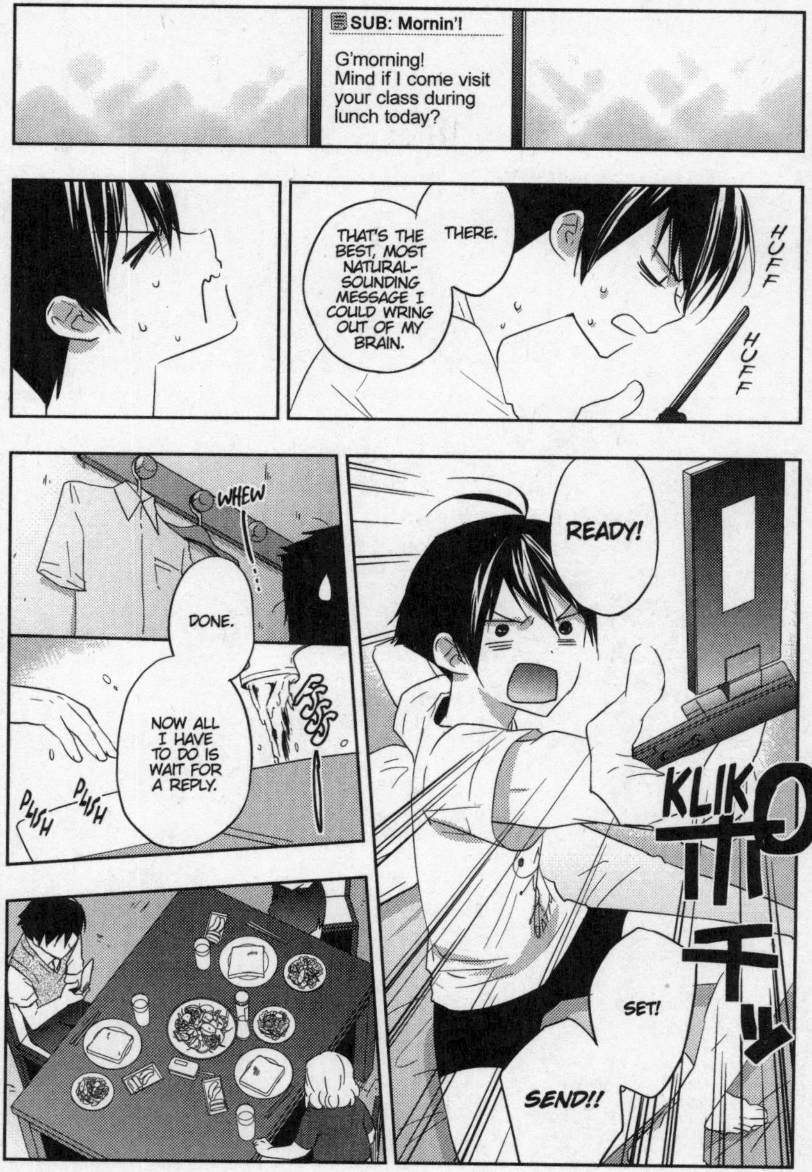
SUB: Mornin'!
G'morning! Mind if I come visit your class during lunch today?
HUFF HUFF
THERE.
THAT'S THE BEST, MOST NATURAL-SOUNDING MESSAGE I COULD WRING OUT OF MY BRAIN.
READY!
KLIK
SET!
SEND!!
WHEW
DONE.
FSSS
NOW ALL I HAVE TO DO IS WAIT FOR A REPLY.
PLISH PLISH

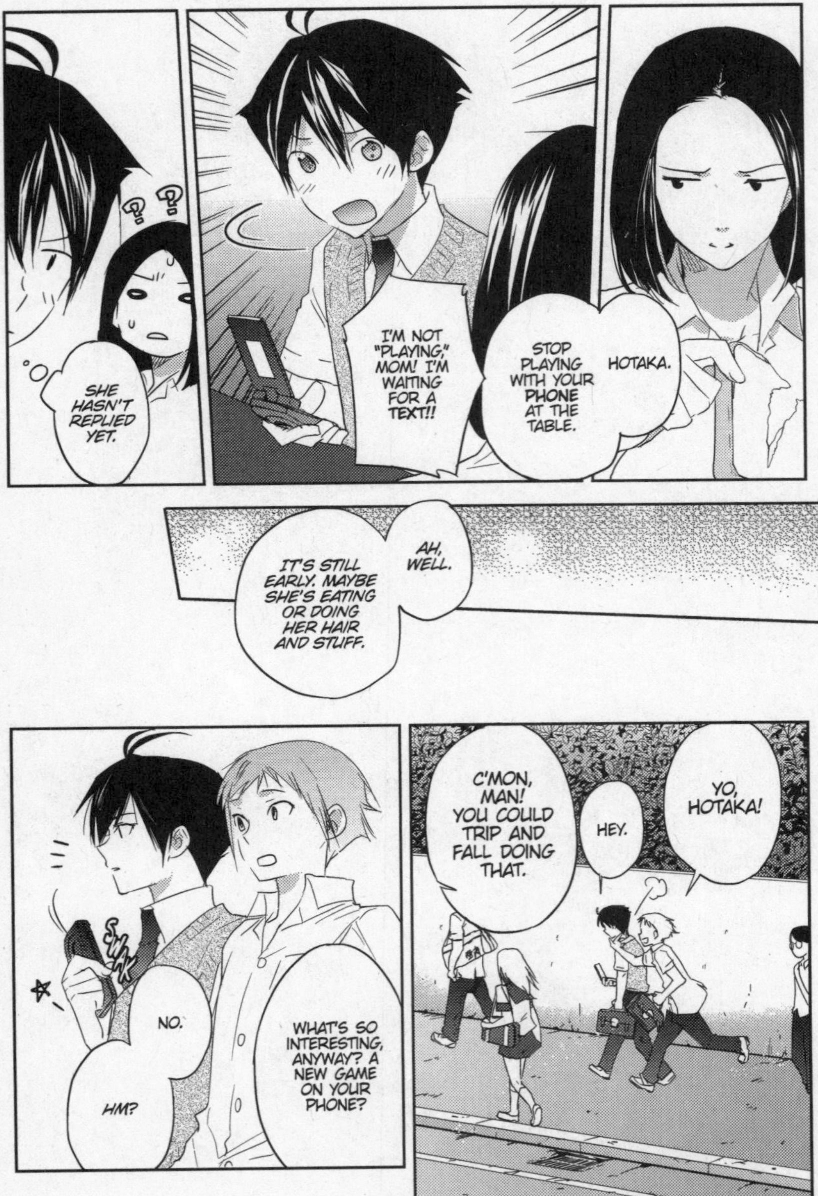
HOTAKA.
STOP PLAYING WITH YOUR PHONE AT THE TABLE.
I'M NOT "PLAYING," MOM! I'M WAITING FOR A TEXT!!
SHE HASN'T REPLIED YET.
AH, WELL.
IT'S STILL EARLY. MAYBE SHE'S EATING OR DOING HER HAIR AND STUFF.
YO, HOTAKA!
HEY.
C'MON, MAN! YOU COULD TRIP AND FALL DOING THAT.
WHAT'S SO INTERESTING, ANYWAY? A NEW GAME ON YOUR PHONE?
SWAK
NO.
HM?

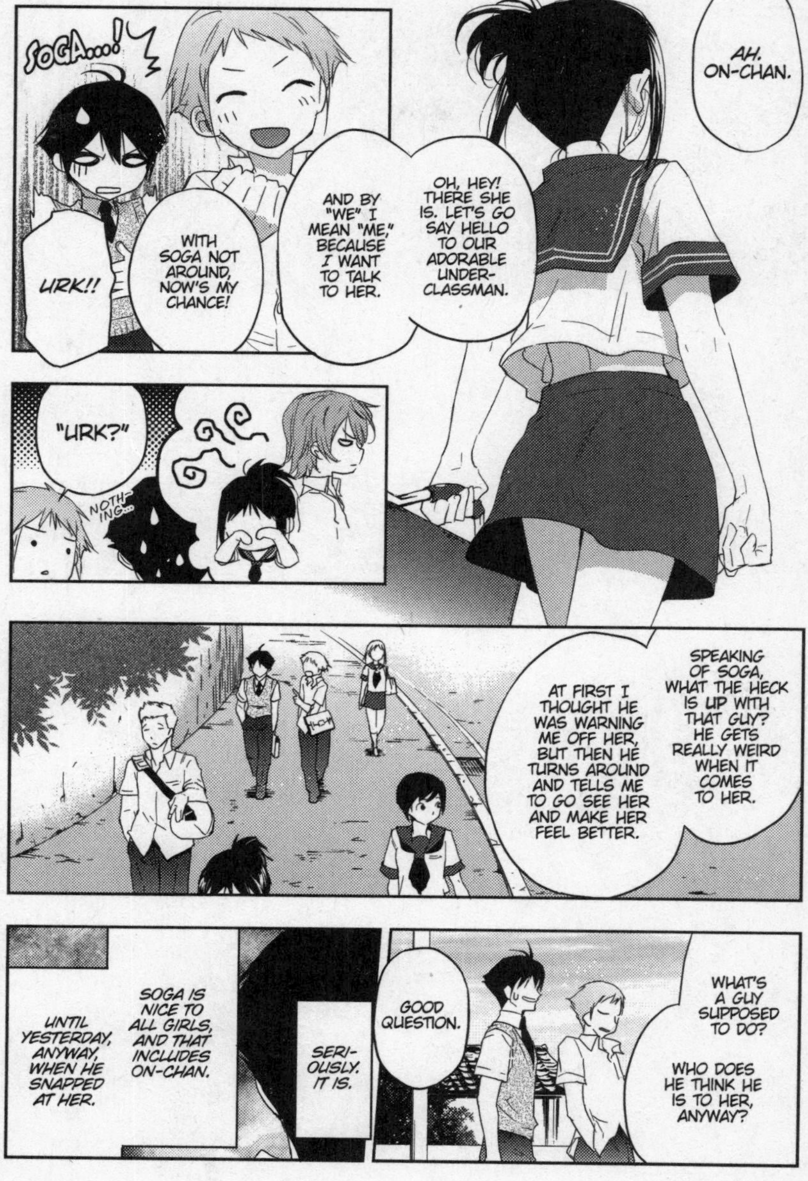
AH. ON-CHAN.
OH, HEY! THERE SHE IS. LET'S GO SAY HELLO TO OUR ADORABLE UNDER-CLASSMAN.
AND BY "WE" I MEAN "ME," BECAUSE I WANT TO TALK TO HER.
WITH SOGA NOT AROUND, NOW'S MY CHANCE!
SOGA...!
URK!!
"URK?"
NOTH-ING...
SPEAKING OF SOGA, WHAT THE HECK IS UP WITH THAT GUY? HE GETS REALLY WEIRD WHEN IT COMES TO HER.
AT FIRST I THOUGHT HE WAS WARNING ME OFF HER, BUT THEN HE TURNS AROUND AND TELLS ME TO GO SEE HER AND MAKE HER FEEL BETTER.
WHAT'S A GUY SUPPOSED TO DO?
WHO DOES HE THINK HE IS TO HER, ANYWAY?
GOOD QUESTION.
SERI-OUSLY. IT IS.
SOGA IS NICE TO ALL GIRLS, AND THAT INCLUDES ON-CHAN.
UNTIL YESTERDAY, ANYWAY, WHEN HE SNAPPED AT HER.

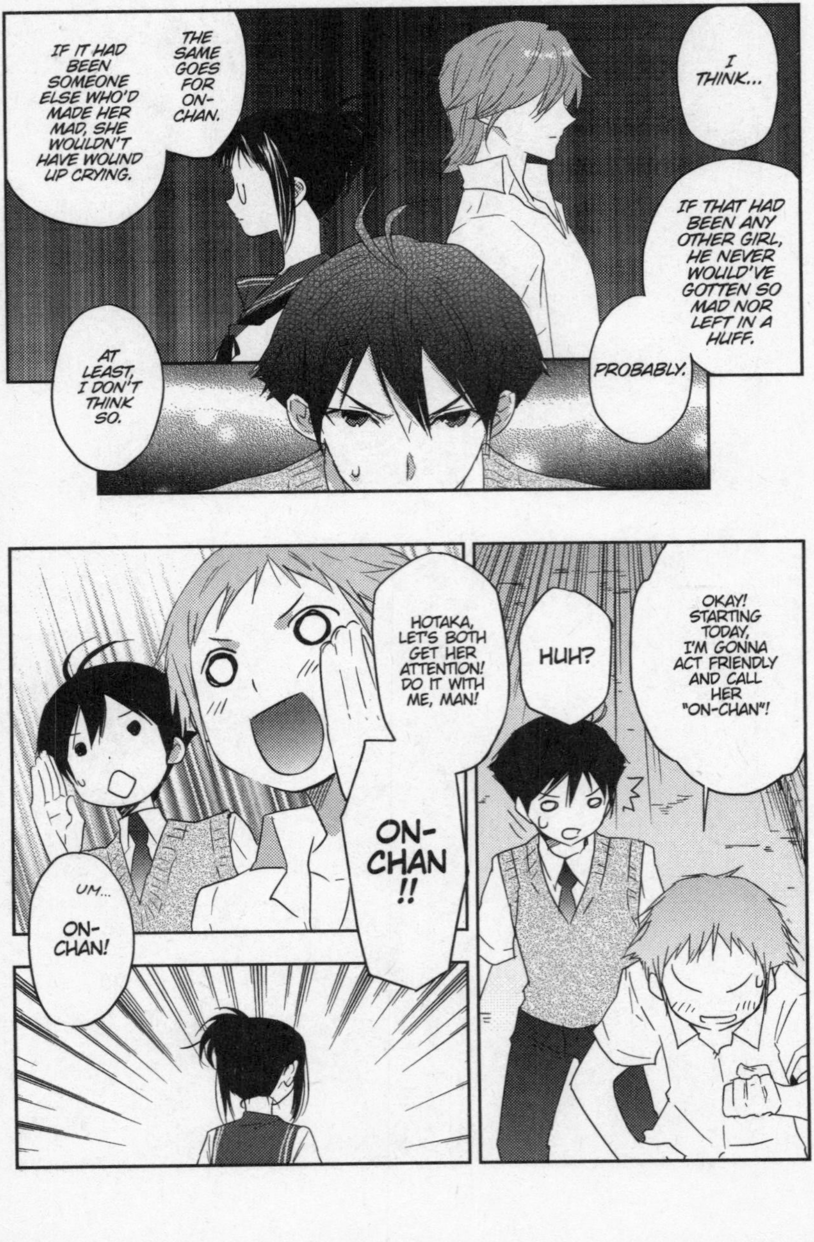
I THINK...
IF THAT HAD BEEN ANY OTHER GIRL, HE NEVER WOULD'VE GOTTEN SO MAD NOR LEFT IN A HUFF.
PROBABLY.
THE SAME GOES FOR ON-CHAN.
IF IT HAD BEEN SOMEONE ELSE WHO'D MADE HER MAD, SHE WOULDN'T HAVE WOUND UP CRYING.
AT LEAST, I DON'T THINK SO.
OKAY! STARTING TODAY, I'M GONNA ACT FRIENDLY AND CALL HER "ON-CHAN"!
HUH?
HOTAKA, LET'S BOTH GET HER ATTENTION! DO IT WITH ME, MAN!
ON-CHAN!!
UM... ON-CHAN!

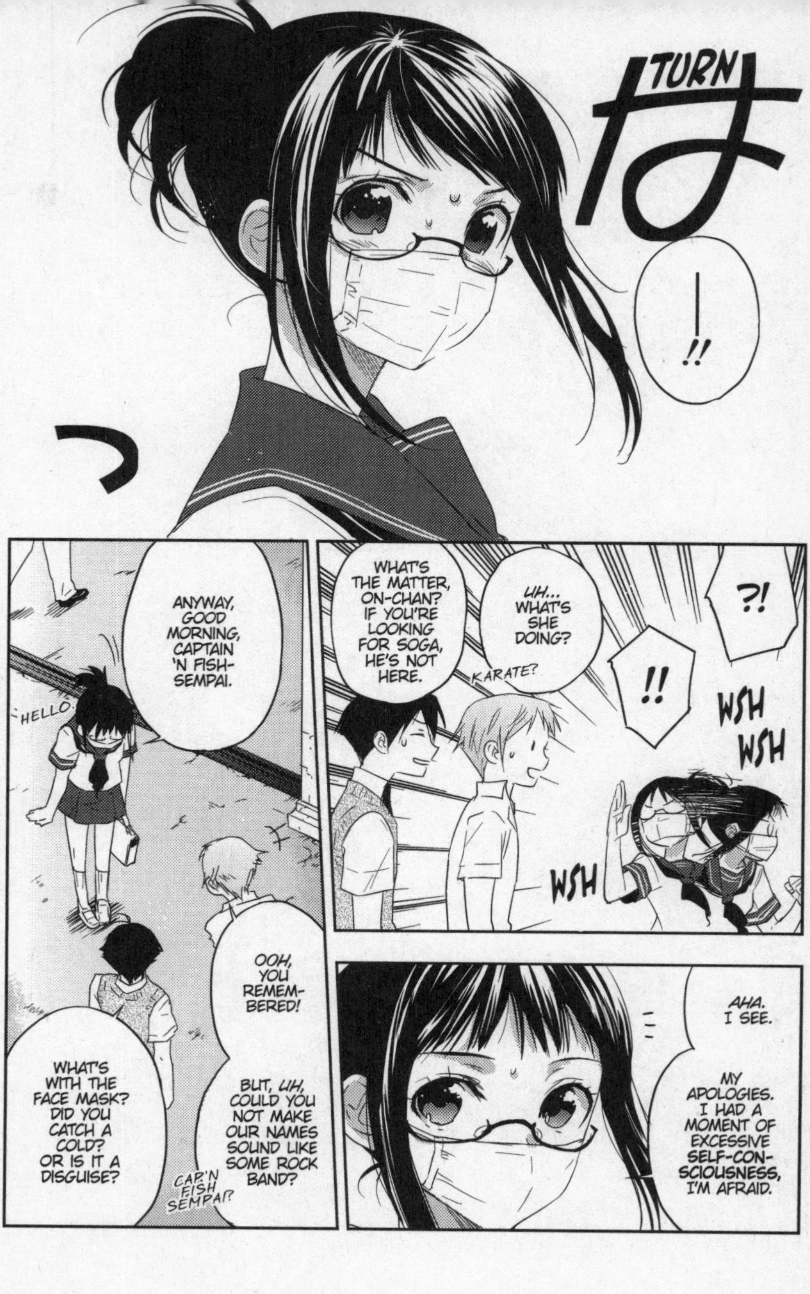
TURN
—!!
?!
!!
WSH WSH
WSH
UH... WHAT'S SHE DOING?
KARATE?
WHAT'S THE MATTER, ON-CHAN? IF YOU'RE LOOKING FOR SOGA, HE'S NOT HERE.
AHA. I SEE.
MY APOLOGIES. I HAD A MOMENT OF EXCESSIVE SELF-CONSCIOUSNESS, I'M AFRAID.
ANYWAY, GOOD MORNING, CAPTAIN 'N FISH-SEMPAI.
HELLO.
OOH, YOU REMEMBERED!
BUT, UH, COULD YOU NOT MAKE OUR NAMES SOUND LIKE SOME ROCK BAND?
CAP'N FISH SEMPAI?
WHAT'S WITH THE FACE MASK? DID YOU CATCH A COLD? OR IS IT A DISGUISE?

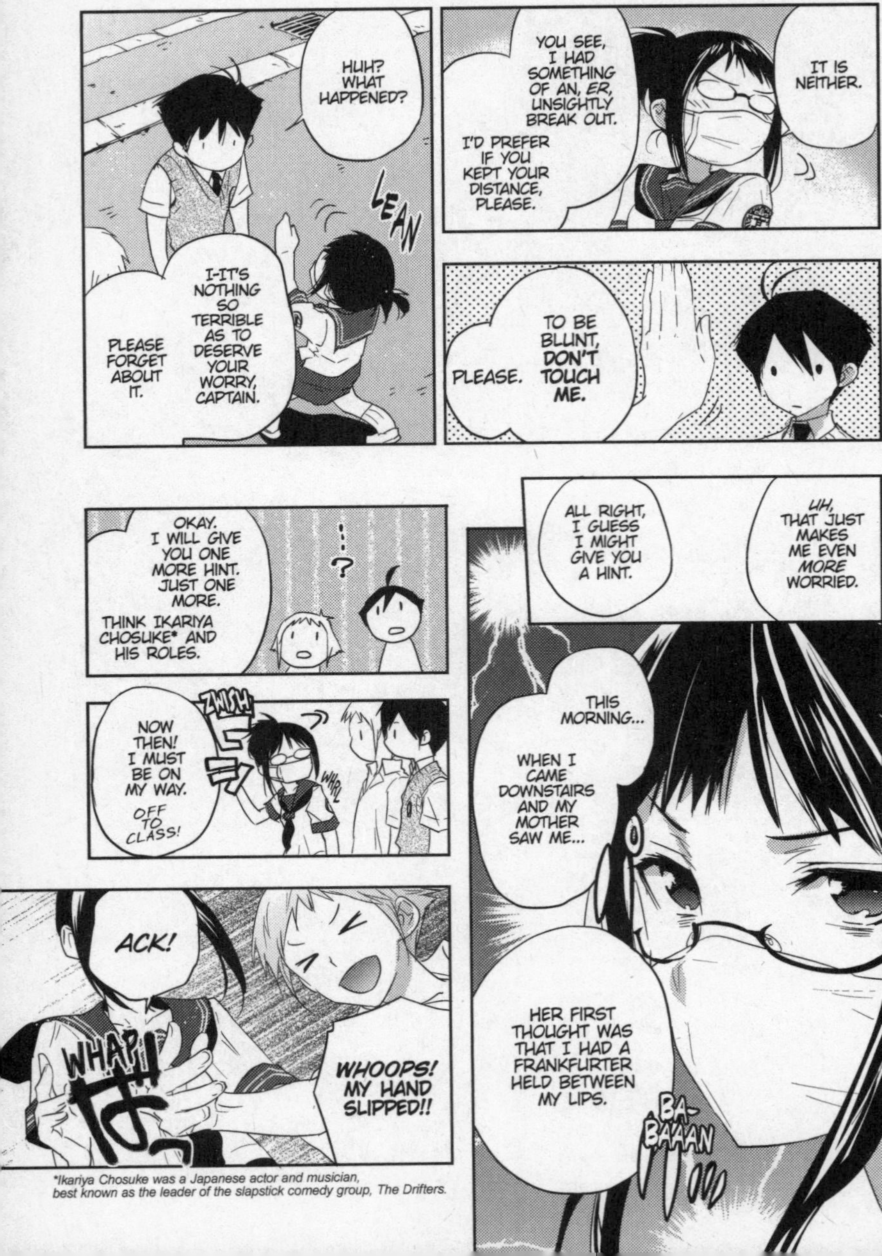
IT IS NEITHER.
YOU SEE, I HAD SOMETHING OF AN, *ER*, UNSIGHTLY BREAK OUT.
I'D PREFER IF YOU KEPT YOUR DISTANCE, PLEASE.
TO BE BLUNT, **DON'T TOUCH ME.**
PLEASE.
HUH? WHAT HAPPENED?
LEAN
I-IT'S NOTHING SO TERRIBLE AS TO DESERVE YOUR WORRY, CAPTAIN.
PLEASE FORGET ABOUT IT.
*UH*, THAT JUST MAKES ME EVEN *MORE* WORRIED.
ALL RIGHT, I GUESS I MIGHT GIVE YOU A HINT.
THIS MORNING...
WHEN I CAME DOWNSTAIRS AND MY MOTHER SAW ME...
HER FIRST THOUGHT WAS THAT I HAD A FRANKFURTER HELD BETWEEN MY LIPS.
BA-BAAAN
OKAY. I WILL GIVE YOU ONE MORE HINT. JUST ONE MORE.
THINK IKARIYA CHOSUKE* AND HIS ROLES.
...?
ZWISH!
NOW THEN! I MUST BE ON MY WAY.
OFF TO CLASS!
WHIRL
ACK!
WHAP!!
***WHOOPS! MY HAND SLIPPED!!***

*Ikariya Chosuke was a Japanese actor and musician, best known as the leader of the slapstick comedy group, The Drifters.*

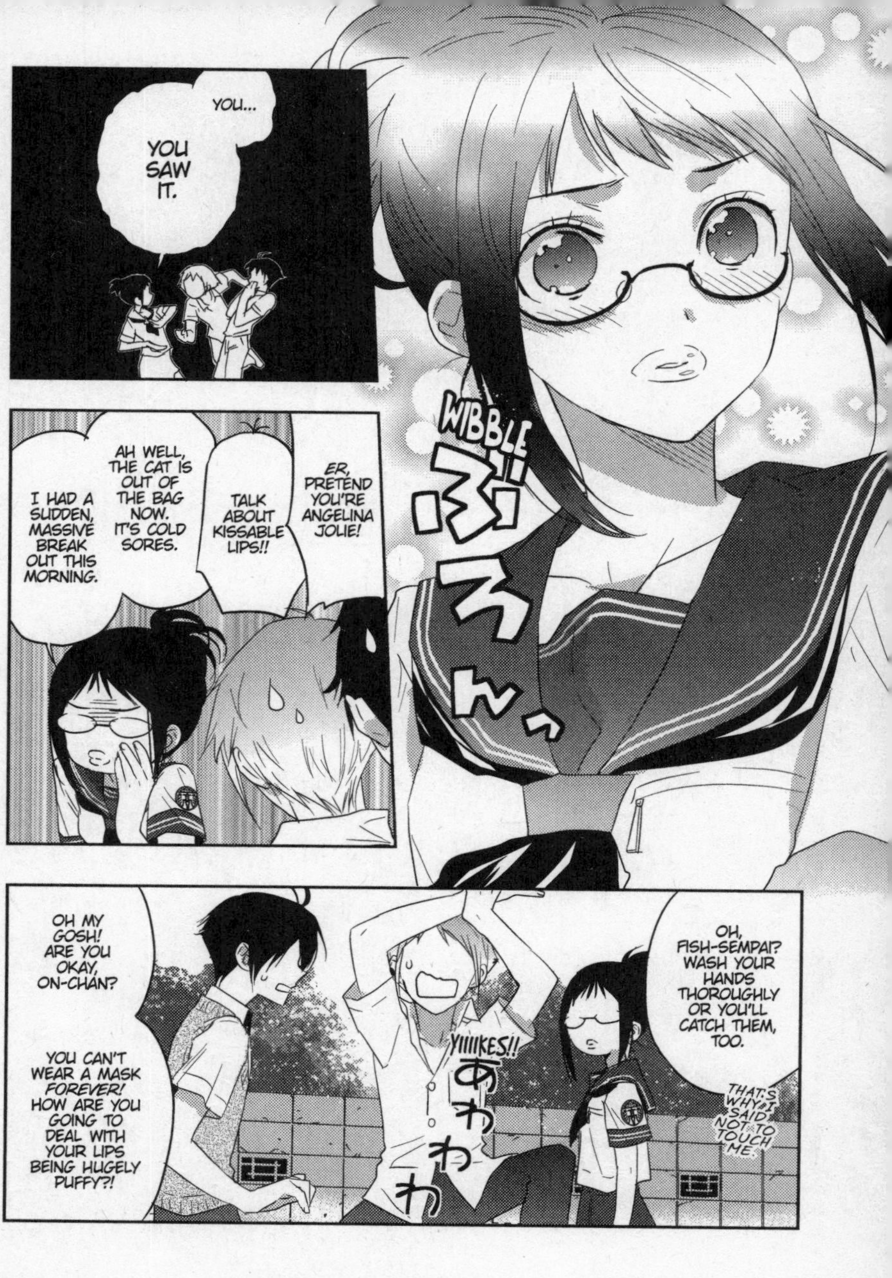
WIBBLE
ぶるん
YOU...
YOU SAW IT.
ER, PRETEND YOU'RE ANGELINA JOLIE!
TALK ABOUT KISSABLE LIPS!!
AH WELL, THE CAT IS OUT OF THE BAG NOW. IT'S COLD SORES.
I HAD A SUDDEN, MASSIVE BREAK OUT THIS MORNING.
OH, FISH-SEMPAI? WASH YOUR HANDS THOROUGHLY OR YOU'LL CATCH THEM, TOO.
THAT'S WHY I SAID NOT TO TOUCH ME.
YIIIKES!!
あわわわ
OH MY GOSH! ARE YOU OKAY, ON-CHAN?
YOU CAN'T WEAR A MASK FOREVER! HOW ARE YOU GOING TO DEAL WITH YOUR LIPS BEING HUGELY PUFFY?!

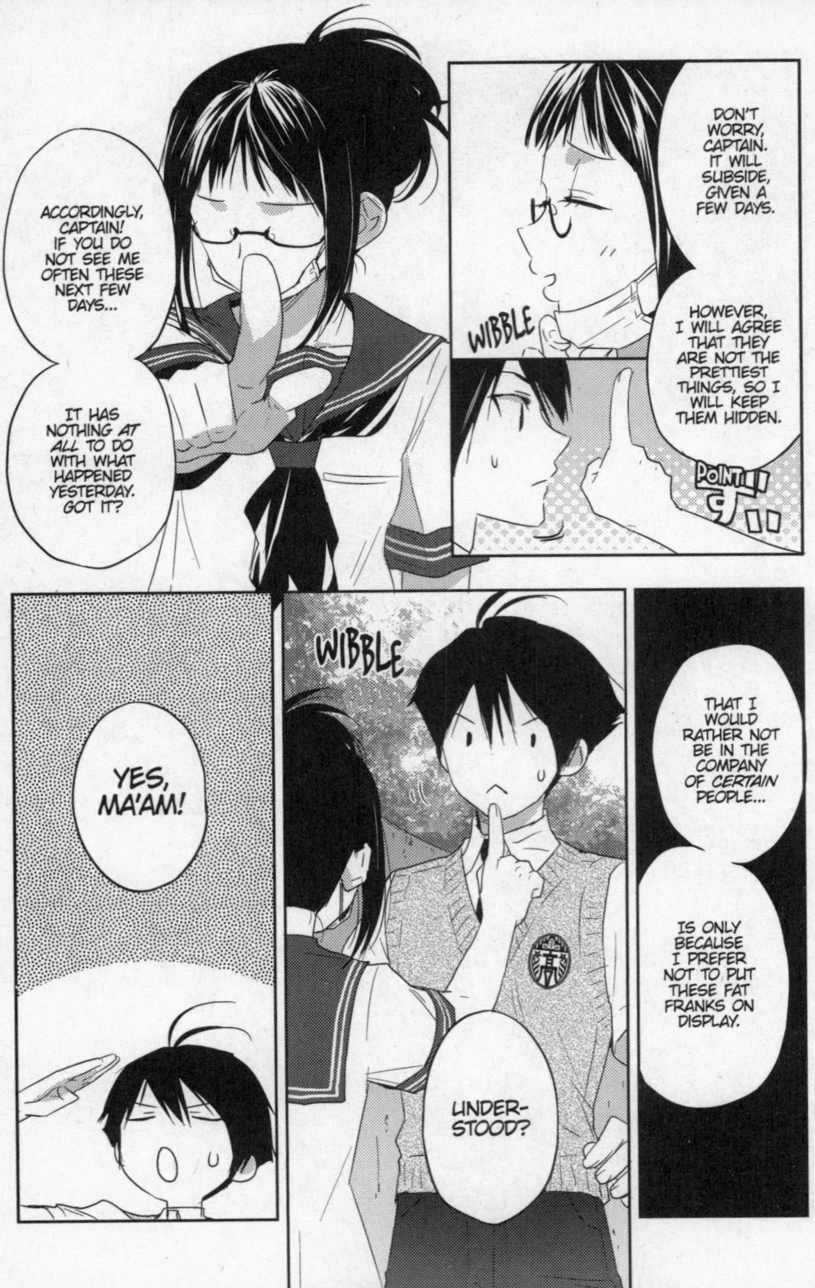
DON'T WORRY, CAPTAIN. IT WILL SUBSIDE, GIVEN A FEW DAYS.
WIBBLE
HOWEVER, I WILL AGREE THAT THEY ARE NOT THE PRETTIEST THINGS, SO I WILL KEEP THEM HIDDEN.
POINT!!!
ACCORDINGLY, CAPTAIN! IF YOU DO NOT SEE ME OFTEN THESE NEXT FEW DAYS...
IT HAS NOTHING AT ALL TO DO WITH WHAT HAPPENED YESTERDAY. GOT IT?
THAT I WOULD RATHER NOT BE IN THE COMPANY OF *CERTAIN* PEOPLE...
IS ONLY BECAUSE I PREFER NOT TO PUT THESE FAT FRANKS ON DISPLAY.
WIBBLE
UNDER-STOOD?
YES, MA'AM!

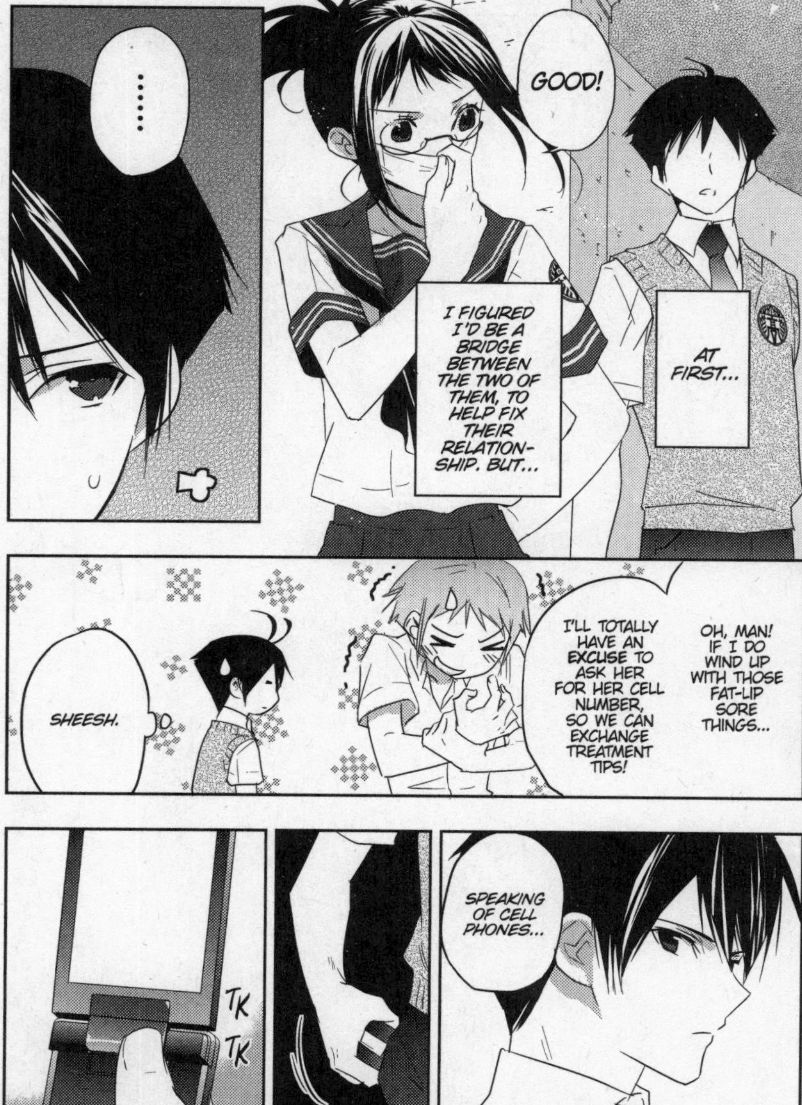
GOOD!
AT FIRST...
I FIGURED I'D BE A BRIDGE BETWEEN THE TWO OF THEM, TO HELP FIX THEIR RELATION-SHIP. BUT...
......
OH, MAN! IF I DO WIND UP WITH THOSE FAT-LIP SORE THINGS...
I'LL TOTALLY HAVE AN EXCUSE TO ASK HER FOR HER CELL NUMBER, SO WE CAN EXCHANGE TREATMENT TIPS!
SHEESH.
SPEAKING OF CELL PHONES...
TK
TK

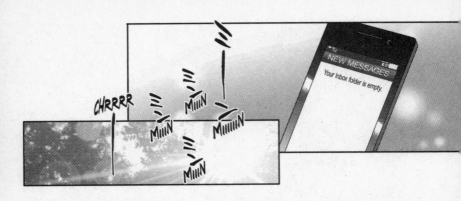

NEW MESSAGES
Your Inbox folder is empty.

CHRRRR

MiiiiN
MiiiiN
MiiiiN
MiiiiN

YO! MORNING!

SHOOP

STILL NOTHING? WEIRD!

DID I MESS UP AND SEND IT TO THE WRONG NUMBER?

HEY! MORNIN'!

HEY!

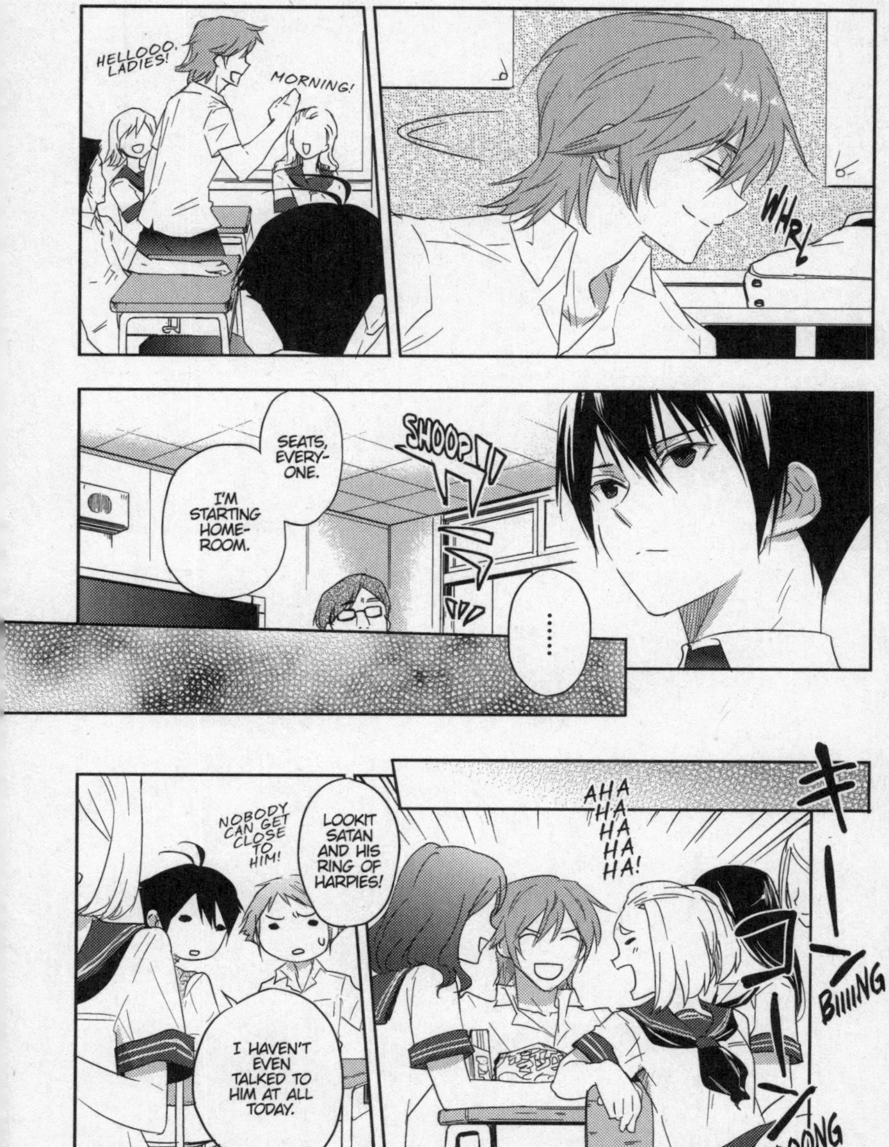
WHRL
HELLOOO, LADIES!
MORNING!
SHOOP
SEATS, EVERYONE.
I'M STARTING HOMEROOM.
......
BIIIING
BOOONG
AHAHAHAHAHA!
LOOKIT SATAN AND HIS RING OF HARPIES!
NOBODY CAN GET CLOSE TO HIM!
I HAVEN'T EVEN TALKED TO HIM AT ALL TODAY.

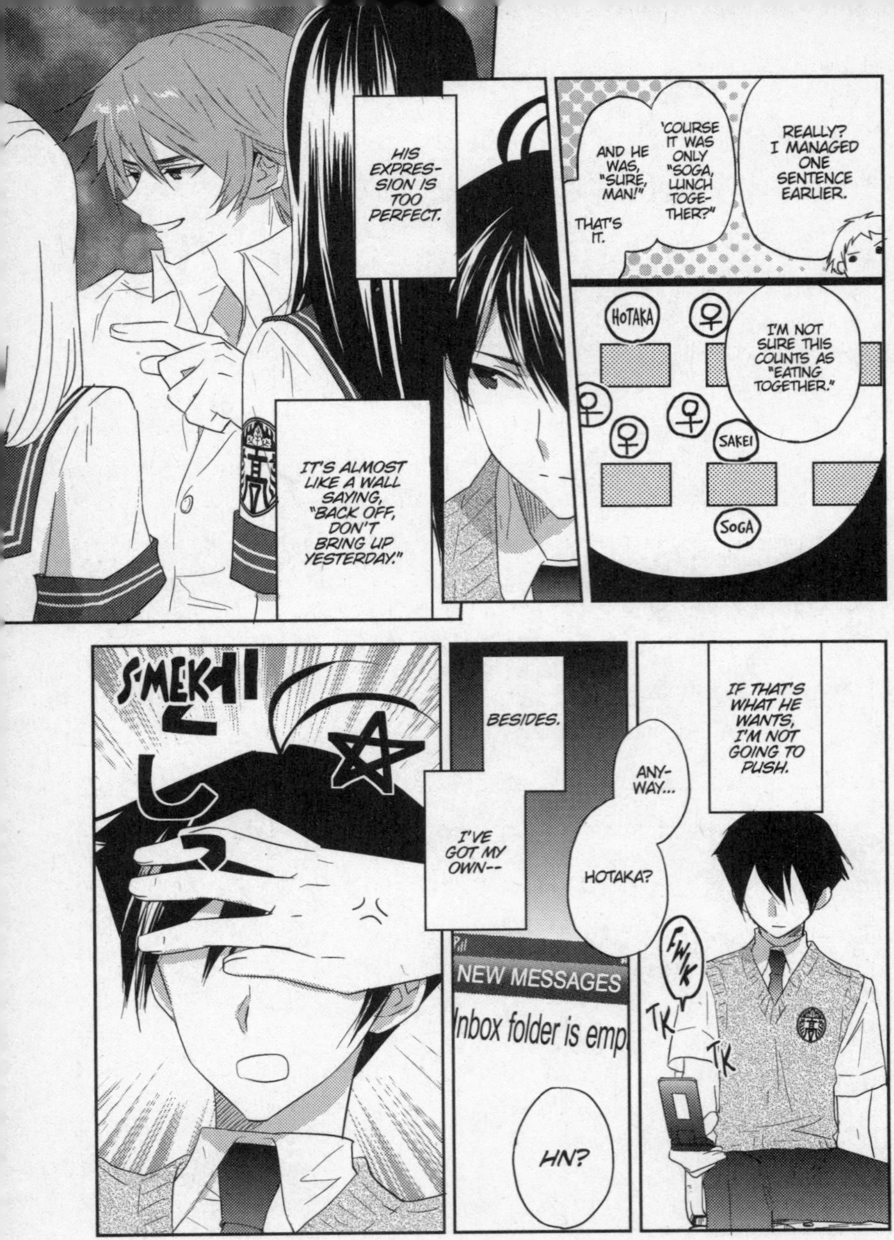
REALLY? I MANAGED ONE SENTENCE EARLIER.
'COURSE IT WAS ONLY "SOGA, LUNCH TOGE-THER?"
AND HE WAS, "SURE, MAN!"
THAT'S IT.
I'M NOT SURE THIS COUNTS AS "EATING TOGETHER."
HOTAKA
SAKEI
SOGA
HIS EXPRES-SION IS TOO PERFECT.
IT'S ALMOST LIKE A WALL SAYING, "BACK OFF, DON'T BRING UP YESTERDAY."
IF THAT'S WHAT HE WANTS, I'M NOT GOING TO PUSH.
ANY-WAY...
HOTAKA?
FWIK
TK
TK
BESIDES.
I'VE GOT MY OWN--
NEW MESSAGES
Inbox folder is emp
HN?
S-MEK-I

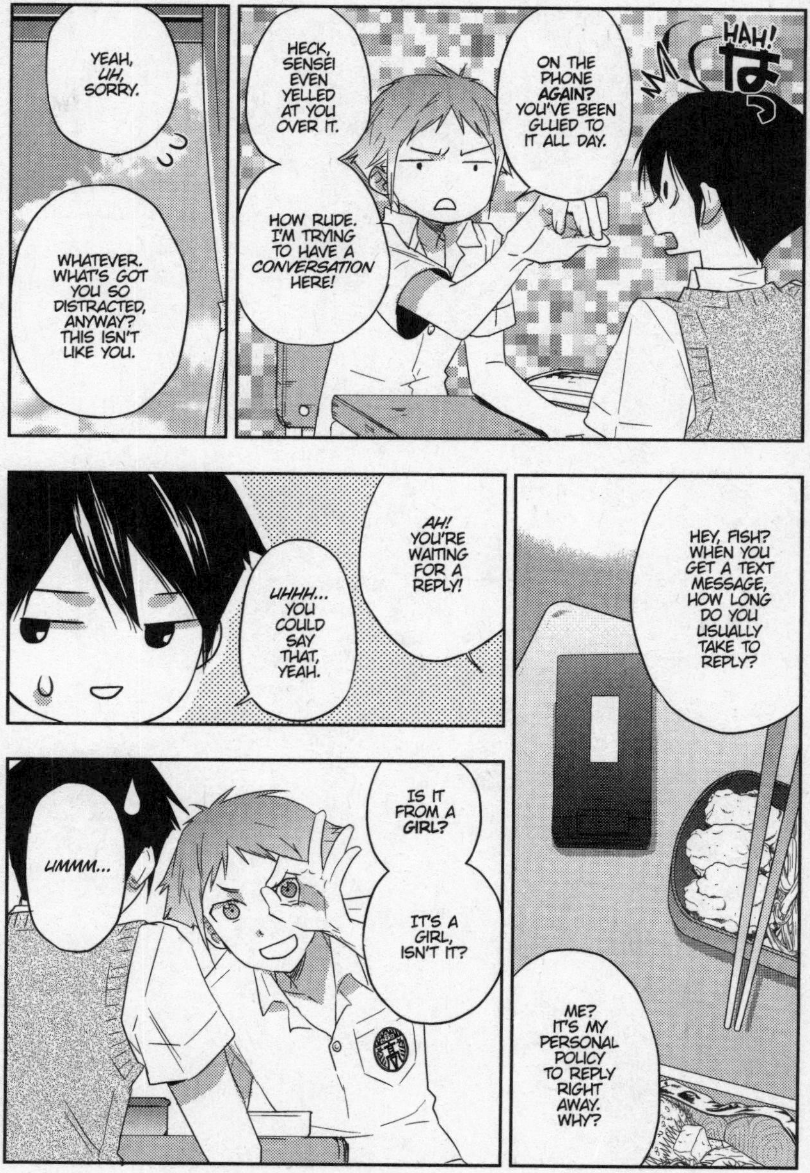
HAH!
はっ
ON THE PHONE AGAIN? YOU'VE BEEN GLUED TO IT ALL DAY.
HECK, SENSEI EVEN YELLED AT YOU OVER IT.
HOW RUDE. I'M TRYING TO HAVE A CONVERSATION HERE!
YEAH, UH, SORRY.
WHATEVER. WHAT'S GOT YOU SO DISTRACTED, ANYWAY? THIS ISN'T LIKE YOU.
HEY, FISH? WHEN YOU GET A TEXT MESSAGE, HOW LONG DO YOU USUALLY TAKE TO REPLY?
ME? IT'S MY PERSONAL POLICY TO REPLY RIGHT AWAY. WHY?
AH! YOU'RE WAITING FOR A REPLY!
UHHH... YOU COULD SAY THAT, YEAH.
IS IT FROM A GIRL?
IT'S A GIRL, ISN'T IT?
UMMM...

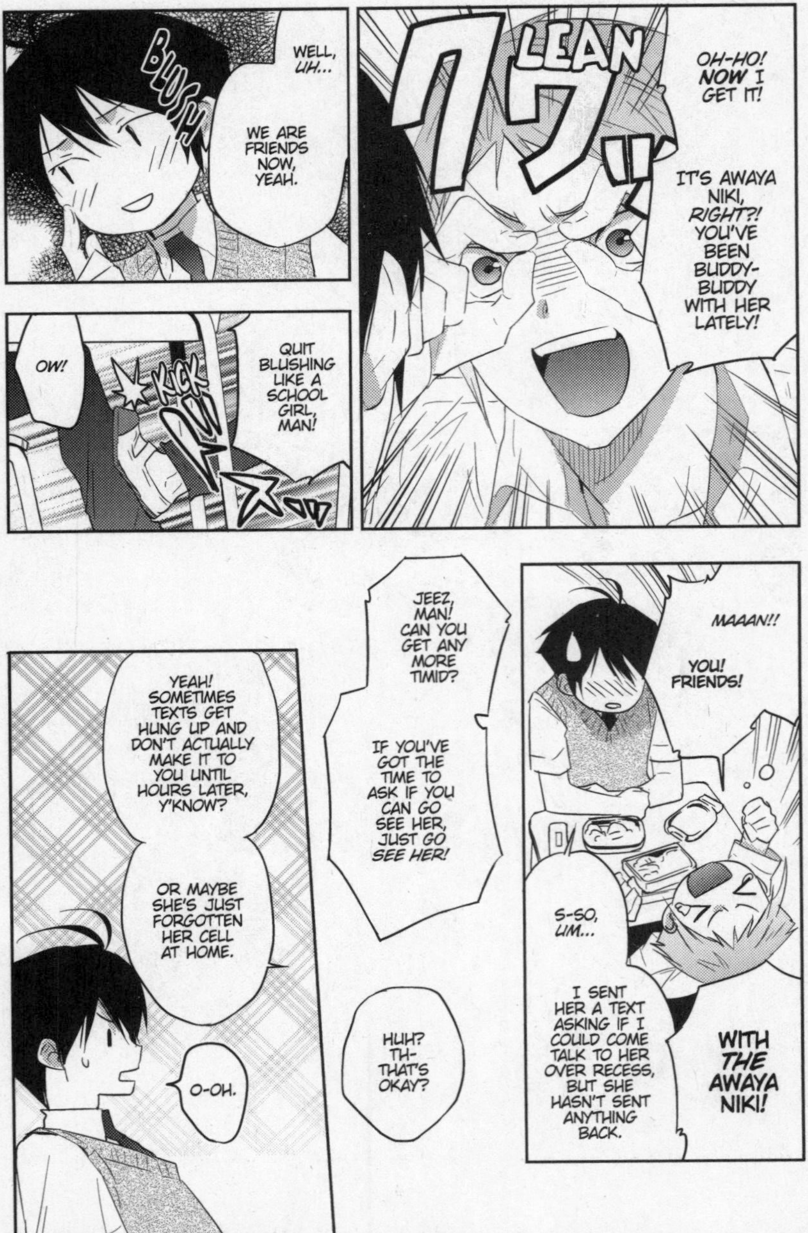
LEAN
OH-HO! NOW I GET IT!
IT'S AWAYA NIKI, RIGHT?! YOU'VE BEEN BUDDY-BUDDY WITH HER LATELY!
BLUSH
WELL, UH...
WE ARE FRIENDS NOW, YEAH.
QUIT BLUSHING LIKE A SCHOOL GIRL, MAN!
KICK
OW!
MAAAN!!
YOU! FRIENDS!
WITH THE AWAYA NIKI!
S-SO, UM...
I SENT HER A TEXT ASKING IF I COULD COME TALK TO HER OVER RECESS, BUT SHE HASN'T SENT ANYTHING BACK.
JEEZ, MAN! CAN YOU GET ANY MORE TIMID?
IF YOU'VE GOT THE TIME TO ASK IF YOU CAN GO SEE HER, JUST GO SEE HER!
HUH? TH-THAT'S OKAY?
YEAH! SOMETIMES TEXTS GET HUNG UP AND DON'T ACTUALLY MAKE IT TO YOU UNTIL HOURS LATER, Y'KNOW?
OR MAYBE SHE'S JUST FORGOTTEN HER CELL AT HOME.
O-OH.

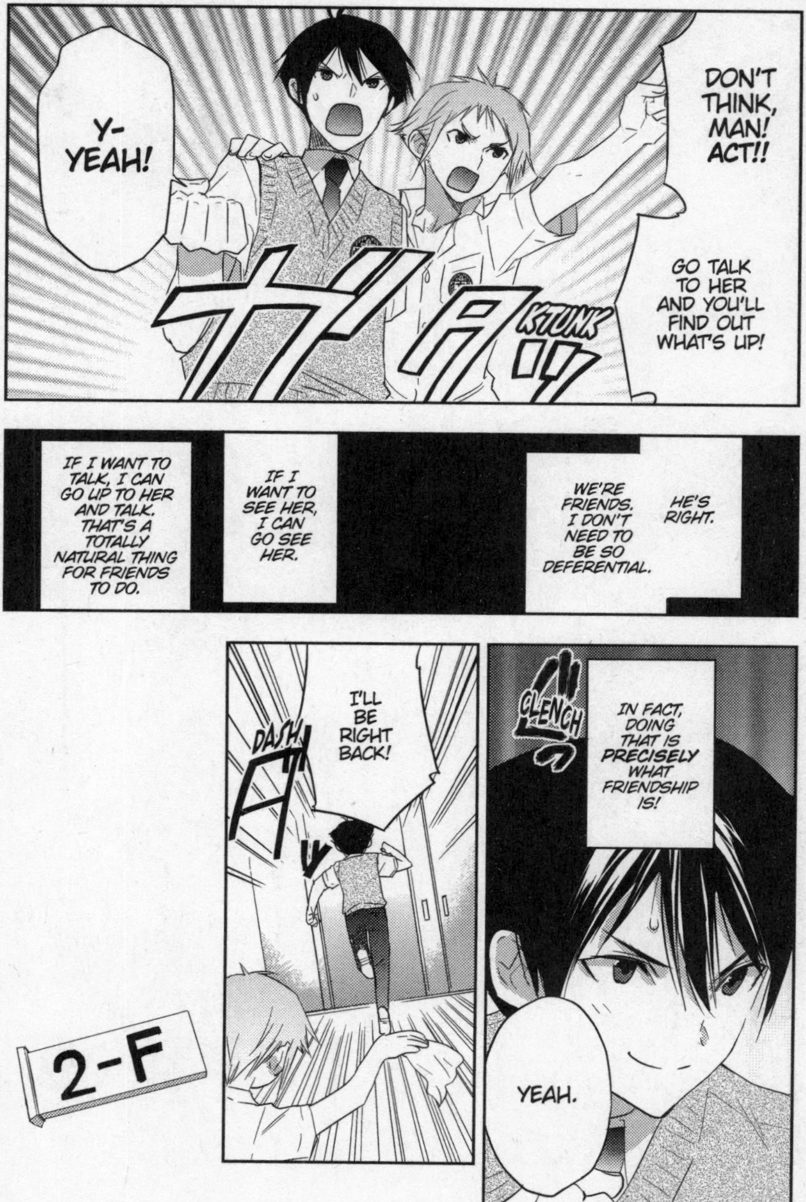
DON'T THINK, MAN! ACT!!
GO TALK TO HER AND YOU'LL FIND OUT WHAT'S UP!
KTUNK
Y-YEAH!
HE'S RIGHT.
WE'RE FRIENDS. I DON'T NEED TO BE SO DEFERENTIAL.
IF I WANT TO SEE HER, I CAN GO SEE HER.
IF I WANT TO TALK, I CAN GO UP TO HER AND TALK. THAT'S A TOTALLY NATURAL THING FOR FRIENDS TO DO.
CLENCH
IN FACT, DOING THAT IS PRECISELY WHAT FRIENDSHIP IS!
YEAH.
I'LL BE RIGHT BACK!
DASH
2-F

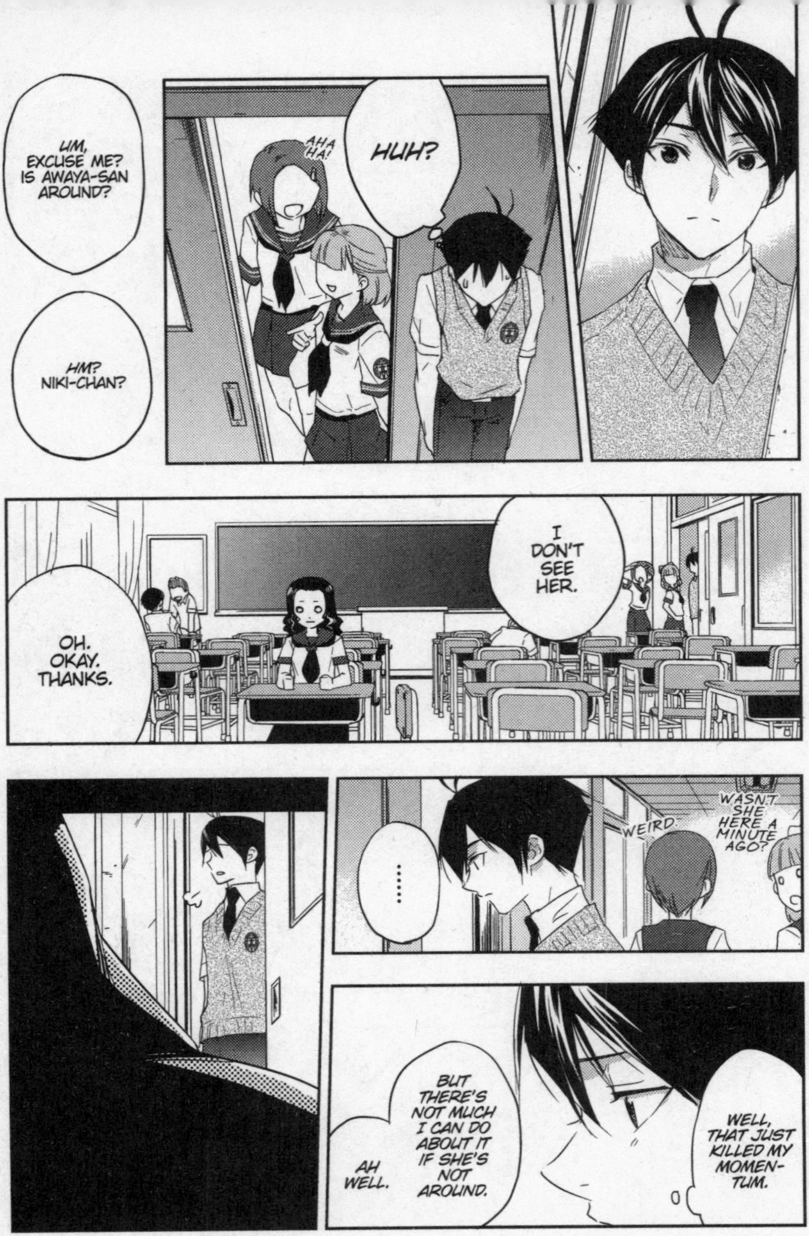
HUH?
AHA HA!
UM, EXCUSE ME? IS AWAYA-SAN AROUND?
HM? NIKI-CHAN?
I DON'T SEE HER.
OH. OKAY. THANKS.
WASN'T SHE HERE A MINUTE AGO?
WEIRD
......
WELL, THAT JUST KILLED MY MOMEN-TUM.
BUT THERE'S NOT MUCH I CAN DO ABOUT IT IF SHE'S NOT AROUND.
AH WELL.

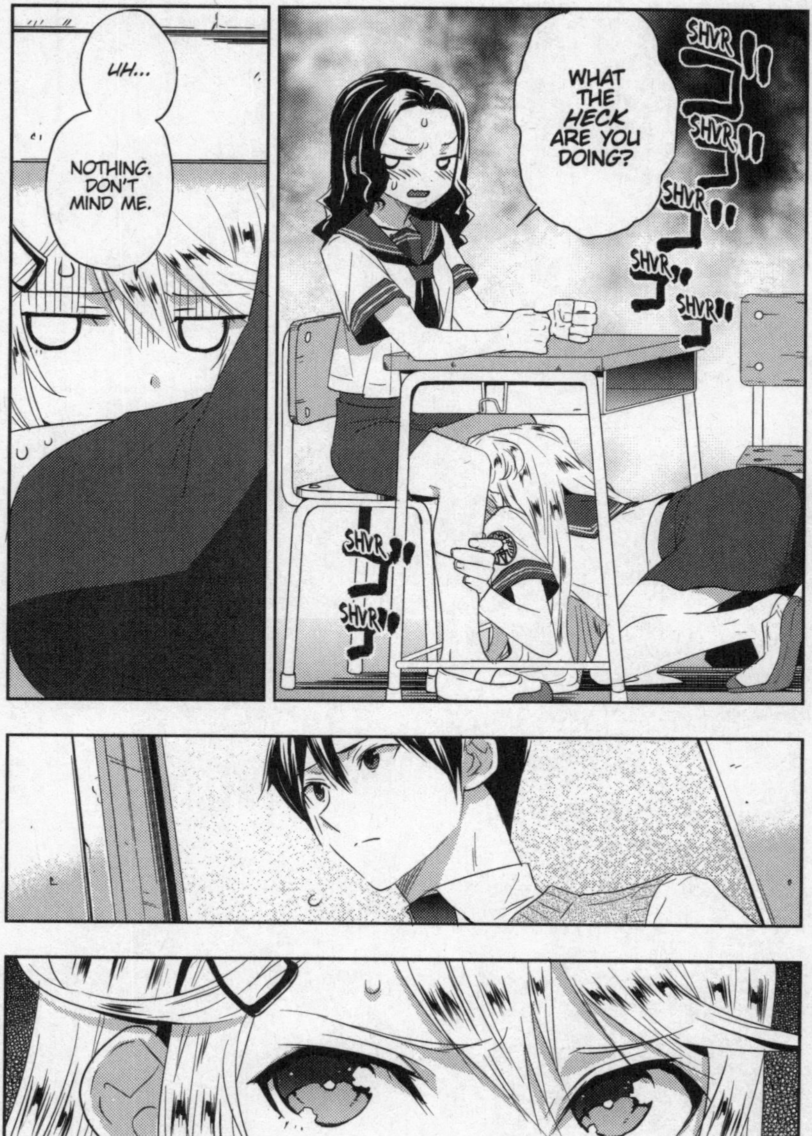
WHAT THE HECK ARE YOU DOING?
SHVR
SHVR
SHVR
SHVR
SHVR
SHVR
SHVR
UH...
NOTHING. DON'T MIND ME.

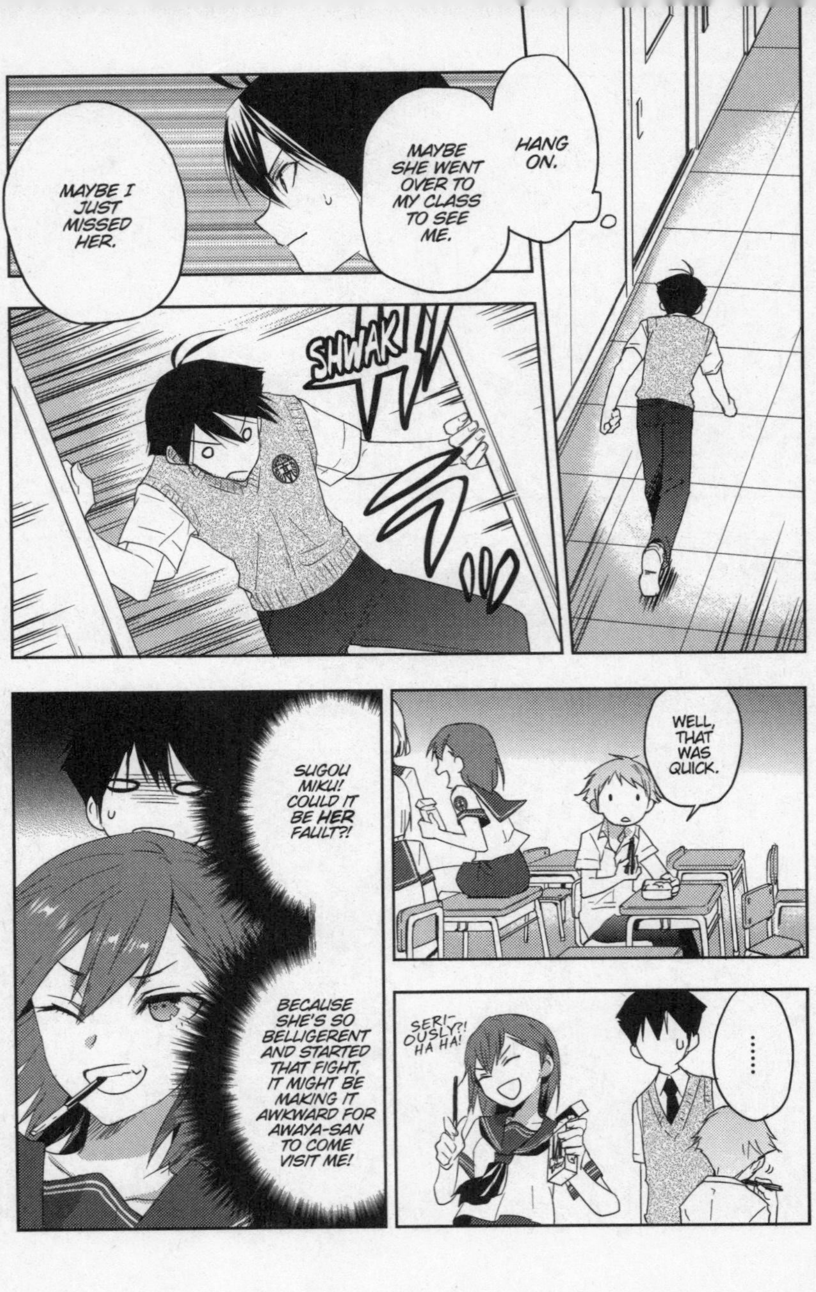
HANG ON.
MAYBE SHE WENT OVER TO MY CLASS TO SEE ME.
MAYBE I JUST MISSED HER.
SHWAK
WELL, THAT WAS QUICK.
......
SERI-OUSLY?! HA HA!
SUGOU MIKU! COULD IT BE HER FAULT?!
BECAUSE SHE'S SO BELLIGERENT AND STARTED THAT FIGHT, IT MIGHT BE MAKING IT AWKWARD FOR AWAYA-SAN TO COME VISIT ME!

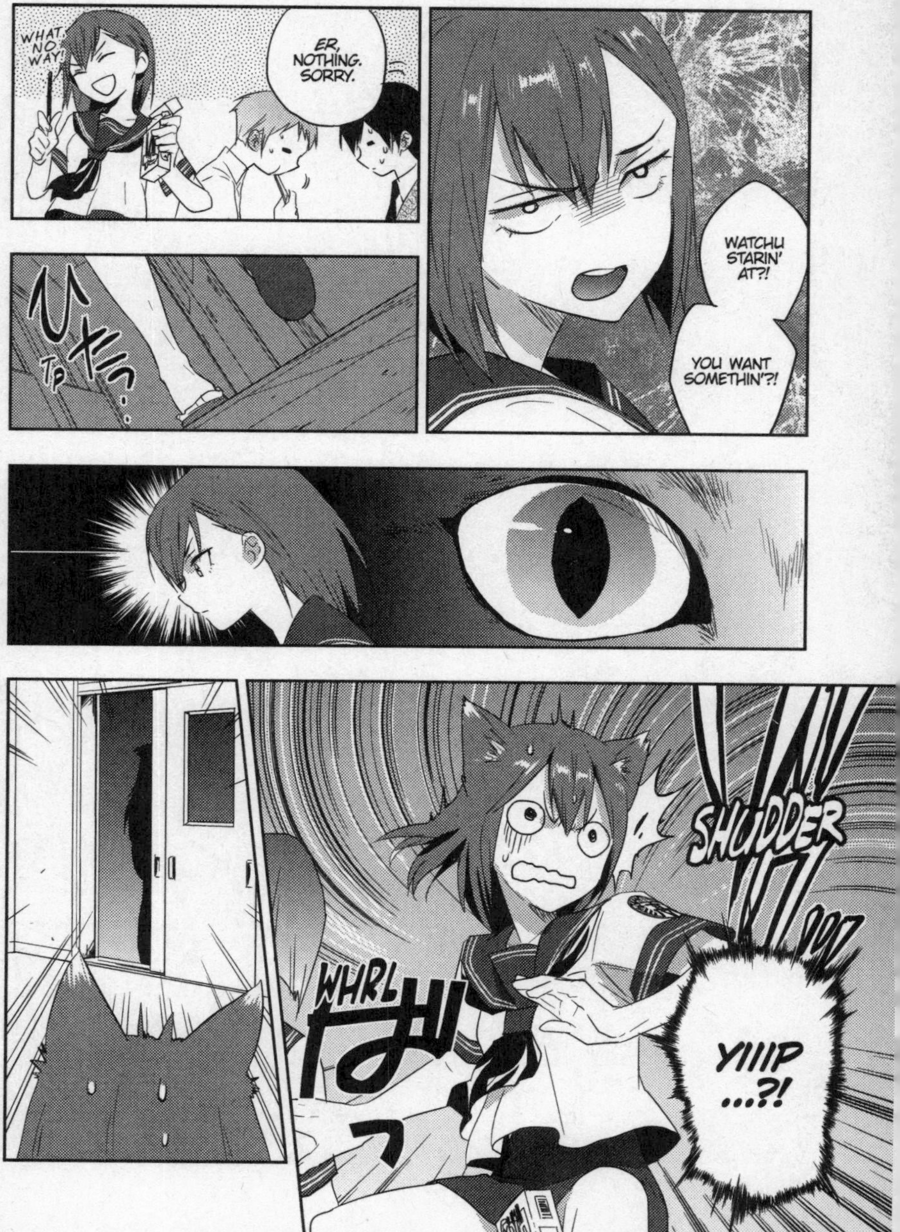
WATCHU STARIN' AT?!
YOU WANT SOMETHIN'?!
ER, NOTHING. SORRY.
WHAT, NO WAY!
SHUDDER
YIIIP ...?!
WHRL

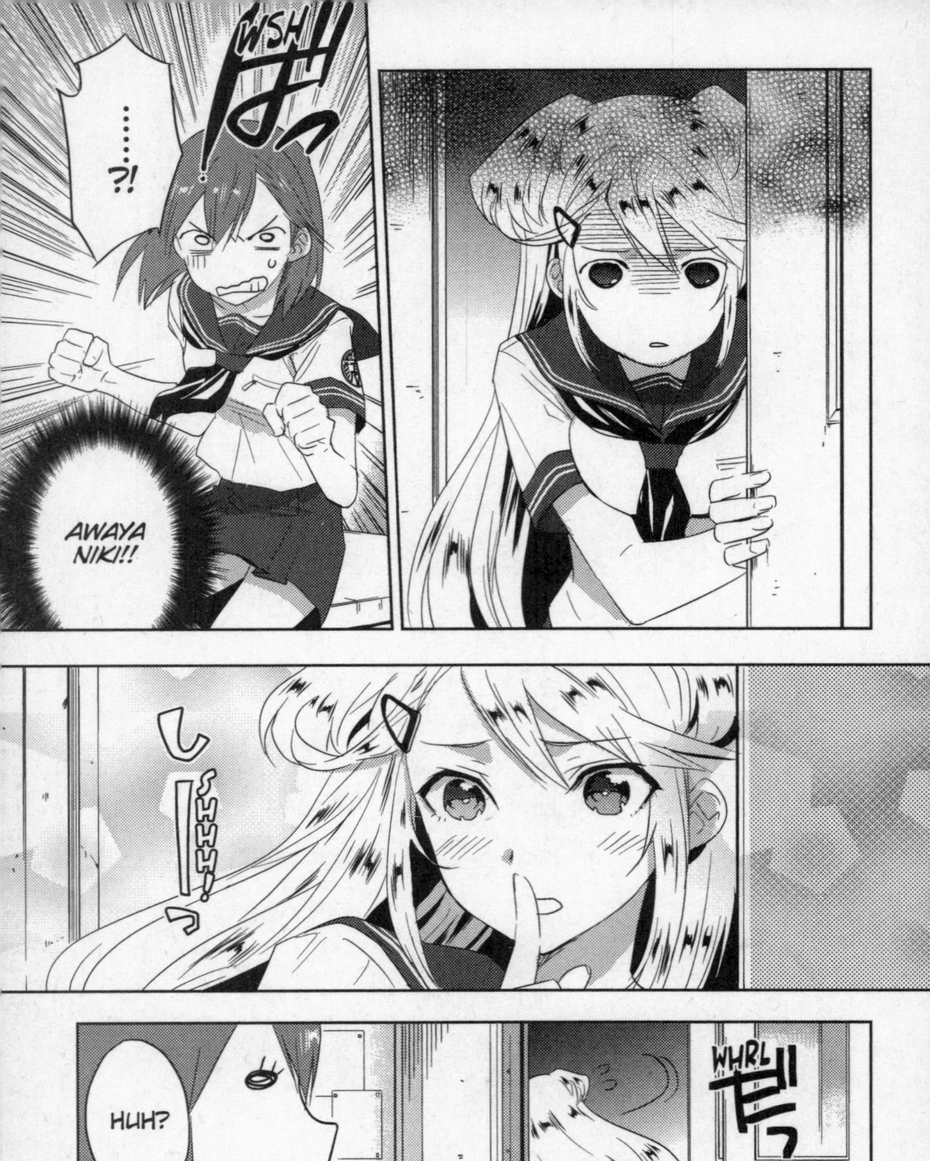
WSH!!
ばっ
......?!
AWAYA NIKI!!
しーっ
SHHH!
WHRL
ぜっ
HUH?

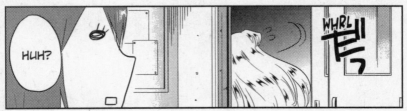

CREEPY.

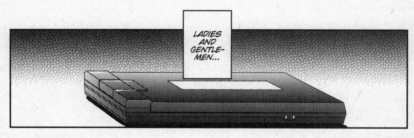

LADIES AND GENTLE- MEN...

IT HAS BEEN THREE DAYS SINCE THEN.

I WAITED FOR A REPLY FOR THREE FULL DAYS.

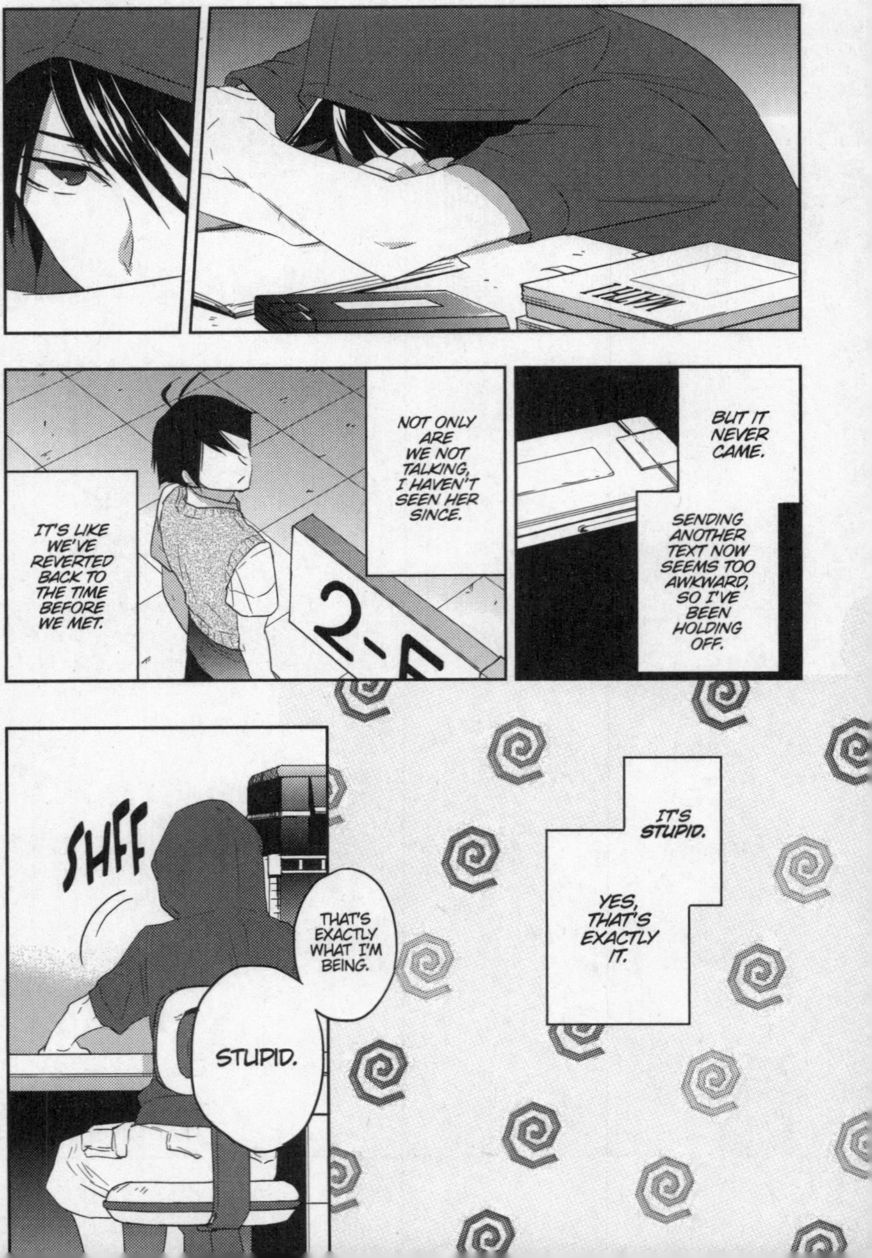
BUT IT NEVER CAME.
SENDING ANOTHER TEXT NOW SEEMS TOO AWKWARD, SO I'VE BEEN HOLDING OFF.
NOT ONLY ARE WE NOT TALKING, I HAVEN'T SEEN HER SINCE.
IT'S LIKE WE'VE REVERTED BACK TO THE TIME BEFORE WE MET.
IT'S STUPID.
YES, THAT'S EXACTLY IT.
SHFF
THAT'S EXACTLY WHAT I'M BEING.
STUPID.

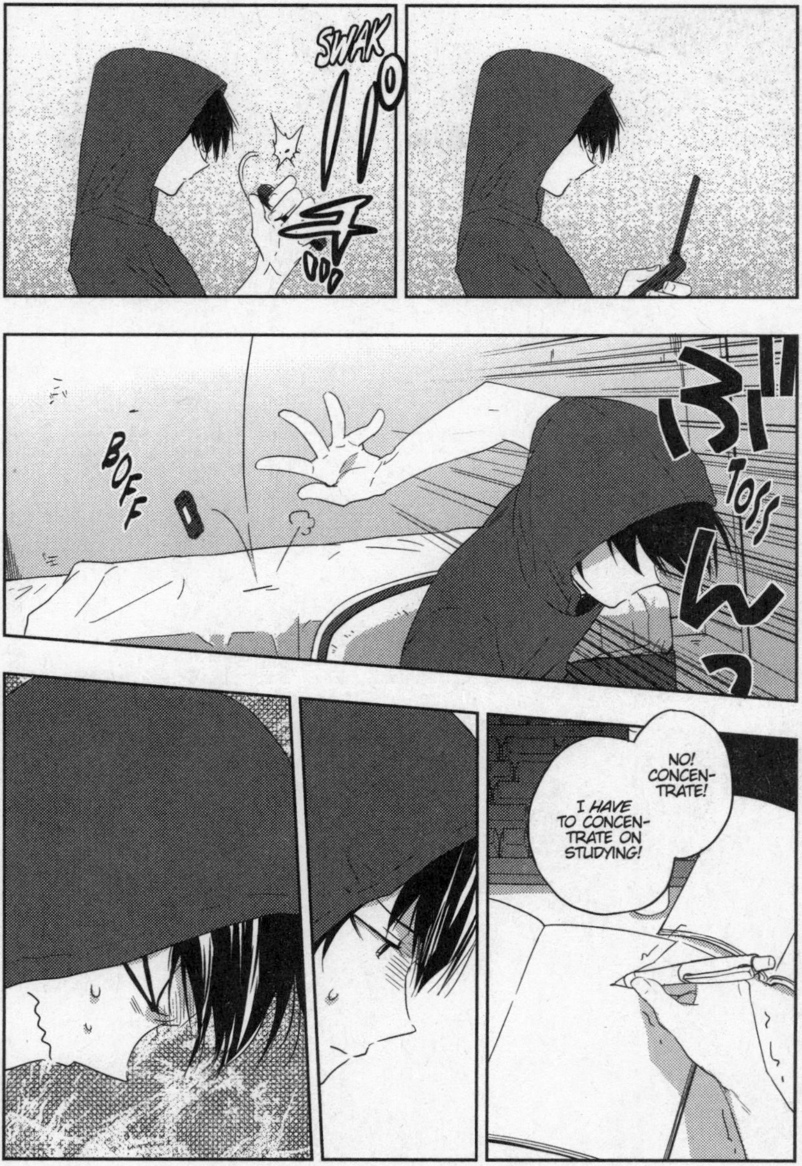
SWAK
TOSS
BOFF
NO! CONCEN-TRATE!
I *HAVE* TO CONCEN-TRATE ON STUDYING!

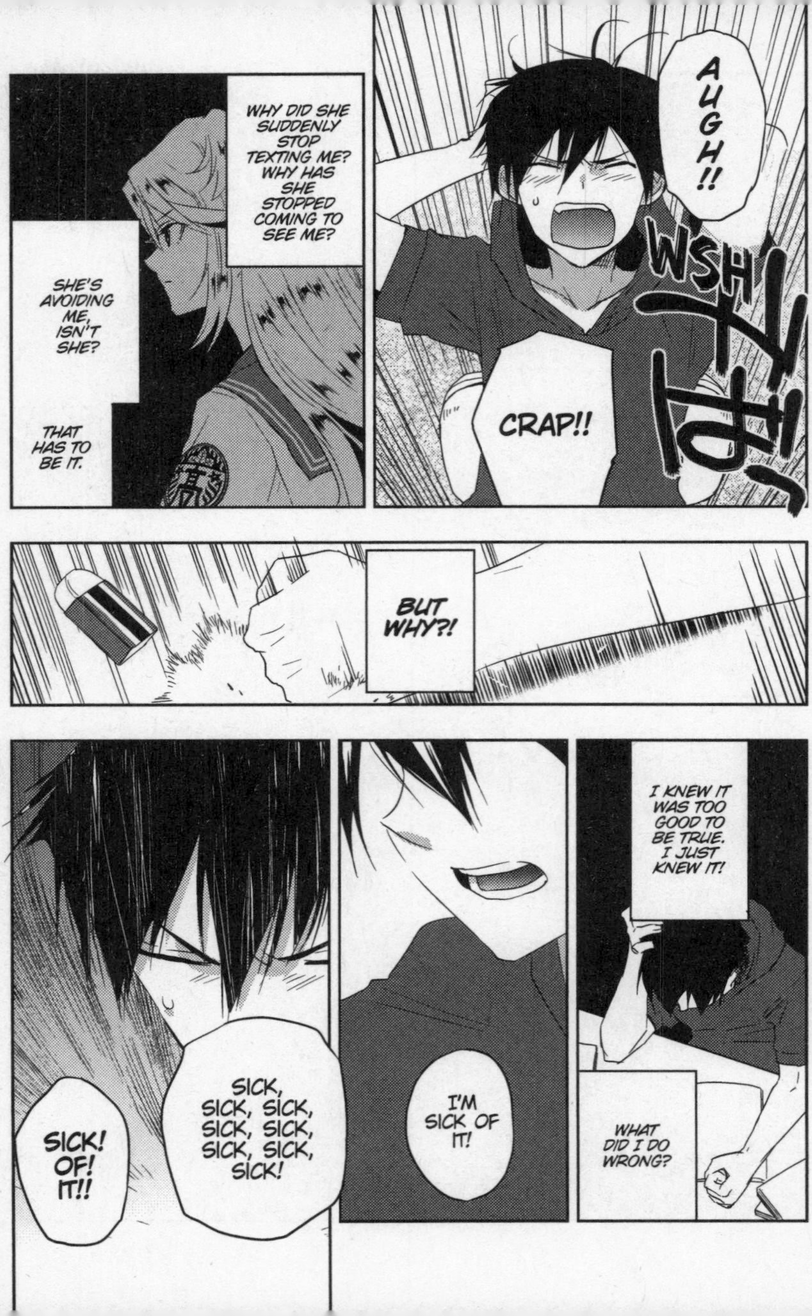
AUGH!!
WSH
CRAP!!
WHY DID SHE SUDDENLY STOP TEXTING ME? WHY HAS SHE STOPPED COMING TO SEE ME?
SHE'S AVOIDING ME, ISN'T SHE?
THAT HAS TO BE IT.
BUT WHY?!
I KNEW IT WAS TOO GOOD TO BE TRUE. I JUST KNEW IT!
WHAT DID I DO WRONG?
I'M SICK OF IT!
SICK, SICK, SICK, SICK, SICK, SICK, SICK, SICK!
SICK! OF! IT!!

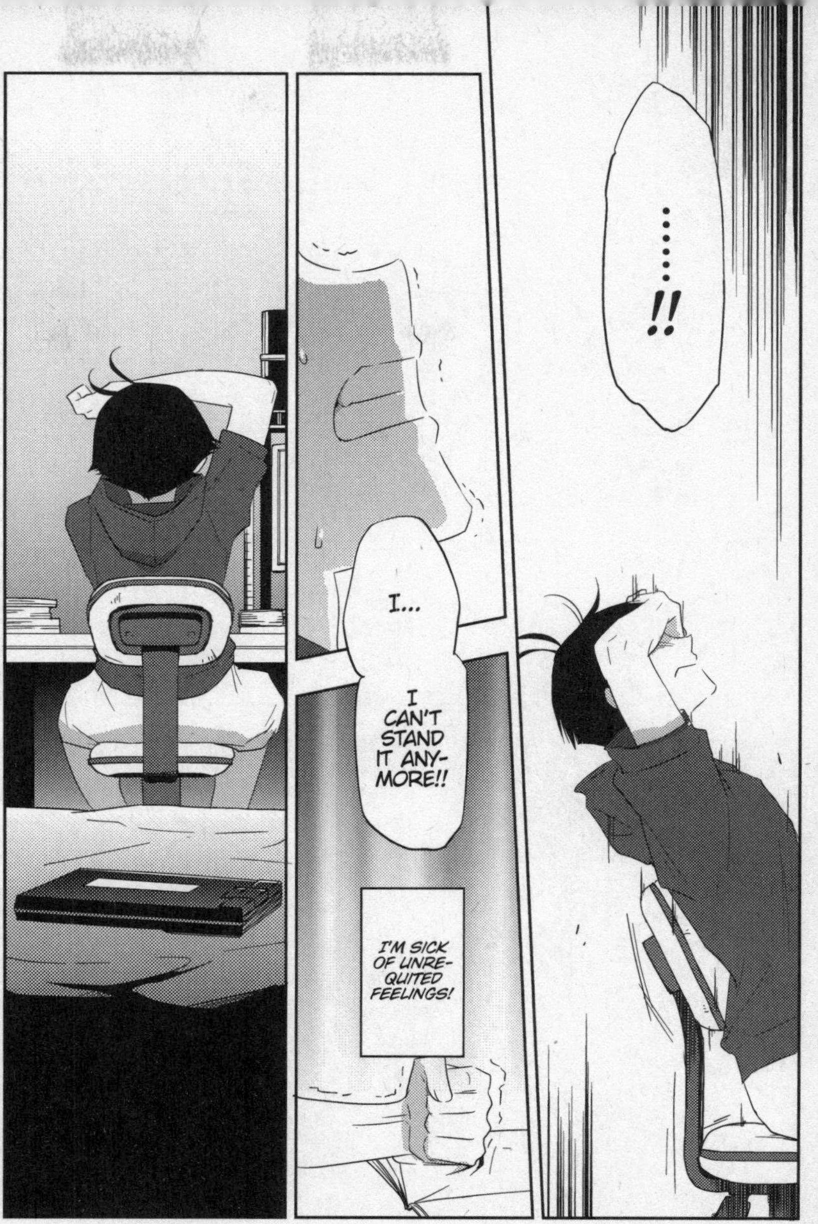
……!!
I…
I CAN'T STAND IT ANY-MORE!!
I'M SICK OF UNRE-QUITED FEELINGS!

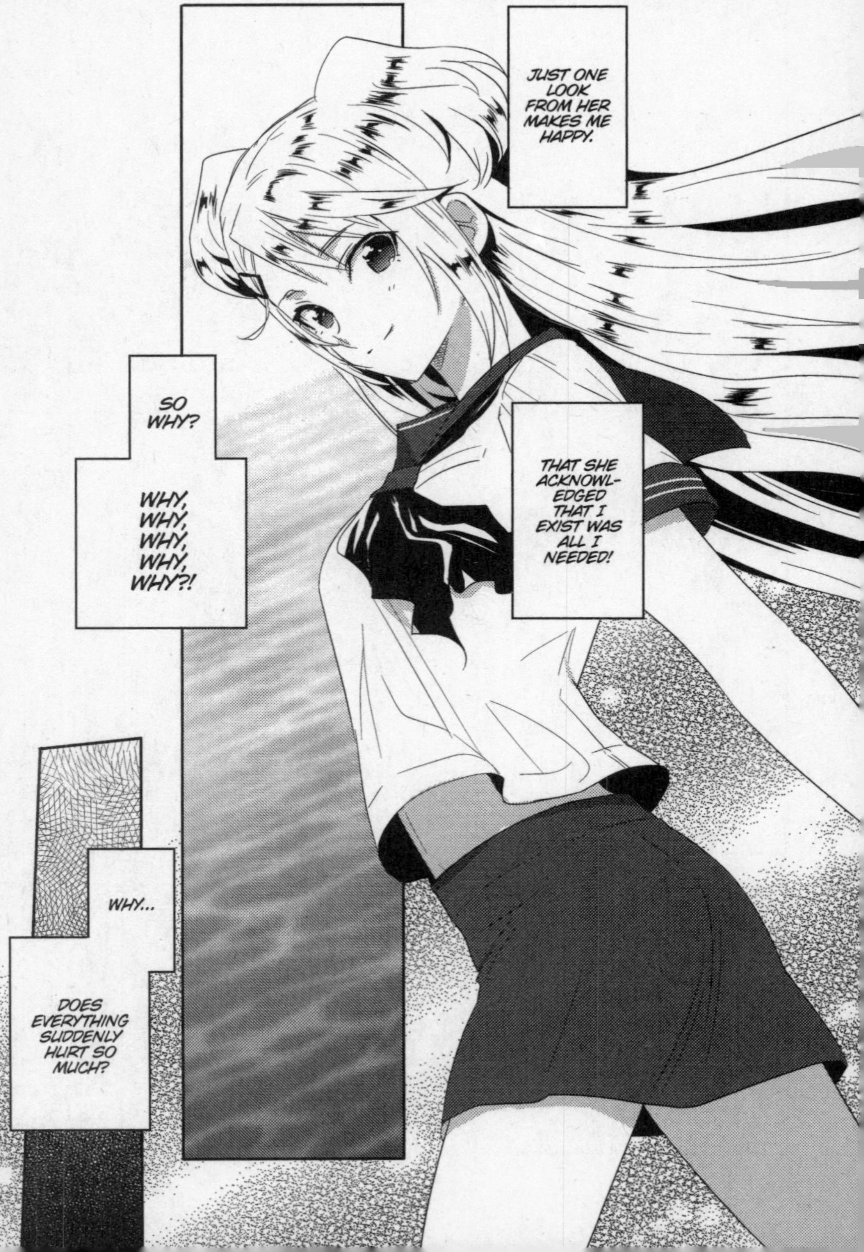
JUST ONE LOOK FROM HER MAKES ME HAPPY.
THAT SHE ACKNOWL-EDGED THAT I EXIST WAS ALL I NEEDED!
SO WHY?
WHY, WHY, WHY, WHY, WHY?!
WHY...
DOES EVERYTHING SUDDENLY HURT SO MUCH?

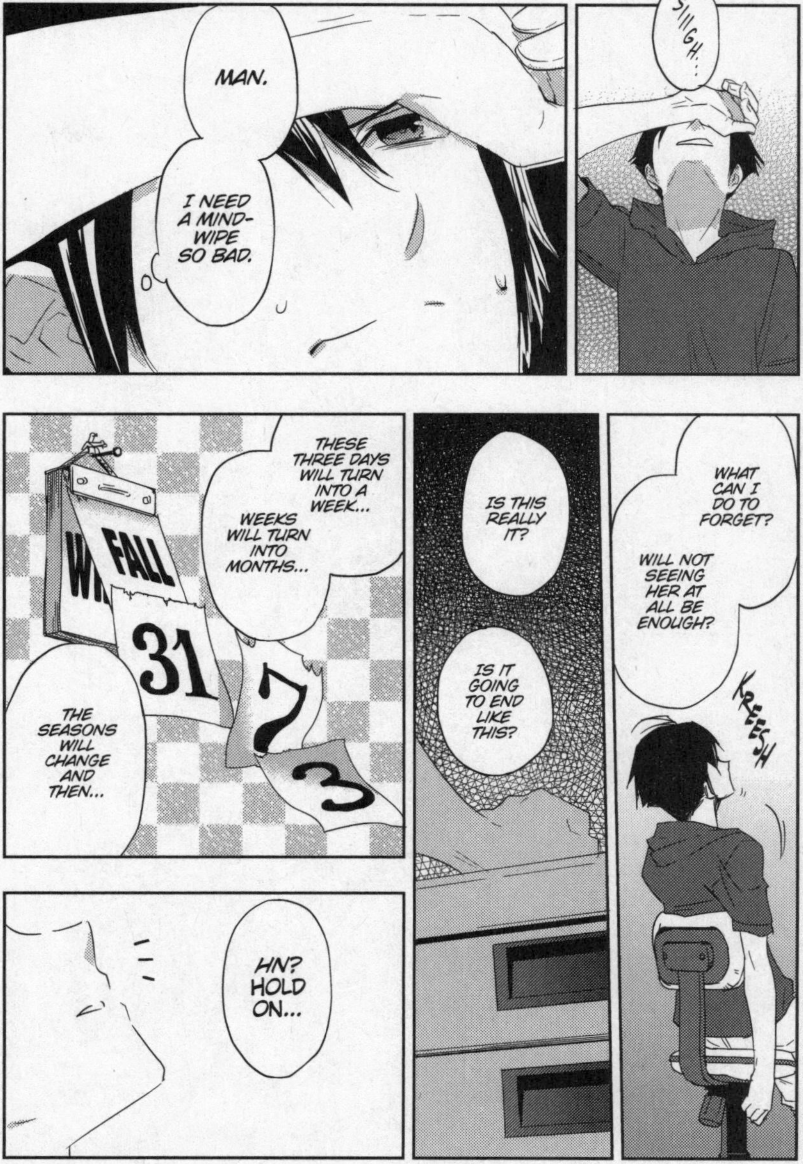
SIIIGH...
MAN.
I NEED A MIND-WIPE SO BAD.
WHAT CAN I DO TO FORGET?
WILL NOT SEEING HER AT ALL BE ENOUGH?
KREESH
IS THIS REALLY IT?
IS IT GOING TO END LIKE THIS?
THESE THREE DAYS WILL TURN INTO A WEEK...
WEEKS WILL TURN INTO MONTHS...
FALL
31
7
3
THE SEASONS WILL CHANGE AND THEN...
HN? HOLD ON...

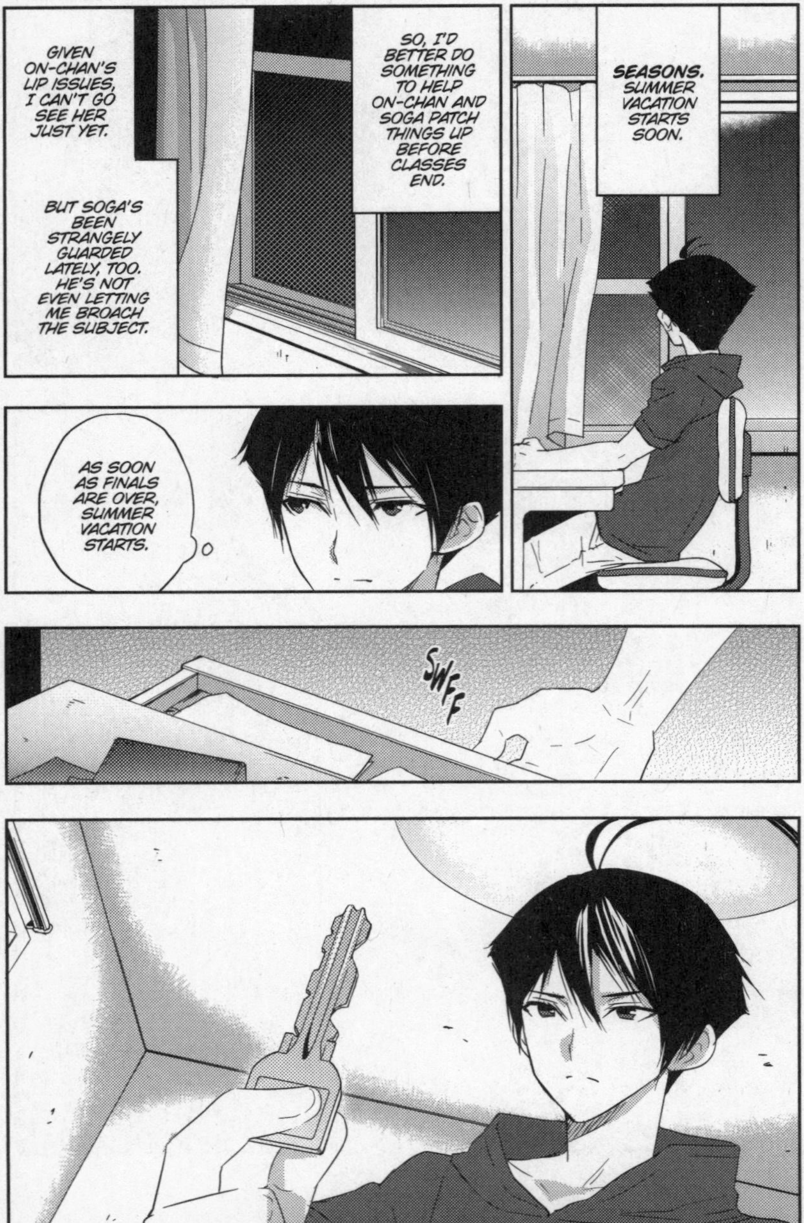
SEASONS. SUMMER VACATION STARTS SOON.
SO, I'D BETTER DO SOMETHING TO HELP ON-CHAN AND SOGA PATCH THINGS UP BEFORE CLASSES END.
GIVEN ON-CHAN'S LIP ISSUES, I CAN'T GO SEE HER JUST YET.
BUT SOGA'S BEEN STRANGELY GUARDED LATELY, TOO. HE'S NOT EVEN LETTING ME BROACH THE SUBJECT.
AS SOON AS FINALS ARE OVER, SUMMER VACATION STARTS.
SWFF

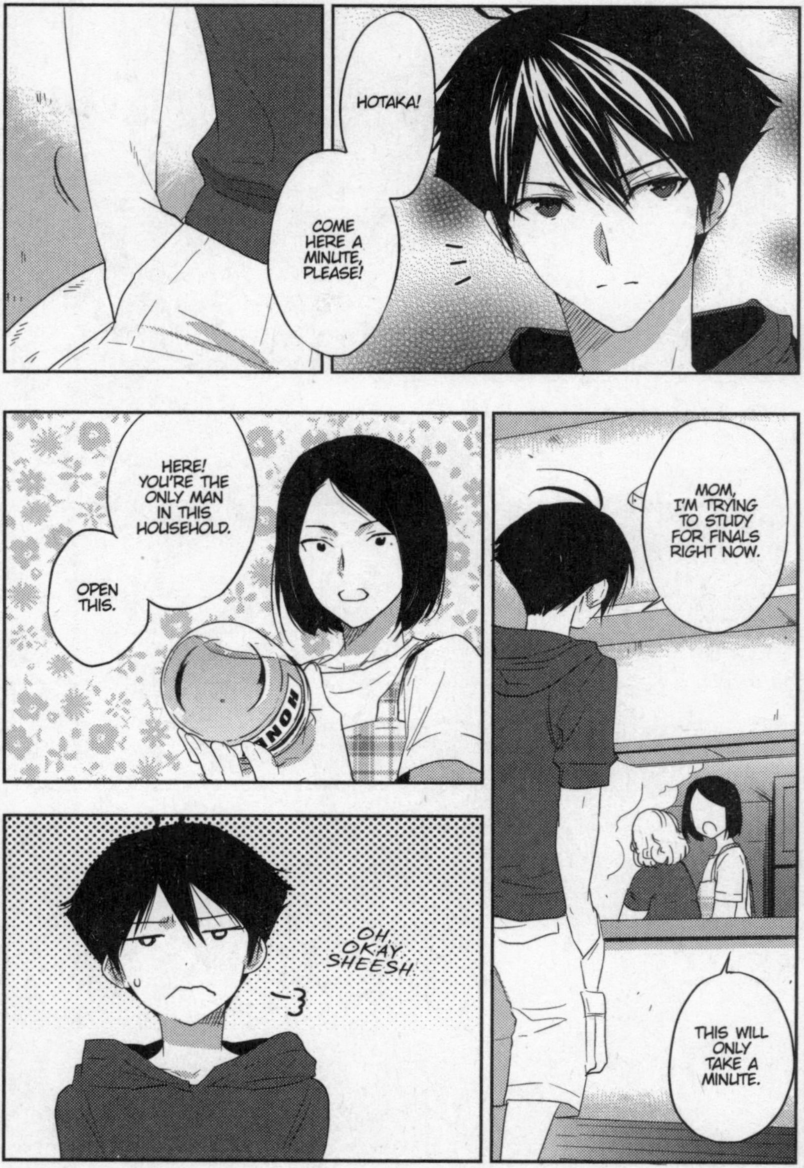
HOTAKA!
COME HERE A MINUTE, PLEASE!
MOM, I'M TRYING TO STUDY FOR FINALS RIGHT NOW.
THIS WILL ONLY TAKE A MINUTE.
HERE! YOU'RE THE ONLY MAN IN THIS HOUSEHOLD.
OPEN THIS.
OH, OKAY. SHEESH.

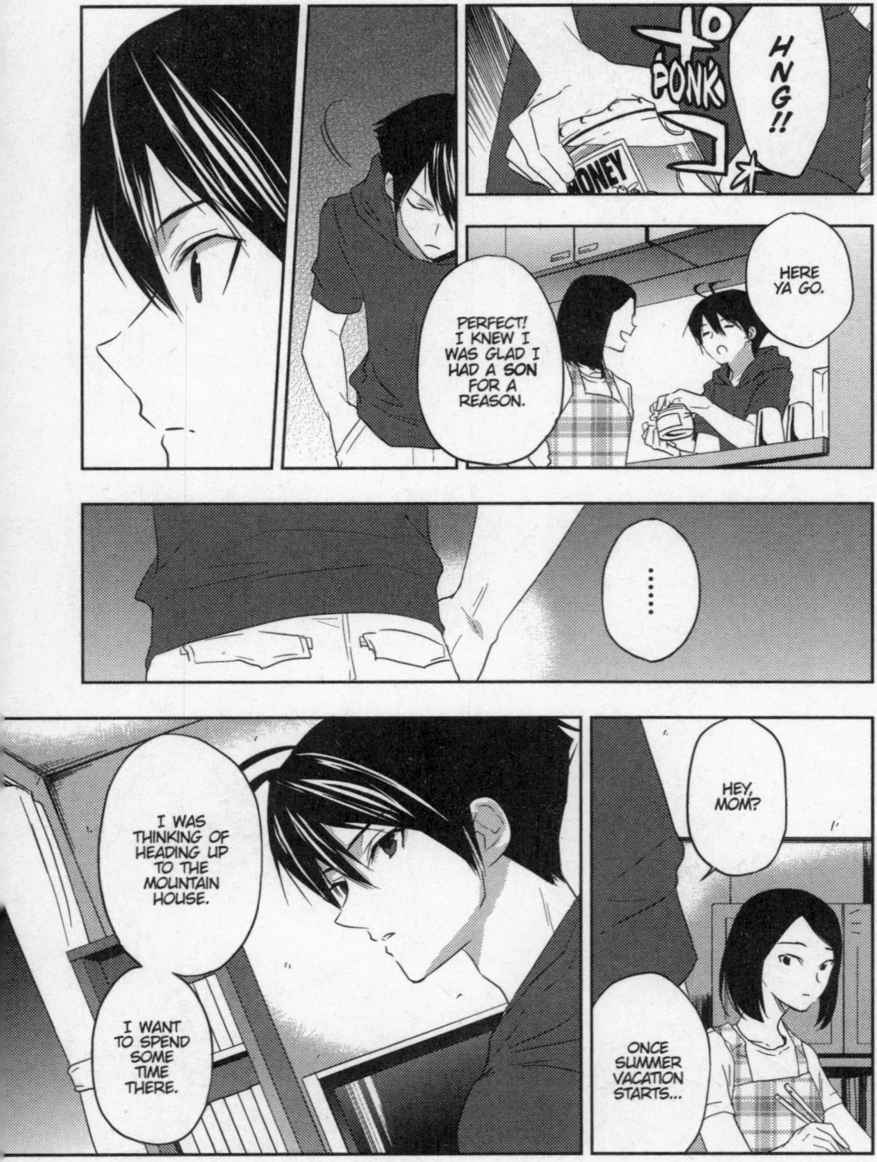
HNG!!
PONK
HERE YA GO.
PERFECT! I KNEW I WAS GLAD I HAD A SON FOR A REASON.
......
HEY, MOM?
ONCE SUMMER VACATION STARTS...
I WAS THINKING OF HEADING UP TO THE MOUNTAIN HOUSE.
I WANT TO SPEND SOME TIME THERE.

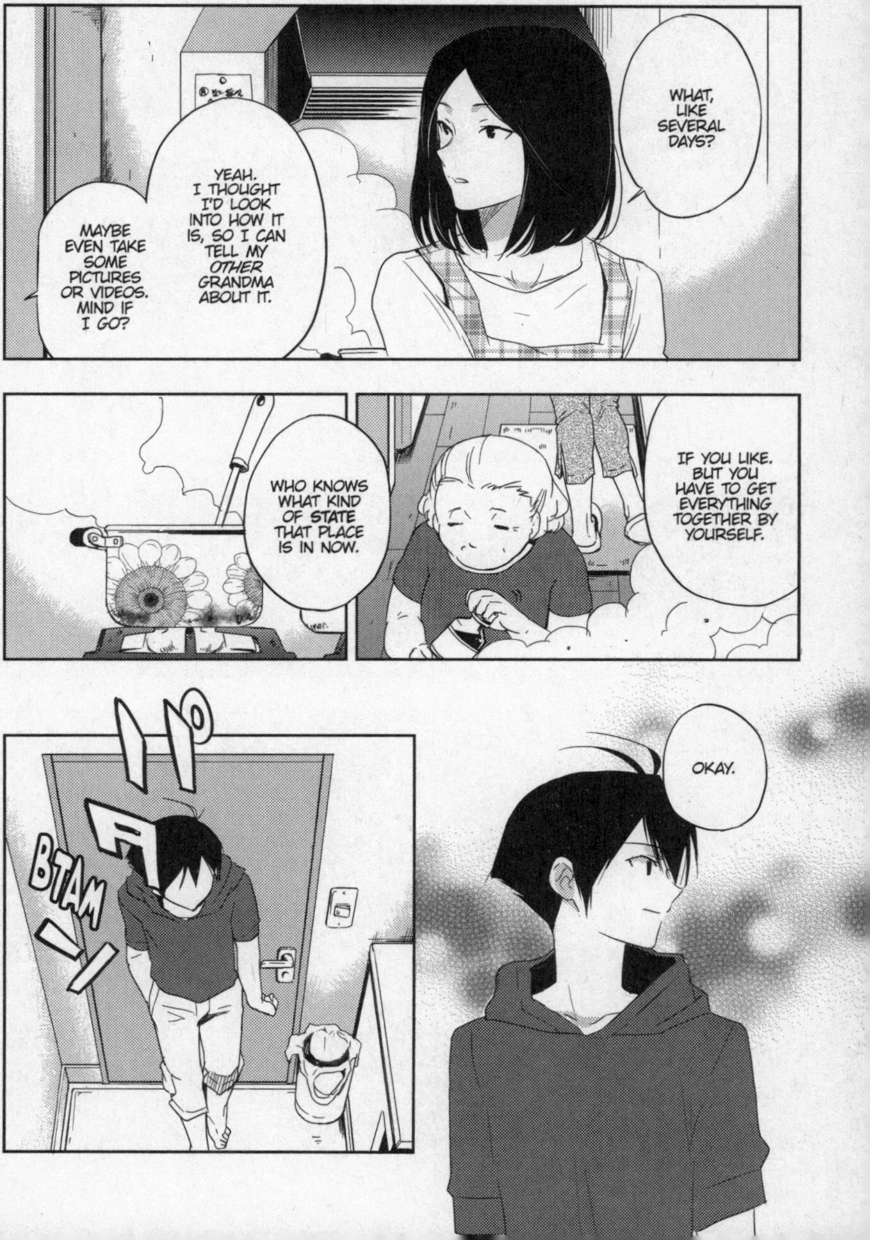
WHAT, LIKE SEVERAL DAYS?
YEAH. I THOUGHT I'D LOOK INTO HOW IT IS, SO I CAN TELL MY *OTHER* GRANDMA ABOUT IT.
MAYBE EVEN TAKE SOME PICTURES OR VIDEOS. MIND IF I GO?
IF YOU LIKE. BUT YOU HAVE TO GET EVERYTHING TOGETHER BY YOURSELF.
WHO KNOWS WHAT KIND OF STATE THAT PLACE IS IN NOW.
OKAY.
BTAM

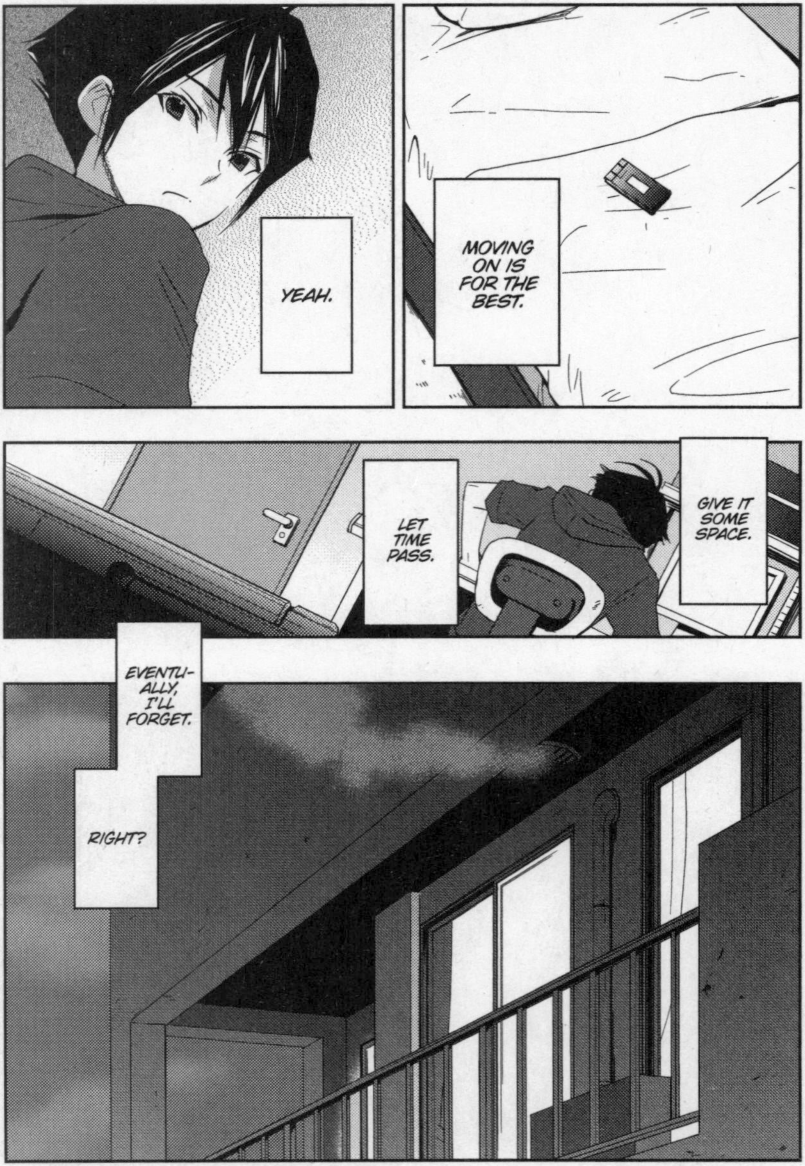
MOVING ON IS FOR THE BEST.
YEAH.
GIVE IT SOME SPACE.
LET TIME PASS.
EVENTU-ALLY, I'LL FORGET.
RIGHT?

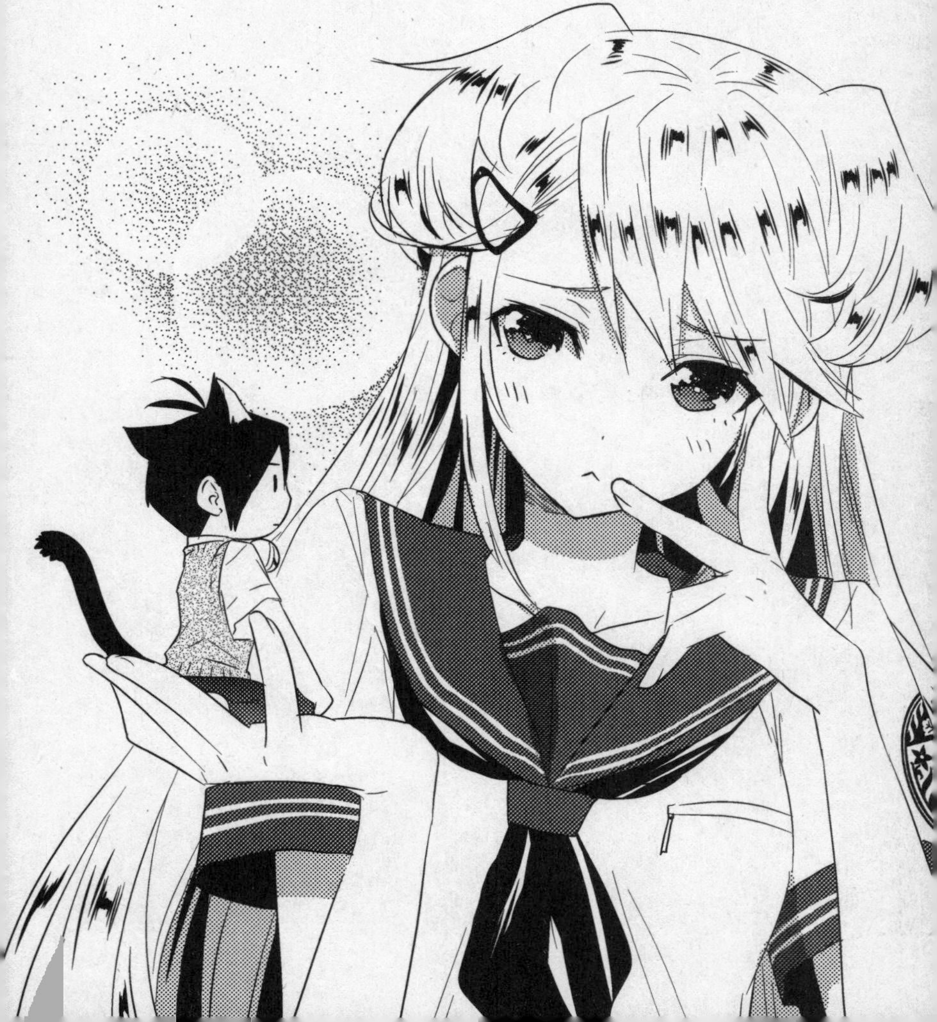

# Chapter 10: I Haven't Studied At All

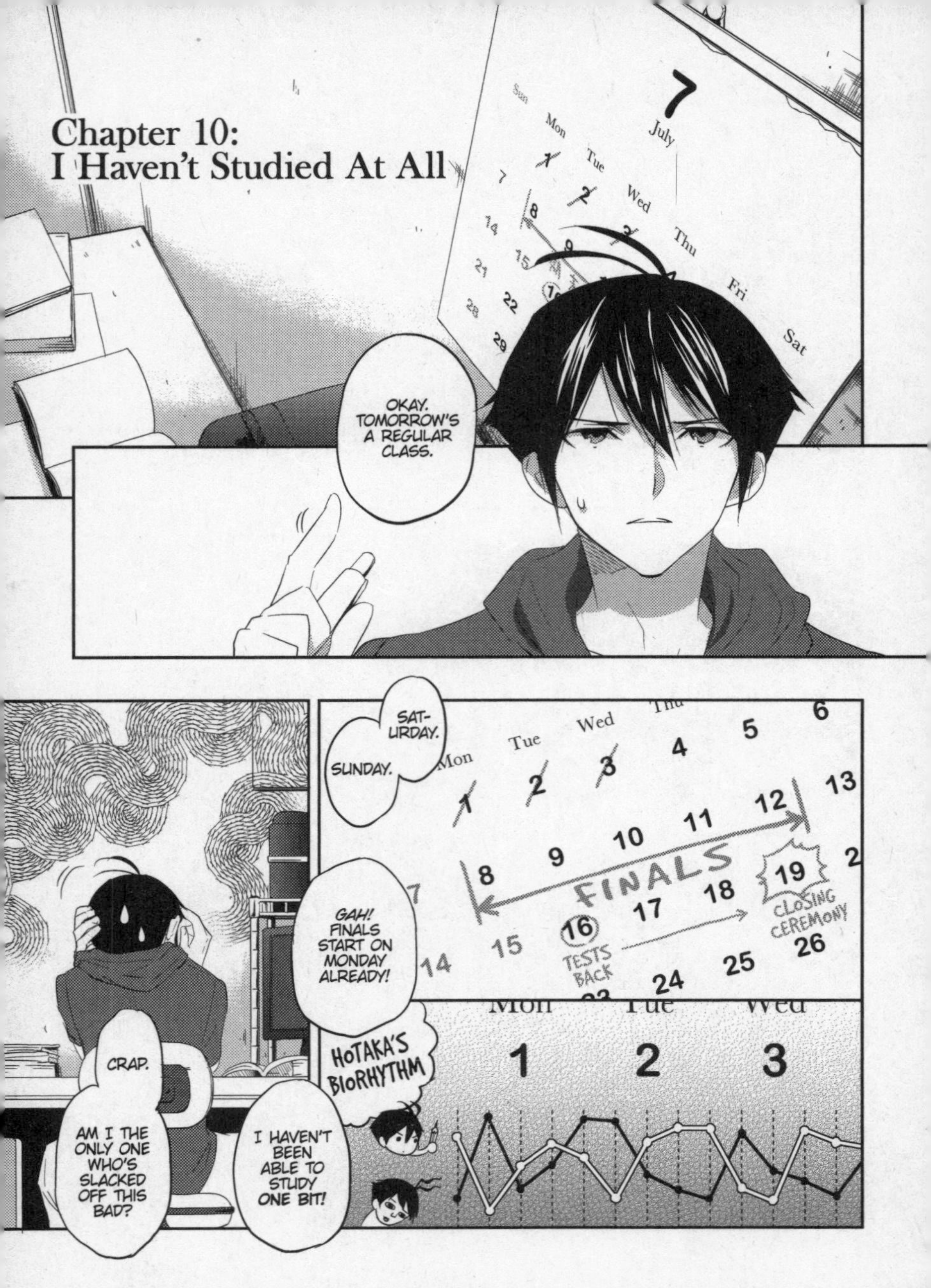
7
July
OKAY. TOMORROW'S A REGULAR CLASS.
SAT-URDAY.
SUNDAY.
FINALS
TESTS BACK
CLOSING CEREMONY
GAH! FINALS START ON MONDAY ALREADY!
HOTAKA'S BIORHYTHM
CRAP.
I HAVEN'T BEEN ABLE TO STUDY ONE BIT!
AM I THE ONLY ONE WHO'S SLACKED OFF THIS BAD?

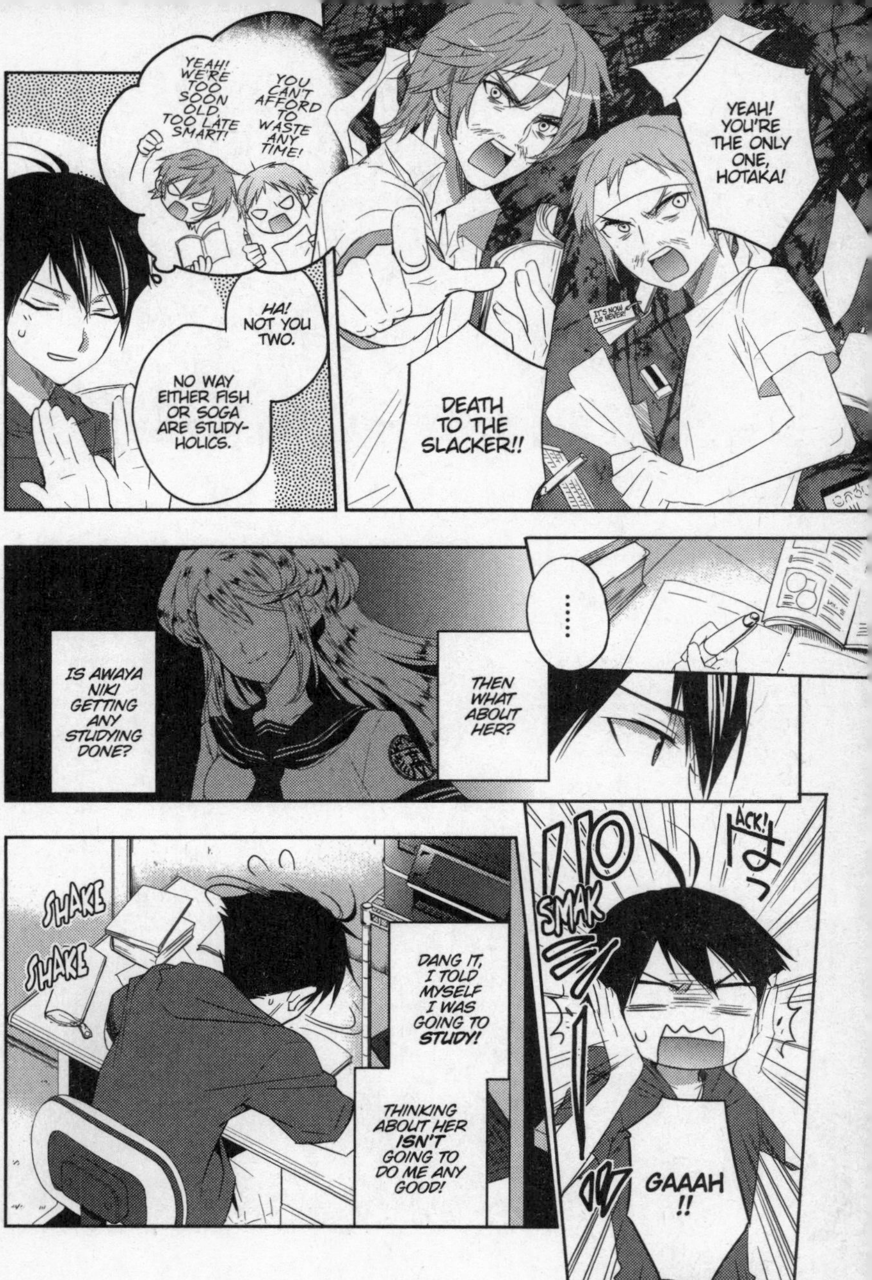
YEAH! YOU'RE THE ONLY ONE, HOTAKA!
IT'S NOW OR NEVER!
DEATH TO THE SLACKER!!
YOU CAN'T AFFORD TO WASTE ANY TIME!
YEAH! WE'RE TOO SOON OLD, TOO LATE SMART!
HA! NOT YOU TWO.
NO WAY EITHER FISH OR SOGA ARE STUDY-HOLICS.
......
THEN WHAT ABOUT HER?
IS AWAYA NIKI GETTING ANY STUDYING DONE?
ACK!
SMAK
GAAAH!!
DANG IT, I TOLD MYSELF I WAS GOING TO STUDY!
THINKING ABOUT HER ISN'T GOING TO DO ME ANY GOOD!
SHAKE
SHAKE

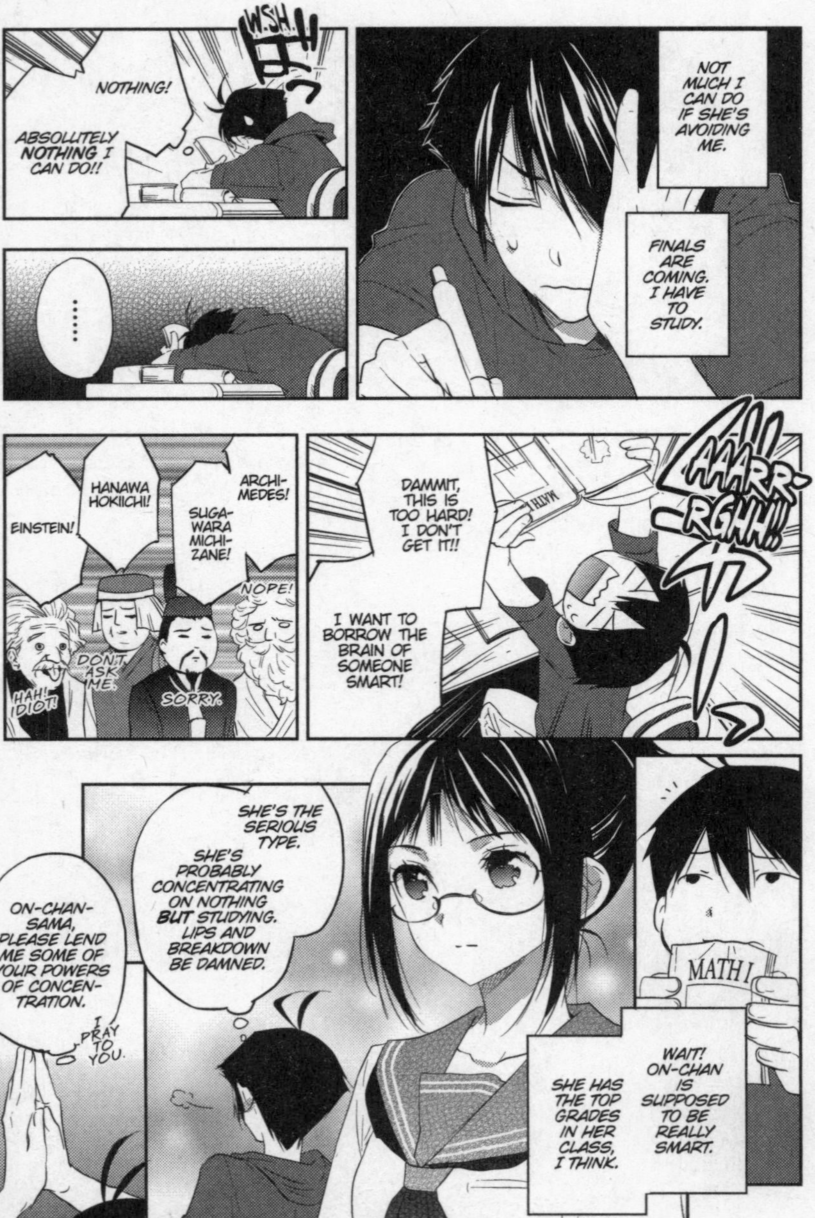
NOT MUCH I CAN DO IF SHE'S AVOIDING ME.
FINALS ARE COMING. I HAVE TO STUDY.
W.SH.
NOTHING!
ABSOLUTELY NOTHING I CAN DO!!
......
AAAARR-RGHH!!
MATH
DAMMIT, THIS IS TOO HARD! I DON'T GET IT!!
I WANT TO BORROW THE BRAIN OF SOMEONE SMART!
ARCHIMEDES!
SUGAWARA MICHIZANE!
HANAWA HOKIICHI!
EINSTEIN!
NOPE!
SORRY.
DON'T ASK ME.
HAH! IDIOT!
MATH I
WAIT! ON-CHAN IS SUPPOSED TO BE REALLY SMART.
SHE HAS THE TOP GRADES IN HER CLASS, I THINK.
SHE'S THE SERIOUS TYPE. SHE'S PROBABLY CONCENTRATING ON NOTHING BUT STUDYING. LIPS AND BREAKDOWN BE DAMNED.
ON-CHAN-SAMA, PLEASE LEND ME SOME OF YOUR POWERS OF CONCENTRATION.
I PRAY TO YOU.

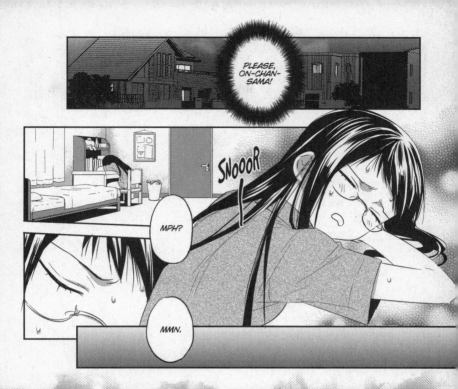

PLEASE, ON-CHAN-SAMA!

SNOOOR

MPH?

MMN.

PAT

HRM?

PAT

HUH?

ODD. I DON'T...

WAIT. NO. IMPOSSIBLE!

PAT

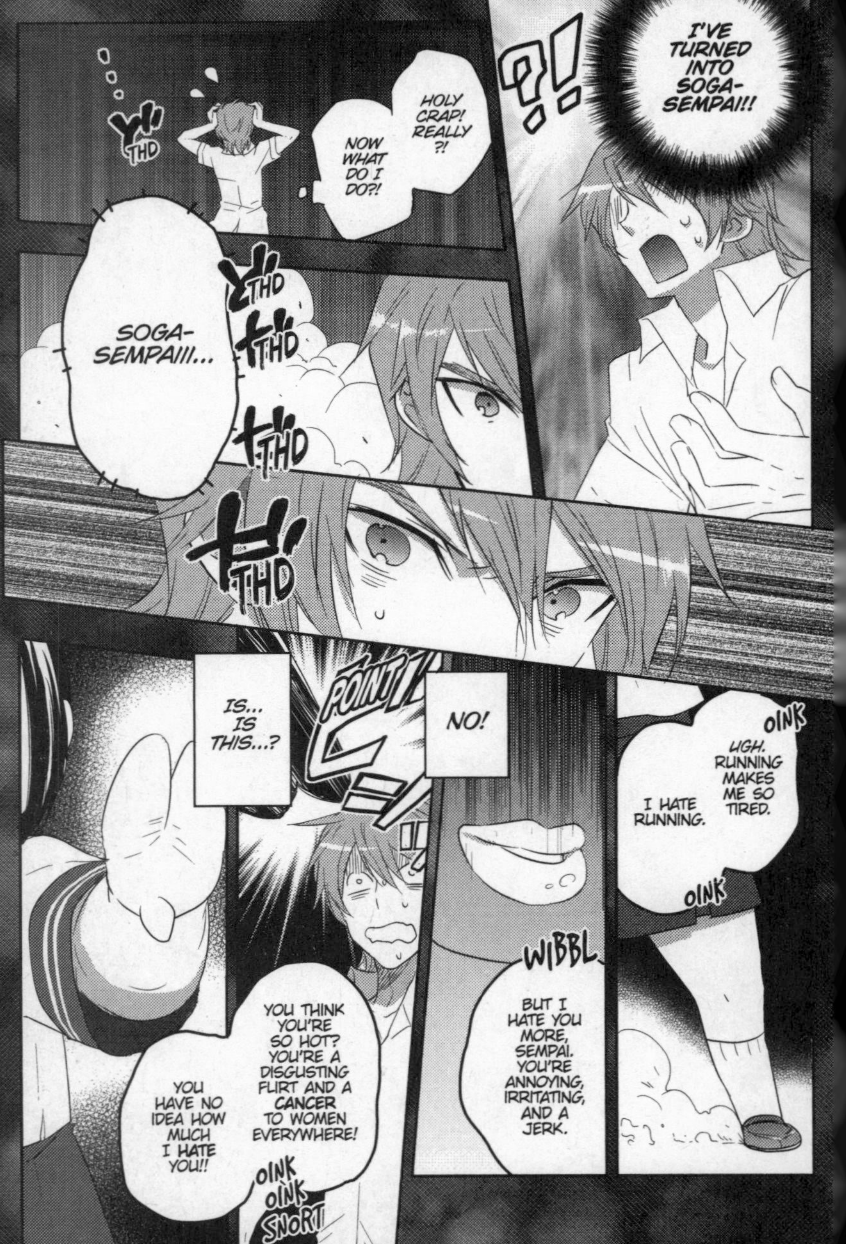
?!
I'VE TURNED INTO SOGA-SEMPAI!!
HOLY CRAP! REALLY ?!
NOW WHAT DO I DO?!
THD
SOGA-SEMPAIIII...
THD
THD
THD
THD
OINK
UGH. RUNNING MAKES ME SO TIRED.
I HATE RUNNING.
OINK
NO!
WIBBL
BUT I HATE YOU MORE, SEMPAI. YOU'RE ANNOYING, IRRITATING, AND A JERK.
IS... IS THIS...?
POINT
YOU THINK YOU'RE SO HOT? YOU'RE A DISGUSTING FLIRT AND A CANCER TO WOMEN EVERYWHERE!
YOU HAVE NO IDEA HOW MUCH I HATE YOU!!
OINK OINK SNORT

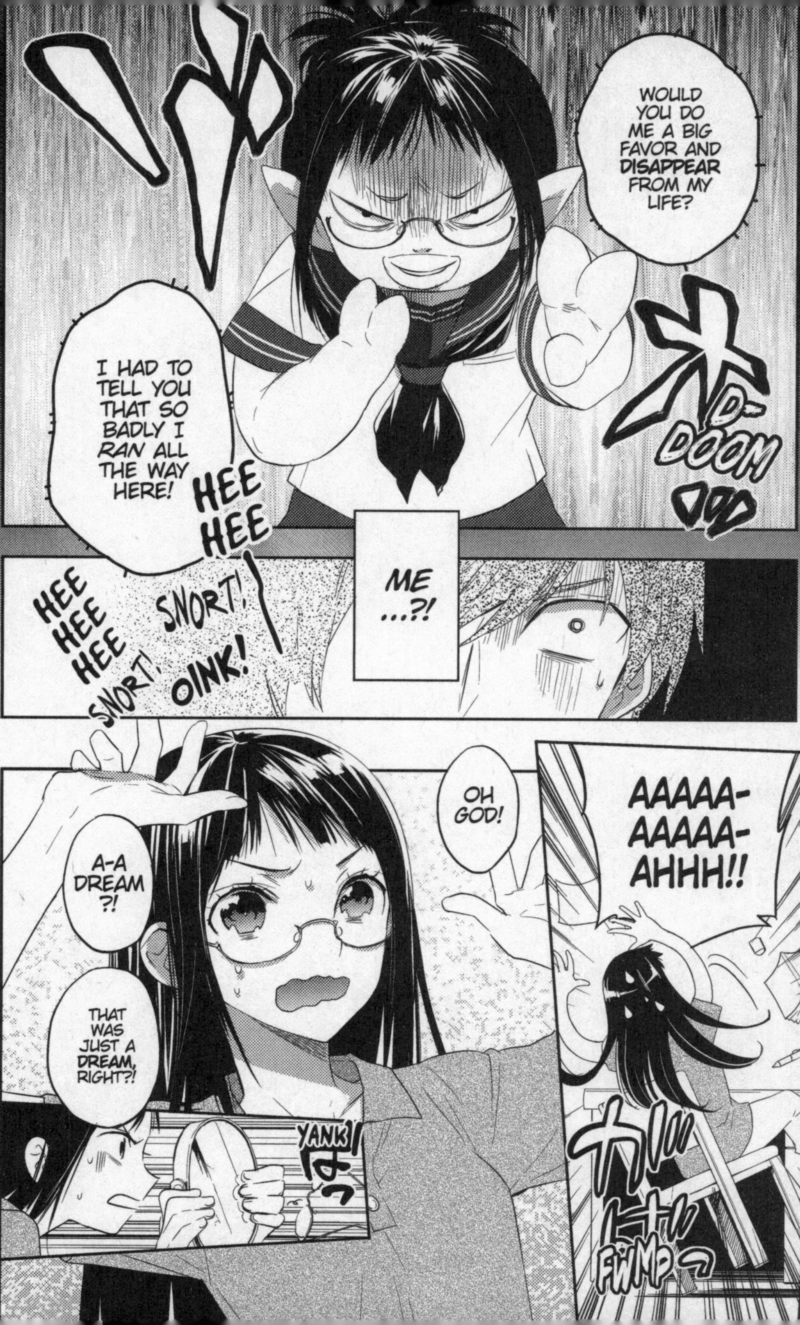
WOULD YOU DO ME A BIG FAVOR AND DISAPPEAR FROM MY LIFE?
D-DOOM
I HAD TO TELL YOU THAT SO BADLY I RAN ALL THE WAY HERE!
HEE HEE
ME ...?!
SNORT! OINK!
HEE HEE HEE SNORT!
AAAAA-AAAAA-AHHH!!
FWIMP
OH GOD!
A-A DREAM ?!
THAT WAS JUST A DREAM, RIGHT?!
YANK!

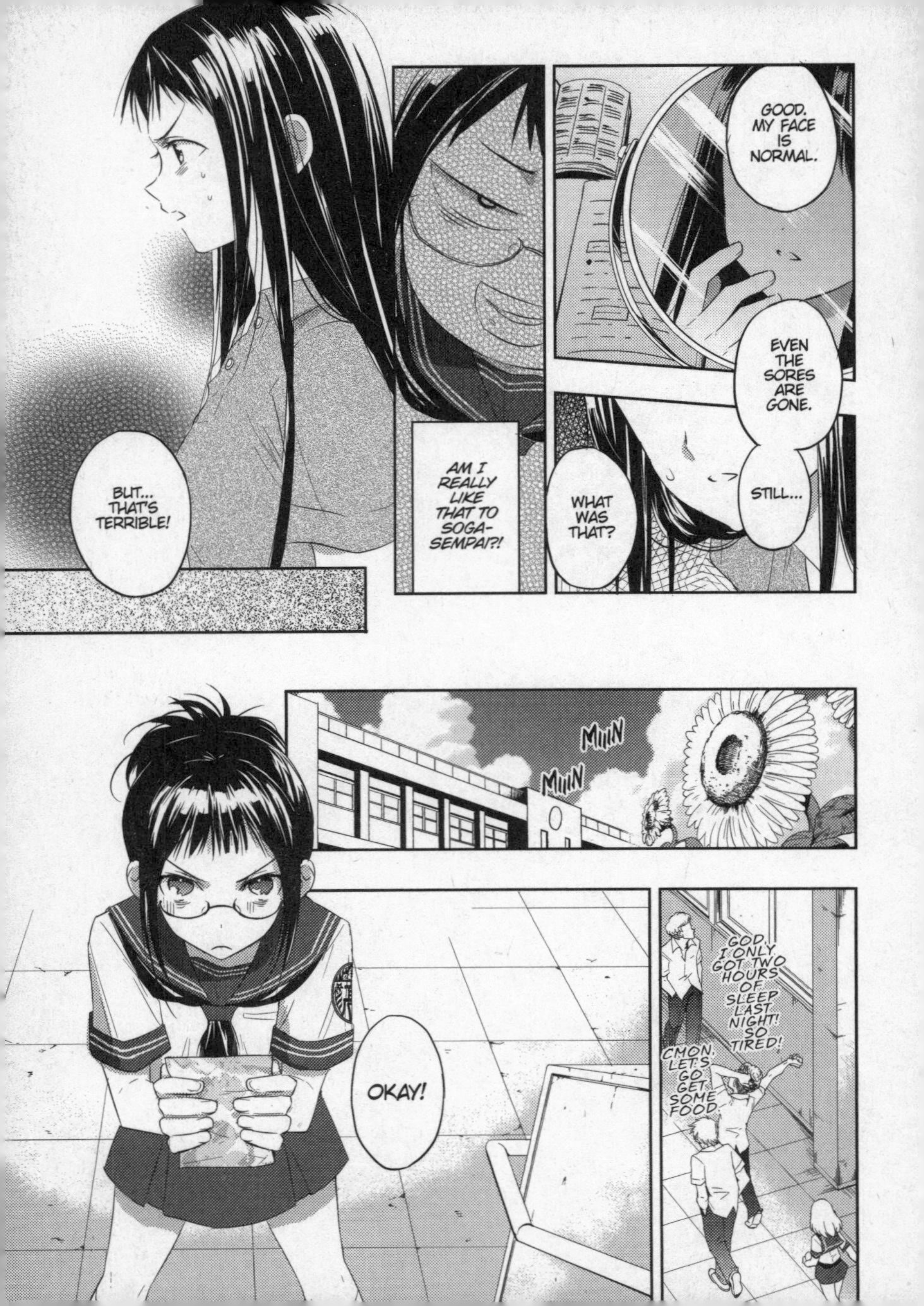
GOOD. MY FACE IS NORMAL.
EVEN THE SORES ARE GONE.
STILL...
WHAT WAS THAT?
AM I REALLY LIKE THAT TO SOGA-SEMPAI?!
BUT... THAT'S TERRIBLE!
MIIIN
MIIIN
GOD, I ONLY GOT TWO HOURS OF SLEEP LAST NIGHT! SO TIRED!
C'MON, LET'S GO GET SOME FOOD.
OKAY!

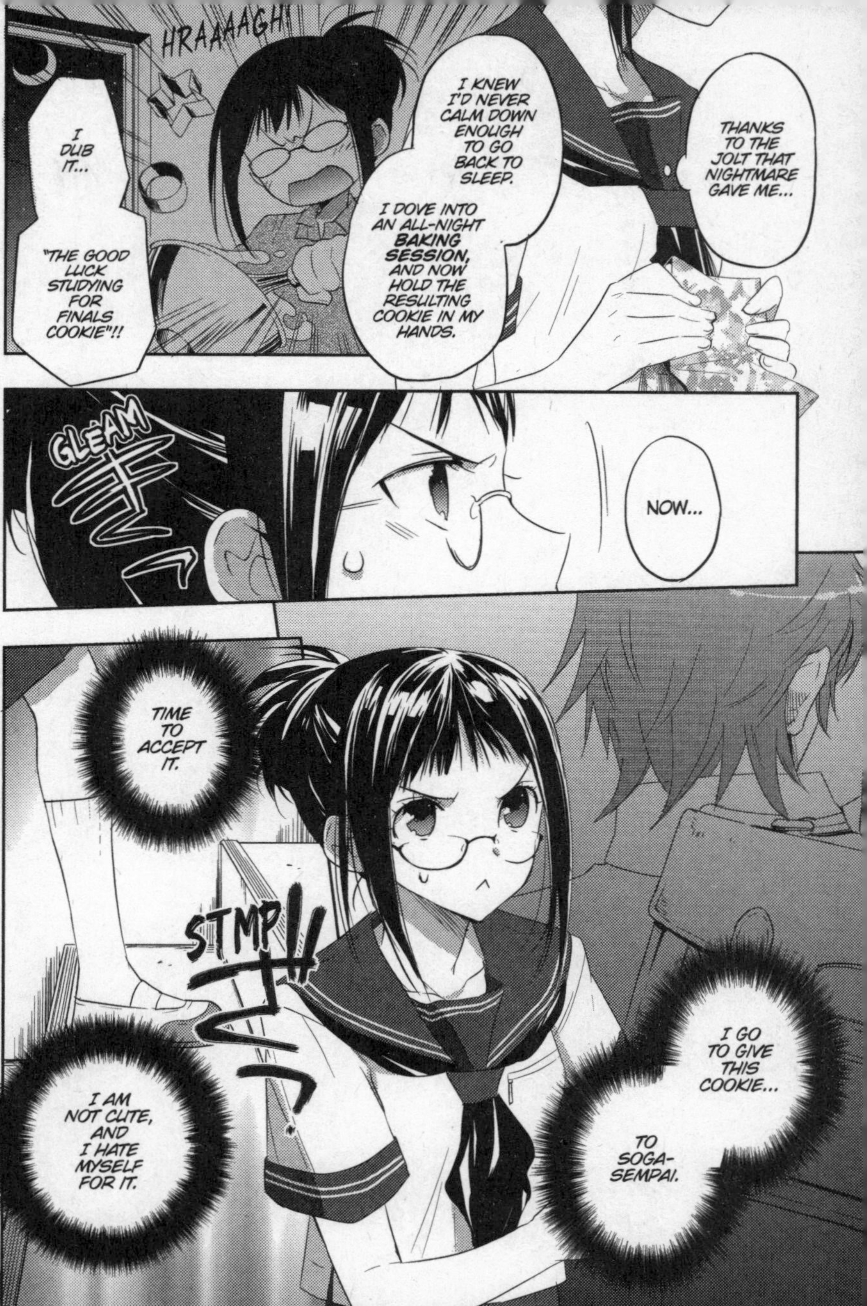
THANKS TO THE JOLT THAT NIGHTMARE GAVE ME...
I KNEW I'D NEVER CALM DOWN ENOUGH TO GO BACK TO SLEEP.
I DOVE INTO AN ALL-NIGHT BAKING SESSION, AND NOW HOLD THE RESULTING COOKIE IN MY HANDS.
HRAAAAGH
I DUB IT...
"THE GOOD LUCK STUDYING FOR FINALS COOKIE"!!
NOW...
GLEAM
TIME TO ACCEPT IT.
I GO TO GIVE THIS COOKIE...
TO SOGA-SEMPAI.
STMP!!
I AM NOT CUTE, AND I HATE MYSELF FOR IT.

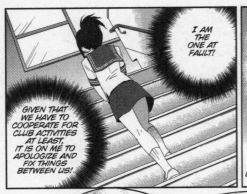

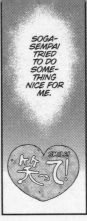

SOGA-SEMPAI TRIED TO DO SOME-THING NICE FOR ME.
笑って!
SMILE!
BUT I RUDELY TURNED MY NOSE UP AT IT, MAKING THINGS AWKWARD BETWEEN US.
I AM THE ONE AT FAULT!
GIVEN THAT WE HAVE TO COOPERATE FOR CLUB ACTIVITIES AT LEAST, IT IS ON ME TO APOLOGIZE AND FIX THINGS BETWEEN US!
SORRY FOR WHAT I DID.
I ACTUALLY REALLY LIKED THE COOKIE. THANK YOU! HAVE THIS IN RETURN!
IT ISN'T NEARLY AS GOOD AS THE ONE YOU BAKED, BUT I COULDN'T STOP MYSELF FROM MAKING IT!
HERE! ENJOY IT WHILE STUDYING FOR FINALS!
YES! JUST LIKE THAT!!
ZING
THOUGH, IT HAS AN UNFORTU-NATE "WHAT THE HECK ARE YOU DOING?" VIBE.
WSH
ANY-WAY!!
I MUST BE HONEST! AND STRAIGHT-FORWARD!!

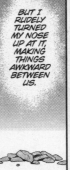

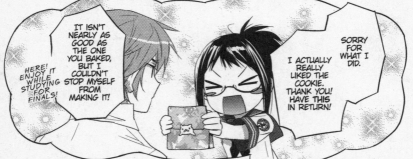

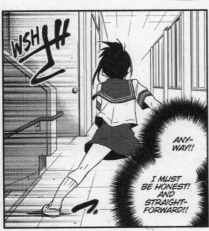

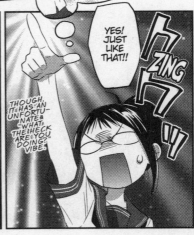

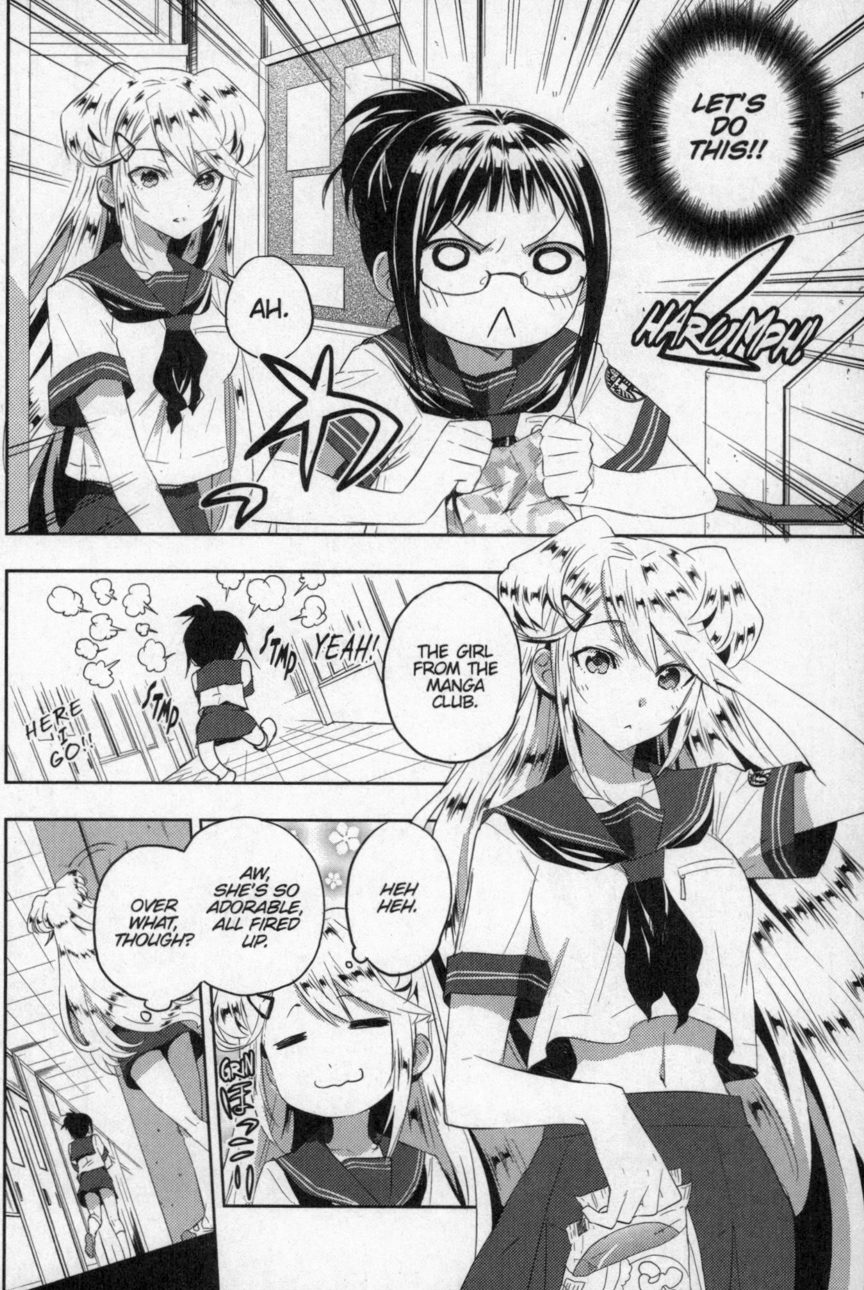
LET'S DO THIS!!
HARUMPH!
AH.
THE GIRL FROM THE MANGA CLUB.
YEAH!
STMP
STMP
HERE I GO!!
HEH HEH.
AW, SHE'S SO ADORABLE, ALL FIRED UP.
OVER WHAT, THOUGH?
GRIN

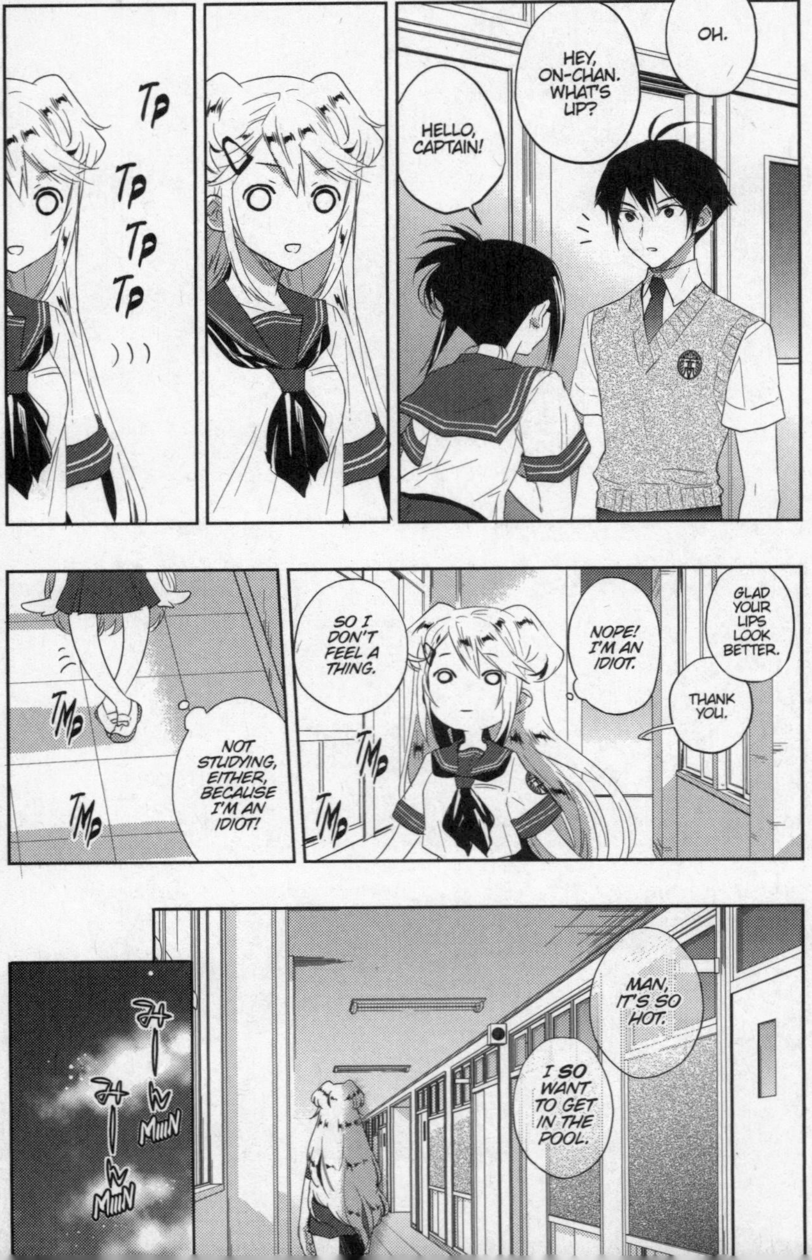
OH.
HEY, ON-CHAN. WHAT'S UP?
HELLO, CAPTAIN!
Tp
Tp
Tp
Tp
GLAD YOUR LIPS LOOK BETTER.
THANK YOU.
NOPE! I'M AN IDIOT.
SO I DON'T FEEL A THING.
TMP
TMP
NOT STUDYING, EITHER, BECAUSE I'M AN IDIOT!
TMP
TMP
MAN, IT'S SO HOT.
I SO WANT TO GET IN THE POOL.
みーん MIIIN
みーん MIIIN

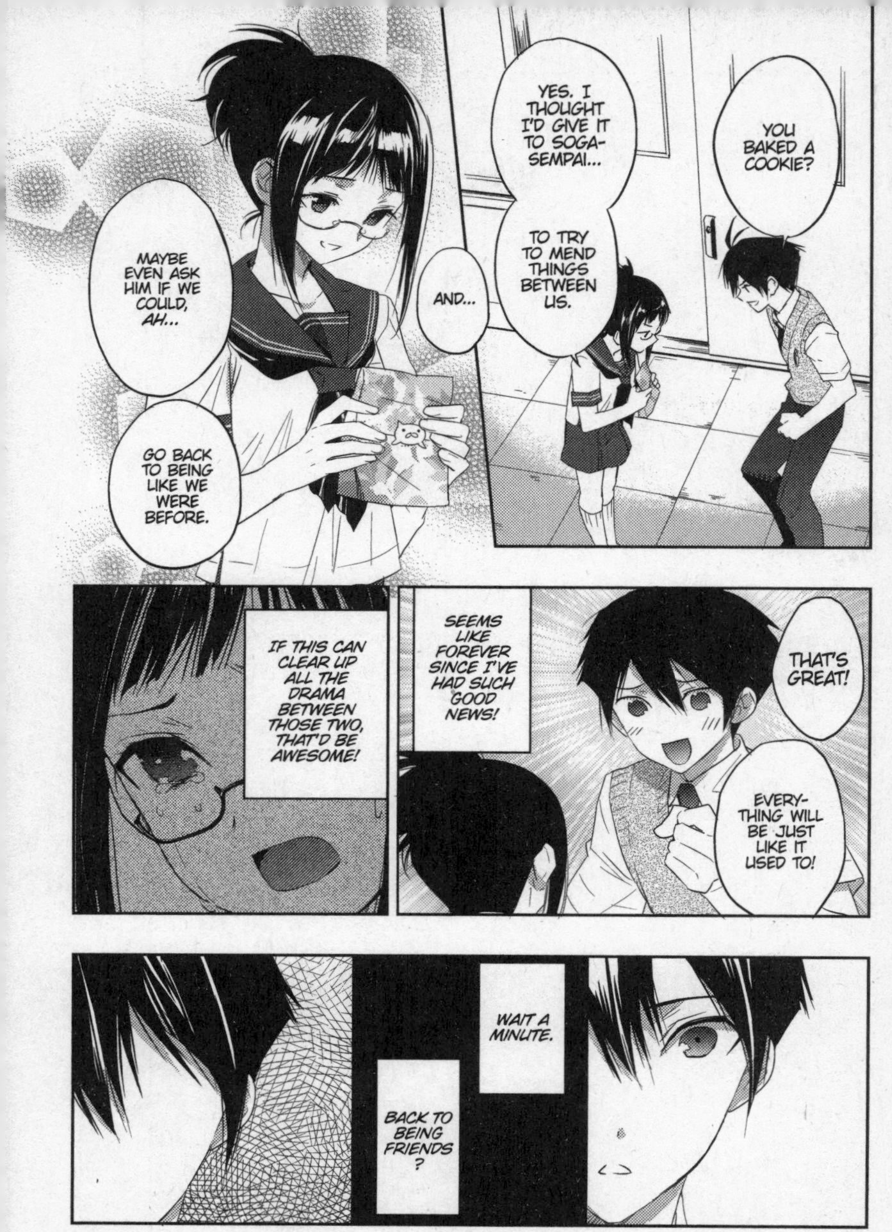
YOU BAKED A COOKIE?
YES. I THOUGHT I'D GIVE IT TO SOGA-SEMPAI...
TO TRY TO MEND THINGS BETWEEN US.
AND...
MAYBE EVEN ASK HIM IF WE COULD, AH...
GO BACK TO BEING LIKE WE WERE BEFORE.
THAT'S GREAT!
SEEMS LIKE FOREVER SINCE I'VE HAD SUCH GOOD NEWS!
EVERY-THING WILL BE JUST LIKE IT USED TO!
IF THIS CAN CLEAR UP ALL THE DRAMA BETWEEN THOSE TWO, THAT'D BE AWESOME!
WAIT A MINUTE.
BACK TO BEING FRIENDS ?

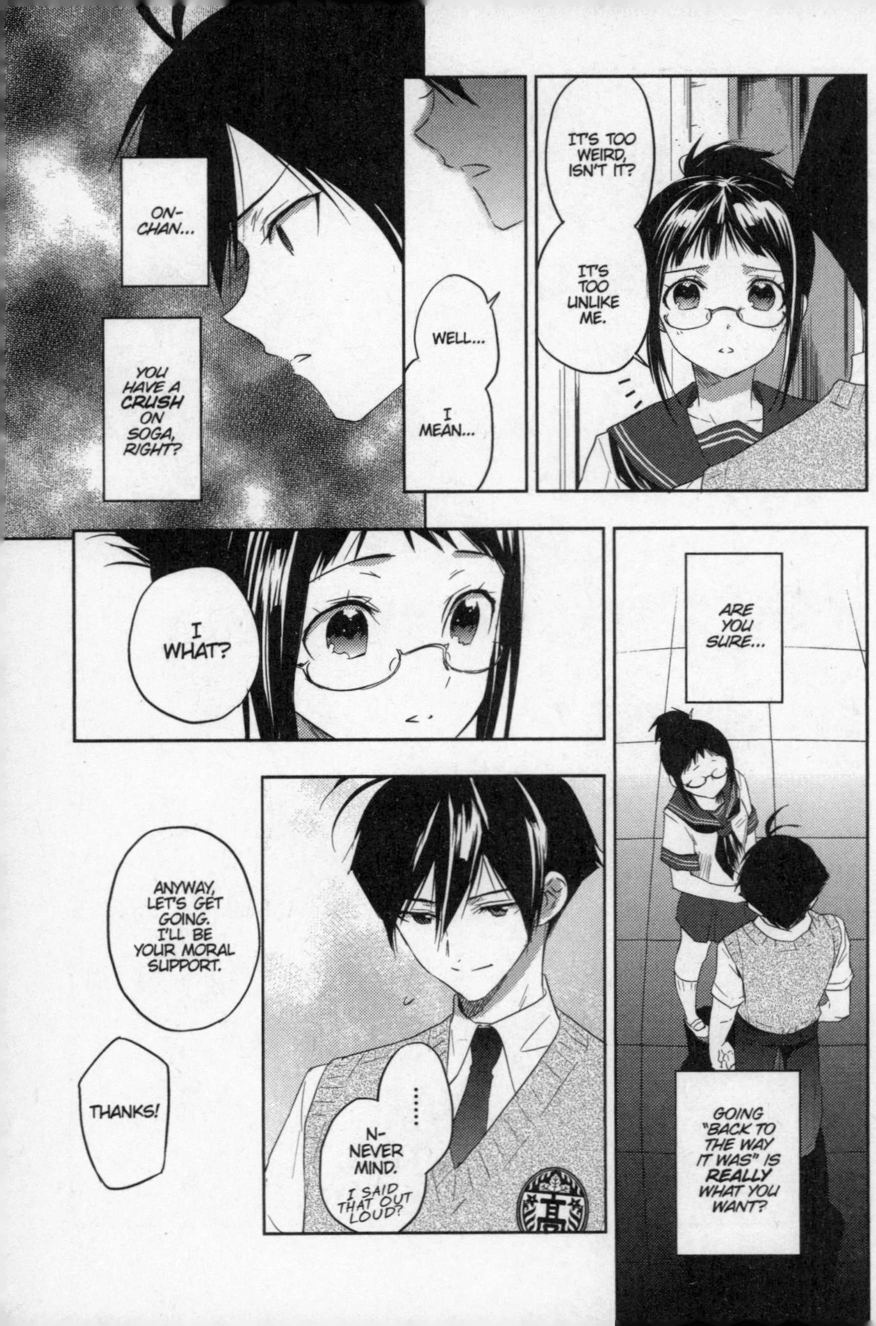
IT'S TOO WEIRD, ISN'T IT?
IT'S TOO UNLIKE ME.
WELL...
I MEAN...
ON-CHAN...
YOU HAVE A **CRUSH** ON SOGA, RIGHT?
ARE YOU SURE...
GOING "BACK TO THE WAY IT WAS" IS **REALLY** WHAT YOU WANT?
I WHAT?
......
N-NEVER MIND.
I SAID THAT OUT LOUD?
ANYWAY, LET'S GET GOING. I'LL BE YOUR MORAL SUPPORT.
THANKS!

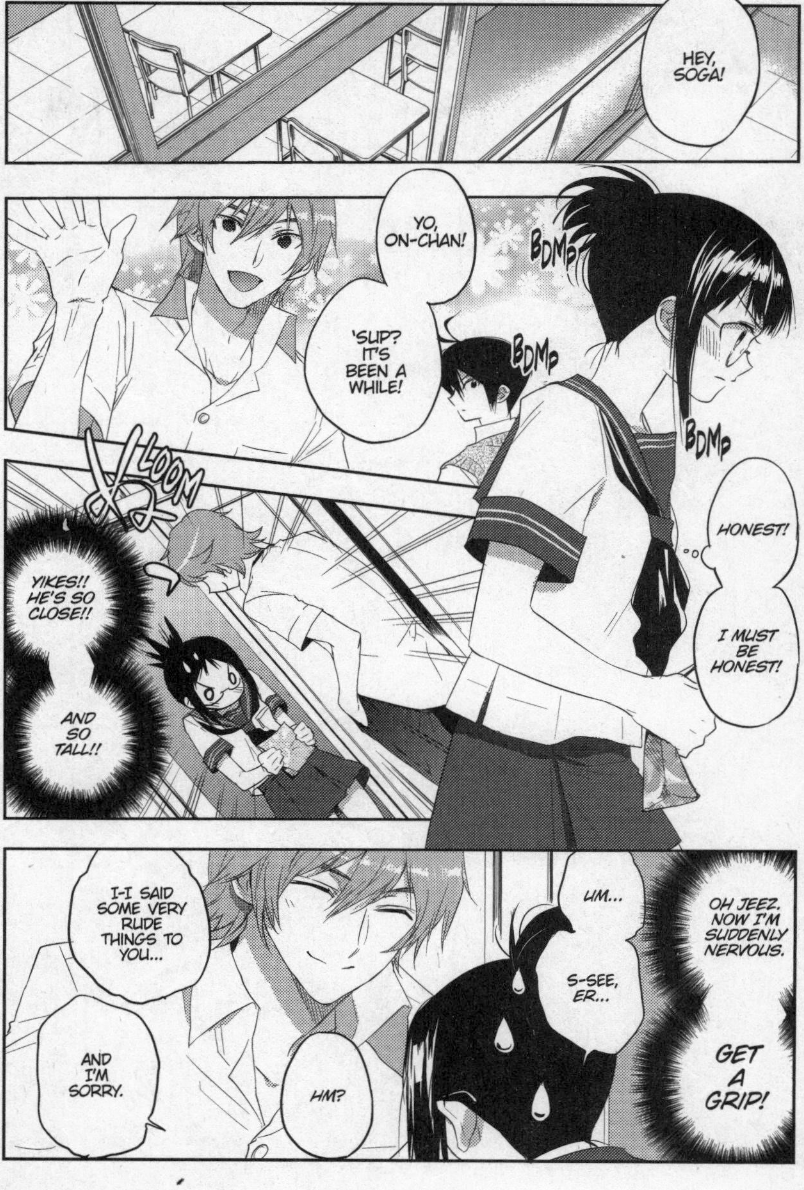
HEY, SOGA!
BDMP
YO, ON-CHAN!
BDMP
'SUP? IT'S BEEN A WHILE!
BDMP
HONEST!
I MUST BE HONEST!
KLOOM
YIKES!! HE'S SO CLOSE!!
AND SO TALL!!
OH JEEZ. NOW I'M SUDDENLY NERVOUS.
GET A GRIP!
UM...
S-SEE, ER...
HM?
I-I SAID SOME VERY RUDE THINGS TO YOU...
AND I'M SORRY.

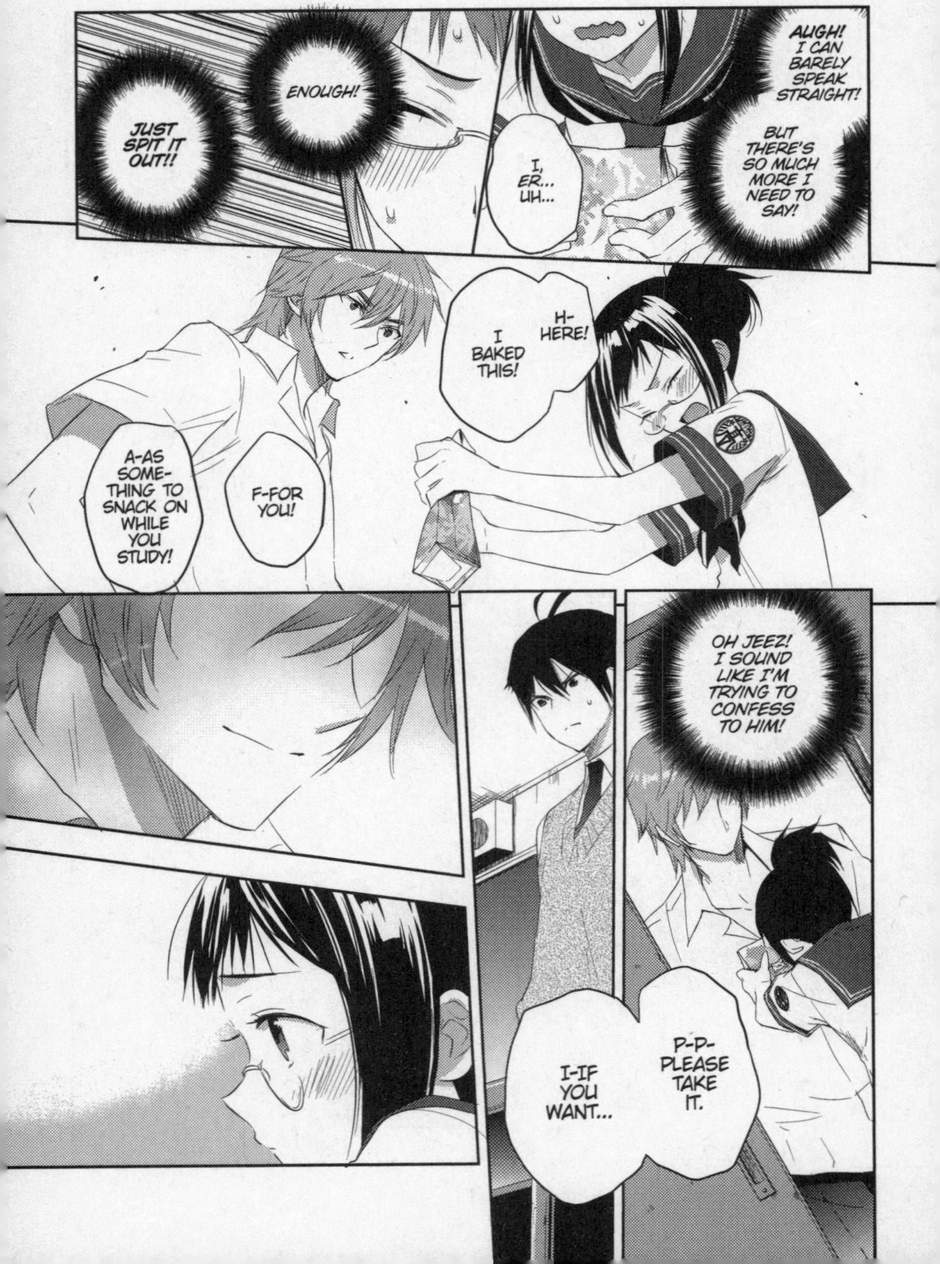
AUGH! I CAN BARELY SPEAK STRAIGHT!
BUT THERE'S SO MUCH MORE I NEED TO SAY!
I, ER... UH...
ENOUGH!
JUST SPIT IT OUT!!
H-HERE!
I BAKED THIS!
F-FOR YOU!
A-AS SOME-THING TO SNACK ON WHILE YOU STUDY!
OH JEEZ! I SOUND LIKE I'M TRYING TO CONFESS TO HIM!
P-P-PLEASE TAKE IT.
I-IF YOU WANT...

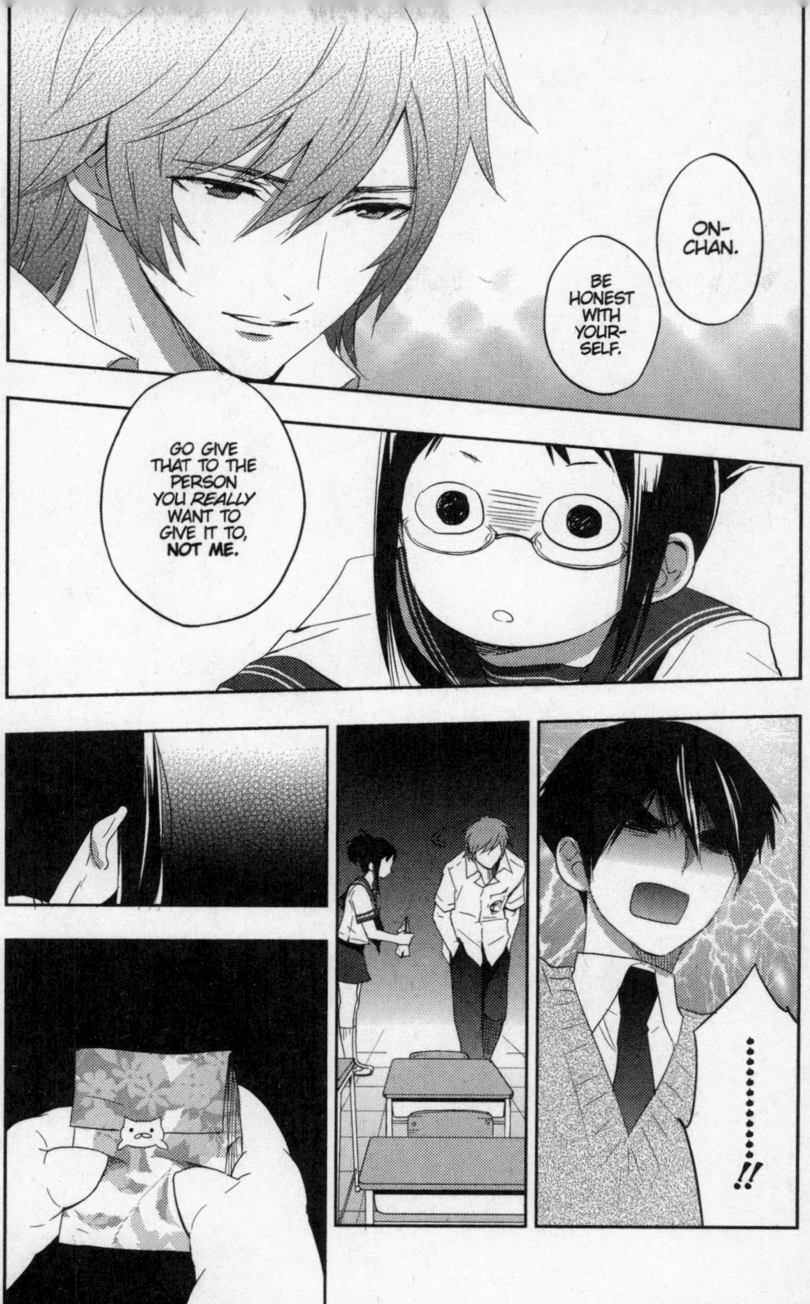
ON-CHAN.
BE HONEST WITH YOUR-SELF.
GO GIVE THAT TO THE PERSON YOU *REALLY* WANT TO GIVE IT TO, **NOT ME.**
..........!!

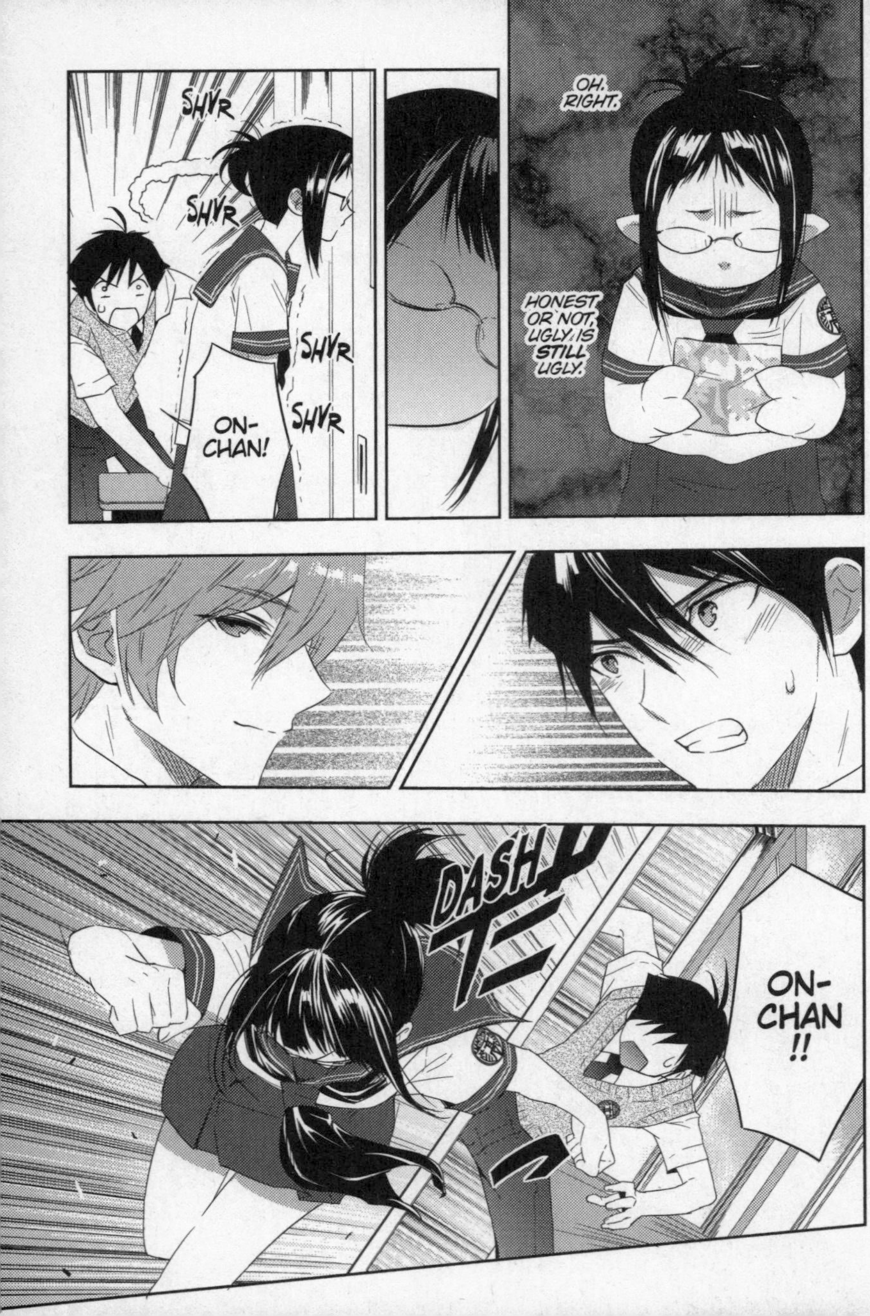
OH. RIGHT.
HONEST OR NOT, UGLY IS STILL UGLY.
SHVR
SHVR
SHVR
SHVR
ON-CHAN!
DASH
ON-CHAN !!

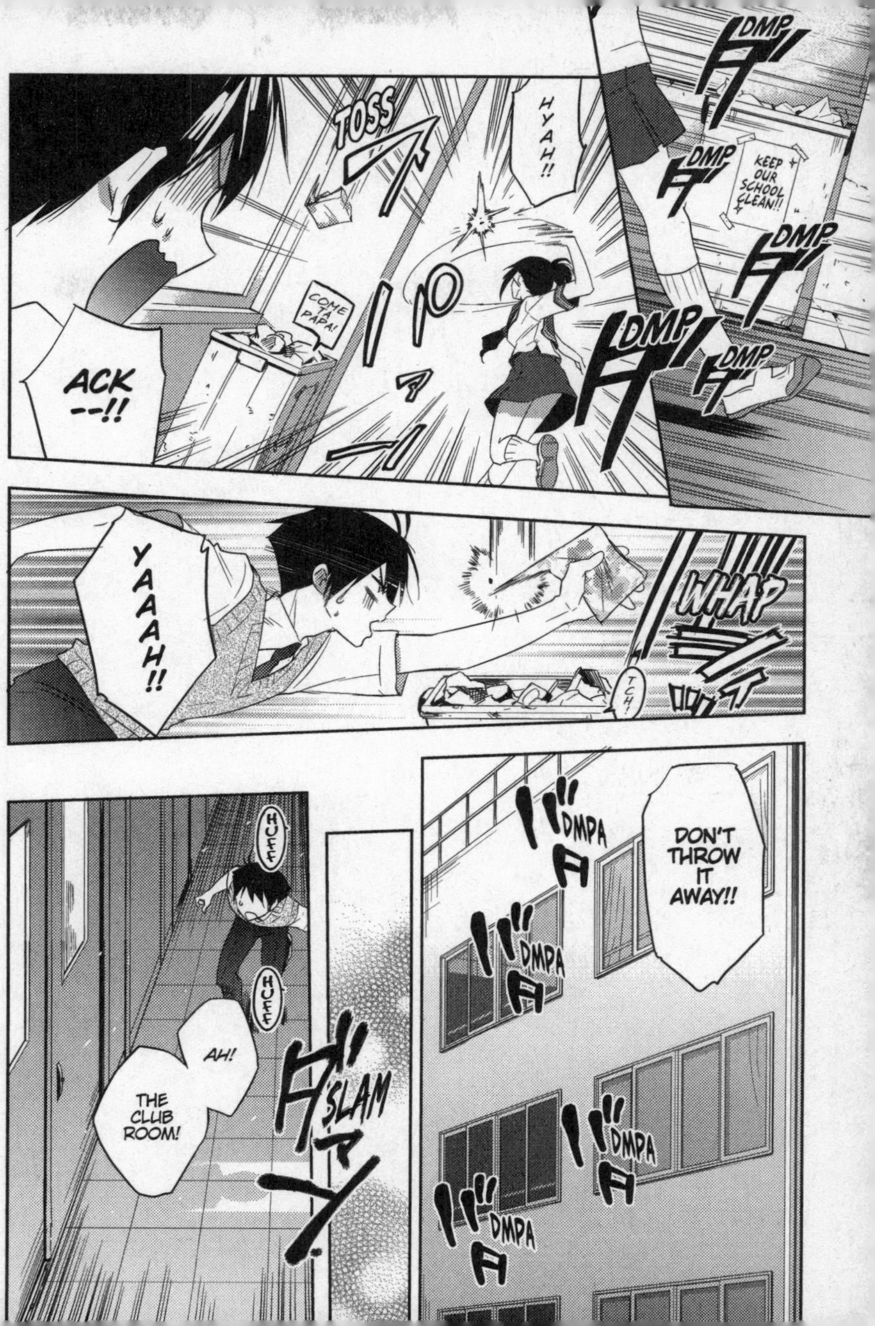
DMP
DMP
KEEP OUR SCHOOL CLEAN!!
DMP
DMP
DMP
HYAH!!
TOSS
COME TA PAPA!
ACK --!!
WHAP
TCH!
YAAAAH!!
DON'T THROW IT AWAY!!
DMPA
DMPA
DMPA
DMPA
HUFF
HUFF
SLAM
AH!
THE CLUB ROOM!

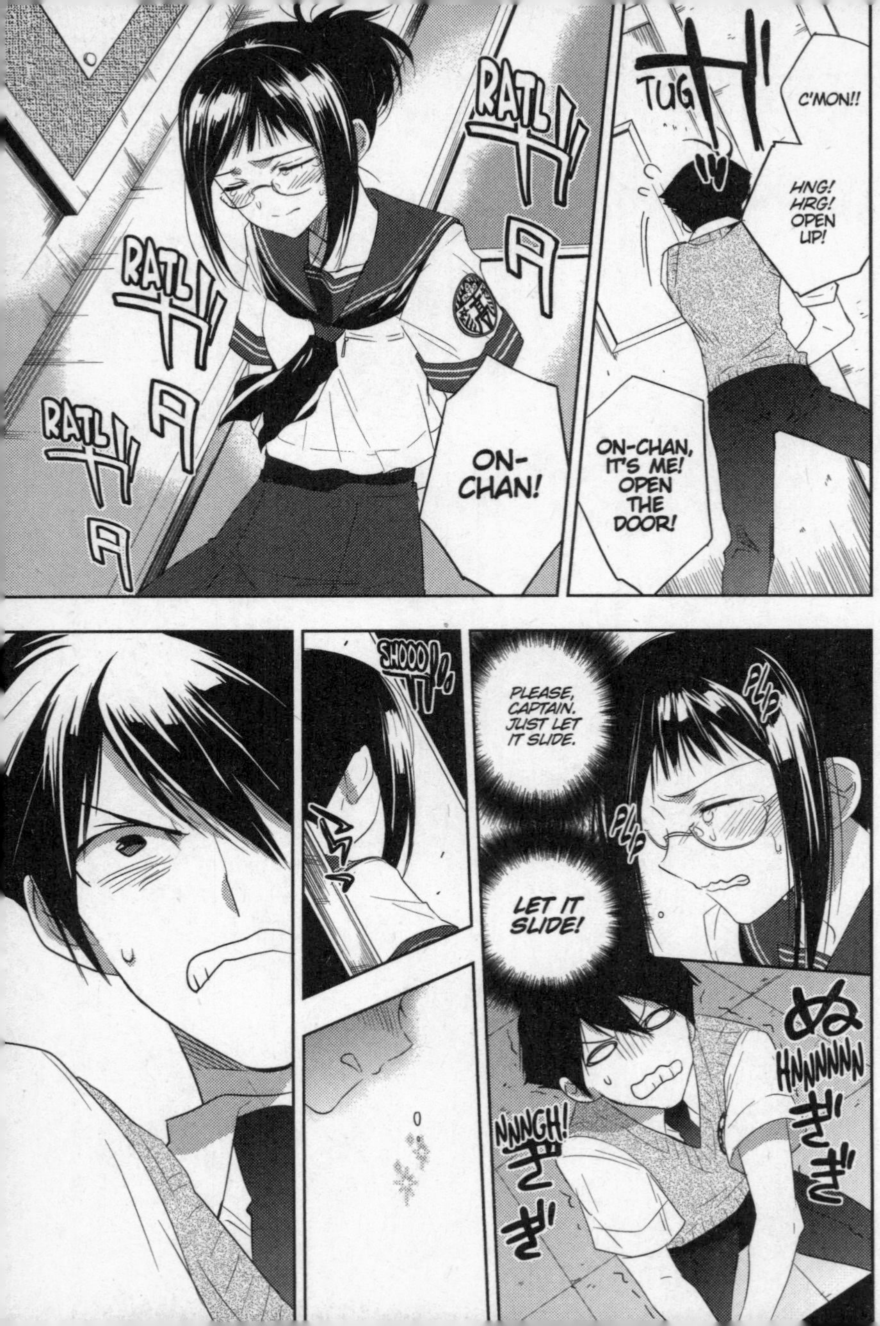
TUG
C'MON!!
HNG! HRG! OPEN UP!
ON-CHAN, IT'S ME! OPEN THE DOOR!
RATL
ON-CHAN!
RATL
RATL
PLIP
PLEASE, CAPTAIN. JUST LET IT SLIDE.
PLIP
LET IT SLIDE!
ぬぎぎ
HNNNNNN
NNNGH!
ぎぎ
SHOOO

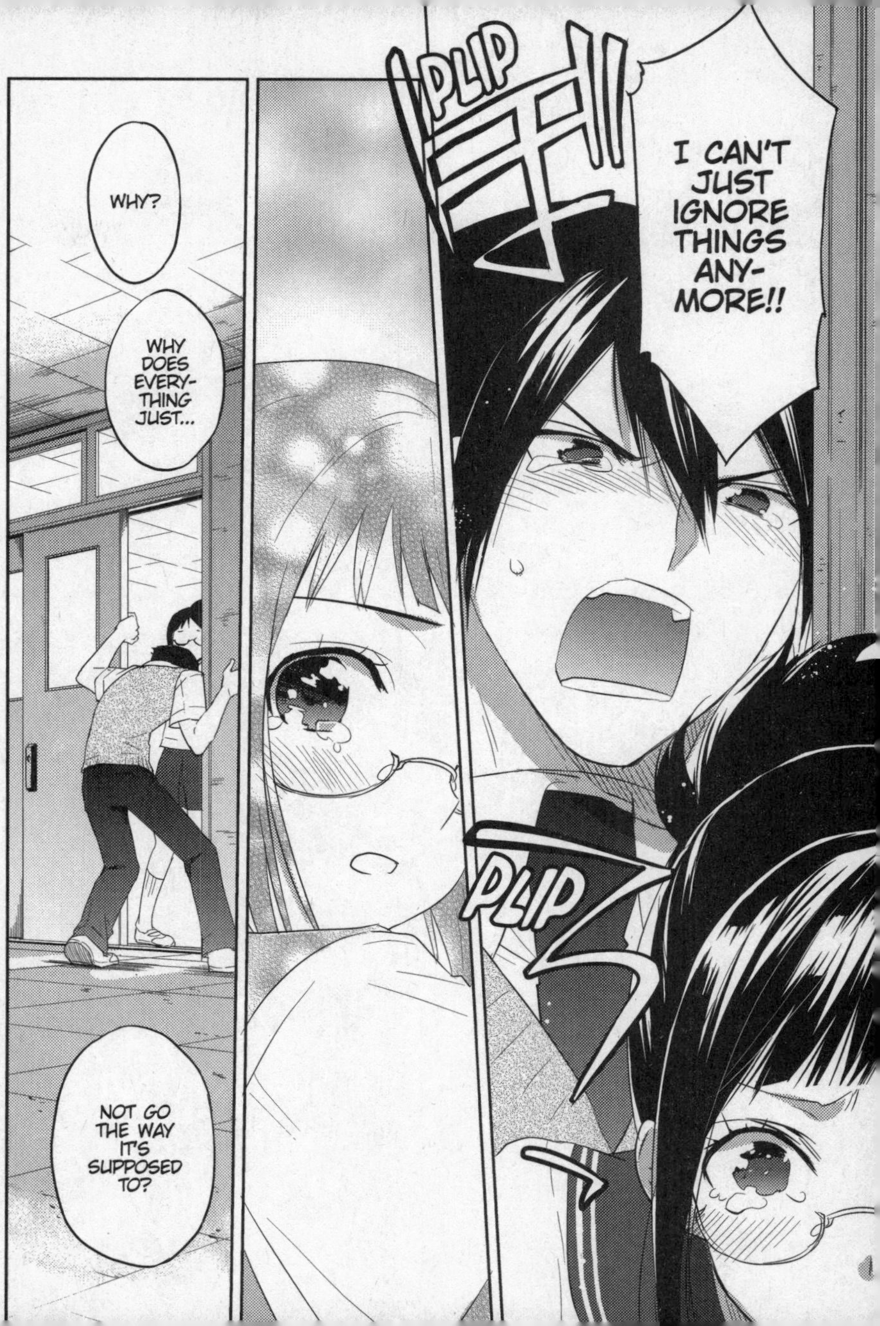
PLIP
I CAN'T JUST IGNORE THINGS ANY-MORE!!
PLIP
WHY?
WHY DOES EVERY-THING JUST...
NOT GO THE WAY IT'S SUPPOSED TO?

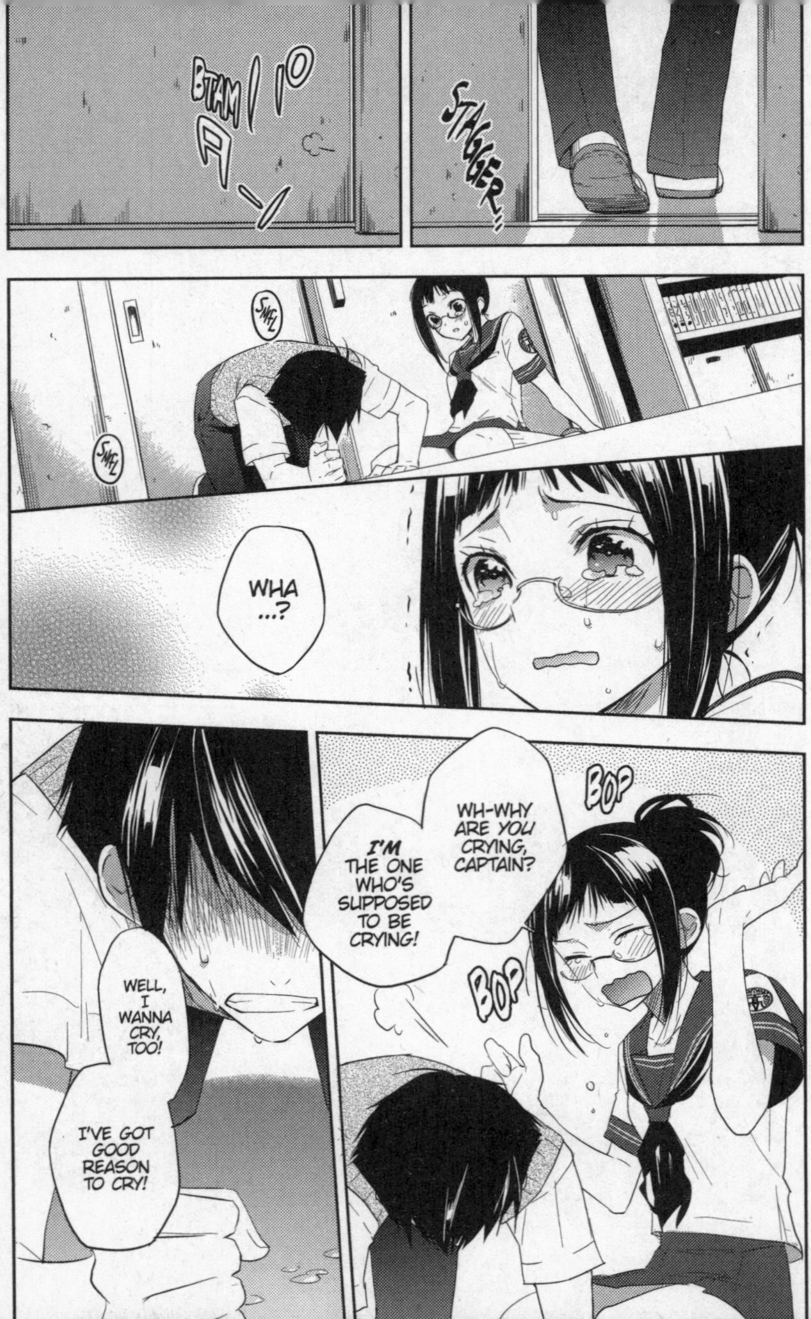
STAGGER..!!
BTAM
SNIFL
SNIFL
WHA ...?
BOP
WH-WHY ARE *YOU* CRYING, CAPTAIN?
*I'M* THE ONE WHO'S SUPPOSED TO BE CRYING!
BOP
WELL, I WANNA CRY, TOO!
I'VE GOT GOOD REASON TO CRY!

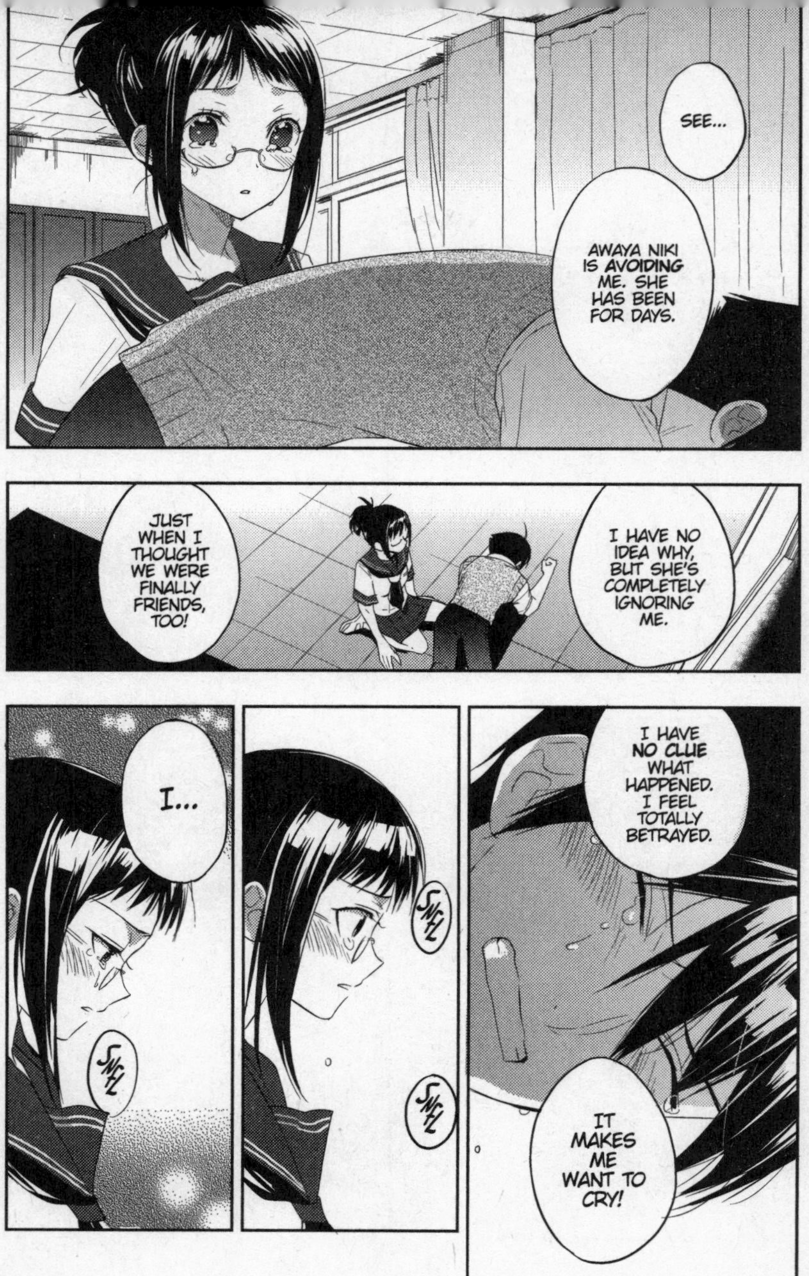
SEE...
AWAYA NIKI IS AVOIDING ME. SHE HAS BEEN FOR DAYS.
I HAVE NO IDEA WHY, BUT SHE'S COMPLETELY IGNORING ME.
JUST WHEN I THOUGHT WE WERE FINALLY FRIENDS, TOO!
I HAVE NO CLUE WHAT HAPPENED. I FEEL TOTALLY BETRAYED.
IT MAKES ME WANT TO CRY!
SNFL
SNFL
I...
SNFL

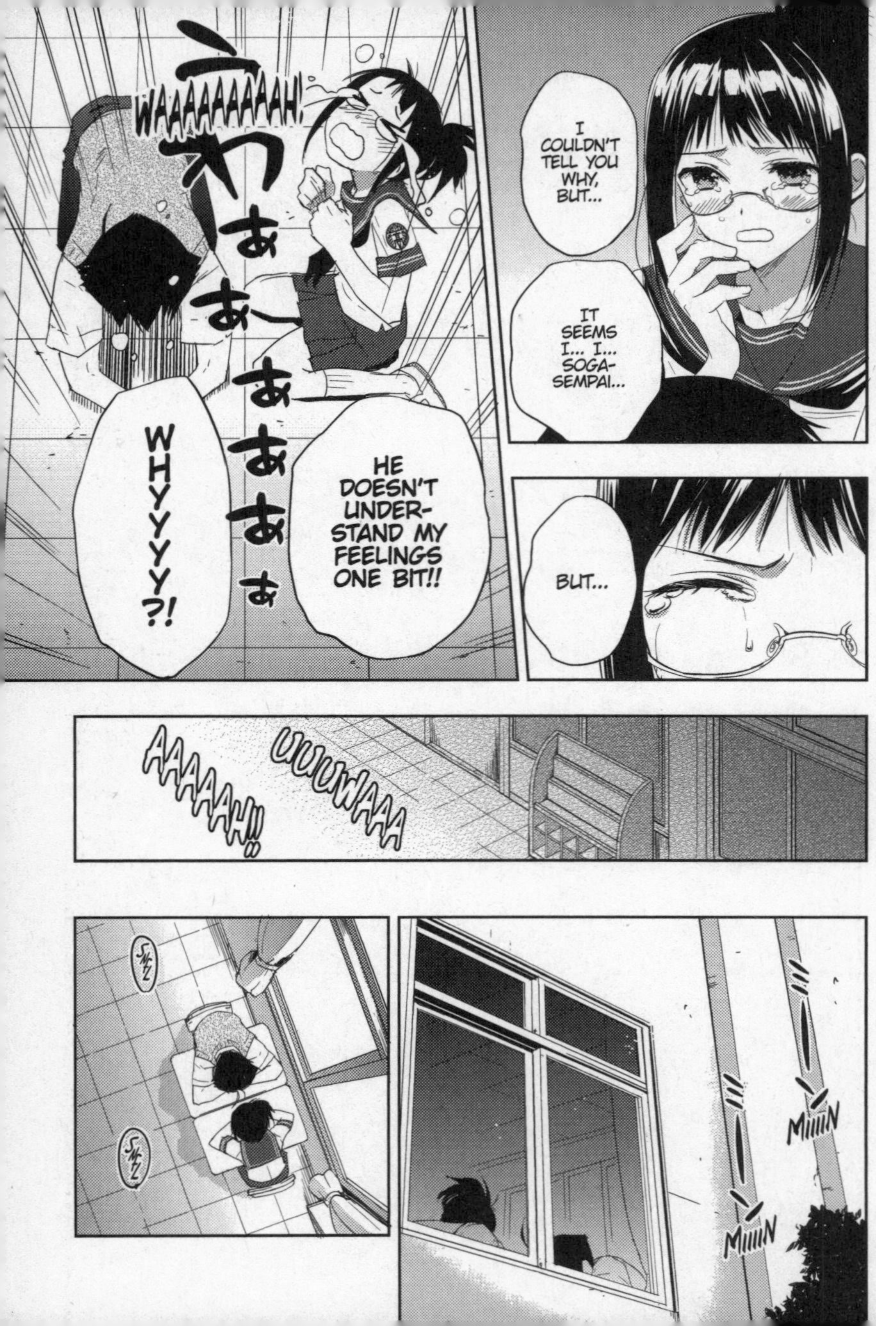
I COULDN'T TELL YOU WHY, BUT...
IT SEEMS I... I... SOGA-SEMPAI...
BUT...
WAAAAAAAAAH!
うわぁあーあーあああぁ
HE DOESN'T UNDERSTAND MY FEELINGS ONE BIT!!
WHYYYYY?!
UUUWAAAA
AAAAAAH!!
MiiiiN
MiiiiN

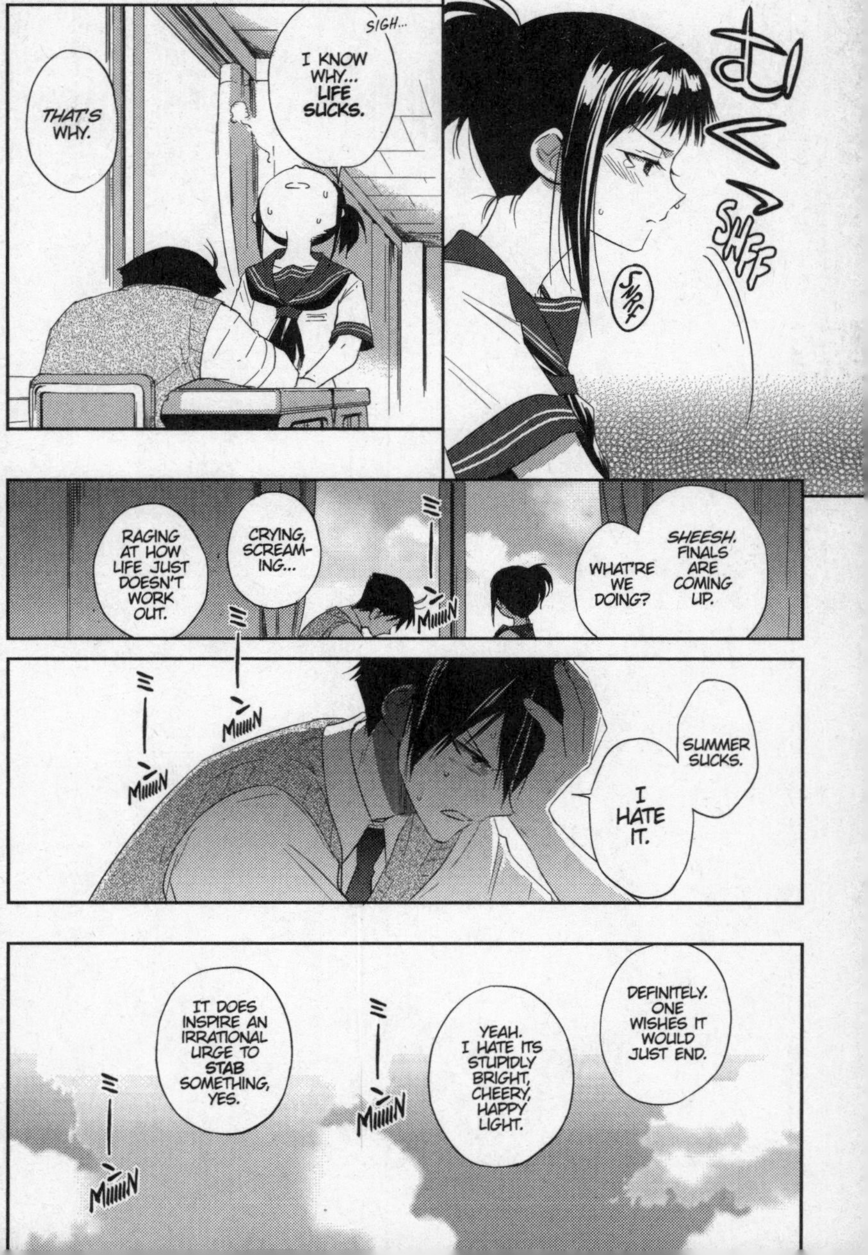
SHFF
SNRF
SIGH...
I KNOW WHY... LIFE SUCKS.
THAT'S WHY.
SHEESH. FINALS ARE COMING UP.
WHAT'RE WE DOING?
MIIIIN
CRYING, SCREAMING...
RAGING AT HOW LIFE JUST DOESN'T WORK OUT.
MIIIIN
SUMMER SUCKS.
I HATE IT.
MIIIIN
DEFINITELY. ONE WISHES IT WOULD JUST END.
YEAH. I HATE ITS STUPIDLY BRIGHT, CHEERY, HAPPY LIGHT.
MIIIIN
IT DOES INSPIRE AN IRRATIONAL URGE TO STAB SOMETHING, YES.
MIIIIN

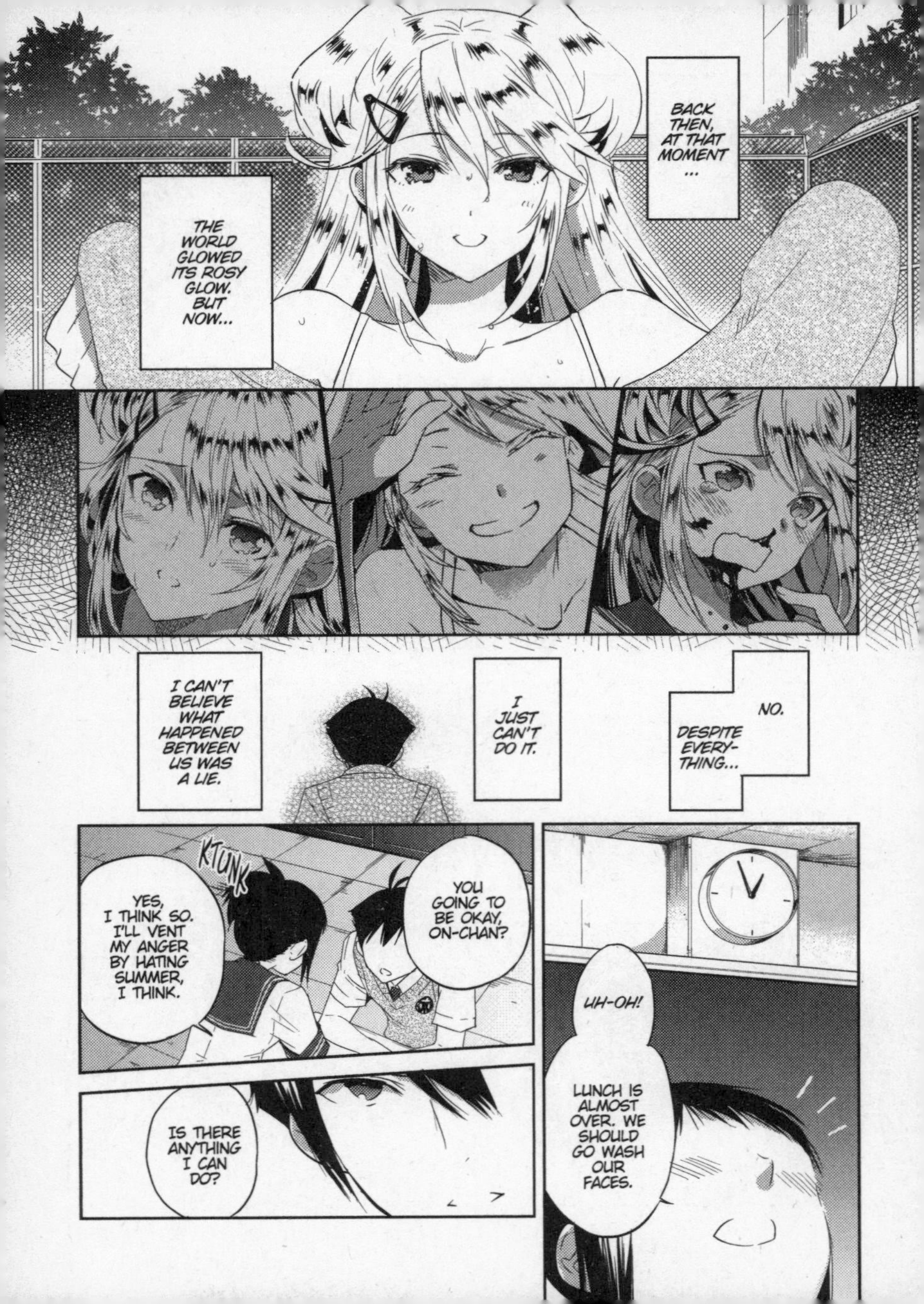
BACK THEN, AT THAT MOMENT ...
THE WORLD GLOWED ITS ROSY GLOW. BUT NOW...
NO.
DESPITE EVERYTHING...
I JUST CAN'T DO IT.
I CAN'T BELIEVE WHAT HAPPENED BETWEEN US WAS A LIE.
KTUNK
YOU GOING TO BE OKAY, ON-CHAN?
YES, I THINK SO. I'LL VENT MY ANGER BY HATING SUMMER, I THINK.
IS THERE ANYTHING I CAN DO?
UH-OH!
LUNCH IS ALMOST OVER. WE SHOULD GO WASH OUR FACES.

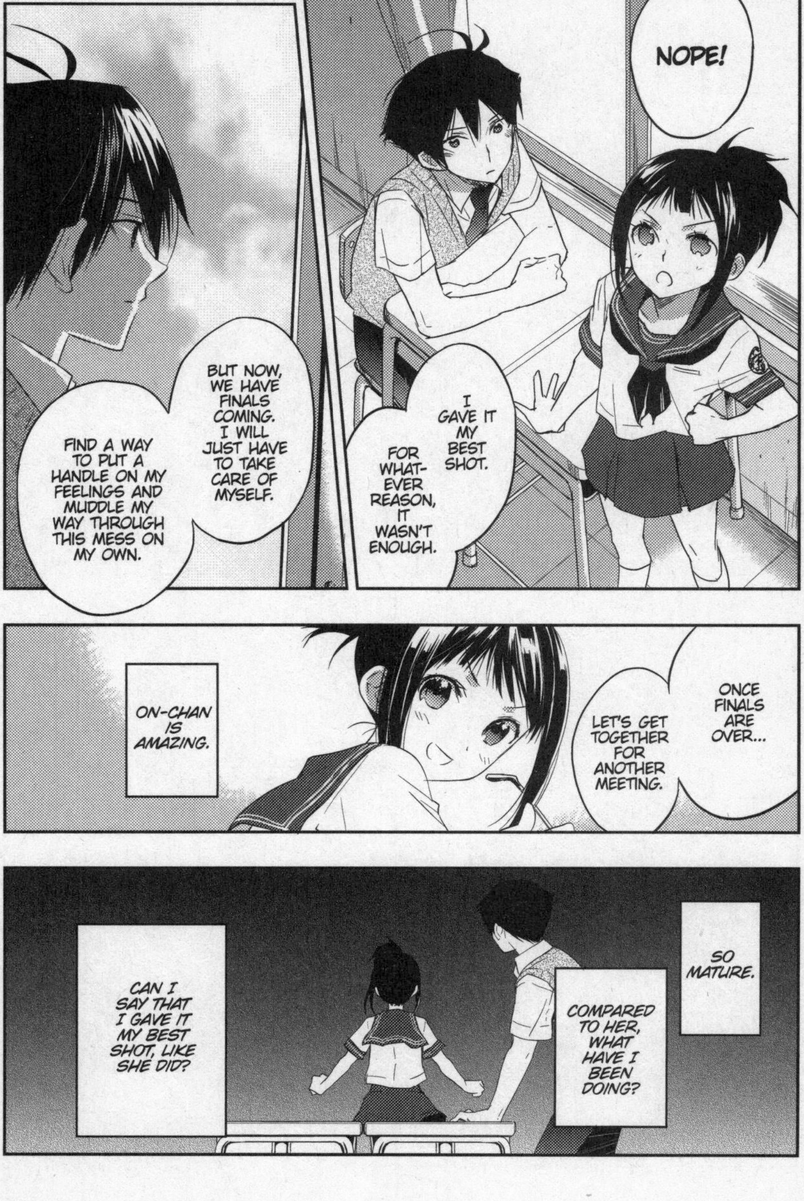
NOPE!
I GAVE IT MY BEST SHOT.
FOR WHAT-EVER REASON, IT WASN'T ENOUGH.
BUT NOW, WE HAVE FINALS COMING. I WILL JUST HAVE TO TAKE CARE OF MYSELF.
FIND A WAY TO PUT A HANDLE ON MY FEELINGS AND MUDDLE MY WAY THROUGH THIS MESS ON MY OWN.
ONCE FINALS ARE OVER...
LET'S GET TOGETHER FOR ANOTHER MEETING.
ON-CHAN IS AMAZING.
SO MATURE.
COMPARED TO HER, WHAT HAVE I BEEN DOING?
CAN I SAY THAT I GAVE IT MY BEST SHOT, LIKE SHE DID?

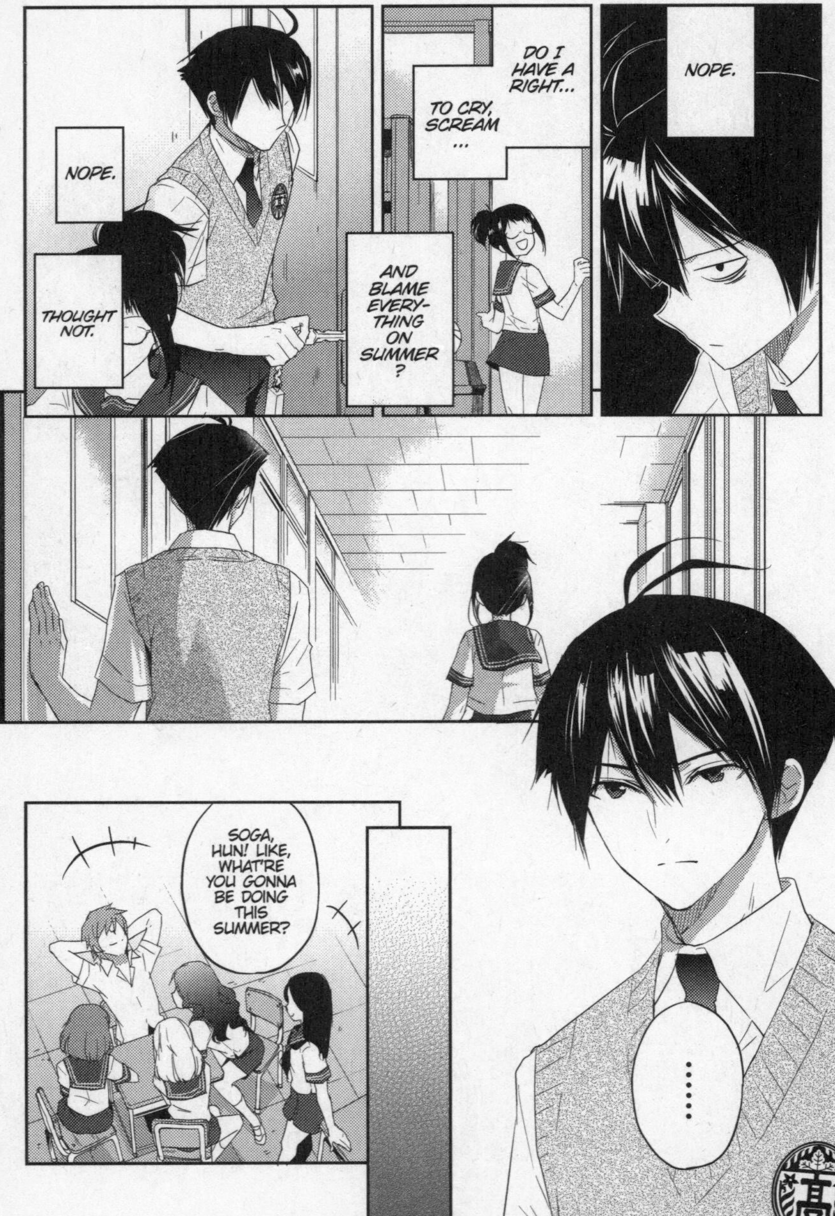
NOPE.
DO I HAVE A RIGHT...
TO CRY, SCREAM ...
AND BLAME EVERY-THING ON SUMMER?
NOPE.
THOUGHT NOT.
……
SOGA, HUN! LIKE, WHAT'RE YOU GONNA BE DOING THIS SUMMER?

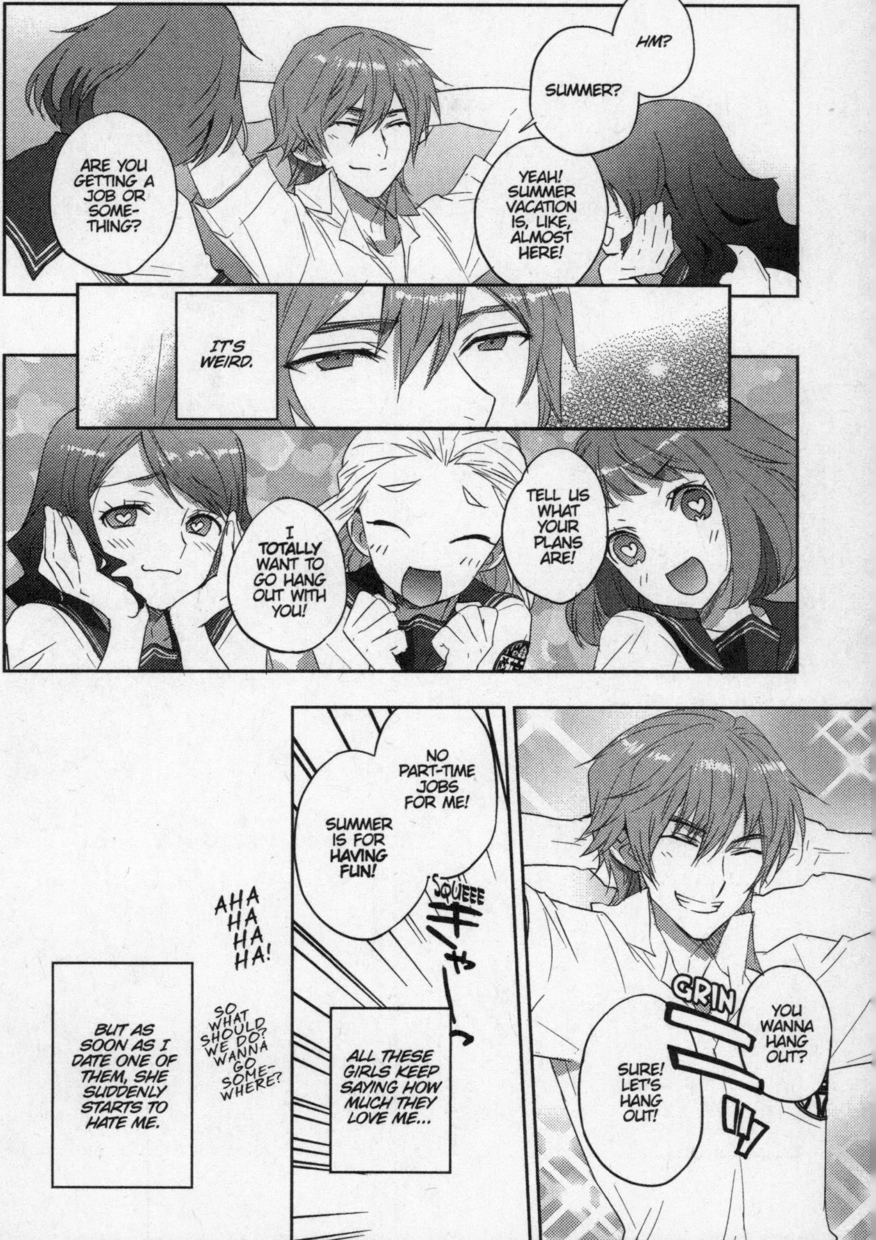
HM?
SUMMER?
YEAH! SUMMER VACATION IS, LIKE, ALMOST HERE!
ARE YOU GETTING A JOB OR SOME-THING?
IT'S WEIRD.
TELL US WHAT YOUR PLANS ARE!
I TOTALLY WANT TO GO HANG OUT WITH YOU!
GRIN
YOU WANNA HANG OUT?
SURE! LET'S HANG OUT!
NO PART-TIME JOBS FOR ME!
SUMMER IS FOR HAVING FUN!
SQUEEE
ALL THESE GIRLS KEEP SAYING HOW MUCH THEY LOVE ME...
AHA HA HA HA!
SO WHAT SHOULD WE DO? WANNA GO SOME-WHERE?
BUT AS SOON AS I DATE ONE OF THEM, SHE SUDDENLY STARTS TO HATE ME.

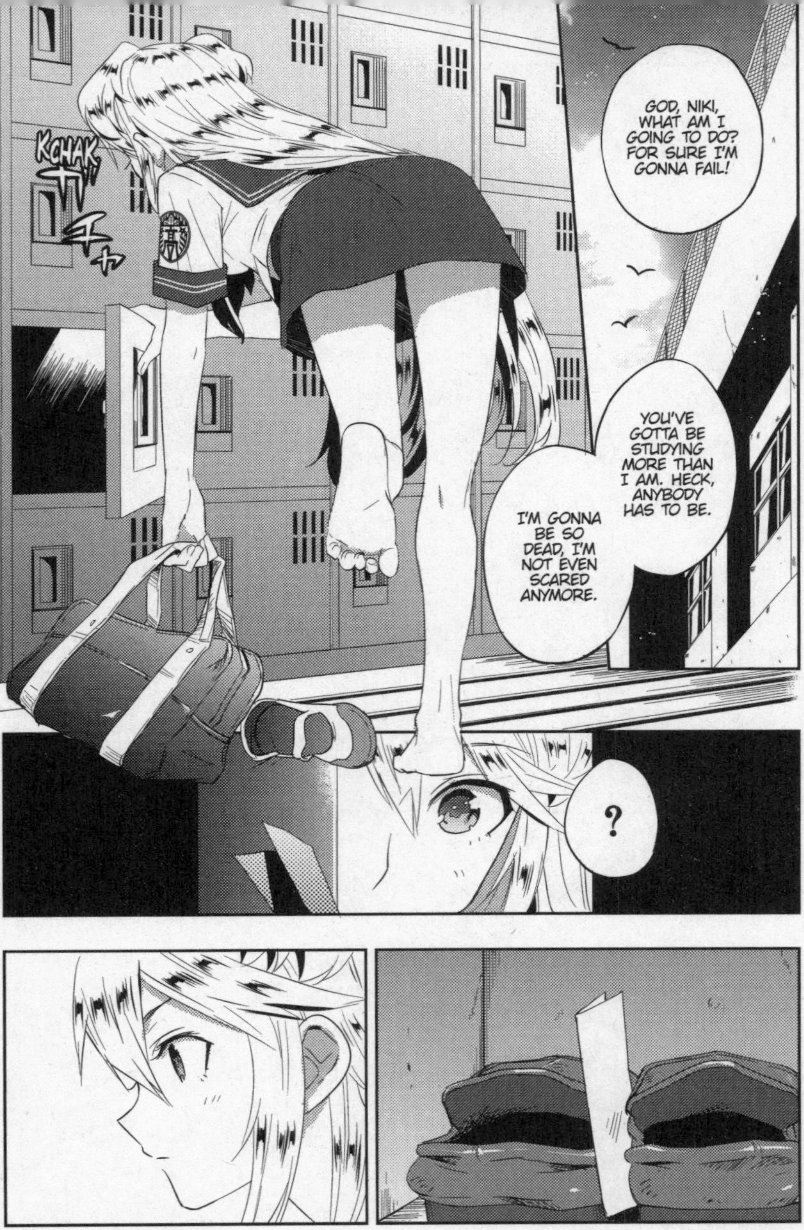
GOD, NIKI, WHAT AM I GOING TO DO? FOR SURE I'M GONNA FAIL!
YOU'VE GOTTA BE STUDYING MORE THAN I AM. HECK, ANYBODY HAS TO BE.
I'M GONNA BE SO DEAD, I'M NOT EVEN SCARED ANYMORE.
KCHAK
ガチャ
?

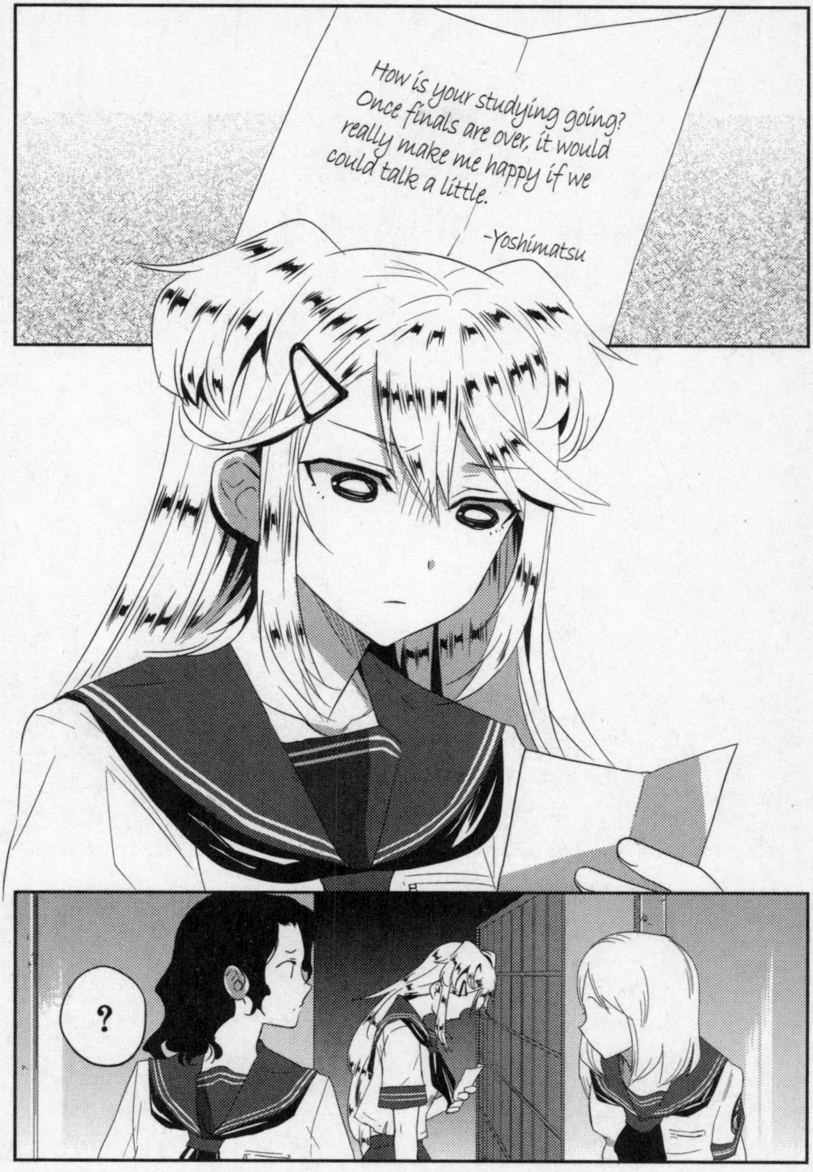
How is your studying going? Once finals are over, it would really make me happy if we could talk a little.
-Yoshimatsu
?

To be continued...

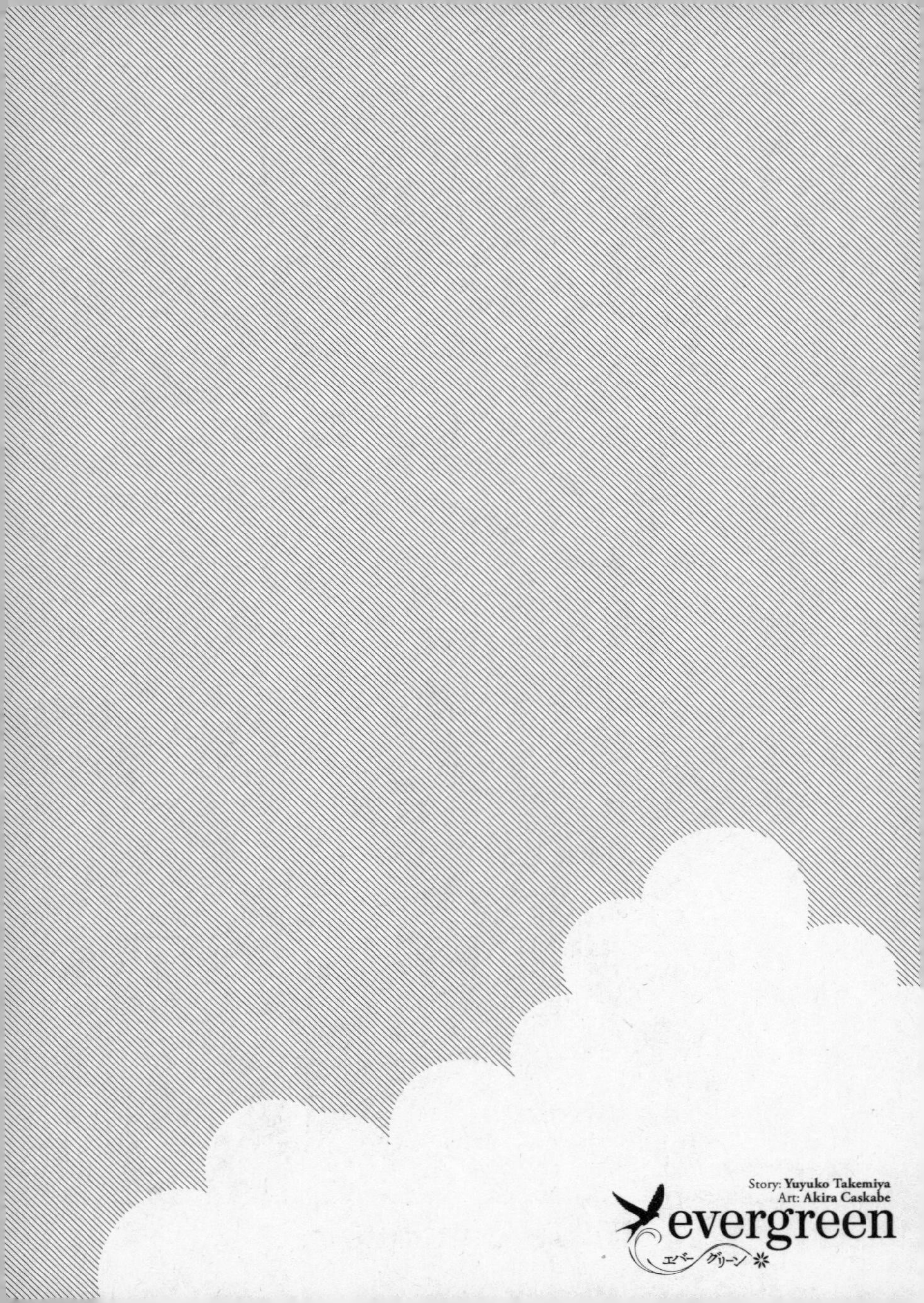
Story: Yuyuko Takemiya
Art: Akira Caskabe
evergreen
エバーグリーン

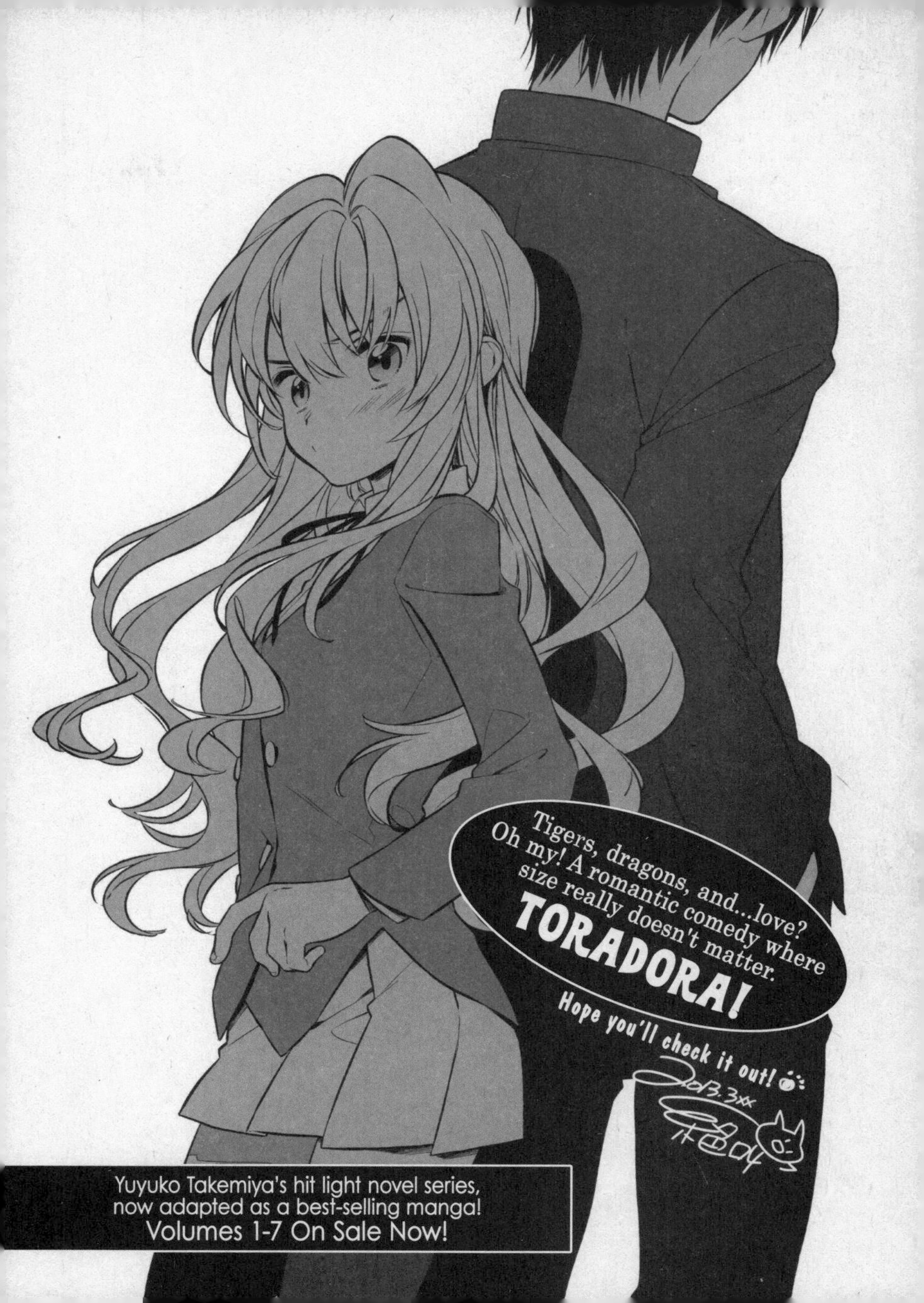
Tigers, dragons, and...love? Oh my! A romantic comedy where size really doesn't matter.
TORADORA!
Hope you'll check it out!
Yuyuko Takemiya's hit light novel series, now adapted as a best-selling manga!
Volumes 1-7 On Sale Now!

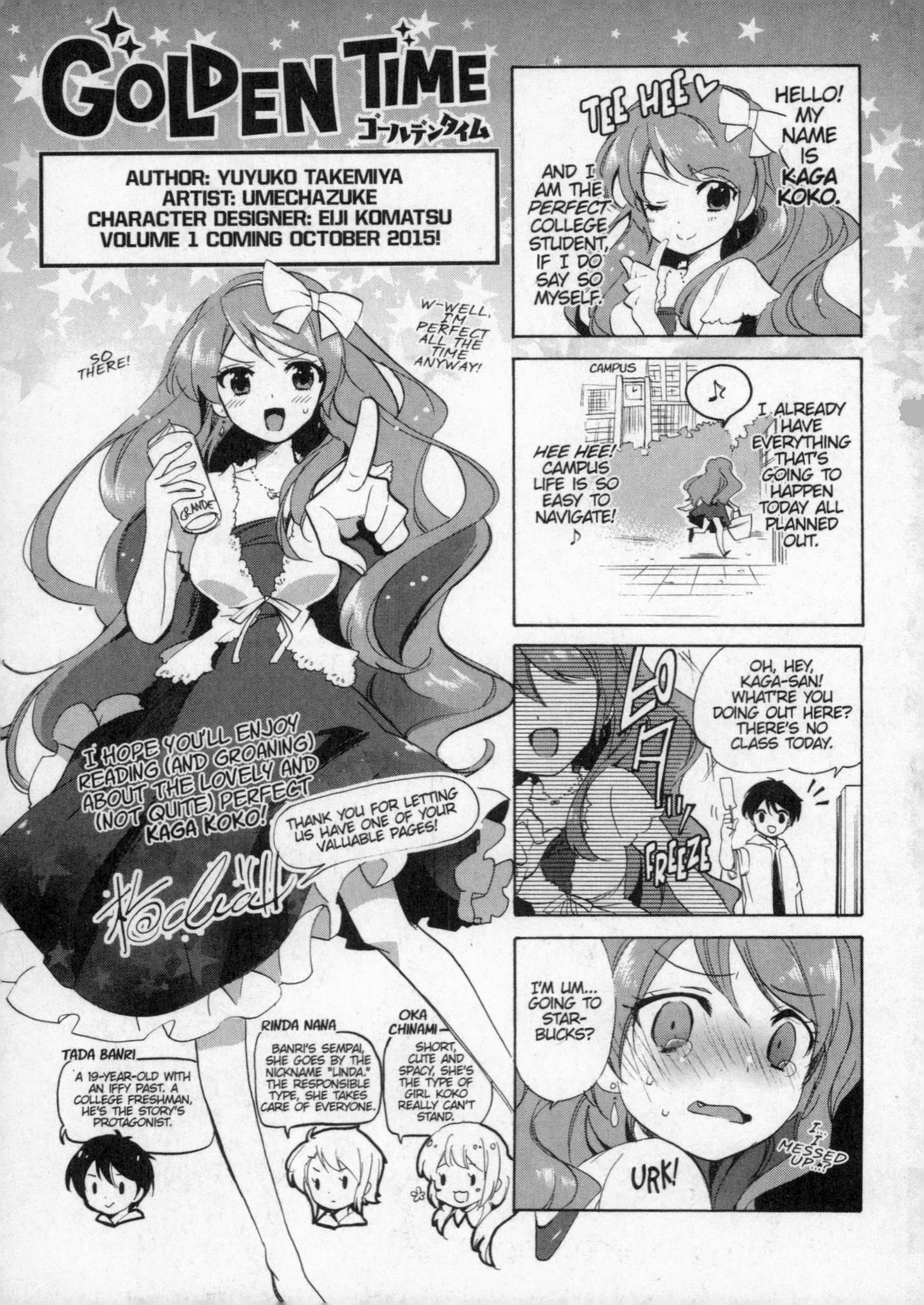
TEE HEE ♥
HELLO! MY NAME IS KAGA KOKO.
AND I AM THE PERFECT COLLEGE STUDENT, IF I DO SAY SO MYSELF.
CAMPUS
♪
I ALREADY HAVE EVERYTHING THAT'S GOING TO HAPPEN TODAY ALL PLANNED OUT.
HEE HEE! CAMPUS LIFE IS SO EASY TO NAVIGATE! ♪
OH, HEY, KAGA-SAN! WHAT'RE YOU DOING OUT HERE? THERE'S NO CLASS TODAY.
FREEZE
I'M UM... GOING TO STAR-BUCKS?
I... I MESSED UP...?
URK!
GOLDEN TIME
ゴールデンタイム
AUTHOR: YUYUKO TAKEMIYA
ARTIST: UMECHAZUKE
CHARACTER DESIGNER: EIJI KOMATSU
VOLUME 1 COMING OCTOBER 2015!
W-WELL, I'M PERFECT ALL THE TIME ANYWAY!
SO THERE!
GRANDE
I HOPE YOU'LL ENJOY READING (AND GROANING) ABOUT THE LOVELY AND (NOT QUITE) PERFECT KAGA KOKO!
THANK YOU FOR LETTING US HAVE ONE OF YOUR VALUABLE PAGES!
OKA CHINAMI
SHORT, CUTE AND SPACY, SHE'S THE TYPE OF GIRL KOKO REALLY CAN'T STAND.
RINDA NANA
BANRI'S SEMPAI, SHE GOES BY THE NICKNAME "LINDA." THE RESPONSIBLE TYPE, SHE TAKES CARE OF EVERYONE.
TADA BANRI
A 19-YEAR-OLD WITH AN IFFY PAST. A COLLEGE FRESHMAN, HE'S THE STORY'S PROTAGONIST.

# SEVEN SEAS ENTERTAINMENT PRESENTS

# evergreen

## VOLUME 2

## story by YUYUKO TAKEMIYA / art by AKIRA CASKABE

TRANSLATION
**Adrienne Beck**

ADAPTATION
**Bambi Eloriaga-Amago**

LETTERING
**Roland Amago**

LAYOUT
**Mheeya Wok**

COVER DESIGN
**Nicky Lim**

PROOFREADER
**Shanti Whitesides**

ASSISTANT EDITOR
**Lissa Pattillo**

MANAGING EDITOR
**Adam Arnold**

PUBLISHER
**Jason DeAngelis**

EVERGREEN VOL. 2
© AKIRA CASKABE/YUYUKO TAKEMIYA 2013
Edited by ASCII MEDIA WORKS.
First published in Japan in 2013 by KADOKAWA CORPORATION, Tokyo.
English translation rights arranged with KADOKAWA CORPORATION, Tokyo.

Seven Seas books may be purchased in bulk for educational, business, or
promotional use. For information on bulk purchases, please contact Macmillan
Corporate & Premium Sales Department at 1-800-221-7945 (ext 5442)
or write special macmillan.com.

Seven Sea
Seven Se

ISBN: 97

Printed

First Prin

10 9 8 7 6 5 4 3 2 1

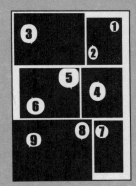

D1532485

## FOLLOW US ONLINE: www.gomanga.com

# READING DIRECTIONS

The manga prelude and epilogue sections that
bookend this light novel read from right to left,
Japanese style. If this is your first time reading
manga, you start reading from the top right panel on
each page and take it from there. If you get lost, just
follow the numbered diagram here. Enjoy!!